STABBED IN THE BACK

*A Private Investigator's
Real Life Experiences*

DUANE W PURDUE

ISBN: 978-1-962363-73-0 (sc)
ISBN: 978-1-962363-74-7 (hc)
ISBN: 978-1-962363-75-4 (e)

Rev. date: 02/28/2024

CONTENTS

ACKNOWLEDGEMENTS

There's a reason we were born with two ears and only one mouth. Most of us know that reason. So we can hear twice as much as we speak. Ah, but how many of us listen to what we hear? It's not easy to do. Many of us hold our own opinion in high regard and want to share that with others. But if we sit back and observe others, we can learn so much in so little time. Most of those teachings will be good positive things. Sometimes we'll be taught ways not to be. Regardless, every time we brush shoulders with someone, we have a chance to learn something. Our character grows and we have them to thank for it. I owe thanks to many and can repay so few.

My wife, the most important person in my life, has taught me much over the past 50 years, and she'll continue to teach me. I couldn't imagine being married to anyone else, and I hope our next 50 years are filled with as many memories and experiences as the last. I love you, Paulette, with all my heart and soul. You are truly my Life, and my Love.

My children have given me things that a father can remember for a lifetime. Each child with his own personality, his own character, mannerisms, likes and dislikes. Each one is an entity unto themselves. No two are alike, and I wouldn't want them to be. Each of them needed contact unique to their own personality. As a father it's my responsibility to know and meet those needs. Irrespective of the challenge or the cost, it all passes away soon after hearing them say, "I love you Dad."

Some people can help you realize where your strengths and weaknesses are. My friend, Griff, is just such a man. A Marine to be sure, we met, we adapted, and we became friends. Griff is like a brother to me. In fact, he's like a brother to everyone else, too. He's black. Since we each left the Marine Corps over 40 years ago, we've stayed in touch, and we always will. Griff and I share much, in fact, everything. I've learned much, and feel I've offered little in return, but we will always love each other.

Other people come into your life, and you know they should be there. Pastor Ralph is just such a man. He's unwaveringly lived for God for over 40 years of our friendship, and long before that. He's withstood the test of trials, heard the best and the worst and never wavered in his commitment to God, nor his friends.

A friend isn't really a friend, until he knows *all* about you, and still considers you a friend. Mike and Judy are just such people. Joining my Search and Rescue Team many years ago, it took little time for me to learn that I could trust my life with this man, and I have. Both Mike and Judy know the meaning of friendship down to its very core and stand by those principles regardless of cost.

Some people make you feel comfortable yet challenge you to be better. That's a task if you hope to avoid pushing people away. Pastor Jerry is just such a man. Middle aged, and young at heart, he's a man on fire and dedicated to God, a man who truly loves people and prays that all will succeed. He's wise beyond his years yet listens and learns whenever an opportunity arises. He's quick to appreciate, slow to anger, and eager to learn. It's a privilege to call him a friend.

If this writing touches one person or improves their life, this two-year adventure has met its goal.

INTRODUCTION

This book is compiled from years of experiences I've had, when I decided to sit down and comprise a list of adventures; some for my own benefit, but generally for the reader's. Each experience carries with it some lessons. As you read each one, you can decipher what lessons can be learned and put them to use in your own life. As you start to read, you'll see that the era I describe is very different from what you may have been used to. There was no Internet, no e-mail, no computers, no cell phones, no microwave ovens, no Styrofoam cups, no cable TV, no CD's, no space shuttles, no telephone answering machines, there was no such thing as an astronaut, no satellite communication bringing the world together, and some of it occurs even before the first man landed on the moon. We had never heard of AIDS, and gas station attendants would pump your gas, wash your windows and check under the hood for you. During my young childhood, we didn't even have a color TV. A week's worth of groceries cost $20.00, you could buy a new car for $5,000; a postage stamp cost 10 cents, minimum wage was $1.00, gas was 29 cents a gallon, there were no drive-thru restaurants, a hospital stay cost $35.00 a day, and a haircut, 50 cents.

You'll follow my course of a life as it progresses into these modern luxuries. Many things have changed even since I experienced them many years ago, Marine Corps boot camp, duty stations, the draft, dirt bikes, race cars, race boats, communications, medical advancements, and on and on. Try to put yourself in the time frame in which the experience occurred. I've gained some knowledge through the years, most of it due to experiences. Some good, some bad. You'll find that I'm a common, average man, nothing more. I don't consider myself exceptional in any way. My personality mandates that I'm a goal-oriented, purpose-driven person. By that I mean I have to have a vision or a goal to aspire to. Without that, I'm stagnant and start to deteriorate. Ambition is a driving force in my life. I find that without something to look forward to accomplishing, severe depression knocks at my door. With a goal to aspire to, I become focused, and it seems to carry me through life. No vision or goals, no life.

You'll find as you read that I'm addicted to adrenaline. Something must always be happening. If it doesn't happen naturally, I create an environment that will facilitate adrenaline. The problem is compounded by being a perfectionist as well. I set a goal and I'm generally not satisfied until it's reached with perfection, "Perfection" in this case meaning, "*the best that I believe I can or ever will do.*" I find myself disappointed many times. These character flaws seem to be a curse more than a blessing, but I've been fortunate to accomplish some things that are considered unusual, or in some cases extraordinary. I believe that most anyone can do the same thing if you have the desire and determination. This book is designed to encourage you to try. In some cases the names of individuals have been changed to maintain their own privacy. Other times, names have been changed to protect the innocent, or the guilty.

You'll find I talk about the spirit world - ghosts, as some would say. Read it with caution. The stories are true, irrespective of how unbelievable they seem. They did happen as I wrote them. My playing in this spirit world was an open door to terrible things that could happen, and sometimes did.

You're going to hear me talk about God, to whom I credit my life. If it weren't for him, I'd be dead now. When I speak of God, you'll find it frank and down to earth. There's no mystery to my belief, or confusion as to right and wrong about him. I refer to him with respect. I'm not a preacher, evangelist, or formal representative of God in any way. In fact, you'll see how I fell short of that. You may also see where I might have pleased God at times. You are the judge. There were significant lessons for me to learn about God. He may have similar lessons for you. Let me assure you that it's easier to learn from reading about my mistakes than making your own. Is this a spiritual book? After reading my disclaimers above I'd have to say, yes, of sorts. Then you'll read about when God abandon me. Guided me and failed to lead. Assured me and failed to protect. Or did he? Was there a lesson to be learned in this adventure as well? Have you experienced a similar situation regarding God? You'll want to read how this ends.

Experiences, if looked at from a different perspective, can be considered as *adventures*. Each adventure offers something for us to learn, or for someone else to learn something from our adventure. The adventures you'll read here will put you in the driver's seat. You'll be able to evaluate whether you'd make a similar decision, or something different. But making your mind up here means you won't have to do it when under your own pressure.

You'll be introduced to this author at a young age and feel the things I felt during growth and maturity. You may have experienced similar adventures. Down to earth thoughts and feelings. You'll see what the young really think and do, and in this case, why. If raising kids of your own, this could help. You'll move forward to see my bare heart as I lose what I love and stay with me as I fall in love with my future wife of 50 years. You'll ride along on my daily routine as a private investigator and see what that life is really like. This isn't James Bond fantasy, but real life work of a private investigator. What it takes to be one, and what you're going to encounter when you are. You'll have a chance to recognize successes and failures, even before they occur. How were these challenges addressed, and would you do the same thing? Have you already been in those shoes and learned the lessons that it taught?

You'll accompany me during my dirt racing career, and later while running the impossible 100 mile foot race, the Western States 100. You'll see and feel the devastation of being innocently accused of a crime, and the lifelong result as an outcome. If you've ever been wrongly accused of something, this will hit home to you. If you haven't, you'll feel the affects of what it does to you and those around you. When you close the back cover and pass it on to a friend to read, this is a book you'll never forget.

Some of the things I've learned can be put into simple sentences; some you've heard before and will recognize, while some I've realized myself. If you know me, you know I believe what I write:

- Life isn't fair. Don't expect it to be.

- No one owes you anything, except a chance. Once it's given to you, it becomes your job to make them wonder what they would have done without you.
- You owe loyalty to those providing an opportunity to you. Anything less is a disservice to yourself and them.
- Those who do unto others will always reap similar results.
- Doing less than your best at anything reaps similar consequences with everything.
- It's a tragedy when your position in life grows faster than your character.
- The value of your reputation is not what you think of yourself, but what others think of you.
- The best method for determining your own character is to learn what others say about you behind your back.
- It's okay to aspire to something better. It's a stimulus to perfection.
- Success is not a sin. Failure to strive for it is.
- Teach others what you know, and you will never starve for an education.
- God made man in His image; not color, shape, or sex, but Spirit.
- God controls everything. Sometimes he allows nature to dictate the results.
- Guilt festers, love grows, laziness stagnates, anger permeates, hatred paralyzes, resentment drains, appreciation multiplies, kindness begets, ambition succeeds, goals dream, and a smile kindles.
- Change is never comfortable, until it becomes the past.
- Your past is a failure unless you've learned something from it.
- Viewing your life as a Positive or Negative is your choice and responsibility. It's not an opportunity to grieve or complain.
- Families should remain families; friends normally will.
- Your heart and your mouth are inescapably intertwined. Learn to control one, and the other will follow.
- Men fall in love with women that they're attracted to. Women become attracted to men that they fall in love with.
- Women control the world. Good ones let men think they do.

- Men are controlled by their head. Good ones know which one to control.
- Being two-faced is akin to betrayal. Not expressing your opinion at all is sometimes a wiser decision.
- Alcohol can tell the time of day. At night it turns mice into men. The next day it's the other way around.
- A true friend is one who would give his life for another, knowing that the other would never learn that he did.
- Hobbies are good; passions are stimulating, control is mandatory.
- Gaming did far more to promote computer advancement than given credit for.
- Drugs are Satan's' favorite tool to control his future population. Our first experiment with drugs gives Satan the key to our home.
- When children reach adulthood, they should make life easier for their parents.
- Ordering God from schools manipulates inevitable results.
- Jesus is real. Those who don't believe, eventually will.
- People change as they grow older. Husbands and wives must work hard to change together.
- Prejudice, imposed by anyone, is a way of forgiving themselves.
- Intellectually handicapped people always resort to name-calling.
- Some people are intentionally oversensitive just so they can get attention.
- Killing a baby can happen as early as conception, and it torments God.
- Ronald Reagan was one of the greatest Presidents we've ever had.
- Love is selfish. You never love someone who does nothing for you.
- None of us should try to amend the acts of our ancestors. It's difficult enough to be responsible for our own actions.
- There are ugly men and women, but it usually starts deeper than their skin.
- Affirmative Action successfully promotes prejudice and hostility.
- A racist is anyone who thinks that your skin being dark or light is important.

- Profiling is appropriate. If it's proven that one group of people commit substantially more crime, they, whoever they are, should be targeted to protect the public. When the same group of people are successful, statistics should keep just as accurate track of the improvements.
- Black people aren't. White people aren't. Negro isn't a slanderous term, honkey is. African American is a way of isolating those who might just rather prefer to be called a human being.
- Most policemen are good. Good policemen are heroes. We sleep because heroes don't. Being afraid of a policeman is generally an admission of guilt.
- Never allow yourself to be satisfied when you've practiced something until you finally get it right. Rather practice it until you can no longer get it wrong.
- If Jesus were to walk through your home tomorrow, you shouldn't have to stay up tonight preparing for him.

The following read is written from the heart, hoping that it'll touch yours.

CHAPTER 1

Starting Young

Life starts young, as so they say. But life is really little more than memories and future experiences. Memories from the past, coupled with future experiences yet to be had. We all have good and bad memories, and our future experiences will surmount to the same thing. It's our job in life to look at those and turn them into positive things, lest the temptations befall us to wallow in the bad, or sometimes make bad out of good. Sounds strange that someone would expend the energy to look at something in a negative light, rather than find the positive in it. Nevertheless, it happens. We all do it. Why? Is it possibly a way of giving ourselves attention, getting attention from others, or forgiving ourselves for our own shortcomings? It's hard to say. I suppose there are as many reasons as there are people who commit the act. The old axiom, "Is the glass half full, or half empty?" is a larger, more revealing question than most of us consider it to be. I would answer, "Neither. There just isn't enough glass."

As a common man I've had many experiences in life. I'm fortunate. Maybe there'll be more in the future, maybe not. Each step in life has a corner. I've found that looking around it is a difficult thing to do. Maybe you have too. However, common denominators to all future experiences are hope and vision. Without either, the human spirit begins to die. The death can come slowly or quickly, but death will come. As a Born-Again Christian I can say with confidence that the loss of either is not something that God wants for any of us. We allow it to overtake us. Why would we do that? Again, there are many answers. Each of us who succumb to that tragedy does so for their own set of reasons. Regardless, each of us must face the reality that losing hope and vision is our own surrender. I too, have been there. Let's look at life, for a time, though the eyes of my own memory.

I was born in 1949, a baby boomer. My Mom and Dad were very much in love. Mom idolized Dad; he was a good man. No, he was a great man. He was a man of many talents of which art was only one. His talent to enjoy people, another. Many liked him, and he had few enemies. He enjoyed life, and enjoyed making what he could out of life. A bad experience to him was only a way of learning how not to do something. He enjoyed doing things for other people and enjoyed their appreciation. Mom was his queen; we were his little soldiers. My thoughts of Dad are always good. I can recall as little as 3rd or 4th grade in school, how going somewhere with Dad was generally an experience. I enjoyed how both friends and strangers would admire him, complement him, and talk to him. Dad was my hero. I was a lucky little boy.

We lived in an old small two-story farmhouse with decaying brown shingles extending from the top of the roof, down the walls, all the way to the ground. The old decaying white trim around the windows was badly faded and needed paint. The house had its own smell both inside and out, but it was home. The hardwood floors were chipped and faded. I'd sometimes play in the gaps between the wood. Filling them up with any dust I could find, or pushing something down in to see how far it would go. There was a narrow creaky staircase behind a door that led to the attic. My, there were a lot of things to see up there. Mom and Dad stored their world of treasures up there and I could look around at the boxes with curiosity and adventure. At the far end of the attic was a room. I don't know whether Dad built the room or not, but my oldest brother claimed it as his bedroom. There were only two bedrooms downstairs, so he got this privilege by natural selection. I was eight years younger than Mike and wouldn't challenge his right. Besides, I slept closer to Mom and Dad and that attic was a scary place to call home when you were alone. Mike was a brave brother.

There was no garage at our home, but Dad was quite a worker and inventor. If he couldn't buy something he needed, he'd find a way to make it. We had a creaky wood covered porch in front of our house that wrapped around to the side. Dad found room to enclose the side and put his tools in there. I remember how old it seemed, dust and cobwebs everywhere. But there was Dad, in his workshop diligently working on a project that I didn't understand at all. How comforting it was to walk into his shop and see him quietly working. Often, he'd be at a project on a crowded workbench with many busy things around. Or other times at his metal lathe, creating and shaping. He was changing something. I couldn't put together anything more than that, but I remember he'd always look down at me with a gentle smile and go back to his project. I liked Dad and went into his workshop often.

The rugged old dirt road leading to our house wound around a small grove of oak trees, along the side of a hill, and down to our house, sitting on acreage overlooking rolling hills, apple orchards, pear trees, and in the far distance, an amazing view of night lights from several towns touching shoulders with each other, where there always seemed to be a lot of people. That was something we didn't have at home, a lot of people around. The rolling hills seemed to keep most neighbors at a distance. We lived there in a world of our own. The houses we could see always stayed at a distance. My two younger brothers, Cliff and Jack, were outside boys. All of us were. Inside the house was only a place to eat and sleep. Our world was outside, rain or shine. When we'd come in the house dirty, wet, or muddy, Mom would simply say, leave your close at the front door and go get into the bathtub. We had no showers then, or at least I didn't know of any. I became very experienced at muddying up a bathtub and Mom and Dad never complained, it was just one of life's experiences.

I don't remember when things started going bad. It just seemed as though I always knew that Dad had a bad heart. There were times during my childhood that I remember Mom and Dad sleeping together in the same bed. Then there were times when they didn't. There were even times when I slept in my bed in their bedroom. They never seemed to fight, and I never heard a cross word from either of them. I knew Mom and Dad were friends, they always were.

Dad wanted a swimming pool for us, and we certainly had the room to put it out behind the house. I was too young to remember any of it, but Mom often bragged about Dad having a tractor come in to dig his pool. The sandstone clay was so hard the tractor just spun its tracks. Undeterred, Dad sent the tractor home. He started digging the pool by hand. Several months later we had a full-size swimming pool to enjoy forever. Thanks Dad.

I remember little about Dad's first heart surgery. Mom talked about it a lot, but I don't remember him being away from home. It's sad that I didn't miss him. I remember more the surgery on Dad's hands. He looked at them often. His fingers balled up and he couldn't open his hands. Muscles were holding his last three fingers closed and Mom was more sympathetic for him than he was for himself. Dad was an artist; more so, he was a perfectionist by nature. Everything he did had to be done at his best, or it wasn't good enough. His hands frustrated him, for he knew he could do better. How could his pictures be any better? They looked like photographs. Each detail looked real and exactly in a place where they should be. He'd spend months on a single portrait, mostly his horses. Dad loved his horses, but his painting and pastels covered a gambit of subjects, each of them looking more perfect than the last. Yes, Dad was an artist.

I don't remember Dad going in for surgery on his hands. But I do remember the ball of bandaging on his hand when he came home. His hand was covered in a protective ball for weeks. He needed help doing things, but I don't remember Mom ever complaining. She served him with thoughtful care. Months later Dad's bandages were off and I could see the scars on his hands. It hurt me to see him scarred like that, but he said it was okay. His hand was better now. That was comforting, until he came home again with the other hand bandaged in a ball. Dad was a brave man.

Dad was a man who enjoyed sharing what he knew. He could do that without making someone think that he thought he was smarter or better than others. He was just willing to offer knowledge to those who asked, and never forced his opinion on anyone. I remember remarking one time about how pretty a flower was. Dad didn't say, "Yes, it is, son," nor even let my comment pass without recognition. Instead, he stopped what he was doing and said, "Well, let's go take a look at this flower." He guided me over to it and took me very close. He showed me how the flower sprung from the stalk of the plant, how it grew from a fresh green stem into something remarkable. He showed me where the bees go to reap their reward, and explained about the chlorophyll that makes up the color for each plant. In a little time, this pretty flower became much more, it was an entity. Wow, Dad was smart.

"Dinner," Mom would call outside, and we all went inside, to wash up of course. All sat at a long table with Mom at one end and Dad at the other. Mike, Cliff, Jack, and I never sat at the same place at the table. Dinner was always a new experience. I listened as everyone talked. Afterward, we watched TV for a little while, no color. Wouldn't it be beautiful in color? "Someday," Dad would always say. "Someday I'll get you kids a color TV set." But Dad was sick, and somehow, I knew that the color set would never be.

Dad stayed home more often and didn't seem to go out in his shop much. He'd sit outside for a while, and have to go back in. He walked slower and didn't play with us much anymore. He didn't wrestle with our Great Dane, and the horses were gone. Mom and Dad were in separate beds now. Mom woke me up late one night to come out and give Dad a hug. He was sitting in his favorite chair with no shirt; a towel was draped across his back. His head was low, and he had trouble breathing. This was my all-encompassing, ever-present Dad, who wasn't feeling good. I didn't know why, but I knew it was important. Shortly after, Dad brought home an oxygen tank. This green and yellow thing looked like what I saw on black and white TV for divers who were able to breathe underwater. He showed it to all of us and told us not to be afraid of it, that things were okay. He'd often use the oxygen tank and he covered his face with a fighter pilot's mask to breathe. This was important somehow, and I spent much time with Dad after this. He couldn't carry the tank himself, so Mom put it in a box. I'd carry the box to and from the car, or keep it near Dad, wherever he was. Dad needed this tank and whatever it was doing for him, I would be there to help.

Mom had planned a special trip somewhere for us kids. We were looking forward to it very much, but as the day got nearer to leaving, Mom came to me and asked if I'd stay home with Dad. "Yes," without hesitation I agreed. I don't even remember missing the event that Mom took Cliff and Jack to. I remember Dad taking me with him and I'd pack his oxygen tank in the rear of the car. I have no regrets. I felt important.

Dad went in for his second heart surgery. There was much talk beforehand, but I paid little attention. My immortal Dad could overcome anything. Mom and Dad talked about how they were going to try a new method for surgery. The Doctor's were going to chill him to slow his heart down enough to do the surgery. That's what he wanted. Mom and Dad talked a lot about it, but I didn't understand much of what they were saying.

Mike was in the Marine Corps now. He was doing great and was sent to Viet Nam, assigned to a helicopter gun ship. We wrote occasionally, but I was too young to realize where he was and what he was doing so I didn't really know what to say to him. My letters said little more than, I love you. Mike couldn't come home for Dad's surgery, and I know that distressed him.

My brothers and I visited some neighbors overnight. That was unusual, we hadn't done that before. Mom and Dad went somewhere that day and I wasn't sure where they were going. I remember Dad at the front door giving us the usual hug and kiss before he walked out, nothing unusual. Dad was going to the store I guess, but my spirit told me Dad wasn't comfortable. Things weren't as normal as they looked. Oh well, we're going to stay overnight at the neighbors. Cliff, Jack, and I took a long hike that day. That wasn't unusual for us. We spent a lot of time in the hills near our house, hiking, exploring, and searching for lost treasure. I remember all the seashell fossils that abound in the sandstone rock on each hill. Like an ocean had covered the land, we could see distinct shells in the rock. They were plentiful everywhere we looked. During our first year of hiking, we learned to accept them as normal and went on to seek other adventures. We came home later than usual this evening, home to the neighbors. We expected to be in some trouble for that, but our neighbor was nice. They asked where we had been and were quickly forgiving. My spirit told me something was wrong here, too.

Later that evening Mom came to get us. It was nice to see Mom, even though we had a good overnight stay. Mom was quiet and her face was red and wet. That wasn't like her. She was always a beautiful woman. Many friends told her so, and I always agreed. Instead of gathering us up in the car, Mom sat us down on the couch. She was preparing us for something, but none of us knew what. "You know Dad can't always be with us, don't you, kids?" She started out. "He had surgery today," she paused and choked while clearing her throat, "and he didn't wake up." She started crying uncontrollably. My younger brothers must have caught onto what she was saying right away. They too started crying but I just looked and stared at Mom. This wasn't possible, and I wasn't going to have it. My hero would always be there, and nothing anybody could say was going to change that. My Dad would come home.

The first night without Dad was tough. Mom cried, my brothers were quiet, and I was confused. The second night, third, fourth, and on didn't seem to get any better. I never got angry with Dad; I just couldn't understand and wasn't going to accept that he was gone. I suppose I haven't to this day. Who was I going to play baseball with? Dad taught me how to be a catcher, and I was very good. Some said I was far ahead of my team, but Dad taught me that. I was so proud when he watched me play. He'd sometimes get as close to me as he could behind the backstop and quietly give me a tip. Yep, it worked, thanks Dad. I didn't really want to play much baseball after he died. I did for Mom, but not much for myself anymore. I eventually grew out of Little League and went out on top as the best catcher in the league. I hope Dad knew. Even today I can't help but cry, almost out loud, when I watch Field of Dreams. I wish Dad could come back.

Mom struggled on. I grew into my adolescent years and Mom was a miserable woman without Dad. I didn't know why she was so angry and upset all the time, but life was different now. Mom seemed to have little patience for us kids, and after working full time and commuting home, she was too tired to give us the attention we felt was deserved. Trouble was brewing at our home, and I was the cause of most of it.

Mom started dating after about six months of Dad's death. These guys weren't Dad, and Mom shouldn't be with them. I never hesitated to let her know how I felt about it, and we grew apart. I became unmanageable and out of control. I did what I wanted when I wanted. Nobody seemed to care, and nobody could stop me.

I wasn't there when Mom married Tom, none of us kids were. They came home together to break the news. This couldn't be true. Tom was going to move in with us? He was loud, noisy, and bragged a lot. He drank every night and argued with us kids. He married Mom for Mom, and we came along as baggage. I did little with Tom, and stayed away from him as much as I could. I was in 7th grade now, Intermediate School as it was known then, now called Middle School. This was a tough time for me. I didn't know who I was, or even what I was. I was a loner and focused on myself. I drifted away from my brother's companionship, Mom was focused on Tom, and Tom made me his target. I didn't play baseball anymore and I missed the feeling of being good at something. One day I started playing on the parallel bars at school doing pull ups and trying to climb up on top of them. I was a thin but stout young boy and it seemed easy for me to do these things that other kids were only trying to do. I played a little longer and enjoyed quickly excelling over the others. Day by day and week by week I went out to the parallel bars. Every recess and every lunch found me there and it didn't seem to take long before I was performing before other kids who came over to watch. Flips, turns, forward falls, dismounts. I made things up and perfected them. This was starting to get fun. Even a teacher or two came by to quickly watch for a minute. It was a task to think up new things. I was a small center of attention and I liked that. I had to do better. It wasn't long before another young boy, Roger, joined me and I taught him all I had learned. I wasn't resentful that he was good. I enjoyed having the company and teaching him. Eventually, Roger learned some new things, and taught me. We didn't compete, we shared. The small crowd who watched enjoyed it and that is where I met Cheri.

She was a bright girl in my class who sometimes came out to watch and talk to me. She was pretty, with dark hair and bangs, and very popular at school. She was outgoing and had a lot of friends. I was glad she talked to me. Seventh grade was a tough place to be alone. Becoming friends with Cheri was a slow process. She was either busy talking with others, or I was busy on the bars, but whenever we spoke, we knew we liked each other. I had to keep impressing her on those bars. I don't know why, I just enjoyed her attention.

It was a Saturday morning, and I woke up early, as I frequently did. Mom and Tom were in bed sleeping and I was anguished as I walked by their bedroom. I went to the kitchen and then to the TV room. Sometime later the phone rang. It was Cheri. By now we often called each other. We were good friends, buddies. She'd chat about her life, and I'd get little chance to chat about mine, but that was okay. I liked listening to her. I liked her liking me. Cheri was my outlet in life now. My only comfort where I felt I was a person. I felt important when talking to her and I needed to feel that. It felt good and there was little of that now.

I heard Tom get up in the background and he was in the kitchen making coffee. I had to get off the phone or he'd yell at me, so I hung up. I didn't want to, and I was mad at him that I had to give up my world so he wouldn't be mad. I walked into the kitchen and saw him sitting in the dining room. His eyes were drooping and red. His hair out of control, his head tilted sideways. I saw this often. Tom had a hangover. I started smelling the coffee he was preparing when he said something to me out of the side of his mouth. I couldn't hear it, but I didn't like it, and I told him. He accepted the challenge and bit back with a course snap of the mouth and vulgar cussing. That justified my response and I replied in childish kind, as I had done so often in the past. Tom wasn't up to contention this time. He had slapped us on the head before, pushed us around, and sometimes manhandled us to our bedrooms. But Tom was sick this morning and wasn't to be argued with. My arrogant mouth was intolerable as he jumped up off the chair and came toward me for what I knew was going to be another slap in the head. But he was angrier than I expected, and he grabbed me by the throat and while choking me, opened the sliding door outside. My head rocked back, and my hands were on his arms. There was little I could do to stop him other than hope he would stop himself. Tom was a big strong man who outweighed me by 100 lbs. I wasn't up to the task of fighting him at my age anyway. I hoped this wouldn't be too bad as my head leaned far back and I could see the hill behind me, upside down, the hill where I liked to hike and build forts. We were outside only a brief time before Tom slipped on the morning dew that had gathered on the wooden walkway. Over the side of the walkway we went, down onto the grass. He still had me by the throat, and I landed first on the ground, on my side. He fell on top of me, and the pain quickly stabbed me in the shoulder. I heard a snap but didn't focus on it as much as the fear of what was going to happen next. Tom pushed himself off of me and walked back into the house. Nothing was said as he walked away. Maybe this was over now, but not until I could get up and get away. Mom was still in bed and I'd have to do this alone. I couldn't move my arm. I knew something was wrong but ignored it in favor of getting away from Tom. I got myself up but knew that I had been hurt. This was bad. What was I going to do? I went to my bedroom to lie down and wait for all of this to pass.

Hours later I still hurt, but Mom was up now and maybe she could keep Tom away from me. I couldn't move my shoulder and the pain was more than I had felt with other injuries I've had. This one was going to take some time to get over.

Mom and Tom argued that day, as they often did. I stayed away from them both. By that night I was pretty sure that Tom hadn't told Mom about the incident this morning. He'd be in a lot of trouble if he did, and maybe we could be better friends if I didn't tell her either. I bandaged my shoulder and put a shirt on over it. At dinner I ate with my left hand and Mom asked why. "No reason," I casually said and avoided looking up at Tom. Everyone went on to eat. I hurt, but I wasn't about to say anything to Mom. Days went by and eventually Mom caught on that something was wrong. I told her I had hurt my shoulder on the bars at school, but that it'd be okay. She accepted that without giving me the attention of looking at it, but that was okay too. All I wanted was for this to go away. I was missing day after day on the bars at school, and Roger was continuing on. My fame and attention was dwindling. Two weeks, three weeks went by and I couldn't pick anything up or move my shoulder. Mom said it's time to go to the doctor. She was shocked and cried when he told her that I had broken my shoulder, and the healing process had already started. He'd either have to leave it that way or break it again and then set it. Somehow the doctor knew that this didn't happen on the parallel bars and asked me how it was really broken. With my head held low, "Tom," was the only thing I could get out.

I don't remember Tom much after that. Mom told him to leave, and they had a monumental argument. He called her occasionally after that, but Mom was steadfast in not talking to him. She was alone again, and very miserable.

From then on, I never went back to the parallel bars. I lost my distinction there and I was just another kid at school. Cheri was still there, and we continued to talk. I liked talking to her. She was more mature than I, who thought in more infantile ways. She'd correct me when she thought I did something stupid or childish. She was making a better person out of me.

Seventh grade was over, and I'd miss Cheri for three months, but we would talk on the phone every day. Sometimes two or three times a day. Other than that, day by day went by with nothing to do. Life seemed to have few experiences.

Eighth grade came and went too fast. I knew that Cheri would be going to a different High School than I. I hated that thought and didn't know what I was going to do. It seemed as though she didn't like it either, and that made me feel closer to her. Where was life going to go now?

Mom started going to bars again and I resented her for it. Her loneliness and desperate need for companionship was beyond my understanding, or maybe I just didn't want to understand. This wasn't what Dad would have wanted, nor was I the person that Dad would have wanted me to be either, but I forgave myself for that. I was, however, holding Mom to task for her needs. I just couldn't understand or accept how she could go out at night and meet strange men. Most of which were interested only in sex. Mom seemed to accept that. It was companionship, of sorts. Few of them would come back and I was glad. But Cecil was a different story.

Cecil was a rugged, wrinkled man, but stout and strong. His skin was baked and dry, especially on the back of his neck. His arms were that of a man, one who used them frequently for heavy work. He had a pouch for a stomach, but not as big as other men his age. His salt and pepper hair sometimes stuck straight up like it was rebelling on its own. His large mustache was seldom trimmed or groomed. His teeth were straight, those that were there, but faded more than I would expect of a man his age. He was a carpenter, and he was loud. He spoke loud, laughed loud, coughed loud, yelled loud, and loudly made sure everyone heard what he had to say. Cecil was just a loud sort of guy, and he was an alcoholic. Mom and Cecil got along great when they were sober. After a few drinks, things around the house were in turmoil. This wasn't a healthy relationship, but it was companionship for Mom. After a few months of dating him, Cecil moved in with us. I wasn't surprised, nor was I happy. I accepted what this stage of life was offering, but I wasn't embracing it. Cecil paid some attention to Jack, Cliff, and I. Not much I admit, but some. All of us brothers took to that quickly. All of us needed a man's attention. I had Bill's, but Cliff and Jack had no one. Bill was Sister Donna's husband. He was a unique case of his own. A grown child would have been a complement. Bill suffered with the character flaws of having few morals and less conscience. I wish now that I, too, would have had no one rather than Bill. However, to look on the positive side, had I not been exposed to a man like Bill, I may have acquired some of his foul traits myself without recognizing them. But Cecil was now our stand-in father, and I had hopes, albeit small, that things would be okay now, or at least better.

Cecil was a hard worker, and a hard drinker. He'd come home from work, open his beer, and find something to do outside. One project or another, he rarely finished any of them, but he seemed ambitious to me. Mom would frequently get angry with him for starting something else without finishing the last. She was right. But Cecil would drag me along with him from one project to another. I learned a lot from his knowledge. Not that he tried to teach me anything. He didn't. He wanted me there to do the grunt work, and I did. I learned by watching him and being quiet. But I was a teenager now and I had other things on my mind, so those learning experiences would have to wait. Getting Cecil mad was always a memorable experience. I did get a chance to watch him work though, and I quietly enjoyed that. He wasn't at all like Dad. He was no artist, or perfectionist, nor did he take pride in his work, but he did know things about carpentry, and I enjoyed watching and learning. I've always had an affinity toward learning something. I enjoy learning very much. It was difficult in school because I had so many other things on my mind. As the years grew on, I found myself fascinated by things I didn't know, and was learning from someone else. I haven't lost that to this day. I pray I never will. Going to school or college has been a secret quiet desire for as long as I can remember, but it will never come to pass. My road has been paved in other directions.

Cecil liked to hunt and took advantage of that in the open hills where we lived. Pheasant, quail, and dove were his prey of choice. He could walk up the dirt road and come back with two or three quail for Mom to cook. He would clean them himself and seemed to even enjoy it. Mom never balked at cooking them. He'd sometimes walk out into the large fruit orchard, acres and acres of apples, pears, cherries, and other fruit trees. They were old and desperately in need of pruning or picking of their blessings. I have no idea who actually owned that vast acreage of trees. Maybe Dad did. We had treated it like it was ours, and now Cecil was. During the appropriate season he'd walk out in the orchard and would almost always bring back a pheasant. He liked living at our house. As time grew on, and I grew taller, Cecil brought out one of my Dad's shotguns. He taught me how to shoot it, but not much about the do's and don'ts. I had to learn that on my own. I think he just wanted company when he went out on his hunting walks, someone who could crawl through the berries and bushes to flush out the birds. I did as I was told.

I had a gun too, and maybe I'd get a shot myself. Crawling through the dry grass and brush was never fun. I hate snakes, and it seemed like I'd always run into one somewhere. Fortunately, they were king snakes, garter snakes, or an occasional large gopher snake. Never any rattlers, although that was always my fear, and neither Cecil nor anyone else took the time to teach me that there were few, if any, where we lived. I grew up with that fear of snakes and, except for my manly denials, still do to this day.

The neighbors were getting angry with Cecil and my periodic hunting trips around the property. They didn't like hearing the gunshots. They were much too far away to get peppered by any errant shotgun blast, but it disrupted their comfort zone, and one day they came out to let Cecil know about it. I was curious to learn how Cecil was going to handle this, politely, tactfully, peacefully, with concern for others maybe? Nope, it wasn't to be. I cowered down as he returned his answer to our neighbor. "He's shooting doves, quail, pheasant, or anything else that's in season," he loudly retorted. "And when deer season opens, he's going to hunt them, too." Our neighbors were no longer our friends. Maybe that taught me something that I'd unconsciously remember for the rest of my life. To this day, friends are important to me. Everyone can and does say that, but I fear my philosophy goes a step farther. I never want to argue with a friend, and although it happens on rare occasions, I feel that pain for hours, days, and weeks. I can't let it go until the problem has been addressed and settled. It pains me to have bold or cross words with friends, and it's arguably said that I feel the same way about family. I hold that hurt close to my chest, but I carry an argument for what seems like an eternity. Until it's settled and finished, my mind goes back to it over and over. It's tormenting to me to feel that something is left unfinished.

Mom spent years with Cecil. Eventually the arguing, yelling, and drinking became more than Mom felt was worth the price of companionship, and she made him move out. They still talked to each other, and occasionally even saw each other. But as they did, Mom grew farther apart from him. He loved her and had a difficult time being away from her. But Mom eventually had suffered enough with him and refused to talk to him again. His phone calls went unanswered, and their periodic accidental run-ins met with her immediate retreat. Cecil and Mom were through. Mom stayed alone from then on, for the rest of her life.

CHAPTER 2

Dad is Gone - Life Changes

The oldest in the family was Donna. She was always "Sis". Donna and I were close, which was mostly her doing. She looked out for me, checked on me, and cared for me when I needed it. Donna was a fiery red head with a laughing personality. She was always doing something good for somebody and laughing at their jokes. Donna found something funny in nothing funny at all. She was 10 years older than I and lived in a different world. She seemed to always enjoy seeing me and I liked seeing her, too. When she got married to Bill, she moved away and although I didn't know what the void in my heart was, I knew it was there. Mom didn't like Bill and I couldn't figure out why. He was a big, good-looking man who often acted my age. I could relate to him when he did. We had something in common and I seemed to latch onto that. I liked Bill. Mom was wrong.

When Bill and Donna moved back to a nearby town, I spent as much time at their home as I could, after school, weekends, and overnights. It didn't matter, I was always there. Mom didn't care and most of the time I never bothered to call to tell her. She just knew. Bill took me places with him, did things with me, let me do things with him, and talked to me like I was on his level. We were getting to be good friends. He taught me his ways and I listened. He taught me how to steal, how to cheat on your wife, how to take advantage of others, and how to deceive. He had the moral character of a gross ignoramus, 144 times worse than an ordinary ignoramus, but I didn't know any better, and didn't care. I found a home with Bill. I hoped Donna wouldn't find out I did these things, but Bill thought they were okay. I rode along with Bill as he found women to flirt with. I watched him scheme on them, and anyone else he could get something from. Dad was long gone now, and I tried not to think about him much. Bill took his place. I was glad Dad wasn't

15

around to see. However, for some reason, a voice always talked to me in my mind. It said that what I was doing was wrong. It was wrong, it was wrong, it was wrong - but I didn't listen. Bill was my friend.

I was deeply rooted in Bill and his ethics before Mom caught on. Mom and I argued a lot now. She wasn't the person I knew, nor was I the son she raised. We were at odds, and of course it was all her fault. I forgave myself, but not her. There was no foreseeable repair in either of our eyes. I was a pre-teen brat and could rightfully be identified as worse. Cliff was growing older too. He was two years behind me. Jack was a year behind him. Jack and I were far enough apart that we got along well. Cliff and I were always at odds. Cliff was his own person and had morals like Bill, and sadly like me. Cliff was bolder about it. I didn't like that, and he didn't like me. We didn't talk much anymore and didn't go hiking in the hills together. We just argued with each other. Cliff was sorry that he wasn't older, and he always tried to act like he was. That crossed into my territory, and I wasn't going to let him invade that. Jack was the content one who never seemed to cause any trouble. He just went along with everything and never seemed to complain. I hoped he would stay that way. He clung onto Mom and stayed out of Cliff's and my trouble. I couldn't put the words together, but I knew that was good.

My life with Bill was getting worse, and certainly I was getting bolder. Mom could see it, and I didn't like her for that. She couldn't control me any longer and I took advantage of it. I did what I wanted, went where I wanted, saw what I wanted, and said what I wanted. I was raising myself by this time, and still in the eighth grade. Cherie and I still talked, and it was with her that I could be my real self. I didn't know who my real self was, and I was experimenting, but never with drugs. To this date, I've never fallen prey to that invitation. In fact, I've never even had the temptation to try them. Maybe God was looking out for me there, too. I imagine that had I started, I would have had to try them all, sell the most, and be the best at it. God watches over fools and children.

Mom had suffered enough of me by the time I graduated from eighth grade. I was strong headed, and she knew this would be a task bigger than she could handle. Mike was still in the Marine Corps but was back from Viet Nam. He suffered war wounds and was sent back stateside.

Although I didn't know the importance of it then, I was impressed when I learned that he was assigned to the "President's Own", a Marine Corps Band that played for the President in Washington, D.C. I played the drums a little bit and was in awe of the Band that was so good. He sent records home for us, and I played them by the hour listening. They were perfectionists and even at that young age, I appreciated it. Mom was very proud of him and talked of him to others frequently. I would never achieve the accomplishments that Mike did. He was my big brother in the Marine Corps.

Mike's tour with the Band at "8th and I" in Washington, D.C. was over. He was sent to Bremerton, Washington, on the Puget Sound. I didn't know anything about that and wasn't interested very much. He was married to a Filipino woman whom I had met, and who seemed pretty nice. Mike and I got along well when he made his few trips home to visit. Mike could see I was growing up and heading in the wrong direction.

I picked up the phone by accident one day and heard Mom talking to Mike. She was telling him secrets about my life. She revealed things to him that I didn't want him to know. I was mad at Mom for doing that. I listened as they arranged for me to come up there and stay with him through summer vacation. Mom was clearly pleased as they made the arrangements. When they hung up, she said little to me other than that I was going to Bremerton. I was mad and I resented it. I would be away from Bill and Donna. More so, I would be away from Cheri although she and I had never been the girlfriend/boyfriend type, even though I wanted that very much. Instead, she would tell me about the boys she liked and how they treated her. She would routinely confide in me as her best friend, and I listened. She had many boys that liked her, so I listened a lot. It was a painful friendship, but I didn't want to give it up. She was very important to me, even at age 14.

I was really alone for the first time on the trip to Washington. Mom made it clear that things would be okay on the plane and told me how I was to find the ferry and get on it to cross the Puget Sound to Bremerton. I knew I was a grown-up kid, but this was a little more than I wanted. I was scared as I said goodbye to Mom at the airport and climbed the steps to get onto the plane. The stewardess took me right away to find a seat. Maybe the excitement of being on a plane for the first time would take this lonely feeling away. I didn't know how to put it into words, or even have a cognizant thought, but I knew my life was changing once again, and I was scared.

The taxi took me from the airport to the ferry. At least I hoped he was taking me there. What if he wasn't and left me somewhere else? How would I know where the ferry was, and how would I get there? What would happen to me if the taxi driver didn't do what he was supposed to? It seemed like a long ride in the cab. Eventually, it came to an end and the driver got out. He took my bag from the trunk and opened the door for me. I'd now see whether I was really at the ferry or not. When I got out, I could smell the salt water and see the birds in the air. It was a big boat, and cars were driving on. I guess this was the ferry I was to get onto. "Bremerton" I said as I bought the ticket. "OK, son," the man returned and took my money. He directed me to the ferry, and I walked on next to the cars. "I'll do what I'm told, and see where it gets me," was my only thought.

There was a mighty rumble when it left the dock. I couldn't tell whether I was impressed or scared. I stood at the side rail and watched as it moved out toward a vast open waterway. "This is big," I thought quietly to myself. People were all around me and I didn't know any of them. I was by myself in a whole new world. What would I do if Mike wasn't there when I got off? The last instruction from Mom was to wait for Mike to pick me up. I wasn't very secure in that for some reason. I didn't know why, I just hoped Mike would be there.

The ferry sailed through the waterway with no apparent end. I walked around both inside and out. I was taking in what I could see and learn, the distant land, the birds in the air, the waves on the water, the sound of the engines, the metal walls, and the wind blowing strongly against me at the bow of the ship. I thought of home and tried to decide whether I'd rather be there or here, and I thought of Cheri.

It seemed like a very long ride, and I was getting hungry. I'd seen everything I could look at on the boat and I hoped it would stop soon. Eventually we pulled up to the dock and the huge ramp lowered down. Cars started pulling off and I knew this was Bremerton. I walked into the building where all the other passengers were going and there was Mike. I was safe again.

He took me to my new home. It was small, almost a bungalow of sorts. It had a kitchen, small living room and one bedroom. It was easy to see that my bed would be the couch. That was okay; I slept on the floor at Bill's and Donnas'. I was more grown up here, Mike treated me that way and I liked that. I soon learned that he expected more of me, too. What do you mean I have to wash the dishes? No dishwasher? I have to help clean the house too? This stay could turn out to be a bummer. It'll take me an hour a night to do this. Well, I'd better get to it rather than just stare at it. The job isn't going to get done until I make it that way. It wasn't so bad.

I was certainly impressed by the military uniforms hanging nearby as well as the belt buckles on the table and the Marine manuals lying around. There was no doubt I was in a Marine Corps environment, the best of the best. I was proud to be near it. I wanted to see more, see the Base where he worked, see other Marines, and be near what they do. Mike said that Bremerton had the world's largest dry dock for ships. I was going to get to see a ship out of water. That would be interesting. Mike's tour playing the trumpet in the "President's Band" was over. He now played for a small Marine Band here on base. When he wasn't doing that, he worked in the laundry. Not a very glamorous job for my brother, but he didn't seem to mind, so I wouldn't either. As time went on, I enjoyed calling him on the phone when he was at work. Whoever answered called me, 'Sir'. I'd ask for Cpl. Purdue and they'd always say, "Wait one," and put him on the phone. Yes, I liked that.

I had little to do at home but watch TV, and that's what I did during the day, all day. Julie, Mike's wife, and I just sat and watched TV. I didn't know anybody, and there certainly weren't any kids my age around, so I stayed to myself in the house. That must have bothered Mike, as after a few weeks, he asked me to start going out and doing something. "What?" I would ask. "Bowling, skating, or something else," he replied. He didn't know either but was trying to help. Now, I have to guess that he was hoping to get some time alone with Julie, but I didn't catch on then. I just stayed home and got in their way.

Eventually school started and Mike got me enrolled. This was high school. I was a freshman and didn't have any idea what to expect. Was I going to get beaten up, ignored, made to scrape gum off the bottom of lunch tables, or what? On my first day, I was ready for trouble, but it never happened. After several days it wasn't so bad at all. I had no difficulties other than what I brought on myself. I was a junior Marine. I saluted to say hello to a passing acquaintance, and would march myself from class to class, squaring the corners at every turn. I looked like an idiot to anyone watching but was completely content within myself. I don't think I'd do it again though.

At home I became quite proficient at shining brass belt buckles and spit shining shoes to a mirror black glaze. Not only could I see myself in Mike's shoes, but I could see detail in my face. Now that's a spit shine. Mike liked it, too, although probably not as much because of the quality of the shine, as because he didn't have to do it himself. It wasn't long before he had a second or third pair for me to shine. I complied and spent two or more hours per shoe while watching TV. There was sure getting to be a lot of shoes around here. They couldn't all be Mike's. What's this, a different size? And over here, a NAVY pair? Yep, Mike's friends were taking advantage of my services too. After I caught on, they started slipping me a couple of dollars for the spit shine. I appreciated that, but probably more than the money, I appreciated their recognition. I was growing up.

I don't remember much about the Base except seeing some incredibly huge ships up on stilts, out of the water. Everywhere you looked, inside and out, men were working on them. It was quite a sight. There was a small base bus that would carry passengers around and I took advantage of that. Slowly I got to know a handful of people. Most of them were very nice, and I didn't have Bill nearby to teach and encourage me in his ways. Mike wouldn't tolerate that kind of behavior and I had no temptation to violate Mike's standards of living. I was glad for the clean, decent lifestyle.

"Want to go fishing?" Mike asked one day. *Did I??!!* This was going to be great. Mike checked out a ski boat from the Base Special Services and off we went, Mike, Julie, and I. All in all, we must have gone a dozen times out on Puget Sound. The water was remarkably clear by the bank. We would cruise slowly just about 30 or 40 feet offshore and lay on the bow just looking at the sea life under the water. We could see all the way to the bottom, and it was a beautiful thing to watch. I couldn't get enough of it. I could have stared underwater all day and not missed fishing at all. But alas, fishing was what we came for and soon we'd steer out to deeper water. I didn't know the Marine Corps had fishing poles, but Mike checked one out for me, too. I was just like he was, and we'd fish for whatever would bite, except sharks, and that's all that seemed to be around. We saw one shark after another. They were only a couple of feet long, but sharks, nonetheless. We'd finally have to weigh anchor and go someplace else if we were going to catch anything other than sharks. I can't remember how our fishing normally ended up. I was just happy to be where I was.

Ah, but there was a void in my life that I couldn't pinpoint, until I got the letter. It was from Cheri. She missed me, not as a boyfriend I could tell. She was telling me about her boyfriends at home and I had a lot of things I could write to her about, too. "I'm a Marine up here, you know." Mom even wrote occasionally, and she'd send me a few dollars with assurance that she loved me. I was happy about both the letter and the money.

I did okay in school, academically, but my real forte was physical education (PE). I just seemed to do well. That was a surprise to me and everyone else. I grew up with asthma and had attacks frequently. There were no meds or inhalers for it then. You just gutted it out until it went away. I was allergic to dust; mold, odors, food, the cold, and so many other things that I didn't bother to keep track of it any longer. Asthma had controlled my life for so long that I found a way to work around it, or better, ignore it. When we ran during PE, I tried harder than most of the others. I wasn't any better, I just tried harder and that made me better. When I was done, I'd walk away alone so no one could hear my asthmatic breathing. I was generally too weak to shower with the rest of the class, so I'd sit on the bench in front of my locker and try to get dressed, one piece of clothing at a time. OK, that's on, now slowly work the next piece on. By the time my next class started I was usually getting my breathing under control, but I always felt so very weak. Well, maybe tomorrow will be better.

Wrestling was a lot of fun. We had a good teacher, and I took to it naturally. He'd show us a move and I understood it right away. It wasn't long before I was eliminating my competition one by one and was getting a name for myself. I liked that. But I quickly learned that I had to beat them quickly. The shoulder that had fallen prey to Tom's assault sometime back was weak and started to hurt during longer matches and I didn't want anyone to hear me struggling to breathe. So, while they were still gearing up for a longer match, I'd go for the pin, and usually win. Mike would have been pleased had he ever seen me.

Several months went by and some of the kids in class had been gone for a couple of weeks or more. I didn't realize until later that going hunting was an accepted reason to miss classes. That was a common practice in Washington. You certainly couldn't get by with it back home. But here, to bring a note to school saying you'd be out on a hunting trip wasn't something unusual. What a great experience that would be.

"Want to go hunting?" Mike asked one day. "You've got to be joking," was my only thought. "A couple of Marines on the Base and I are going to go this weekend, and I thought you might like to come with us." This was too good to be true, a hunting trip, and with other Marines. I didn't sleep that night or the next. The weekend took too long to come. Friday night I sat on the couch looking out the window for hours. Mike was late. But when he finally got home, he was packed and ready to go. So was I. I climbed in the car with him and the other heroes and off we went. After we arrived in the woods, we unfolded a large tent and started a campfire. This was living at its finest. Still, I was probably the first one who crawled into a sleeping bag. Taking one last breath of the fresh crisp air and the distinct smell of a tent and sleeping bag, I fell asleep.

It was still dark when Mike shook me awake. The campfire was again a pleasing and comforting sight when I stepped out from the tent. An old beat-up coffee pot was on the coals and I recognized the smell of fresh coffee. I'd never had any, until that morning, but I had to have a cup just like the others. Daylight was breaking and without anything being said, everyone loaded their rifles. I was just going to walk along, and I was happy with that, but Mike went into the tent and came out with a .22/.410 over and under two barrel. A .22 on top and .410 shotgun on the bottom. "Here, you carry this" he said with quiet sincerity. Oh man, the trip was now unexpectedly perfect.

I walked beside Mike for hours looking for deer. One of the other Marines shot one and had it hanging when we got back to camp. It was my first experience seeing a deer, or any other animal for that matter, gutted and skinned. I was a little uncomfortable with it, but I didn't say anything. I was going to learn something, and I wanted to take it all in. When he was done, he wrapped it up to keep the flies and bees off it and buried the hide and innards.

We stayed another day and walked for many more miles up and down the mountain sides. No one else took a deer and Mike never even got a shot. Before coming home, we got some target practice on an old tree stump. I fired the 'over and under' for the first time, and watched as they fired their deer rifles. We packed up and came home. Mike and the others drank a few beers on the way and occasionally offered me a sip. I took it of course. We unpacked when we got home and the next day my assignment was to clean the rifles, which I did without complaint. In fact, it was an honor. Mike showed me how to do it and I followed his instructions to the tee.

I was getting some attention from a few girls by now and I was comfortable in talking with them. Mike would tell me some ridiculous things to say to them and thinking he was serious I followed his instructions. He and his friends must have had some good quiet laughs figuring either I had a lot of guts or was incredibly naive. I suppose I was a little of both. But I became popular, and bold.

I had a couple of male friends, one of whom had a motorcycle. Actually, it was more of a doodlebug than a motorcycle, but it got us both over to the town of Port Orchard where he had a girlfriend. To my excitement she had a friend who was prepared to meet me. It was through Dolores that I learned some of the differences between men and women. We spent a lot of time in Port Orchard. High school was over for the summer, and I graduated from freshman to sophomore. Staying in Washington for another school year was not to be. Mom wanted me home and I'm sure Mike and Julie wanted their privacy back. As the summer started, I flew back home. Mom was very happy to see me, and I was happy about that. I was happy to see her, too.

Life had changed in that year. I had learned a lot, and had a lot of memories, but I never wrote a letter to Washington. Soon after getting home, Cheri called me, and we started talking again. We had a lot to catch up on, and she certainly wanted to tell me about her most current boyfriend. I wanted to contact an old school buddy, Dave, and it wasn't long before we were palling around again. Mom was treating me like I was older, and I was acting like it. I could see that everyone in the house was now pretty independent, Mom, Cliff, myself, and even Jack. We all seemed to have our own separate lives going on while living in the same house. Mom was still working as a bookkeeper and trying to make ends meet. It exhausted her and there was little energy left for anything else. We accepted that and went about our own way. We came and went as we wished, and pretty much did what we wanted to do. Mom tried to keep track and even some control of us, but all to no avail.

Cliff was getting older and had bolder ideas. He was now planning on having a gambling party at an old abandoned house just below our property. He made up poker tables, got some ice chests, and even put together a roulette table. In school he put the word out and invited everyone to come on Friday night. Everyone did, including the cops. Needless to say how that turned out, but this brush with the law was not to be Cliff's last. His life was headed a little different direction than mine, or maybe I just didn't get caught like Cliff did. There were times coming in the future when I certainly deserved to. Like the time Dave, Bud, and I stole some roadside warning, blinking sawhorses. We took the yellow flashing lights off of them and put them up on the dash of the car while driving up Mt. Diablo at night. Dave was great at sound effects and easily convinced cars in front of us that we were the police. Then there was the time we emptied the back of a produce truck sitting alongside the road and gave away hundreds of pounds of vegetables, (including to Mom, who pretty much figured what we had done), or the gas that we siphoned, or the shotgun that I carried on the front seat of my car just because the law (then) would let me do it.

I loved Donna and it didn't take long before I started spending time at her house again. Along with spending time with Donna came Bill, and Bill hadn't changed. He was still the friendly, amoral crook that he had always been. It was easy for him to relate to and use kids my age, which he did frequently. Bill had a Tree Service and I worked for him after school almost every day, for free of course. He would occasionally give me some money when Donna insisted on it, but he enjoyed the opportunities to have me work for him for nothing, so I did. I had his friendship and I liked that.

I became progressively more popular in school during the next three years. Even though we went to different schools, Cheri and I talked every day after I got home, sometimes for hours. Girls in my own school liked me and I had to pay attention to them, too. It was a very confusing time.

I had my share of fights down by the backstop behind the school. I bested each opponent and got a reputation. I'm not sure that this reputation was good for me. The admiration came from the wrong type of people, the ones who liked to fight. I could see that this was not the direction I wanted to go, and it always made Cheri mad. She'd learn about it even before I got home, I have no idea how. There were no cell phones then. You'd just beat the drums or look for smoke signals. The last fight I got into at school was with a poor kid who challenged me to it. I have no idea why, and I was never mad at him for anything. In fact, I thought he was a pretty good kid. Someone must have put him up to it. I couldn't help but think all day long whether there was something about this kid that I didn't know. If not, he's in a world of hurt. Word was out before lunch about the scheduled fight. When school ended, a large crowd had gathered down at the backstop. I arrived to find my metal shop teacher standing off at a distance. I thought he was going to have me arrested. "No, I'm just here to see the fight," he said. I couldn't believe it, but he really was. I met the kid face to face, trying to get mad enough to fight, but he didn't make it easy. He was visibly scared, and I knew he didn't want to be there. I really didn't either, but for different reasons. "Well, let's get started," I thought, and raised my arms for the usual push against their chest to get things going. He stepped back and his fists came up in front of his face. I hit him three or four times in rapid succession as speed was a natural thing for me. He didn't like getting hit and danced around hoping it wouldn't happen again. I danced with him, popping him at will. He'd take an occasional swing, but to no avail. They were simple to avoid, and I'd go back after him again. "How long is it going to go on like this," I thought? The poor kid got so tired of holding his hands up in front of his face that he dropped them down to his chest, leaving me a target to practice on. I was getting tired of this and was feeling sorry for him. His face was bloody, his nose bleeding, and his lips cracked. I didn't want to hit him anymore, and thankfully someone stepped in between us to stop it. It was the shop teacher. "He's had enough." I dropped my hands and agreed. The poor kid had tears in his eyes and said his mother was going to kill him for getting home late from school. I couldn't help but think she was going to get mad at him for more important things, too. Bud walked up to me and asked if I wanted a ride home. I said, "Yes, but we're going to give my foe a ride home too." We put the kid in the front seat of the car, and he directed us to his house. His shirt was bloody so I took mine off and gave it to him. He was thankful and apologized before getting out of the car in front of his house. For the rest of the school year we were friends. I wish I could remember his name. He taught me a lesson. I didn't like to fight anymore, but there was one more fight coming.

Bill watched wrestling a lot and he must not have known how staged it was. He wasn't very smart, you know. Bill was pumped up over wrestling and kept saying how he wanted to drop kick someone. He was a big muscular man. If he were to drop kick someone, that someone was going to get hurt. He was so focused on it that I knew a fight was looming somewhere in the future for Bill.

One night, we were all watching TV at Bill and Donna's when the phone rang. Bill got excited by the caller and soon hung up, "Come on, Duane," he mumbled while he grabbed his keys and went out the door. I had no idea what the call was about or where we were going but in short order we were at a bar in a nearby rough and hard core area. The type no one would go to for a quiet drink. This was a notorious fighting bar, and we were going inside. I was a teenager and had no business legally or morally inside that bar. We sat down with some friends of Bill's and the one who made the call to Bill. They pointed out the bad guys over at the bar. There were several of them and only a few of us at our table. Bill ordered beers for everyone, and the waitress looked down at me for only a moment before saying, "Okay." We all had two or three before the bar closed at 2:00 a.m. At 17, two or three beers were all I could drink and still stand up. Bill's friend rose from the table and walked outside. One of the men at the bar followed. Everyone else rose at once and even with my oncoming asthma attack I knew I was about to be protecting my face from flying fists. Bill stepped to the door, and I was right behind him. I could see Bill's friend out in the parking lot, down on the ground, with his adversary standing above him kicking him in the face. Bill ran outside, down the steps, across the lot, at a dead run and punched the man in his face. The man's legs immediately went limp and without breaking his fall, he went down to the pavement. Everyone inside ran out and each one picked a foe. The parking lot was full of fists and feet. I, however, wasn't sure that I wanted to play an active part in that, and I backed up against the wall so as not to let anyone behind me. I awaited my attacker or attackers. One by one, the brawl wound down, and I could hear sirens in the far distance. Most of the combatants ran away, except for four. Two were holding a third man by his arms. They had him pinned up against a car, while the fourth man punched him in the face over and over again. The man's head was down and he was clearly unconscious. The sirens were getting closer, and the fourth man was ready to quit and run, but only after he kicked the unconscious man in the face. The parking lot was dark, but there was enough light that I could see who the unconscious man was; it was Bill. That was more than I could take, and I ran out into the parking lot after the fourth man, or the first or second, or whoever I could get to. I wasn't quick enough. They dropped Bill to the ground and ran, not from me of course, but from the approaching police sirens. I got to Bill and picked him up. He was semi-conscious and didn't want to be in the parking lot when the cops got there. I couldn't blame him. I helped him across the street into a large field of dry grass. From there, we walked several miles home. He could hardly talk and mumbled only slurred words. I kept telling him I couldn't understand him, so he took my hand and put it to his face. His jaw was like a bag of marbles. The sensation haunts me to this day. It was so badly broken I couldn't envision how a doctor could fix it. He spent a few days in the hospital with his jaw sewn shut by his gums. Bill wanted to drop kick someone, but never did, before he got the notion out of his system, and I witnessed a sadistic beating of another human being.

I lived two lives then, one at home with Bill and Donna. That was the same life I lived at school and with my two school pals, Dave and Bud. Different from the life I lived around the girls that were attracted to me, or me to them. With them I was a funny, likeable guy, always trying to make them laugh. It did my heart good to see a grin on their face. If I could get them to laugh out loud, I would get warm inside. Sometimes that meant acting like a fool, other times it meant being quick witted. Whatever it took, I adapted and took advantage of every opportunity. I didn't like being a clown and I avoided that at all costs. To be admired for my humor seemed to be my goal. I had a lot of friends, mostly girls. I liked that. My other life was with Cheri. We both went into our sophomore years in different schools and it would stay that way through our Junior and Senior years. We were growing older now and I was growing wearier of hearing about her boyfriends. I liked Cheri. Much more than any other girl who liked me at my own school. Then something happened while she was between boyfriends. I told her how I felt. She acted shocked, but I don't think she was. She had to have known. I couldn't hide things very well, but I was shocked beyond belief when she announced that she liked me, too. I said it, I got it out. And she felt the same way. This was too good to be true.

From that time on, I invested every emotion I had in Cheri, but as the months passed, I learned that this was a dangerous thing to do - very dangerous. Cheri was a pretty and outgoing person. She talked and flirted with everyone, and she was going to a different school. All my feelings and all of my heart became tied up in her. Yet I didn't know from one day to the next whether her flirting would find her a new boyfriend or not. Or worse, keep seeing me and see him, too. Cheri was a year older and hung out with kids that were her age, both boys and girls. This was a real threat to me, but I couldn't change it, and I couldn't endure it. I needed her to convince me that our relationship was secure, and she thought only of me. She never really put much energy into doing that. Compounding the problem was her inability to be convincing, even when she tried. She would calmly or quietly say she wasn't seeing anyone else, or didn't do this or that, but I needed much more. It led me to hysteria. I questioned her constantly. The more I did, the less she tried to be convincing. Cheri liked attention. She liked to be the center of attention. She had an "A" personality, and it was easy for her to be in a crowd and, in short order, have all eyes on her. I couldn't live with that, and I couldn't stop her, I couldn't tolerate it, and I didn't know what to do about it. I became a tormented, scared, threatened young man, with all his eggs in one basket.

High school created strong mixed emotions. I wanted to grow up, but not get beaten up. I was distraught over Cheri going to a different school. I learned long ago that Cheri was a person who needed and demanded to be the center of attention. She had a pleasant personality, and she was growing up to be a beautiful young woman. All my feelings were tied up in her and our relationship was seriously threatened by the distance between our two schools. It seemed natural to cover up and hide the pain that I felt daily. I accomplished it by laughing or trying to make someone else laugh. I enjoyed making people laugh, and it made me popular even as a young freshman at Pleasant Hill High. I enjoyed the friendship of my long-time pals, Dave and Bud, and girls seemed to enjoy me. I had what I would deem my share of potential girlfriends. Most of them I kept on the string because I liked their attention, but I wouldn't get any closer to them because of Cheri. There are exceptions, and I'm ashamed to admit that I tried to keep those exceptions from Cheri, but as a Freshman I was generally a well-behaved young man. School was tough for me as I never learned to study, and there was little encouragement at home. I enjoyed the shop classes and PE classes most. Metal shop, wood shop, and auto class were all enjoyable, but PE was my ace in the hole to make up for academic bad grades. I could always depend on PE's high grade to balance out the bad ones.

There was really nothing exceptional through my Sophomore, Junior, and Senior years in high school. I suffered the pain of broken relationships, ignored crushes, bickering friends, and jealous arguments. I grew, learned, experienced, fought, made up, and made love, but the latter was more special to me than it was to other friends who were doing the same thing. Cheri and I were close, and slowly getting closer, but never any closer or faster than she wanted things. She took the lead in our social and private lives together. I did little more than follow that lead. She liked that and it drove me crazy. She may have liked that, too.

For the next two years of school, Cheri and I broke up, got back together, and broke up again, only to reunite as two magnets with opposite poles. I was attracted to girls at my school, and she to boys at her school, but we always came back to each other for more hard times. We had more love for each other than we had for anyone else. We had fallen in love, or found ourselves that way, I'm not sure. But this love was painful. I couldn't figure out why and I quit trying. Her parents would ask her why, Mom would ask me. We had no answers, but we knew we really did love each other, even though the fights and discontent. We weren't friends anymore, as we had been while growing up. Instead, we were lovers, and my insecurities were making us miserable.

Bill had taught me and was still teaching me to get what you could, when you could. He was talking about women. He liked Cheri, but encouraged me to go out on her, date others behind her back, and have several girls on the side, which I did for a while. There were Teresa and Shirley, but I wasn't attracted to them as much as I just thought it was the manly thing to do. Right or wrong, it was manly, so saith Bill. And why not, he was cheating on Donna as often as he could. My guilt level rose to another level each time he did, and each time I went out on Cheri.

I had a different view on some things than other guys my own age did. I learned that from the way they talked, and things they did. They'd talk boldly and openly about their escapades with their girlfriends, and who did what to whom when they went out Friday night and parked. That's what they called going someplace to kiss and neck back then. "Park". We called it "making out," and it was a great thing to do, but that was unique and special to me. It was not something to be talked about, bragged on, or shared with others. It was private, very special, and all your emotions should be invested in it, and the person you're with. Oh, I kissed other girls and occasionally went farther than that in my teenage years, but I was always uncomfortable with it. It wasn't the "Something Special," that I had with Cheri. It wasn't the all-encompassing investment of emotions toward a special person that I felt this kind of thing should be. I could never tell Bill how I felt. I would only imagine his laughter and Bill detouring me from revealing my deep inward thoughts about kissing or doing anything further than that. I cherished my encounters with Cheri and was forever threatened that they would cease. Yet I, myself, was causing problems by my mistrust. I had no one to turn to, no one to get advice from, and no examples to emulate other than Dad. Cheri didn't cherish me like Mom did Dad, and our relationships were very different.

Cheri and I were serious about each other, but we had no set plans for the future. In fact, as a Senior, I cut more school with Bud and Dave than I attended. I barely graduated. Had it not been for taking two periods of PE to get the A's, I probably would have failed. Cheri on the other hand was a good student. For her, graduating was not going to be a problem. The other boys she was attracted to were the problem and I lamented day and night over the girl, who was becoming a woman, who I loved.

Cheri was a great actress and was in drama class throughout high school. She auditioned for a play in her Senior year and won the lead role. She rehearsed frequently, both day and night. I was uncomfortable with that. I didn't want her away from me for long. Even if she were at her home, and I at mine, I knew we were by the phone and could talk, which we frequently did when she was home. The play was finally ready to show, and two nights were scheduled at her auditorium. She asked me to come and see her and of course I went, but the play wasn't what I had expected to see at high school, nor from my girlfriend. It was about a girl and her boyfriend, or maybe it was her husband. During the final act they embraced and ended with a long kiss. This was devastating for me to see. She had already told me that they had rehearsed many times and he wanted to rehearse a lot more, but I thought it was the play they were rehearsing. Now, even this one long passionate kiss was too much for me to withstand. I got up and ran out into the parking lot, wanting to cry and scream at the same time. Cheri quietly later said, "Oh, it didn't mean anything," and left it at that. Well, THAT wasn't enough. I needed more assurance, more comforting, and it was never to come.

Graduation came, and I was lucky to be sitting in the audience with the other more deserving students. My behavior, coupled with my failing grades in history and other subjects, were almost my downfall, but my school counselor got a hold of me in time to scare me into buckling down to finish those classes with passing grades. As a result, I was the first in the family to graduate. Cliff would not. Jack would follow me when it was his turn, but with better grades and less stress. Mom had never pushed or encouraged me to go on to college. Neither she nor I had made plans for the future, and I was to let each day see its own sunset. I had no job, no plans, no goals, and nothing to do. I spent most of my time over at Bill's and Donnas' helping Bill work at his Tree Service. I cleaned up brush, passed equipment up to him in the tree, and loaded the brush onto the truck. It was hard physical work, but I didn't mind. In fact, I enjoyed it. I liked being with Bill, I liked accomplishing something, and I was buff. Although Bill wasn't teaching me, I watched him long enough to teach myself how to climb and trim trees. Bill knew it, and it wasn't long before I climbed the trees and came back down to clean the brush too. Why Bill didn't help out in that I don't know. Sometimes he'd pay me, sometimes he didn't. I never knew from one week to another whether I'd have any money to take Cheri out or not. Sometimes I'd tell him all I needed was gas money, and that's all I got, but I stayed at Bill's and Donnas' often, and I ate a lot of their food.

I never went hunting with Bill, but we did go fishing for Sturgeon and Stripers out in Suisun Bay. Bill was a great fisherman and a lot of pleasure in my life involved fishing with Bill. We'd catch fish when others didn't, mostly due to Bill's knowledge and luck. A lot of people at the dock and bait shop knew Bill and the guy who tagged along with him.

Cheri's parents tired of our fighting and of me. As all parents with daughters, I suppose no man was good enough for their little girl, but in Cheri's case, maybe her parents had a good point. I was, so far, worthless, with no direction in life and apparently no ambition or abilities. I'd spend the rest of my life in a tree, they thought. Her parents' dislike of me was both insulting and a challenge. Cheri on the other hand was torn between them and me. Not a good place to be. She'd sneak to see me, and lie to them, but they weren't as naive as we thought. They finally gave Cheri an ultimatum. If she were to continue to see me, they'd kick her out of the house. She continued, and they kicked. Cheri moved in with Mom and I, but that wasn't going to last long. Our bickering bothered Mom a lot, and of course she blamed Cheri. How could her son be at fault? Well, maybe he was, but not as much at fault as Cheri. It wasn't long before Mom decided enough was enough. She wasn't going to kick us out in the street, but what she did was frightening enough. She rented an apartment for us by paying the deposit and the first month's rent, then took us shopping. She bought a week's worth of groceries, bundled up anything at the house that she could that we might need to start out, and drove us over to the apartment. We loved her for setting us up, but staying at home living off her would have been easier.

I needed a job now, but it wasn't the only problem I had. My faded white 1957 Desoto convertible could pass the first gas station, but I shouldn't ask it to pass the second one. The holes in the top let the wind in and it blew the holes bigger. The engine missed and popped, and the exhaust had holes from the header pipe down to the tail pipe. Everyone knew I was coming, and they always knew when I had left, yet my old Desoto had to take me to and from a new job, any job. I needed a job and I took the first one that came up.

"Knock, knock, knock" became a familiar sound to me. I carried a small suitcase from door to door for Fuller Brush. "Foolish Brush Man," I'd announce, and I usually broke the ice. This was an embarrassing job, but it was a job. I couldn't expect to do any better than this. I hoped it wouldn't be my career, like the older gentleman who trained me, but it was paying the rent----sometimes. If Cheri shopped for groceries every few months and didn't spend much, we could get by, but I was always in a bad mood over money. In fact, I was angry every time we had to spend money, not because I begrudged Cheri the money, but because we didn't have any, and yet it was my job to produce it. Buying groceries only depleted what little we had. I hated grocery shopping with Cheri.

In between our arguments, Cheri and I spent time making up. We argued a lot and made up a lot, sometimes carelessly, and Cheri got pregnant. She had to tell her parents, and I had to tell Mom. We didn't know what we were going to do but there was no doubt that my job was going to be easier than hers. Her parents had kicked her out of the house because of me and now she was pregnant. The stress of her pregnancy, telling her parents, my job and lack of income, marginal transportation, and every other everyday problem in life was overwhelming for both of us. Cheri decided that living without me was better than living with me. I came home one day to find she had moved out and gone back home to her parents. Devastated, I called and called. She wouldn't talk to me, and her parents supported and encouraged her in that. I was beside myself and drank myself to sleep for weeks. I tried to manage day by day, but as time went on my guilt overtook me. I was without the one I loved, the one who also made me miserable. I couldn't take it anymore. I tried calling her again but found out from her mom that Cheri didn't live there anymore. They had put her in a home for unwed mothers, and fathers were not allowed to call or visit. In fact, her mom went on, THIS father wasn't even going to know where she was.

This couldn't be, I told myself. If only I could talk to her and hear from her that this is what she wanted and this is where she wants to be. But where is she? As a teenager I found myself immersed in my first investigation. It took weeks and many contacts with friends and relatives of Cheri's outside of her house. It took dozens of phone calls to all types of homes that might cater to unwed mothers. Her name finally surfaced in San Francisco at a Catholic center. I drove there immediately, but the trip took a lifetime. Should I, or shouldn't I? What if I do, what if I don't? Can we live together; can we live without each other? There were no answers in my own mind.

I learned upon my arrival that no-one outside her own family was to visit Cheri, especially me. The Nun was a no-nonsense bull who was not used to being questioned or challenged. So, I didn't do either - I pleaded. She wouldn't budge. I implored her to just take a message to Cheri, to tell her I love her and please call me. The Nun agreed, if I would leave and never come back. I agreed.

Two days went by and I seemed to live in a Hell of my own, until the phone rang. It was Cheri. Breaking the ice was hard and she wasn't about to make it easier. She may have enjoyed the attention of my groveling, or maybe she was just convinced that I was wrong and she was right, but we did talk for hours, over several days. With both of us believing that we could make it work, she came home to our small apartment, made even smaller now that she was larger.

Our wedding was in a Judge's Chambers in Concord, CA. on May 3, 1968. No fancy wedding for us. Neither Mom nor I could afford any more than this, and her parents certainly weren't going to pay for Cheri to marry a bum like me. Mom and Cheri's parents came to the wedding. My old buddy Dave was best man, but a short and sweet ceremony it was, brief and to the point. We were married, and now back to the apartment, neither one of us knowing how long this would last.

It wasn't long before my tax refund came in and I had decided I was going to spend it on classes, Karate classes. I joined a local Dojo and within the first two or three classes I was hooked. I knew this was for me. I started out like most everyone else, thinking I'll learn this and then go beat the heck out of my enemies. Week after week went by and eventually I was allowed to come into the Dojo for group classes, or train on my own as much as I wanted. I was there every day, some days all day long. This wasn't a hobby to me; it was a passion. Eventually the usual instructors took a liking to me and taught me their secrets. Sometime after that, Bob, the top instructor, owner, and Sensei, started teaching me. I enjoyed every minute of it. Once a week, we'd have matches at a group class. I looked forward to these, and took on all challengers, or appointed opponents. It didn't matter. If they bested me, I'd study why. If I beat them, I'd consider myself lucky and study their techniques. One of the instructors who taught me much had a deadly spinning rear kick. He could stand facing you in a defensive posture and look at you square in the eyes. Without warning, you were looking at his rear leg coming around and you were staring at the bottom of his bare foot an inch from your face. He had great technique and was deadly accurate. This opponent could hurt you if he chose to. He never did and I was always able to pull his kick before the crippling strike to your head. I knew there had to be a flaw in his movements somewhere, and whenever he battled another opponent, I watched. I watched, and I watched some more. Eventually Bob quietly moved alongside me. We both stood against the wall watching the movements on the mat. "You figured it out yet," he asked? "I think so, Sir." "What is it?" He tested me with a follow-up question. "Well, Sir, if you watch his rear foot closely, you can see him come up on his toes just before he strikes, but it happens very fast." Bob just cracked a small grin and walked away as quietly as he had approached.

It wasn't long before Dennis, the threat to all who bowed to the mat, had beaten another opponent with his spinning rear kick, and both bowed to each other in respect, turned to Bob and bowed to him as the black belt overseer that he was, and prepared to take their place against the wall. "Dennis, you stay out here," he said in his normal quiet tone of voice "Purdue, on the mat." Oh great, I was being brought to task to see if I could put into practice what I thought I had observed. I stepped up, bowed to Bob, turned to Dennis and while looking at him square in the eyes, we bowed to each other. I learned long ago that the match starts without warning, and that included the time during your respectful bow of honor to your opponent. Bob taught all his students that nothing is off limits when protecting yourself. Take your opponent to the ground and continue to beat him until you're sure he won't get up. I wonder even today whether that philosophy is sound or excessive, but I never saw Bob lose a match in a tournament. He was very good at what he did. Our style of Karate was focused on defending yourself against a street fighter, and that's sometimes the toughest kind. You don't know what they'll do. A stylist has forms and techniques he follows. Many times you knew what to expect. Bob's teachings were against the unexpected. I liked that.

I raised my head and dropped back into a right-side Rear Horse, a common defensive stance for any style. Bob's hand came out from between us, and our match was on. My eyes never left Dennis's chest. I don't look at my opponent's face or eyes. His chest lets me see his hands and his feet. I can strike to the head without looking at it. Dennis started first with some hand movements and strikes that missed their target. No points. I aggressively responded by side stepping his direction of travel and attacked his front. Two strikes and I moved out. "One point," Bob declared. Dennis had been my instructor in the past, and I could see he wasn't taking this casually. His eyes lowered down on me, and I knew things were going to get more serious. Three strikes, one to the head, two to the chest. Dennis gained a point, and we were tied. I knew he felt better now. I hoped he felt confident, too confident. He moved in for another strike and I sidestepped his motion again, this time to his back. With a forceful strike with my elbow, my target was his lower back, his kidneys. "One point," Bob declared again. It was two to one now, and all I needed was another point. Dennis wasn't going to let that happen and I knew he was going to reach down deep. His deadly forte was his spinning rear kick and there was no doubt he was preparing to unleash it soon, with its full fury. I'd have to curtail my normal response to an attack by moving in and attacking back or I'd move right into his powerful rear leg thrusting toward my face. He could effectively rearrange my good looks.

We squared off again, and I felt Dennis looking at me square in the eyes. He saw me looking at his chest and probably felt I was afraid to look at him in his face. I had never told him my secret of where I looked at my opponent. Hands up, we slid toward each other almost simultaneously. Blows were exchanged and each was blocked by the other. It was getting hard for me to breathe now, but I wasn't going to reveal that weakness. I forced myself to breathe slowly and quietly, but I really needed air, and I wasn't going to stay alert very much longer. I'd have to move in for my final point, but only after he launches his spinning rear kick at me. I stared at his chest, he at my eyes. His rear foot moved slightly, but it moved. His heel came up and he was on his toes, all in a microsecond. I saw the blur of his heel and I knew it was me or him. I sidestepped his forward motion, to his front this time, and his spinning rear kick struck the air, where I had been. With one leg planted on the mat, and the other thrusting out at head height, he was an open target. A simple basic move, a snap kick to the groin, took Dennis to the mat. The match was over. I leaned over to help my past instructor up and I said quietly in his ear, "You'll never try that on me again." He nodded in agreement, and both of us went over to take our positions against the wall.

From that point on I was a respected member of the Dojo. Students would ask me how to do things, or what to do "if". I was pleased that my practice and devotion were paying off. Bob, too, was pleased. A short time later I became an instructor myself. There was little income in it. I traded teaching for my own lessons, and I graduated up the ranks, proud to be where I was. We traveled throughout the Bay Area to different matches and even hosted some at our Dojo. I participated and beat most of my competitors. I can't remember one I lost, but I'm sure I did. What I won the most was confidence and compassion. I knew what I could do, and soon learned that it was more difficult to not hurt a man, than it was to hurt him. That scared me. My hot temper grew quieter, and I was able to walk away from a challenge out on the streets. I was comfortable with myself, and only smiled if challenged by an unknowing unfortunate. This was a good time for me in my life. Much had been accomplished.

CHAPTER 3

Tough Times

I was married to Cheri now, my childhood friend, high school sweetheart, and longtime combatant. Adults could see our fate. Her parents, Mom, friends and family, all prophesied our demise, but we were in love and weren't about to listen. Our inability to dissect and evaluate our love didn't mitigate the self-destructive path that we were on. How can you love someone for the qualities that they have, yet live in fear because of the same qualities? For the next three years or so I was going to experience a love/hate relationship and its most volatile times. Much of it was my fault. If there's a Satan, and I believe there is, he romped through my insecurities like a child experiencing their first play yard. Cheri and I were doomed from the beginning. We were both set on our ways and forgave ourselves for our own shortcomings. If the other one would change to what we wanted them to be, we could get along. Has anyone else ever felt that before? Many of us secretly have. The word "secretly" being a key description here. For if we know it's wrong yet can't, or don't want to change, we keep it a secret to ourselves. Both Cheri and I did just that although I'd be at fault if I allowed myself to be so presumptuous as to outline her thoughts and feelings and align them with mine. I never really knew her thoughts, and it was hard for me to gain wisdom to deal with her feelings. Either I wasn't listening to her, or I didn't believe her, or she wasn't relaying her feelings in a way that I could understand. Regardless, the results were inevitable. A head-on collision was in the making. The saddest thing about it is that I believe we did love each other, but it was appropriately once said, "What God doesn't put together, he's faithful to destroy." This destruction was a long, slow, painful, torturous demise, for both of us, I'm sure.

Cheri and I lived in a small one-bedroom apartment during her pregnancy. I continued working as a Fuller Brush man for as long as I could endure the experience. I'd come home each night angry at myself and distrusting her. There were the usual self-proclaimed studs living in the complex that targeted one lonely woman after another and boasted of their conquests. We've all run into them before, but they were a significant threat to me. Cheri was vulnerable to them, and in my view, coveted their attention. She was still the flirt she had always been, a teaser of sorts. She just did it generally to get attention rather than solicit a male friend or sexual encounter, but that was enough for me, and I considered it a violation of boundaries. I'd come home to find her talking to one of the good-looking hunters in the apartment building and my insecurities would grasp me like a vise squeezing my head and chest to a point of exploding. Cheri was not the kind to respond to a quiet question and I wasn't the type to pose anything to her that way. I'd be angry and ready for a fight, probably because I wanted her to know how serious this was, how upset I was, how important this was, and have her assure me that it was genuinely nothing and that it wouldn't happen again. That scenario is mostly laughable now. It was never to be. Cheri was not able to convincingly reassure me, nor did she try. "Oh, nothing's going on," she'd haphazardly say, and that wasn't nearly enough to take the supposed threat to our relationship away. First, I needed her to convince me that nothing happened or was happening and, second, that it would never happen again, but Cheri enjoyed attention, and even thrived on it. Because I didn't give her enough of the right attention, she sought the wrong attention, be it either from another man, or from me in my anger. Hence, I think her enthusiasm to adequately reassure me was contrary to her own desires. I knew that my own problem was incurable. I couldn't live if she cheated on me, I couldn't live without her, I couldn't stop her, and I couldn't get her to quit flirting. This was a nightmare straight from Hell. Did she play with my emotions? Maybe. Did she want to torment me? No, I don't think so. I'm sure that today she has a different perspective on our relationship. I can't speak for her and although we occasionally write now, she doesn't speak of her shortcomings or motivations.

Our first child was born August 31, 1968. I loved the name Tammy and Cheri agreed that this name would belong to our little girl. I didn't share the excitement of being a father that a real father should have and even deserves. We had no medical insurance, and I had no job. We were barely surviving week to week or month to month. I now had additional responsibilities that I couldn't meet. What was I to do? This fear preyed uppermost on my mind and robbed me of the ecstatic joy of having my first child. Cheri didn't understand and I couldn't make her. That's not to suggest that I didn't love little Tammy; I did, very much. However, like my love for Cheri, my love for Tammy would hurt. I couldn't meet the requirements that she certainly deserved. Food, diapers, clothing, furniture, the list went on, and my failures became more agonizing.

I was afraid to hold Tammy. She was so small and fragile. I'd never been around a baby like this, and I had no experiences to draw on. As time evolved, I grew more comfortable, but always feared that I'd bump into something with her, drop her, or do something else to accidentally hurt her. In short order, I did enjoy her very much. I watched her movements, her sounds, her responses, and I was amazed that this was my little girl. God, I wished I wasn't such a failure and could take care of her better. She was so cute. I loved the things she did, and later the things she said. I enjoyed it when she learned to crawl and would climb up on my lap to cuddle. I remember her sleeping on my chest while I napped. I didn't know how to be a Daddy. I had no examples around me to emulate. I could only remember my own Dad, who by now had reached the occasional memory stage. This new experience of being a father was daunting to me. And with it came more pressure and more failures.

Dave, Bud, and I remained friends even after high school. Dave had joined the Air Force and I heard from him through the occasional letter or when he was home on leave. Dave was making something of himself, and I was pleased. Bud wandered from job to job and lived alone in a small nearby house, close enough that he could walk over to visit. Bud was simple minded, but a nice guy. He had a big heart and was loyal to our friendship. He always had a plan or a scheme for something. His newest one was to become a cowboy. Bud wanted a horse. He had a small field behind his house where he could keep a horse, but the problem was --- getting one. Like me, Bud had little money. He frequently talked about getting a horse and I played with the idea myself, but in a less serious fashion. Bud approached me one day to say that he had found a horse. In fact, he had found two, one for him and one for me. He had already come up with saddles, tack, and all the other essentials. And now he had the horses. "Forget it, Bud, I can't afford a horse," was my usual response. This time Bud said he was going to buy both of them. He didn't want to be a cowboy alone. It was a crazy idea but that was little deterrent to me. I was a young adult man who didn't do many logical things anyway. So, off we went to get our horses. No, we didn't have a trailer or any other way to get them back home. They were 20 miles away. We were going to ride them home. Logic again escaped us both as we drove to San Ramon during the afternoon hours. Bud bought Sarge and Forsythe and we saddled them up for the long ride home. Sarge was mine from here on out, while Bud claimed Forsythe. The rancher just grinned and shook his head as we rode out his driveway wearing our cowboy hats. We hit the main road and turned north, toward home. There was no shoulder or sidewalk along the roadside, just a 5-foot drainage ditch for miles. The horses were fine, until it got dark. Headlights shone in our eyes as we negotiated the small space between the roadway and the drainage ditch. Cars honked and I waved back with my finger. I'm sure that both horses were talking back and forth about the idiots they were now going to have to obey. I swear they both shook their heads and laughed. Hours went by and we finally made it to Walnut Creek. We had to ride through town and out to Bud's house. It was daylight before we arrived, and my butt was calling me names that even a butt shouldn't say.

I don't think Cheri ever rode the horse. She didn't really have an interest. I remember Tammy walking around his head when he lowered it to eat, his big eye just casually looking at Tammy's head. Tammy had no fear, and I should have been more protective. I gave her rides on the horse and she liked that. He was very spirited and loved to run. He was hard to stop when he did and hated it when Bud's horse came along side. He always wanted to be in front, so I didn't take Tammy along very often.

Cheri and I had few peaceful times and at 19 years old I had many driving forces. Like Cheri, one of them was for attention. I wasn't a bad looking young man and occasionally got attention from other girls. Bill had effectively taught me the techniques of cheating on your wife but failed to relay the moral violations of it. Although it rarely happened, it did occur, I shamefully admit. I'd go home feeling guilt ridden and distraught. There was no victory or excitement in the deceit. I'd see Cheri and Tammy and feel worthless. This was not a quest I was proud to print in the history books. My shame stayed with me for weeks afterwards.

Teresa was a small Indian girl with long, course black hair who liked me in high school, and tried to stay in touch even after I was married. I shied away from her as I was only temporarily attracted to her in high school. Contrary to Cheri, she was quiet and rarely spoke. She was submissive and almost obedient, but she had little personality. I had to drag a conversation out of her, and my interest in her in high school had been fleeting. We ran into each other in town one day and I had just had an exceptionally hard morning with Cheri. Teresa and I talked some and she was still clearly interested in me. I needed that at the time and found it comforting. She gave me her phone number and for the next few months we talked. On rare occasions we'd see each other, but I really didn't know why I was doing it. I didn't want to, and I wasn't sexually interested in her. I suppose I was just responding to her declaration of love for me. It was not something that I valued, and I wanted out of this illicit friendship. I was looking for an excuse to end our encounters. She had a boyfriend out of town and visited him on the weekends or as often as she could. She became pregnant and chose to identify me as the father, hoping I would make a commitment to her. I was angry. Our rare meetings took precedence over her actual boyfriend, who was much more likely responsible. I asked for a blood test, and she rarely contacted me again. Little David was born to her alone and I met him once when she brought him to one of my rare part time jobs at a gas station. Only a few months old he certainly was a cute baby. Did he resemble me? Opinions differ.

I wandered from job to job displaying my own sense of values, or lack thereof. If I didn't like something at work, I believed it was my duty to announce it and quit if need be. I was generally liked by most employers except for that trait. It cost me a lot of job security, especially when I needed it most. Cheri was pregnant again.

I was no better off in life now than I was when Tammy was born. I struggled to make ends meet. Generally, they didn't! I cringed each time Cheri said we had to go grocery shopping. I'd go with her to try to keep things under control and always failed. "What do you mean you need milk?" "Can't we get along without laundry soap?" "This stuff is going to cost us over $100.00!" A hundred dollars took a long time to earn during the days of my youth. You'll think the same thing about today's wages when you snuggle up against your retirement years too. I'd be despondent and angry at Cheri every time we left a grocery store. I thought she always spent too much, and I had to find a way to get the check to clear. Cheri never really did spend too much on groceries. Accusing her of it was my way of saying we could have done with less. I guess we could have eaten air.

Cheri grew bigger, and I grew angrier. I didn't know how I was going to meet this additional responsibility. I didn't object to her pregnancy; I objected to the overwhelming imposition of how I was going to pay for it. That bled over into the appearance that I resented another child. I was unable to make this clear to Cheri and she always believed I was hostile towards her for getting pregnant. Little help came from family or friends. Her parents offered a bassinet and some other incidentals. I resented that I couldn't provide that myself. It seemed like only weeks went by before it was time.

July 19, 1970, "It's a boy," the nurse came out to announce. I was dazed and numb. A girl was difficult to raise, how was I going to do with a boy? I hadn't even considered it before. I had assumed with certainty that Tammy was to have a sister. I was wrong and surprised again. Lee was named after my father, Leo. Cheri wanted that and I agreed. I didn't know how I was going to treat a boy or what I had to do differently than with a girl. I just didn't know, and I hated not knowing. I didn't resent Lee for being a boy. Instead, I had to gather my thoughts as to how I was going to raise him. My only education to male companionship was Bill. I wasn't about to do that to Lee. I had a lot to think about and it kept me in solitude, away from Cheri, and even Lee.

Cheri and the baby were home from the hospital for only a couple of weeks. We fought and argued every day. It may have been the height of our discontent with each other. We were deep into confusion as to what the other was thinking, and we were unable to communicate our own thoughts or emotions to the other. She was up and walking around and healing from the birth. I had planned a hunting and fishing trip long prior to the birth. Cheri never went with me in the past. I didn't feel she'd miss me if I left now. I packed up my gear, hooked up my small wooden fishing boat, and left for a long three-day weekend with my brothers. We all loved to hunt and fish and figured that during a hunting season an employer was just going to have to do without us for a while. We each lost more than one job because of our erroneous presumptions that our bosses would understand, but this trip was cut short. Weather moved in, our camping spot was less than dry or comfortable, the hunting was miserable, and there was certainly no place to fish. Making an unusually difficult decision to go home early, we packed up Saturday afternoon and headed for home. As we got closer to town, each in our own cars, we broke off and went in our own directions. It was late now, nearing midnight. Cheri always stayed up late and no doubt she'd be awake when I got home. I stopped at the head of the gravel driveway to turn around and slowly backed the boat down alongside our small one-bedroom house. The moon was shining, and it helped me park the boat. There was a carport at the side of the house but it was too difficult to get the boat turned and parked inside it, so I usually left it in front. The small house was more of a cabin and sat parallel to the driveway. There was only one bedroom and it had a back door that led out to the carport. The gravel creaked and crackled as I put the boat in its place. Something was wrong, and I couldn't quite decipher what it was. Why did I think something was wrong? Was it just a feeling, or was there something more? The front of the house is what I found unusual, and it was easy to see that the porch light was off. It was never off at night. I don't understand why it would be off now. And the small light in the carport was off. It was left on most of the time, but not as faithfully as the front porch light. In fact, all the lights in the house were off. The house was dark inside and out. I stopped the boat, shut the car off and

45

looked behind at the carport once more, wondering why. As I looked, the full moon lit up a dark figure of a man leaving the carport and walk out into the dry plowed field behind the house toward a group of houses in the distance. He was well lit and I could see he was a large man with dark hair, and looked similar to Steve, a karate teacher I worked with at the Dojo. What was he doing, and why was he in my carport? I jumped out of the car, but too late. The man was gone, lost in the distance. I ran to the front door but was stopped by the lock. The door was never locked, even when I wasn't home. I pounded on it for Cheri to open the door. She didn't answer, and now I didn't know if she was alright or not. She was a very light sleeper and would frequently get up to check on a small noise or a creak in the house. If she didn't, she'd wake me to do it, or she'd just get up to watch some TV for a while, but I couldn't get her to come to the door now. I ran around to the carport door leading into the bedroom and found it locked too. I pounded on it, but I couldn't wake her, and I went to the back of the house to the kitchen. A window was always open there as it was an old wooden frame and very difficult to close. I'd crawl in through that, but as I approached it, it was easy to see that this window, too, had been forced closed and locked. This couldn't be. "Please God, this can't be." I ran around to the front of the house again to pound unceasingly on the front door. Minutes later, it was unlocked, and Cheri opened it. She was in her nighty and robe, and she quietly let me in.

To this day, I know not whether Cheri was with another man that night, but it was the end of our marriage. My anger, my assault, and my threats were more than she could take. Within days, she had moved out of the house with Tammy and Lee and went back home to her waiting parents. They were right; our marriage was not to last. The next few months were the most difficult I had encountered in my 20 years. I didn't know if or how I was going to live through it, and on more than one occasion I contemplated how I would not. Cheri was 21 now and I learned that she was going to nightclubs. She was moving on with her life; I was not. I couldn't live with her, without her, near her, or away from her. This trauma overwhelmed me hour after hour, days into weeks, and slowly into months. On occasion, she would call and tell me she still loved me and would casually assure me that nothing happened and that I had let my imagination run amuck. I didn't believe her, but it kept me on her string for a little while longer. I tried calling her, too, but usually she wasn't available, according to her parents. Life was not good. I was a miserable young man. To this day Cheri has told me in a detached manner that there was nothing that happened that night. Wouldn't it be a shame if I unjustly accused her? Or an equal shame if she had a chance to get it off her chest, and let the opportunity pass her by? I would very much have welcomed the engagement of hearing what had happened and that she was sorry. No-one but her knows whether anything actually occurred that life-changing night or not, and like anyone else, she is to be considered innocent first.

Donna finally left Bill, or more appropriately put, kicked Bill out. She learned of his ways and caught him at it. She could take no more and she divorced him without turning back. In time, she met another man, Jim. Jim was a good man, quiet and not at all like Bill. Jim fell deeply in love with Donna, and she with him. As many relationships evolve, theirs' too had its rocky periods. It's difficult to surrender your own life to someone else and be happy doing it. Each had their own habits, likes, and dislikes. It took time to learn the other's ways, and then pursue the best one. But they worked at it and were eventually married. I liked Jim and was happy for Donna. She started to be her old smiling and laughing self again. Her misery from living with Bill, and then losing him, was fading. She was commencing a new life with Jim.

Donna and Jim lived in a nice rental house in Concord with a little cottage out back. I lived alone in the house Cheri and I shared, and I was miserable. Their suggestion that I move into the cottage out back was the first break of separation that I took from my life with Cheri. I lived alone in the one room cottage and never remember having any company or female companionship. I had a job driving a delivery meat truck in Hayward and worked from 3:00 a.m. until, many times, late in the afternoon. The drive home was all the energy I had left and I slept until time to make the 1 hour drive back to work. It kept me busy, but I didn't like the hours I spent alone in the truck. 'I kept to myself anyway, so what was the difference?' I'd ask myself. I had no logical answer, so

I endured long hours of solitude. I got used to it. There were no cell phones at that time. You were alone for the duration with nothing to break the monotony. There wasn't even a radio in the truck. I had many hours to ponder my self-inflicted pain.

Eventually, I was offered a job driving a tow truck on the Bay Bridge. Mike already worked there, and he was the driving force behind getting me on board. I was hired as a temporary driver but hoped it would become permanent. It was an 8-hour, 5 day a week job. The first I ever had and I liked it. It was adventurous, exciting, somewhat dangerous, and kept my mind busy. There was still the long drive back home to Concord but that was manageable. I had a respectable job, I was with my brother, and life was looking a little better. I wished Cheri could see me making something of myself, but I knew I had to get past her. Our separation was now long term and without communication. It was over and I was sure she had a boyfriend by now. I didn't want to hear about it or know about it. It would take something remarkable for me to forget her forever. Much of my torment was spawned by guilt. There was a lot of guilt for the way I had treated her. If only I could say I was sorry, I could close that book, but I would feel guilt for many decades to come.

My six-month temporary hire at the Bay Bridge came to an end. There was a hiring freeze and I wasn't going to get picked up. I got along well with most of my co-workers, and even supervisors. They were sorry to see me leave and I was sorry to go. It was a good feeling to know I was accepted there and would be missed. I liked that feeling and would strive for it at every job I would ever have in the future.

I answered an ad in the newspaper for a tow truck driver in Orinda. This was a high-class, high-income neighborhood in the Oakland hills. I didn't care where it was, I needed a job, and they offered it to me. I went to work right away. I was soon to learn that this job at a gas station driving a tow truck was not as glamorous as working on the San Francisco Bay Bridge. At that time, we pumped gas and washed windows for customers and checked their oil and tires. We greeted them and served them. Many were ungrateful and looked down on a "pump jockey". There was really no reason why they should look at me with respect, but I wished they would. Day in and day out, I pumped gas, washed windows, checked under the hood, and drove tow trucks. This wasn't what I had in mind for a career, but then again, I had never thought about a career other than a secret desire for law enforcement. That was something I had only dreamed about. Certainly nothing I could ever achieve myself. Since I had no schooling, no education, no opportunity, and no encouragement, that dream would have to stay a dream. I resigned myself to whatever life was going to offer. I had no idea how to make it any different.

In time, the tow jobs became more frequent and my gas pumping days less imposing. There were times when I'd do nothing but drive all day. We were a AAA service outlet and I did a lot of tows. As other drivers fell by the wayside and went on to do other things in life, I moved up the food chain. I was offered night calls and took it. Night calls required working on a stand-by basis and you had to respond to a call within minutes of being notified. I was still living in Concord and couldn't make the trip to Orinda in time, so I slept in the back of my station wagon at the gas station several nights a week. I built this station wagon to fit my needs, starting from a junker. Because I had no life other than the gas station I had time to rebuild a Corvette engine and shoehorned it under the hood. I took the automatic transmission out and replaced it with a 4-speed stick shift on the floor. I replaced the carburetor with three deuces and chromed everything the engine compartment could stand. I cut a mattress for the rear of my station wagon and hung curtains inside. This was my home six nights a week, but many nights I enjoyed it for only a hand full of hours at a time. Night calls were busy times, but the commission was good. Following up the nights with a full day shift and getting ready for the night shift again was reminiscent of driving the meat truck. I found myself tired all the time but paid little attention to it. There was work to be done and I was happy to be working. My thoughts of Cheri were farther and fewer between now, but the pain wasn't subsiding. It may never go away, but maybe it's not supposed to. At least I could get through a day without crying or hurting. My guilt still haunted me.

I dated occasionally but nothing serious, and rarely would a second date ensue. I may have been boring or uninteresting. It was likely that I was uninterested myself. I was over Cheri, although she came to mind quite frequently. More so, the kids came to mind. I realized I was taken with Tammy and never got to know Lee. He was only weeks old when Cheri left. Tammy was almost two, and she was so cute she captured my heart. I was too young and inexperienced as a father to know what that meant, or what to do with those feelings. I didn't know how to direct or manage them. I just knew they were there, and they were my weakness. To let it show would mean control given to someone else and disaster for me. For self-protection, I always kept my emotions for Tammy, and the one's developing for Lee, hidden. In hindsight, I don't think anyone would have deliberately used the kids as a tool to hurt me. It was certainly on my mind as a young adult, and I acted on those feelings. 'I didn't care.' 'I'm not interested in seeing them.' 'I'll get to them when I can,' was my outlook, but inside I missed them very much. I had no one to tell. In fact, I had no one to talk to at all. Cheri would reach me periodically to tell me the kids missed me, and I should see them. I consented, but inside I was excited. Cheri was still living with her Mom and Dad and I'd have to see the kids over there. They wouldn't let me take them anywhere out of their sight, so I was relegated to visiting them in their quiet living room, or out on the lawn. With nothing to do, or toys to play with, I found it uncomfortable at best, and the kids found me boring. They soon wanted to go inside or to their bedrooms to play. Cheri was never around, and her parents were entirely uncommunicative. They were doing the right thing by letting a father see his children, but they weren't going to participate in the visit in any fashion. This was so uncomfortable for everyone involved that it soon came to an end. Cheri went on with her life. Her parents didn't have to endure me around their house. The kids were left to grow up with Grandpa filling in as Dad. I paid every cent in child support that I was ordered to pay, but visitation rights were neither ordered nor refused. Reasonable visitation was granted at the grandparents' discretion.

There were many months ahead of me filled with loneliness, desperation, guilt, sadness, blame and self-confessions. My inner emotions were full of turmoil. Since Dad died I really had to place where I felt at home. Yes, people tried in whatever ways they each knew how. I didn't blame them and you won't find me doing that now. Life brings with it its own experiences and each person has an assignment to make the best of whatever ones they have themselves. I'm no exception to that rule. It's important to note here that there's a difference between blaming and recognizing. My biggest male influences in life from a growing child into adolescence were my Dad, who I still consider a hero to me, brother Mike, in the Marine Corps and not able to mentor me or shape me into a young man with integrity, and Bill, Donna's husband, who did shape me into a mirror of himself. The things I learned and the values I developed were to lead me down a very dark path overgrown with trials, hurt, and infliction of that same hurt. When would I mature enough to realize that I'm not a victim of life? I created my own issues and consequences. If Cheri had been disloyal to our marriage, and the jury has never come in on that, then was it only her fault? Of course not. If I had treated her like the woman and wife that a spouse deserves to be treated, she would have had no reason for wandering eyes, or a yes to her headshake. If I had espoused a decent set of morals during my growth to this stage I'd have had more and better friends, employers who wanted to keep me on. Family who were proud to have me drop by, and a pleasant wave hello from casual acquaintances. No, the devastation I feel and the loss of the only person or woman who I was able to pour out my inner thoughts and feelings to is gone, and I did it. Now, as if to lay a final jewel on an enemy Kings crown, I have to lay awake hours at a time knowing that this woman is or will be giving all those precious emotions and love to another man. I could not get over this easily, and my nights were distraught with guilt. Guilt that I couldn't admit to anyone, but Cheri. And she was gone. I wished each hour that I could tell her how sorry I was.

My turmoil seemed to last an eternity. Each day, each hour, there seemed to be no peace. Eventually, after many many months, this pain subsided some. It didn't go away, and probably never would, but through God's mercy, it got a little numb. I started to work and function as a human being. I was still very lonely, and very guilty, but I could start talking to people, and I started to establish new grounds for my moral character. Things I would no longer do, and things I would start doing.

Each one, in my mind, was designed to make me a better person. One even I could respect. This improvement didn't manifest itself overnight. It took months for me to develop. It would take years to perfect, if ever I could do that. I didn't know, but these were consequences I never wanted to experience again. If I did, I pray I wouldn't have the guilt that burdens me now. Yes, my personality and character were improving now that there was no more Bill in my life. "In fact," I thought, "I wish Cheri could see it." But she wouldn't, and no other woman would either. I wasn't interested. I was alone and it was going to stay that way. At least until I get me under control. Sure, I found the occasional woman attractive, I wasn't ready to become a Nun. But women would have to wait. There's going to be a new me. One nobody has seen before. Especially me. Life was hectic yet boring, but I was headed for a dramatic change. God had a surprise for me that I neither wished for, nor expected. But God knows what's best for all of us, even me. This surprise was months down the road, but the clock was ticking, and my life was headed for another dramatic change.

CHAPTER 4

My Life, My Love

I was tired and sleepy from several night calls in the tow truck. The calls usually started coming in around 2:00 a.m. when the bars closed, police impounds, lock outs, misguided directional changes into a ditch. There were all types of reasons a tow truck was called. I experienced most of those reasons at one time or another. Last night seemed like a particularly busy night, and Sid, our garage mechanic who so faithfully woke me up in the back of my station wagon when it was time to start the day, let me sleep in an extra half hour. I thanked him for it and really needed the sleep. I'm sure I looked like a feature role player in a horror drama as I walked across the parking lot toward the restroom to wash up. I'd been working the day and night schedule for weeks, and it turned into months, I felt like I was in somebody else's body, and they didn't want me to do anything.

The all-too-familiar gas station bell rang as someone entered the pumps and ran over the hose. Ding-ding was the bell's announcement as they pulled to a stop. No one was there to service our newest arrival and I was annoyed. Me, a tired tow truck driver, would have to do it. I patted myself on the back and changed direction toward the pumps.

"Fill it up, please." was all I heard as I peered down from over the top of the white 1965 Mustang. Its black vinyl top looked like it had just enjoyed a fresh drink of Armorall. The voice was pretty and feminine. I liked that. It was always nicer to serve a woman than a grumpy ol' man who looked down on mere earthlings. "Regular or Ethyl?" was my routine next question as everyone always forgot to mention their preference. I was looking down into the window, but I could only see from her shoulders down. Car manufacturers must have orchestrated their design solely for gas station attendants. I could see right down to her white skirt underneath the black steering wheel. I've seen this many times before and rarely paid attention any longer, but her short skirt, worn in the fashion for the day and time, revealed the attractive nylons embracing her beautifully formed legs. This was an eye-catcher and I took pleasure in taking the time to ask her "Regular or Ethyl." "Regular please," was the response from this pretty voice and I stretched that brief conversation into a look through the window. Her beautiful wavy dark hair gracefully touched her shoulders in a gentle fashion and swayed slightly as she turned her head toward me to repeat again, "Regular please." Her eyes were dark, with makeup perfectly outlining them. Her face was formed in a peaceful, pleasant fashion that perfectly complemented the rest of her body. Nothing was out of place, and she clearly took time to prepare herself for the day ahead. She looked at me straight in the eyes as she turned her head toward me, and a smile graced her face. It complemented an already perfect woman. Her teeth, white and straight, seemed to have a glow to them that one could expect to see only on a TV show. I was momentarily paralyzed. I couldn't move, nor did I want to. I must have appeared to be the old Foolish Brush man that I used to be. "I, ya, okay, Ethyl, no you said Regular, okay, I'll get it, thanks." I stammered around for a useful word to say, just to stare through her window a moment longer. My face probably looking like an over ripe pomegranate ready to pop, I gave up my manly stature by stumbling over to the pump. "Check under the hood, Ma'am?" I asked, hoping she'd consent so I could keep her a few minutes longer. I knew I was going to check under her hood whether she said yes or not. "Yes, please," was the right answer as her beautiful smile once again adorned her face like an elegant human ornament. I wasn't ready for this, I didn't want this, and I was very uncomfortable with this. Click, went the handle of the pump, and I knew this fleeting moment was about over. I hung the pump handle up and thought quickly. "Check your tires, Ma'am?" I asked, hoping it'd give me time to think of another way to keep her there. I'd have rebuilt her engine if she'd stay long enough. "They're fine," was the disappointing end. I told her how much the gas was and went to get her change. My face was red hot. My hands even shook. I hoped she couldn't tell. This was embarrassing. I stuttered a little as I counted her change back for her. I think she knew what she had done to me. How could I hide it? Did I hide it? Did I make a fool of myself? I heard the engine crank over and I knew this was the last second of my encounter with the most beautiful woman I had ever seen. She smiled again as she started to pull away, but it was a special smile. A look-back-over-her-shoulder smile. A go-out-of-her-way smile. My knees got weak standing in the middle of the islands. She must have liked my uniform I said to myself, a "pump jockey/tow truck driver" uniform. Must have been what it was. A disheveled, just woke up, tired tow truck driver in a wrinkled uniform must have caused that last smile. My mouth must have still been open as I reacquired my route to the rest room. I'd remember this morning for a long time to come. Thoughts of this woman preyed on my mind throughout the day. I couldn't tell anyone about her and didn't want to. These thoughts were to be kept to myself. I wasn't the type to reveal myself in such a way anyway. My mind kept wandering back to this morning. I'd probably never see her again. I had no idea who she was or where she lived. She may have worked in Orinda or have just been passing through. I wasn't the aggressive, go-get-her type, even if I had known where she was, but it would have been tempting to have some idea how I could prearrange "accidentally" running into her again. Everyone has their own personal idea what a number 10 is to them. Mine just stopped in for gas. It was a good day.

I had no illusions that this chance encounter was not a one-time event - it was and that was okay. Women were not high on my "To Do" list. I wasn't hunting for one and I still felt the pain of losing my wife and family. Other than the occasional unimpressive date, I seemed to feel numb toward any need for companionship. It was something like holding your hand over a flame - once burned; all of us flinch at the thought of doing it again. I had a lot of thinking to do about why it went wrong. Whose fault was it? Why? What caused it? What could I have done differently? There were a lot of questions I had to sort out, but inwardly, deep inside myself, I knew that my character flaws were a major contributing factor to the destruction of my relationship with a woman that I really cared about, and I couldn't change. Her actions triggered my reactions. Regardless of whether her actions were wrong or not, my reactions certainly were, and I couldn't control them. I had a long way to go before I was going to be able to admit that to myself and a longer way before I could confess it to others. I had a lot of baggage to carry. I sifted my way through it daily, but little got resolved in my mind other than my wife and family were gone. I caused it and I might never see any of them again, certainly not on good terms if I did. There were no forgive-and-forget abilities with either Cheri or me. Our separation was permanent and painful. I went back to pumping gas and my mind dwelled on superficial things the rest of the day. The following day was uneventful, and I worked my night shift for AAA. I usually woke up with my own alarm as I was very uncomfortable getting out of the back of my mobile motel with employees around, especially the owner, Bill. I was there with his permission, but I was still uneasy about it.

Two days after the event with my number 10, I awoke as usual, dressed myself while lying down in the back of the car as I always did, made a trip to the restroom, and commenced my pumping gas duties while waiting for a tow call. It wasn't long before a white Mustang with black vinyl top pulled in and we all heard the familiar loud "ding, ding," that was common in the gas station world. I had already started helping a customer and as usual, another employee came out to make their services available. I have no idea what was said, but he turned around and walked back to the mouth of the station bay where we frequently stood to chat and wait for our next customer. It wasn't long before I finished with mine and walked over to the waiting Mustang. "Hi, can I help you?" was my normal unique opening question? "Fill it up, please." I knew that voice, and yes, of course, THIS is the white Mustang. I quickly lowered my head to look inside the window and it was her, my number 10, my fantasy woman. I couldn't help but smile at her. It was obvious that my smile was uncontrollable. She must have read my excitement all over my face. "Yes Ma'am," was the only thing I thought to say. I hope I didn't tangle that up. I went back to start the pump. "Check under the hood, Ma'am?" "No, you did that two days ago. I think everything is fine." Oh great, now what am I going to do to keep her here? It was only a minute or two before the all too familiar click was heard, announcing the completion of the gas flow. It was a disappointing sound this time. It almost made me angry. I hung up the nozzle and approached her window for payment. I was glad that she hadn't prepared, as she reached for her purse. Okay, here it goes, was my thought. "You work around here?" was my novel, educated-sounding question. "Yes, over at the College," she answered me. She really answered me. She spoke directly to me and was looking at me when she did. She wasn't annoyed in her response, and her answer came with that beautiful smile. She went back into her purse but answering me was a sign of approval that I had to have to try to speak to her again. I don't remember what I said or how the conversation progressed. It'd be silly of me (and silly of you to believe me) to think I could detail the entire conversation, but we talked for over ten minutes there at the pumps. That was one of Bill's taboos, but in this case, I didn't care. I tried hard to keep her talking, and hence, keep her there. She went along with it without noticeable hesitation. She certainly couldn't have been interested in me, but she was so pretty and polite. We knew by each other's participation in the conversation that it was winding down. "What's your name," she asked, as though I was wearing somebody else's shirt. "Duane," I responded without pointing to my name tag and possibly make her feel she had asked a dumb question. "Hi Duane, I'm Paulette." I had never heard that name before, but I liked it. It fit her. I openly exposed to her that I hoped she'd come back again, and she smiled as she pulled away. I walked back to the open bay door happier than I remembered being in a very long time. Paulette, I said to myself over and over. I didn't want to forget that. She might come in again. Paulette. I wrote it down and stuck it in my shirt pocket. "Why didn't you help her?" I asked the other attendant who first approached her when she arrived today. "Because she asked for you," was his answer. She DID? Then it hit me. I was a born investigator. Her car only took a couple dollars in gas. She filled it up two days ago. If she was going to work at the college, her fill-up would last all week, so why was she in today and why did she ask for me? I don't understand. What am I missing? I'll think about that later. I was in a great mood the rest of the day.

It was Saturday. The weekend was starting, and I'd be working day and night, as usual. The days would be busy and the nights busier. This schedule was catching up to me and I was getting tired. I'd often go to the restroom as though I needed to sit down for the usual reason, but within seconds of sitting, I was sound asleep. I couldn't help it and went in the bathroom so I could rest for just a minute. Someone would pound on the door, and I knew I'd been in there too long. I'd go out to the islands for another hour or so. It was so difficult to stay awake. I walked across the parking lot to get something out of my car and was standing alongside it when I saw someone walking from the sidewalk up into the gas station, toward the office. I remember my focus of vision was low. I was looking down. My eyes caught the woman because of her short skirt, worn so frequently at that time as the style of choice. I was very happy for that style. I was uninterested as I looked at her shoes, and up her legs toward her face. I was forced to stop at her legs. They were beautiful, eye catching, even mesmerizing. "Wow," I thought to myself, "that's beautiful, perfect, exactly the leg shape I like." I was a leg man, I guess. I followed her figure up to her face and hair when I stopped with amazing surprise. It was Paulette. She was so pretty. Although I hadn't practiced it before, I quickly walked across the parking lot to her without looking like I was walking quickly. That was difficult to do, but by taking slow steps and very long ones, you can cover a lot of ground. It isn't enough to walk slowly though; you have to look around with your head, like you're interested in things other than your destination, and be sure to look up at the sky. That's important, to show how cool you are! The heck with that! I have to get to her before someone else does.

"Hi," I said with a smile and far too much enthusiasm. She couldn't have helped but think so too but responded with a smile and a return "Hi". "My Mom and I are having lunch down at Lightner's. I was just wondering if you'd like to come down with us." I think that this was truly a gift from God. "Sure," I responded without hesitation. It wasn't quite time for my lunch break, but I didn't care. I was going to lunch. If Bill hadn't given me the time, I'd probably have quit my job. Paulette and I walked the short block together to the restaurant. I ate there frequently but had never seen Paulette there. We walked in and sat down with her mother. She looked so different than Paulette. You couldn't tell by looking at them that they were related. "This is my mom, Lisette," she said. I'd be challenged to remember that name, but I'd try. Lisette was a woman in her 40's, and pretty, but in a different way than Paulette. Her blond hair was natural, and she was well dressed and made up. As soon as she spoke, I could tell that she was German, probably just off the boat. Her accent was very thick, but she was pleasant and smiled frequently. She dominated the conversation for the next hour, and I willingly indulged her. I didn't get to hear anything from or about Paulette, but I think Lisette was taking a liking to me, and that was good. In fact, I liked her, too. We were about halfway through my short one-hour lunch break when a customer got up to pay her bill. She was a young attractive blonde-haired girl, but she didn't catch my eye until she turned to the front door after getting her change. Someone had just walked out, and she wanted that open door too, so she ran over to it and grabbed the edge with her hand. It happened to be the edge that closes against another edge, and it did its job, on her finger. It was a dumb thing for her to do, but funny only because I had done the same dumb thing before, myself. I started to laugh out loud, unable to give the girl the courtesy of letting her make a mistake without notice. Apparently, Paulette and Lisette had caught their fingers in a door too. We all laughed at the poor girl's expense. She walked out without noticing our appreciation for her entertainment. Paulette, Lisette, and I seemed to have the same sense of humor.

The hour had passed in just a few minutes. I don't know if anyone finished their lunch, but it was time for me to go, and I couldn't avoid it. "I have my tow truck to attend to," was the only thing I could say that might impress them. After embarrassing myself with that, I rose quickly to leave. "Well, you must come by the house sometime," was Lisette's parting conclusion. "I'd love to," was the only answer imaginable. Lisette took me up on my acceptance and set the time and date. This was amazing to me, and I willingly took down her address. I was going to see Paulette again, and with her mother's blessings. Her mother must have liked me, and she dominated the hour's conversation. The invitation was the onset to turning my life in a different direction. I knew it when I walked back to the gas station. I didn't know why, but I knew it would.

They lived in an upper scale home in Orinda, on the side of a hill. Although not as expensive as many of the other Orinda homes, it was much nicer than many, certainly a more glamorous home than I had ever lived in. It was spotlessly clean inside and out, everything in its place. They were good housekeepers. There was no man of the house. Lisette was the only parent to Paulette, the oldest. Dave, Collette, and Yvette were her younger brother and sisters, and I met them all. They were nice but disinterested. My evening entailed getting to know Lisette and Paulette better. It was easy to tell right away that they had more of a girlfriend/girlfriend relationship than mother/daughter. Somehow, I was pleased that they got along so well. I learned that both worked in the kitchen at St. Mary's College.

Paulette made no effort to impress me, and she didn't have to. Maybe she knew that. Lisette was very friendly. She treated me like an adult friend. If anyone wanted to put their best foot forward, it was Lisette. It was interesting and I paid attention to both of them that evening. We ate, talked, and talked some more. Maybe there was something about my personality they liked. I certainly tried to show them I had a good side. We talked about their past, my past, their likes and mine. Mostly theirs. I didn't have a lot to talk about that would contribute interest in a conversation. I learned that Lisette's ex-husband, Maurice, was a dog who walked out on her, or so she said. There was no doubt that she firmly felt that way and wasn't afraid to express herself about it. As years went by, I met and befriended Maurice, who I felt loved Lisette and all his children very much. There must have been more to their breakup than meets the eye, or the mouth. As the evening ended, both Lisette and Paulette saw me to the door. I really hoped I could see Paulette again, but she left no indication as to whether she wanted to or not. I'd have to leave that up to her. I hoped she'd come by the gas station again, soon.

The next day Paulette did come by the station, not just for gas, but to see me. I was so happy, but I had to act cool. I failed and told her how happy I was to see her. We saw each other every day after that and talked on the phone often. I'd go to her house where we'd sit and talk, leaving the tow truck outside while waiting for any calls to come in. It annoyed me when I got one, and I think it did her too, but something was happening that I didn't expect. It was never spoken out loud, mentioned casually, or broadcasted, but Lisette was becoming very comfortable in trying to get attention from me. I gave it to her, and she wanted more. I didn't mind, but at some point in time I couldn't help but feel she may have been interested in having a closer friendship than we had. I have no experiences that would corroborate such a crazy thought. After my focus openly turned toward Paulette, Lisette changed. She was nice, but stand-offish. I was sad about that and hoped I had given her no cause. I was a pump jockey interested in her daughter. Is there any wonder she became a little distant?

Although Paulette and I saw and talked every day, that's all we did, and we spent hours doing it. I enjoyed her conversation, her point of view, and her objectivity, and I listened to her opinions, whether I agreed with them or not. When I wasn't with her, I was thinking about her. Weeks went by and we had never touched each other, not even held hands. We hadn't even been on a date, so I finally asked her out, but not just her. I asked if she and her mother would enjoy going to San Francisco with me and my mother. It was arranged, and we all met and went out to the City. You can't help but have a good time in San Francisco, and we did. All of us talked and laughed. I had never made any moves toward Paulette and was determined that I wouldn't. I wasn't going to put her in a position to have to reject me and compromise our relationship. Maybe she was happy just being friends, and I already knew she never had a real boyfriend in the past, other than Steve. I hated that name. She assured me that she and Steve were close, but not girlfriend/boyfriend. I thought maybe someday I might take Steve's place. On the way home, Paulette sat across the seat from me, as she always had. I was thankful for the bench seat in the car, but I don't think she knew it was there. I looked at her frequently and on one occasion looked down at the space between her and I to see her hand resting on the seat, not close enough to her to be comfortable, but in the middle of the seat, over toward me. Could this be an invitation? I felt like a schoolboy at his first movie. I couldn't stretch or yawn to casually put my arm around her. This would take guts. I laid my hand down beside hers, to very lightly touch her finger. She accepted, and we both held hands for the first time. It was a beautiful moment for me. I was holding hands with her. It lasted for a while before she slowly took her hand back to do something. She never returned it that night and I hoped I had done nothing wrong. I prayed she wasn't sorry. It was a good night, and that's how it ended, with a "Good night," at the door, and I drove Mom home.

We continued to see each other every day, but somehow, we didn't pick it up from the holding hand's stage. We were still friends and growing closer, but I never tried to hold her hand. I don't know why she pulled away, and I didn't want her to tell me.

We were in our sixth month of seeing each other every day and she had become an integral part of my life and I was confident in that, by now, I had become important to her. I cared for this woman deeply, and I had told her so. She was more restrained in making the same declaration, but I knew I was substantial in her life. I don't know how it came about, who caused it or what stimulated it, but finally Paulette had found the middle of my bench seat, and I liked her sitting next to me. I turned to her for the first time while sitting in front of her house, and she turned to me. We were face to face and she didn't turn away. I slowly leaned toward her to give her a chance to turn away. She didn't, and we kissed for the first time. She was like a pool of satin. I melted into her as though I was emptying my inner being into hers. I could feel her enjoying the kiss as much as I was. From then on, I was hooked. I didn't want this woman to ever get away.

We continued seeing each other and learning more about each other day by day, but as boyfriend/girlfriend now. We were well past six months into our relationship and never had a fight or argument. Certainly we each had our moments of unhappiness about something, but we handled it differently than I had in the past. I cared when she was upset, and I let her know. She'd respond by sharing her grief without accusation. She worked on trying to work out a problem and I did too. I tried to sense when she wasn't happy and address it before it festered. She, too, could tell when I was hurt or frustrated and would let me know she cared about that. My insecurities and jealousies had not gone away; I had brought them under control, or was hiding them, I'm not sure which. She never gave me any reason to be jealous. She was very committed to our relationship and clearly wasn't the type to deceive or cheat. I was secure in her devotion, but not so sure that surroundings or circumstances wouldn't interject themselves into our world.

Paulette liked goatees, a wrap-around beard and mustache and asked me to grow one. They weren't popular then, but I agreed and started my growth. It was only a few days before it started to fill in and be clearly apparent. Bill, at the station, didn't like that at all, and let me know. "I wasn't going to present myself to his customers that way" he announced. "You've got three days to shave it off." I was always up to accepting a challenge, especially if I felt the challenger was wrong. On the third day I lost my job. I was thankful in a way. No more working long day and night shifts. Scared, but with quiet amusement, I packed my gear together and drove off, wondering if Bill had given any thought as to who he'd get to replace the hours I worked there.

I had a difficult time finding my next job. I slept at Mom's on her couch for a while but couldn't contribute anything. I was very uncomfortable with that, and finally called Mike in Grass Valley. He wasn't working either but had some ideas as to how we could make some money. I heard his plan and packed my gear. "I'll be back in a couple of weeks," I told Paulette. I almost cried when I left, and she did. Two hours later, I was in Grass Valley and met up with Mike. He introduced me to his local watering hole, and we spent several hours at the bar. Mike enjoyed being the king of the mountain at Red's, and most of the people there steered clear of him. They certainly didn't want to anger him, and now that his brother was there, he was openly confident that we were a team to be contended with. I went along with that. We were a team. I won't say we got into a lot of fights, and I won't say we didn't, but we drank a lot and were available to all comers. We were never beaten, but probably should have been. We needed the lesson.

The next morning after my arrival in town, Mike and I went up to a place above North San Juan, outside of Grass Valley. He had a friend who would let him cut firewood there. I pitched a tent and set up home. Mike drove back to Grass Valley where he lived with Julie. I was to stay in the tent to fall trees and cut and split firewood every day. Mike would take orders in town and bring a truck up to pick it up. We'd split the proceeds, and pay our bar bill, but living in a tent by myself, working daylight to dusk, and eating from a pot on a campfire was less than thrilling. I was thankful that I was making some money, but each time I went into town, I'd run up a bar bill and have to go out to cut more firewood to pay for it. This wasn't working out. It rained, and I'd get wet, but still fall and cut trees. Alone, I kept at it and drove myself to complete each day, but I really missed Paulette and had no way to call or talk to her. I grew very despondent. Then, the tent started to leak. I'd move things around to keep them a semblance of dry but usually to no avail. The dripping would fall on my sleeping bag and in my face. This old tent was leaking everywhere. Sleep was tough, but eventually it overtook me.

I woke up one morning and could barely stand up in the tent. 'What's this?' I asked myself as I reached up to the roof. I knew immediately what it was. I stepped outside to see everything covered with snow, about six inches of it, everywhere. "Well, here's another challenge" I thought to myself. The old muddy road leading up the hill to the main dirt road was covered with snow, and my car was settled into its place in the mud and snow next to me. There would be no getting out of here until the snow was gone. I had no radio and no way to tell how long the snow was expected to last. I took inventory of my food and water, then the chain saw gas and oil, and other essentials. Mike wouldn't be up until the snow was gone, I was sure. I relieved the tent from its burden and cleared the fire pit. The coffee was good; I had no time for breakfast, and I went down to my pile of already cut rounds and started splitting firewood. I had a lot of time to myself for the next few days and disciplined myself to maintain my own work standards and goals. I had quite a pile of firewood built before the snow became mud. I was out of supplies, and the tent was collapsing. I made drinking water from the snow but the fuel for the saws was low, and I needed Mike to get this monster pile of wood down to town so I could get some money. Mike drove in with his truck. "I see you've been busy" was his recognition of the wood pile. I just nodded like any mountain man would. We loaded it up, broke camp, and set about getting my car up the hill. The ground was still frozen, and it was the best time. He pulled while I searched for traction. I'd have left it there had we not been able to get it out, but we won that battle and I saw town for the first time in a while. Mike went off to sell our bounty while I stayed in town for breakfast, then to Red's, where I called Paulette.

"I'm coming up," was the only thing she would say. There was no arguing with her or trying to convince her otherwise. I tried and failed, but I was glad I did. A few hours later I saw her walk into Red's, and I was so happy to see her. I was a mess, and she didn't care. "We're going home," was her comforting decision. I offered a token argument, but she won.

Lisette wasn't as pleasant as she once was. She was troubled and aired her grievances frequently. Sometimes it was because Paulette and I spent too much time together, sometimes about Maurice, but she wasn't a happy woman. She was first generation from Germany, and came over just after the war, and became a citizen. She quickly learned to enjoy the freedoms our Country offered, especially the First Amendment. This put stress on Paulette and I, while she tried to remain girlfriends with her mother, who wanted more of Paulette's attention for herself. Paulette was pulled back and forth and although without malice, I pulled on her myself. This wasn't good for us, nor her family. I didn't want to lose her, nor did she want to leave me. Her Mom was at the point of being angry much of the time, so Paulette and I would sit out in the car to talk for hours instead of going inside. That upset Lisette too, and we didn't know what else to do. Eventually, Lisette gave Paulette an ultimatum. She'd be in before midnight or move out of the house. We tried to comply and succeeded frequently, but not always. Lisette stood by her word and Paulette was forced to move out.

We had no place to go, and I had no house or apartment for us. We moved in with my old friend, Bud, in his one-bedroom cottage. Paulette and I slept on the couch in the living room. It lasted for a season until we found our own small house in Pleasant Hill. I delivered firewood for a tree trimmer with a rented truck, but I couldn't make the rent and it didn't last long. We moved over to Wardlow Lane in Concord. It was a little one-bedroom bungalow. I went to work for an old friend who cleaned pools, and we stayed alive. I learned that the first thing that leaves a relationship is the romance and that's shortly after it meets head on with responsibilities. Paulette had completed her training at Beauty College and was trying to make a go of something she enjoyed very much. I liked her doing that but was very much against her being a barber. I didn't want her cutting a man's hair, my insecurities you know. I was genuinely afraid and adamantly against it, strongly against it, and would fight to my death over it. I was very unfair to her, but I still feel the same way today.

Then the fateful letter came. The draft board had learned that I was no longer married to Cheri and moved my draft status to "1-A". This would mean that I was eligible and would have to watch the lottery, as so many others had, to see where my number came up. It was soon to happen and with trepidation I watched TV during the lottery for my number. The first third, it was said, could be expected to be called immediately and would certainly be drafted into the military. The second third would be on standby status should additional personnel be required. The last third could probably relax unless war was declared, and all personnel called. I watched each number come up like a bingo game when the shock came. My number hit and in the first third. It couldn't be, but I looked again, and it was. It definitely was! I was going into the military, without Paulette. My asthma was still prominent in my life, but I had been able to control it without a doctor. There were no records for the past few years. Could I even make it through the military, or should I try? I didn't know how to feel about this, but I did know that I was looking at another life-changing event. It took a week to absorb what I had seen, and I visited the Army recruiter. "Yes, I would definitely be drafted," was his response. "No question about it." Now that I had accepted that fact, I really didn't want to become an Army soldier. Dad and Mike were die-hard Marines. Dad loved the Marine Corps and nothing could compare to it. I grew up hearing that the Marines were the only military our Country had. They were far and away the best of the best, but not everybody made it through the Corps. Mike was one who did, and I was proud of him. Maybe if Mike did it, I could too. I went to see the Marine Corps recruiter and as soon as I walked in, I knew that this was the place I had to be. There were no options. The Marines would have to let me in. I signed up in short order and didn't tell them about my asthma. They wanted a doctor's note saying I was okay, and I brought one back saying that I suffered with asthma all my life, but I hadn't been treated since High School. That was all I needed, and I signed the papers. I was on a six-month delayed entry program to get things in order. I was to report on January 6, 1972. The clock was running now, and it couldn't be stopped. I had to tell Paulette, Mom, Mike, and others.

The stress and problems we had in life had caused Paulette and I to argue. It had been going on for some time, and we just couldn't communicate as we used to. Our arguing got worse, and our boundaries were deteriorating. We'd say and do things that we didn't mean just to make a point or hurt the other one as much as they had just hurt us. We lost our ability to communicate as we had enjoyed so much in the past. We were destined for a head on collision with disaster. Neither one of us wanted it to happen but knew it would. Paulette had an opportunity to travel back to North Carolina with her sister and husband who were visiting out here. She accepted and we both knew that this was the beginning of the end. We wanted each other but not the life we were living and leading. It didn't look like it was going to change, and I didn't know how to change my feelings. She wasn't going to accept our lives like this any longer and she made the move to start a new life in North Carolina.

I thought it was best, too, for a while. We'd talk to each other on the phone but generally an argument or disagreement ensued. I had just gotten a check from Bill, my pool friend, and asked Paulette to come home. We discussed it and made some agreements and arrangements. I bought the ticket with all the money I had and sent it to her. I waited for her to come home and missed her very much. At the last minute, she decided she wasn't coming. I was so distraught I didn't know what to do. I decided to use the ticket myself. I borrowed a small amount of money from Mom and got on the plane to North Carolina. The plane trip was stressful. I didn't tell Paulette I was coming and didn't know if she'd even see me. I had only one round trip ticket and no idea how we'd get home if she agreed. Maybe I'd have to stay there, too. The plane landed in North Carolina and a nice man offered me a ride into town. I accepted and put my small suitcase with everything I owned in the rear seat. He knew the area and took me to a motel near where Paulette was staying with her sister and husband. I thanked him for the ride and the information and went inside to rent my first motel room. It was more expensive than I had thought, and I was counting each dollar. Barely enough for food and a couple of days here, I thought. I went to the room, which was only modest at best. The first thing I did was phone Paulette to tell her I was in town and that I needed to see her. We talked for some time, and she agreed to come to the motel. I wanted a shower and needed to clean up, but it wasn't to be. I left my suitcase in the man's car. I had only what I was wearing. What next? Maybe he'd bring it back when he found it there. Nope, I guess he liked what I used to own. Whatever was in it he enjoyed and he's probably wearing my clothes now.

Paulette arrived and we were happy to see each other, very happy. We talked about our problems and tried to understand each other and iron them out. We agreed and disagreed. We had a lot of work to do. We talked for hours over several days until my money was running very low. She helped as she could, but she had no money either. It was time for me to go home without her. I had missed my flight and had to cash the ticket in for money. We were at the bus station now, sitting in a row of chairs. Darkness had fallen and my bus hadn't arrived yet, but it would soon. Paulette said more than once that I was not the committed type and couldn't make the commitments to her that she needed for security. I couldn't understand that, as I loved her very much, and she admitted loving me. Then it hit me. I understood what she was saying. In front of everyone at the bus station, I knelt in front of her and asked, no, begged her to marry me right now! She was surprised and didn't believe me. It took some time for me to convince her I was serious and ready, although it scared me even as I was trying to convince her. We looked at a crippled old man with no legs who was sliding himself around on a cart low to the ground. He was dirty and misshapen and both of us felt sorry for him. That seemed to join us a little bit and Paulette got on the payphone to tell her sister she wouldn't be home tonight.

I cashed in my bus ticket, and we bought two round trip tickets to

Dillon, South Carolina, just across the border from North Carolina. You could get married there right away, unlike North Carolina, and we got on the bus together. We made the trip almost without talking, as this was a life-changing bus ride. We got a cheap motel room and waited for the next morning. That night was filled with emotions, happy, sad, scared, unbelief, excitement, and fear. The next morning we found a Justice of the Peace and followed through with our commitment to each other. We were married in a small office by a female Justice on December 21, 1971. It was a very emotional time, the first time that I was making a commitment to someone other than Cheri. I had a fleeting thought of Cheri, but no reservations about marrying Paulette. I loved her very much.

We caught the bus back to Fayetteville, North Carolina, where her sister lived. Her husband was a Green Beret in the Army. I was about to be a Marine and respected his position in the Army. They would be the first to learn of our marriage. They weren't surprised and admitted that they thought that's why she didn't come home. They accepted it with reservations and knew that Paulette was going to leave. Her mother had given some money to Ann to take care of Paulette and there was some of it left. Ann figured out what she had spent and what was left. She gave us enough money for the bus fare for Paulette and I already had my ticket. She gave Paulette an additional $20.00 for the week's trip home, and some Com Rats, Army food, for the trip. They took us to the bus station, and we commenced our ride home. It was a long ride to say the least, and we were going to spend Christmas on the bus. It was okay though, I was going home with my wife. We did spend our wedding night on the bus, December 21, 1971. That was a hard way to spend our first night, in a crowded bus, but we did. Yes, we did.

Station after station we got off when we could, got on when we had to, and changed buses as needed. It didn't take long to tire of this, but there was more to come. We talked about right and wrong, and whether we were doing what was right or not. We were married and that wasn't going to change, but Paulette was a believer in God and wanted to know that she had done the right thing. She told me she was looking for a sign from God that would tell us that what we did was the right thing to do. We were in the mid-west by now at a small bus station in a small town.

Neither of us remember what State or town. They all looked alike as we stopped at one after another across the States. We both became tired and rummy, but something brought our attention to Paulette's prayer for a sign that we were okay. A thousand miles from North Carolina where we first saw him, and days after we had seen him, we saw again the little crippled, legless old man scooting along on his cart. We were shocked to see him, and we both thanked God for the sign Paulette had been asking for.

Our $20.00 didn't go as far as we wanted. I suppose that no amount of frugal spending can stretch a $20.00 bill for a week between two people, even during those times. We had eaten our Com Rats on the bus. Or when we stopped at a Station, we asked the bus café for a bowl and some hot water. They didn't like that, and the waitresses made their thoughts clear on the subject. Our audacity did occasionally get us some dishes and water though, until we ran out of Com Rats, too. We were starting to experience some serious missed-meal cramps and neither of us had eaten since the previous morning. We slept on the bus through some of the night the best we could, but we were getting very uncomfortable. We were tired, hungry, and broke. We were a little more than halfway home and another day was dawning when Paulette and I woke up. We were pulling into another Station. We'd have a one-hour layover, so we went into their café to sit and wait. All the tables were taken except one, so we invited ourselves to sit down. It wasn't long before we had to tell the waitress we didn't want anything, we were just using her table. I'm sure she understood, but the look on her face didn't express it properly. A man had gotten his breakfast and was looking for a place to sit and eat. We were his only option, so he sat down across from us and started eating his plate full of hot bacon and eggs, toast, hash browns, coffee, and orange juice. He didn't say anything to us, he just started eating in front of us. "Hmmmm," I thought, "maybe if I knock him out," no, I couldn't do that. He lifted his eyes to look at us a couple of times and went on preparing his great-looking breakfast. Before he started to eat, he must have felt the need to completely prepare himself, and he rose to walk into the bathroom. Paulette and I watched the door close behind him and briefly looked at each other. It only took a second for us to

70

eat his breakfast and get up to wait for our next bus. The breakfast was good, but it did come with a little taste of guilt.

At some Stations, we got on to find only single seats left and Paulette would take one while I found another somewhere else on the bus. It pained me to do that, and I'd always ask someone if we could trade seats so my wife and I could sit together. Sometimes they would, sometimes they wouldn't.

We finally arrived home, exhausted, as could be expected. We went straight to Paulette's Mom and told her the news. She was angry and beside herself. I didn't expect such a violent response, but Paulette did. I think Lisette was remembering back when she and Paulette were best friends, and this was no longer to be. She didn't say that, but she certainly had some very fixed opinions on our marriage.

We stopped at her father's house to break the news to him. He was much more congenial and accepted what he knew was inevitable. He reached into his pocket and gave us some money, hoping that it would tide us over until I got started back to work. It helped a lot and I thanked him immensely.

The next stop was Mom's. She started out disbelieving it but came around in short order. She was saddened about the marriage and couldn't hide it but wished us both the best. After getting it off her chest, she came around with full support hoping that we'd get our problems straightened out. She was sure that Paulette and I loved each other, and that things would work out. The hard part was now done, and we went back to our Wardlow Lane cottage, but only for a few days. I was to report to the Marine Corps January 6, only a week away. It seemed like only hours from now. The clock was ticking, and we were headed for another life change.

CHAPTER 5

I Become a Man

S leep was not on my mind the night of January 5, 1972. Paulette and I went to bed without saying much to each other. Our relationship was stressed, but we were working on ironing out our personality differences. Neither of us really intended to hurt the other, but we seemed to be in pain anyway. Each wanted our marriage to work out, but hoped the other would come around to our way of thinking. It was logical to think that it was easier for the other one to change than it was for us to change. Besides, we each knew that we were right, or at least forgivable. I still suffered miserably with my insecurities. Was I good enough for the one I loved? How could I keep her? Would she cheat on me? How can I stop her from being interested in someone else? Would she deceive me? Was I physically enough man to keep her happy? Has she had experiences with other men that would keep her mind on them instead of me? All these confessions I candidly make with guilt, shame, and embarrassment. As I lay out my life, integrity mandates I confess the Good, the Bad, and the Ugly.

We spoke little about the future or what she would do while I was away for the next three months. It was both a painful thought and something we handled by avoiding. I set up an allotment of money to be sent to her for rent and food. Her job as a cosmetologist supplemented my income and she'd be okay. Not comfortable, but okay. Mom lived only a few miles away. She and Paulette were getting along fine. Paulette's mother only periodically communicated with her and I knew that would improve once I was away. Everything I owned was in this little house, and it seemed like the fewer things you have, the more important what you do have becomes. Little things that would mean nothing to anyone else, I labored as to what would happen to them.

I planned and wanted to spend a long amount of time with Paulette after we went to bed that night, something to remember. It wasn't to be. She rolled over and without saying anything, went to sleep. It was her way of dealing with the stress. I said nothing, but closed my eyes to ponder tomorrow. Knowing that Paulette wanted to keep to herself and sleep, I finally dozed off.

The knock at the door was early, but I knew who it was. I didn't want to answer it, yet there was a form of excitement. I opened the door to find a U.S. Marine standing outside. His tan shirt was ironed with creases down his pockets to his waist. His blue trousers were a part of his Dress Blues and the blood-red stripe down the side of his leg denoted he was an NCO. Several stripes on his sleeve let me know he was experienced, and a man of stature. He said little, but what he did say was pleasant. He was there to pick me up. I wanted to ride with Mom and Paulette to the airport, but he wasn't going to let that happen. He didn't want an AWOL recruit before I ever got to the base. It was a casual good-bye to Paulette as I knew she was going to the airport with Mom. The ride there was quiet as the recruiter said little to me in route. He escorted me to the boarding area and waited off to the side while I went to Paulette and Mom. Both were trying to hide their fears. I hugged Mom good-bye and held Paulette tight. Paulette didn't know very much about the Marine Corps or boot camp, but Mom did. She would tell Paulette after I was gone. Paulette was to gain great respect for a Marine, a hero of sorts, and I wanted to be the focus of her admiration. I boarded the plane and got a window that let me see the terminal. The plane started to move and I slowly waved my last goodbye to Mom and Paulette standing there watching. I was now on my own. I had been warned about boot camp for many years. I was about to experience it myself. My focus and steadfast goal was to do exactly what I was told, and do it the best I could. Would that be enough? I thought of my asthma, and a wave of fear came across me, would I be able to hide this or not?

One stop after another, one delay creating another, we didn't reach MCRD on the bus until after dark. Well after dark. I saw the Marine at the gate salute the bus as we passed. It made me proud for some reason. My pride would quickly to turn to fear.

I no sooner heard the air brakes when the door opened and a huge hulk of a Marine jumped aboard, his flat-brimmed hat tilted down over the top of his head to just above his eyes. We'd soon learn that it was called a Campaign Cover. "Get off, get off, get off my bus," he yelled as he walked with force down the aisle. Although I knew what to expect, I could see the expressions on the remaining naive civilians who were already standing up. "Boy he's rude," was one comment made. This recruit was about to learn a lot in a short time. Rude was NOT an appropriate description of a Marine Drill Instructor. As expected, we placed our feet on the footprints painted in the pavement outside the bus. We were all a bunch of civilians on a Marine military base, and looked like a herd of disorganized livestock. We were about to see this for the last time. Within an hour we had been issued utility uniforms that had their own unique smell to them. They looked wrinkled and ragged but freshly washed. We were issued a utility hat which would be called a hat for the last time. It was a cover, and would always be known as a cover from here on out. Our next stop was the barber. He wasn't taking requests. Each haircut took less than a minute. His sharp clippers buzzed over your head taking everything off that you had been so proud of only hours ago. The cold air swept across your newly shaved head and you wondered how you would look with this bald head, but as I vowed before I arrived, I would accept this and anything else they had in store for me. I had only been away from Paulette for hours, but I was already missing her. I turned my focus once again on dedicating myself to complying with this life and the education that was ahead. I was steadfast to the commitment to be a good Marine, though I admit, I was getting scared.

We were issued a toothbrush and other personal items to be placed in our shaving bag, in exactly a specific way. We showered all the civilian grime and crime off and went to a wall of mirrors and sinks to shave. I arrived at a mirror shared by three other recruits and peered in to see what I looked like now. There were several heads in the mirror, all looked alike. I stared for moments, looking for the head that belonged to me. I'm sure the other heads were looking for themselves as we all moved our heads in separate ways to make the appropriate identification. It would have been a shame to shave the wrong face.

After all was done, and our initial G.I. issues were given out, including a Bible, we were escorted in platoon formation, that resembled more of a herd, to a squad bay. We had one minute to get into a bunk bed, a "rack," and I quickly jumped onto a top rack. The light went off and I lay there in shock. I was told what to expect from family and other Marines. Experiencing it was quite another matter. Is this real? Am I really here? What's Paulette doing, and is she all right? I don't remember thinking of anything else when the lights came on. "Get out of those racks you maggots." I jumped to the floor which I would soon learn to call a deck, and stood at a poor example of attention at the foot of the rack. "You pieces of crap will go to the head, to brush, shower, and shave. You have 3 minutes, MOVE." Every recruit there was in shock, maybe not so much so by what was being said, but rather the new world they had volunteered for. I was the lucky one. I came from a family of Marines who had coached me on what to expect and how to handle it. I confess though that being told and experiencing it yourself, as we all know, can sometimes be incomparable experiences. I, too, was in shock. When you have 90 days to make a super human out of a common civilian, shock is the first stage to making the change. They did it well, to everyone, no exceptions. And this was but the beginning.

Within a few days, we were assigned a platoon and each recruit went to their own. Mine was Platoon #1007. I'll remember that for the rest of my life. There were three Drill Instructors and a Platoon Commander: Sgt. Burrell, Sgt. Keys, Sgt. Warrell, and our Platoon Commander, Staff/Sgt. Johnson. These were the best of the best, each one a Marine's Marine. They were the heroes that you'd go to war with. Viet Nam was still raging with all but a small number of Marines out of boot camp being assigned to go to. I expected to go as well, and had already volunteered. The entire platoon was in fear of our Drill Instructors, and hated them, save one. I did fear them, but was in awe of them as well. There wasn't a modicum of hatred in me. Yet I still feared what lie ahead. Could I make the grade, or would I fail? My asthma was my weakness and possibly my downfall. My strength was my maturity. I was 22 years old in a platoon of 18 and 19's. I'd use this to my best advantage.

Boot camp had three stages. The entire time we were there was called a "T" day, "T" for time. T-90 for the first official day we started and we counted down to T-1, the day of graduation. It would be a very long 90 days. Each day was a lifetime in itself. From 5:00 a.m. to 9:00 p.m. there wasn't a moment that we weren't doing something or trying to do two things at once. Not a moment of rest, except one. Sunday morning was an hour of prayer at the Base church. I chose the Protestant session and found it comforting. I learned little about God, but did get the exposure and I'm sure that much entered my spirit by osmosis. I'd be glad of that later. For now, I got to spend an hour away from the Hell, and found some peace in the interim. Paulette had always had an open respect for God, and I'd give it a chance. I didn't know much about God, but I believed in him, and in Jesus. I didn't know really what to believe, but I was sure there was a God, and Jesus was his Son who did live on earth and died on the cross. From there my knowledge was limited, and I didn't know why I had to know any more.

5:00 a.m. in January was cold. Getting out of the rack was difficult, but normally I had my feet on the deck before I was awake. Shortly after we commenced training and T-day's started, I was made a Squad Leader. My position was at the front of the Platoon. My rack was at the head of the squad bay. I could "feel" the Drill Instructor when he stepped into the Squad Bay to hit the lights. Seconds later the metal garbage can clanged and banged as it flew down the isle of the squad bay. "You maggots get out of those racks!" was the order of the day. No matter who the Drill Instructor was that day, it was always the same. Standing at attention in our skivvies, underwear for you civilians, trying to open our eyes, the first thing we all thought of was what T-day it was. Shine, shower, and shave, we had only minutes to organize ourselves in preparation for chow, an inconvenience for the Drill Instructor's I'm sure, but a few minutes of relief for the Platoon. Nobody ever spoke to each other. It wasn't allowed. A nod or a look was all we needed to communicate. Chow was a time when we felt somewhat normal. If we spoke quietly enough, we could communicate with each other. But we ate our chow in Marine Corps fashion. We didn't eat what or how we wanted. We ate what we were told, and everything we were served, we ate everything. Starting at the head of the chow line, the last thing we were to eat went on the tray first. The next thing went on top of that, then the next on top, until we learned what we were supposed to eat first. It was always the last thing on top of everything else. Fortunately, I don't remember ever having any soup. We ate our way down to the bottom, immediately picked up our trays and walked past the Drill Instructor, who ensured the tray was empty. If it wasn't, it would be made that way quickly. We took our positions outside, forming the Platoon as each recruit came out, standing at-ease while we waited. At-ease in the Marine Corps doesn't mean what it sounds like. Your left foot is stationary while the right can extend out parallel to your shoulders. Your head can move, but not to a point where it creates attention. You speak nothing, and your arms are to remain at your side. "At-ease" was a misnomer, "Prelude to attention" would have been more appropriate, but it would have been difficult for a Drill Instructor to order us to "Prelude to Attention." The last recruit out meant the Drill Instructor was right behind him. "Platoon, Ten, Huh!" was always the order. Only a Marine can understand a Marine's order. We clearly understood what was being told to us. To me, the best part of boot camp was about to come. It came several times a day, and always gave me a chill. No one could do it like a Marine Corps Drill Instructor, and none of them did it the same, but it was always the identifying sound of a Marine, and couldn't be copied by any other branch of the service. "Righ HUH!" "For Wrd HUH?" We all stepped out at exactly the same time and always heard the familiar heel of our boots hit the deck as though it were one sound, and then it came; Marine Corps cadence; the most amazing and beautiful sound I've ever heard, or ever will. You marched with pride, because you were proud. Sure, we were all maggots, lowest of the food chain, wanna-be Marines, whale feces, civilian scum, but we were marching to the cadence of a United States Marine. We never seemed to march anywhere long enough. It ended too soon. Our next task was waiting, and there were always many more that day to do. March, drill, PT, obstacle course, run, drill again, more running, classes, more running, and more drill. Everything we did was at double time. At times it was hard for me to keep up, but my goal was to excel. That was going to be a whole lot harder.

Many of our classes took place on the floor at the head of the squad bay. Fortunately for me, it was next to my rack. My foot locker was at the foot of my rack, of course. As soon as we were ordered to the front of the squad bay I knew it was a class. While others secured their gear and ran to the front, I got into my foot locker for one of my two pair of boots, my belt buckle brass, and some polish. As we were taught the fine art of killing, or staying alive, I paid strict attention, and spit shined my gear. I always had first class gear. I hoped it was good enough and was afraid to be proud of it.

We marched back from breakfast chow one morning and were told to stand by at the head of the squad bay. We were at attention when Sgt. Keys was walking back and forth in front of us lecturing us on an aspect of training. Suddenly he turned quickly around and looking directly at me, he fixed his cold eyes and I knew he had picked me out for some reason. Pushing the Recruits between us aside like bowling pins, he forced his way to me. I knew he was coming for me, but I didn't know why. His attack came even before he reached me as his arms stretched out to my throat. Grabbing my neck his hands reached entirely around and he squeezed down. I didn't know why he was attacking me, nor what I did for this, but I knew how to get out of it. My training as a karate instructor made it instinctive, but wisdom, this time, told me to remain at attention. No matter what, remain at attention. "You want to eye f--- me, puke?" he yelled. His face was the only thing I could see and his campaign cover down over his eyebrows. "You going to eye f--- me again, maggot?" I was getting weak and I wasn't able to breathe. His strong hands around my throat were closing off my air, but just shy of crushing my windpipe. With all my concentration my hands remained at my side, and I remained at attention. I was going to let him choke me, even if it meant I'd go unconscious. He may have seen that I was going down, or maybe I was just lucky, but he let me go just as my vision was going black. Without saying anything else, he walked to the front of the Platoon and continued his lecture. I spent several minutes regaining my breath, and my composure, but never moved from being at attention. I learned much later that this test was to see what kind of Marine I was to make. My file had warned the Drill Instructors of my training, and Sgt. Keys determined to see whether I was going to make it to graduation or not. Sgt. Keys didn't know what I would do when he came for my throat. He had guts, and I passed his test.

Pit Calls were a form of punishment that came more than once a day. They consisted of sprint pushups, jumping jacks, sit-ups, more pushups, leg raises, and more sit-ups, all at double time, and as fast as could be accomplished. Normally a Drill Instructor would march us over to a dirt pile, mud pile, or a shallow sloppy water pond for our Pit Calls. Sometimes we knew that we had done wrong, many times we didn't. What we did know was that if one recruit screwed up, the entire Platoon was going to pay the price, normally in a Pit Call, sometimes as a run for several miles. We quickly learned who the screw-ups were, and many watched them closely. If they looked like they were trying, I'd offer help. If they weren't trying, rebelling against the Drill Instructor, or boot camp itself, I'd turn away. I knew what may be in store for them. I never participated in a blanket party, but I knew of at least one. A bar of soap inside a sock could be swung with convincing force. After taps, a blanket pulled over a recruit's head and body to cover his face and hold him down by the corners of the blanket, prevented him from seeing anything or escaping. It was a cruel but convincing way of motivating a recruit who could do it right, but wouldn't. That recruit never slacked behind the others again. No one else did either. Everyone knew the Drill Instructors wouldn't have tolerated such a method to improve motivation, and nothing was ever said by anyone.

Phase-1 of boot camp encompassed learning to march, care for our gear, initial drill, indoctrination to PT, running, and discipline. I had learned and accepted all of this as the precursor of more to come. I seemed to excel on the obstacle course. I was physically strong and agile. The obstacle course was a Marine obstacle course, and difficult at best, but I looked forward to it. Running was more difficult, much more. Each time we set about for a run I was scared. Each time I got asthma, and each time I had to hide it. The Drill Instructor sometimes ran alongside the Platoon, and that was easier for me. But if he wasn't there, he was running in front, right in front of me. I stared at the back of his campaign cover, trying to breathe, and trying to hide that I couldn't. Asthma seems to be a unique ailment. You begin to fight for air, just a little air, anything, and with all your strength your lungs take in a small amount. Never very much. Just enough to make you thankful. Now you have to force it out. Your throat won't let it, but you force it anyway. With no air left, you try all over again to suck in whatever will come. Breath after breath, minute after minute, and frequently hour after hour you fight, until you're too tired to fight any more. No position you get in will aid in taking in the next breath, and you get so tired it's hard to keep on fighting. When you make it through another bout, you know things will be better the next time. They have to be.

The Drill Instructor's campaign cover hardly bounced as he ran in front of me. Up one hill, and down the other side, his pace remained the same. Our boots sounded like thunder on the hard pack dirt. Had we been on the pavement, we'd be in tennis shoes, so we always knew what kind of run it was going to be before we started. Running was tough for me.

Our racks were made every morning before we left the squad bay. All exactly the same way, and with a 4" fold at the top. No wrinkles. The blanket pulled tight enough that the Drill Instructor could bounce a quarter on it. He did, and it did. Until one morning when coming back from a run we entered the squad bay to find it completely overturned. A hurricane couldn't have done such a job. The racks were all turned upside down, blankets, sheets, pillow cases and foot lockers were everywhere. There wasn't a place to walk, or any area not strewn with debris, save one. It was a rack at the head of the squad bay. It appeared untouched. The rack was made, the blanket pulled tight, the 4" fold, and pillow with no wrinkles in it. The foot locker was still stationed at the foot of the rack and it was locked. I looked at amazement at the unbelievable condition of the squad bay and thought of how this was going to get cleaned up, and I looked again at the rack at the head of the squad bay, before realizing it was mine. How I got so lucky I don't know. If I had made my rack correctly, I was sure to continue that way.

We all waited for night time. Sure there was training and even running and marching after dark, but darkness meant that "Taps" was getting nearer. Each day seemed like a week in time. It went on until we thought we had nothing left. After dinner chow, we had time to clean our gear, wash our utilities, spit shine, or even write home. This is what I waited for. I always had my gear spit shined so this was my time for home. Mail-call always, always, brought a letter from Paulette. Every day, without fail, I got mail from her. She was so faithful. Mom would write once or twice a week and I even got the occasional letter from Mike and my brothers, but Paulette's letters were the ones I cherished. She'd tell me how much she loved me, what she had done that day, and how she missed me. She made me confident that things were okay at home and Mom concurred. "Paulette is being so good," she'd say. I knew she and Paulette were getting along well, too. That was my saving grace, and had it not been for Paulette, I may not have made it through boot camp. She helped me to remember I had little time for loneliness. It seemed to come most at night, during my time for thought. I'd read her letters and I'd quickly write back. If I didn't have time, I'd make a way later. "GET in your racks," came the order. "SAY your prayers," came next. The Marine's creed was said out loud, *"This is my rifle. There are many like it, but this one is mine. My rifle is my best friend. It is my life. I must master it as I must master my life. My rifle, without me, is useless. Without my rifle, I am useless. I must fire my rifle true. I must shoot straighter than my enemy who is trying to kill me. I must shoot him before he shoots me. I will..... My rifle and I know what counts in this war is not the rounds we fire, the noise of our bursts, nor the smoke we make. We know that it is the hits that count. We will hit..... My rifle is human, even as I, because it is my life. Thus, I will learn it as a brother. I will learn its weaknesses, its strengths, its parts, its accessories, its sights, and its barrel. I will ever guard it against the ravages of weather and damage. I will keep my rifle clean and ready, even as I am clean and ready. We will become part of each other. We will..... Before God I swear this creed. My rifle and I are the defenders of my country. We are the masters of our enemy. We are the saviors of my life. So be it, until victory is America's and there is no enemy, but Peace!"* Then our prayer to God, "The Lord is my Shepherd," is the only one I knew, but I said it like I meant it, and the lights went off. The timing was always perfect. Quietly in the background over the outdoor loudspeaker I heard Taps, a beautiful sound, and one I know will put me to sleep at my funeral. It was finally time for sleep, and during First Phase it came too quickly. I'd try to hear the ending of Taps, but remember little more. Other times when we had classes for a lot of the day I knew I'd have a few minutes after Taps to stay awake and think or write Paulette. That was dangerous, but worthwhile. I'd take my military flashlight to bed. When the squad bay was dark, I'd pull the covers tightly over me so no light could get out, and write Paulette a letter. Sometimes I was too tired to finish it. Other times I could hear the quiet sobbing of a distraught recruit and felt guilty that I was trying to tell my wife how much I loved her, when he was hurting so badly just a few racks away. As boot camp went on, and the training tougher, I learned to stay awake, to force myself to stay awake. With everything I had, I had to stay awake, at least for a few minutes. For as soon as I closed my eyes, the lights would come on and the familiar garbage can would be waking us up again. If I could only stay awake for a few minutes longer, jus fr few mins lgrrrrr...........

I handled my M14 rifle well. I learned to know it well and could take it apart in the dark in 17 seconds. I put it back together in the dark in 23. Yes, I knew it well. We had never fired this killer, but I knew we would. We marched with it, drilled with it, ate with it, and slept with it. "This is my rifle. There are many like it, but this one is mine." Phase-2 would take us to the rifle range, but for now, I'd learn everything I could about this rifle. But marching for some reason took its toll on me. I developed a severe inflammation in my right Achilles tendon. It got bad enough that I couldn't help but limp, but didn't. Each step was filled with pain. I couldn't twist or turn on that foot as mandated during drill. I couldn't say anything as I'd gone too far with this Platoon. A tour in sick bay would set me behind and I'd have to get picked up by another Platoon somewhere. Running and the obstacle course were more of a nightmare. I pressed on as if I had no choice; I didn't. One thing that the Marine Corps was teaching me was that I would do things that, before I enlisted, I thought would have been impossible. I'd be told to do things that I knew were impossible, yet I'd do them anyway. I'd be ordered to accomplish something that was impossible, yet I'd get it done. I'm glad the Marine Corps taught me that.

The Drill Instructors must have been more observant than I thought. Each morning they'd ask who was sick, lame or lazy and needed to go to sick bay. Each morning I fought the temptation and never said a thing, but for some reason, whenever we went out for a run, or headed to the obstacle course, they'd have something else for me to do. I think they looked out for all of us that way, but they'd never admit to it. In time it healed and I was thankful.

Look out for us they did. I woke up in the middle of the night and desperately had to pee. It was cold out from under the blanket, and the deck was always ice cold. Maybe I could wait for reveille. It's only a few hours away. I looked out the black windows and down the squad bay. Everyone was asleep, everyone but one. At the far end of the squad bay lit up by only a shadow of a light behind him, was the Drill Instructor, standing at parade rest, still with his cover pulled down to his eyes. What was he doing there in the middle of the night, in full uniform, watching his sleeping Platoon? I'll never know. Nor will I know either whether it was real or not, but I'll swear to my death that it was.

Phase-2 brought a bus ride and move to Camp Pendleton. The only purpose a Marine has is to kill people and break things. We were about to learn how to do that. The Marines do it best. There is nothing in the world more dangerous than a United States Marine and his rifle. We had a lot in store for us here, and I was looking forward to it.

We were introduced to living in a Quonset hut. It looked like a small sheet metal airplane hangar. It was nothing more than a big half of a barrel-looking building, laying over on its side. An oil stove sat in the middle for heat. Each squad took a hut. We were headed for some cold and rainy nights in that World War II shelter. Each day we learned more about warfare and the use of firearms from small caliber pistols up to Howitzer cannons.

My biggest fear was about to be realized. The gas chamber. As we marched to it, some of us knew what was ahead, many didn't and they were about to learn. We were issued gas masks and told what they protected against, and what they didn't, how to fit them to our head, and how to quickly clear the gas from inside. We put them on and felt for the first time how uncomfortable and awkward they were. It would be difficult to fight in one of these, but it's better than the consequences. The Drill Instructor checked the fit of each mask and moved toward the chamber. It was a building unlike the rest of the small huts in the area, and without windows. A blanket draped over the entry door was there to help keep the gas in, I'm sure. We entered as though we had no fear. We were good deceivers. When the last recruit entered, we heard the door slam. The hasp closed and we heard the door locking us in from the outside. From here on, there would be no escape. A fire pot was in the middle of the floor and we all stood around it. The Drill Instructor was there to put fear in us, and I believe he was enjoying it. Our masks were still off and the room was very dark. Only a few small lights allowed us to see our surroundings, an otherwise vacant room full of scared recruits. We didn't know what kind of gas we were going to be exposed to, or what it would do to us. "You can breathe now, can't you, maggots?" he said in his firm authoritarian voice. "Yes Sir" was our uniformed shout. "You won't in a minute," he boasted with a pleasurable undertone. Only a second later he ignited the gas in the pit in the middle of our circle. The smoke rose and started to fill the room, but none of us moved, not a muscle. The Drill Instructor was closest to the gas, and he just looked around at us recruits as though it were little more than perfume. The effect reached us before the cloud of gas did. The burning was immediate and severe. Eyes, throat, nose, everything was on fire. "Mask up and clear," was his order. We pulled our masks from their sheaths and donned them, pulling them tight to our face. Once secure, we cleared them as instructed. Our next breath, we hoped, would be clean air. Mine wasn't. I pulled tighter on the straps, cleared, and took a breath; still gas. We were ordered to raise our hands if this occurred. I didn't want to, but I did. The Drill Instructor came over quickly. That was a surprise to me. I envisioned him having a sandwich first. He pulled tighter on the straps, grabbed the mask and pushed it to my face, and tightened the straps again. It didn't help and I was choking with a burning throat. Grabbing my arm, he forced me to the door and pounded on it for the Instructor outside to unlock it. We moved quickly outside and the light hit me as he pulled the mask off my face. Fluids were enjoying their newfound escape from my nose, eyes, and mouth. I didn't like this. The Drill Instructor checked my mask and walked over to get another one. "Fit this," he said with annoyance. I did as he instructed and he rechecked the fit. "Get back in there," he ordered and I turned to walk back into that Hell. I took my place in the circle and heard the door lock behind us again. The smoke permeated the chamber now, but the mask was working. I still burned, but it wasn't getting any worse. "Any other of you girls having a problem?" he screamed with anger. "No Sir," was our muffled unanimous reply. "Then take those masks off. You're going to grace my ears with the Marine Corps Hymn." We complied, and this time all of us felt the burning as we sang for our Drill Instructor. He too had his off, and listened as though he was enjoying it. That was the longest song I've ever sung. "Mask up and clear," he allowed as we finished. We did, and heard the door unlock. We walked out of the gas chamber in line as quickly as we could without looking like we were moving that way. I guess the others didn't like this any more than I did. From then on, it would be harder to hide my asthma.

We spent several hours a day learning the basic firing positions and dry firing the M-14. After a week, we marched for the first time to the firing range. There's no sound like an M-14 when you send a round down range. The recoil bites your shoulder and the slap in the face is something you'll remember. Under control, neither is too much to take your mind off hitting the target. We practiced from quick firing at 200 and 300 yards, to slow methodical firing at 500 yards. I don't know how he knew it, but I overheard the Range Master tell my Drill Instructor, "That recruit's going to be good." And good I was. On pre-qualification day, I tied the all-time Marine Corps range record of 248, out of a 250 perfect score. I was excited and couldn't wait for tomorrow's qualification day. I'd do better yet. That afternoon taught me a new lesson. Things weren't always as you envision they will be. By that afternoon the right side of my face swelled up like a melon. My lip, cheek, and eye, all the way over to my ear, was a large mass of mushy soreness. The Drill Instructor said it was because I had a tight spot weld on the stock of my rifle. That's what they taught us to do, but as usual, I guess I took it literally. That rifle kicked me so many times in the face you'd have thought I lost a prize fight. My spot weld would sure be different tomorrow, like it or not. It was, and my qualification score was down in the 230's, still considered High Expert, but not the score I sought. I was considered sniper quality and told that I'd be going to sniper school after graduation to prepare for my duty assignment in Viet Nam. I was ready and looking forward to it.

A rare event was occurring at the base. The "President's Own" band and "Silent Drill Team" were there for a performance. Usually a recruit wouldn't be given an opportunity to do anything else but train, but this experience the Drill Instructors weren't going to let us miss. I had always been in awe of the "Silent Drill Team", and my brother played in the "President's Band" when he was a Marine. This was a day I'd never forget. I enjoyed listening to the Band, but "awe struck" wouldn't have nearly described how I felt about the Drill Team. It was the most perfect thing I'd ever seen; unbelievable at best. What a goal to aspire to! What a duty assignment to have! What proud Marines they must have been, touring the United States and abroad, demonstrating their control over a fully functional M-14 rifle. Yes, that was quite a day for me. They say that most of the dreams we have at night we don't remember in the morning. I was fortunate. I remembered mine, and I always will. I never imagined myself being good enough to wear their shoes, but I was proud to have seen them.

The only recruits who wore something different were the Yellow Shirts. They were a special small group of Recruits who had excelled in PT. Scoring the highest points in physical agility, running, and the obstacle course earned them a yellow sweat shirt. That's what they wore during PT and they stood out as super human. I aspired to wear a yellow sweatshirt, but alas, my asthma wasn't about to give in to such a success. I admired these yellow shirts as they trained with us, but normally in front of us, because they were faster, stronger, more agile, and all around better at what we all tried to do. I was proud of these recruits. They made me want to be better, and I tried.

Our final exercise at Pendleton was an overnight bivouac. Two teams, one red, one blue. The armbands denoted the difference. Using blank ammunition we would hold our flag, or capture the other team's flag. Night fell and I was assigned to take my squad out on patrol. We worked our way down the mountain and I instructed them to stay off the trail. The walking was much more difficult through the brush, but I wanted my squad to stay off the trail. That's where the enemy will be. Half way down, I spread them out close to each side of the trail. I knew the enemy would have to walk up through there. They had an uphill climb to make, and they weren't close enough to their target yet to start their more cautious maneuvers. It was less than an hour when we heard the quiet rustling of movement up through the brush. More brush moved and I knew it was a squad making its way up toward our encampment. They came along side and their night ended. We took one prisoner back with us.

The final days for Phase-2 met with a 30 mile hike over the mountains carrying full field packs, canteen, and rifles. As we saddled up and prepared to head out, I believed there was no way we were going to hike 30 miles with this. I was wrong. We did. Those that didn't qualify on the range carried their rifles over their heads for some of the trip. Some weren't going to graduate with us, and these rifles held high were the ones who wouldn't.

We loaded up for our trip back to MCRD. We were now into Phase-3, the part of our training that would teach us the finer parts of being a Marine. Up to now the only uniform we had were our hand-washed utilities. Phase-3 would let us starch and iron them. We were becoming more proud all the time. We got fitted for our other uniforms and were excited that we could finally see something other than utilities. We stood in line and received our general issue of Greens, Khaki's, and all the other uniforms that a real Marine wears. In the fitting room were tailors who were going to insure that they fit us as a Marine's uniform should. We were starting to dare to feel proud. We wouldn't wear these until after graduation, but getting the issue meant we were nearing our prize. As I was getting fitted, one of the Drill Instructor's approached me slowly. His eyes were on me and many thoughts raced through my head. "Please, God, don't let me have done something wrong. Don't let me get kicked, or deprived of this uniform." There was no doubt he was headed straight for me. That could only mean one thing. I'm in trouble. "Wear this from now on during PT," he said as his hand came out from his side holding a Yellow Sweat Shirt. In the Marine Corps, you don't say, "You're kidding," "No way," or even "Thank you, Sir". "Yes Sir" was my affirmative enthusiastic response. To this day, I don't know how I earned it, but I was proud to wear it. I felt inferior to the others who wore it, but I swore I'd not shame the honor.

"Purdue," I heard called out. "Yes Sir". "Report next door," was all that was said. You don't ask questions as a recruit. You do what you're told, and exactly what you're told, when you're told to do it. I reported next door to find additional clothing issues. This is where they issued and fitted Dress Blues. That was a proud day in my life. I was the only recruit other than the Platoon Guide who was issued Dress Blues. Probably because of my score on the rifle range, I don't know. It was never told to me, and I didn't ask. But what a wonderful surprise this would be to Mom and Paulette.

Staff /Sgt. Johnson was our Platoon Commander and was a little different than the Drill Instructors. He never swore and rarely addressed us like the worm feces that we were. He was rough in his own way, but different. It was a relief when he came on duty to take over the Platoon. We were all standing in Platoon formation, at attention, for quite some time waiting on something, we never knew what. We were probably waiting for a class room to become vacant, as Phase-3 was filled with classes on war tactics, medical aid, the enemy in Viet Nam, and many other things. I was pleased that they also taught us details on how to wear the uniform, how to speak, how to address the public, and a lot of training on manners. We all became polite Marines. "Purdue," I heard my name called. I dropped out of Platoon formation and ran to Staff / Sgt. Johnson. "What do you want to do when you leave here?" he asked. It was a surprising question that I hadn't expected. No one had ever spoken to us like we were human beings before. "I want to do exactly as I'm ordered," was my response. "You know you're sniper material," he calmly said. "Yes, Sir, and the private will be proud to serve the Corps as a sniper." "Viet Nam." he assured me by a nod of his head and cover. "Yes Sir," was my only reply. "You want to be a Drill Instructor?" he asked in almost a human way." I couldn't help allowing my eyes to get big. "Yes, Sir, the Private surely would." "Where are you going on your leave?" he asked and I knew he was referring to the 30 days we were to get once graduated, which was only days away now. "I'm going home to get married, Sir," I responded almost with fear for doing something else not related to the Corps. "Am I invited?" was his next. Knowing that it was a test question, I answered, "Yes Sir, absolutely, Sir." He ended the conversation with "Get back to your squad". I returned to my position in front of my squad wondering what that was about. Why? What did he really want to know?

Staff /Sgt. Johnson wasn't on duty again for another few days, and only a few days after that was graduation. He called me to him again, and with pen and paper in hand asked me where my wedding was. Certainly he wasn't actually going to come to it, but I gave him the date, time and address. Why would he ask me for these things? Could he do something to cancel my wedding? God I hope not. I didn't see him again until graduation day. This is the day I'd see Mom and Paulette again. I was a different person. I hoped they'd like me.

We stood at attention in front of the civilian audience. The ceremony went on for quite some time and I have no idea what was said or done. I stared into the audience looking for the two women that I loved. I couldn't see them anywhere. Maybe they couldn't make it. Maybe they were late. Maybe they're still home. At the last note of the Marine Corps Hymn, we were declared fully trained and qualified Marines, and dismissed to see our families. I stood there momentarily, and they found me. I squeezed Mom, and loved Paulette. Mom was beaming with pride. Paulette stood in front of me so beautiful I couldn't believe she was mine.

The trip home was quick and I couldn't help but fall asleep for a little while. I awoke and we talked about the wedding. Yes, we were already married, but that was in a small chapel in South Carolina some months ago. This was our real wedding, with family and friends, something Paulette could be proud of. I had forgotten to tell the Staff / Sgt. that I was already married and was getting married a second time, but no matter; I'd probably never see him again. That was my loss, but a natural part of life.

While in Boot Camp, it was announced that the war in Viet Nam was coming to an end. Many of us would not have the opportunity to go. I was included in the many of us. Instead of sniper school, as I thought, I was assigned to be an M.P. The military police was a good alternative. I wanted that from the beginning, but my specialty would be Corrections. I was to work in the Brig. Jails or prisons weren't what I had in mind, but I was open. I was a proud Marine now and I'd do whatever I was assigned.

Our wedding was as beautiful as anyone could imagine. I played no part in its design or planning. I had envisioned a Marine Corps wedding with crossed swords as we exited the church, but that was a little hard to ask, for a newly graduated Marine. Neither Mom nor Paulette knew I had Dress Blues. That was my surprise to them. Mom's mouth dropped as I entered the church. Paulette walked down the isle even more beautiful than I envisioned she would. It was unbelievable that this woman was marrying me. We wed as anyone normally does. I kissed my bride as though it were the first time. With my uniform snugly fitting my newly trained body, we turned to walk down the isle as I escorted my wife to the door of the church. "Ten Huh," was a familiar sound, but entirely unexpected. In front of me were six finely dressed Marines in Dress Blues, swords at the ready, they drew and crossed them in air as one movement. These Marines were here for us. I couldn't believe what I was seeing. We passed under with more pride than I can describe. We were now officially married, and I was officially a Marine. But one more surprise awaited me. Approaching in a uniform I was all too familiar with, escorting his wife on his arm, was Staff /Sgt. Johnson. He drove up from L.A. only days after our graduation just to see me married. This was a great man, and I'd learn to respect him even more in the future. Life was good.

My two favorite women

Staff Sgt. Johnson, my Boot Camp Drill Instructor
and Platoon Commander. A Marine's Marine. I'd
soon be proud to call him a friend as well.

Paulette and Mom surprised me with a Marine Corps Crossed
Sword Honor Guard. They went to the local Base to see if anyone
would help. Telling them that a Marine was getting married,
all six in the room stood up to volunteer. Marines are like that.
I'd later be honored to volunteer for others. Once a Marine,
always a Marine. I know that when I sleep for the last time,
I'll be in Dress Blues, with a Marine playing echo taps in the
background, while I stand at attention in front of my Lord.

CHAPTER 6

Growing Continues

Staff /Sgt. Johnson stopped by Mom's house for a moment after the wedding. He wanted to personally give us his wedding present. It took me quite by surprise when we discovered it was a Bible; a full table display-size Bible. This, coming from a Marine, was not what I expected. He impressed me with it, and I thanked him. I didn't know how to use it, nor was I very interested in it, but I was impressed. I was later to thank him over and over for the seed he had planted.

I had only three weeks to see and enjoy home before heading out to my new duty station. I certainly was going to try to see the kids. I called their grandparents and Edie was cordial in a cold way. Unemotional, she agreed to let us see the kids for a day. We arrived on time and picked them up. I hardly recognized them, but Paulette could see me in both of them. The kids were nervous and very apprehensive. I could tell they didn't want to go and I thought about letting them stay and forgoing my chance to see them. Paulette encouraged me that it would be okay, and we took a change of clothes and loaded them in the car. No good-buy's from Grandma or Grandpa, they were just let out of the door. I was sad at that and remember it well. They were very uncomfortable with letting us have the kids. Clearly they didn't like this at all. I'm sure they felt that it was only fair that I, the father, should have a chance to visit with the kids. They were right, but they didn't like it.

I had to think of something unusual for them today, something they would remember. With nothing close by, the only thing I could think of was Marriott's Great America in San Jose and off we went. It took almost the entire trip to get Tammy and Lee to open up. They sat quietly and would hardly speak. We kept telling them how much we loved and missed them. Paulette worked on them for hours. Lee came around first and Tammy followed later. Marriott's was the ice-breaker.

Soon after arriving, they were laughing, talking, running up to hold my hand, and wanting to be carried. This was such a special time for me that words escape definition. Finally, knowing that we'd be late getting them home I called Les to let him know we were on our way. Traffic slowed us down on the way, and we arrived later than promised. I had hoped they'd understand, and it helped that we called ahead. When we arrived, Grandma was outside. She turned to see Tammy and Lee get out of the car. They were excited and may have wanted to share that with Grandma and Grandpa. It wasn't to be. Grandma sent them directly in the house to their rooms and didn't speak to Paulette or me at all. We got in the car and left. It was clear to me that the kids were to pay a price for my visitation, whether intended or not. I understood why the resistance when they got in the car that morning. I vowed then that this wouldn't happen to them again. "This is the last time I'll be here to see my kids," I told Paulette. She tried to talk me out of it, but we both knew why. I would know my kids through letters from then on.

Paulette was determined that she was going to travel with me to my new duty station at Fort Gordon, Georgia. A Marine got paid only $90.00 a week then and I was afraid that I couldn't take care of her. Leaving her behind wasn't a consideration either, so a week before I was to report to Georgia, we left in an old, but newly purchased car that her Dad helped us buy for the trip, something that would make the trip across the Continent, and hopefully back. Her precious Mustang fell victim to lack of needed upkeep, and wasn't up to the task. She hated to trade it in, and to this day loves the 1965 Mustangs, white ones with black tops, of course.

We said good-bye to everyone and headed off. Lisette was the last one we saw before getting onto the freeway, and she was the hardest. She was giving up her daughter, girlfriend, and best friend to a man that she knew was not good enough for her. I may have agreed, but not openly. The drive was long to say the least. We stopped only for gas and occasional groceries to eat in the car. We stopped for breakfast only because it was the cheapest meal to buy, and it gave us a rest. Paulette's endurance wasn't as high as mine, so I was challenged to do the majority of the driving. She filled in where she could, while I slept against the window. This was the start of our being on our own, and we were to have many experiences.

Arriving at Fort Gordon in three days, my first obligation was to find a place to live. We rented the first place offered to us, a single-wide mobile home out on property not too far from the Base. It was furnished and even came with its own cockroaches, better described as COCKROACHES. You could hear them at night and see them scurry when you turned the lights on. They flew, and the more mature ones had to have landing lights. I'm sure they had to have clearance for their final approach, but I didn't speak cockroach. Georgia itself was a different place to live. The people were pleasant, but somewhat stand-offish. We weren't there long enough to make any friends, but if we had been, it would have taken a while. The town was small, and the weather was humid. There were many ponds and pools around and I was informed to be careful of the water moccasins. I never saw one and I was happy with that. Paulette couldn't do much while I was at school. It was a boring time for her, and it tested us. I, on the other hand was going to Military Police School and had my hands full, classes, books, studying, and watching prisoners. The latter was to be my occupation for he next three years. I'd rather have been in the trenches as a direct Military Policeman, but they thought that this might be the place for me. I'd be the best Correctional Officer I could be, whether I liked the job or not.

Graduation came weeks later, and I graduated in the top three in my class. Because I did, rather than being assigned my next duty station, I got to choose it from a list. That list was long and I had no idea what State was better to choose than the other. North, South, East or West, the choices were many. One that rang a bell was Treasure Island, California. T.I. is between San Francisco and Oakland, only miles from Lisette in Orinda. If I chose that, Paulette would certainly move home with her mother and I might have to, as well, to be with her. That wasn't a good idea. I chose the opposite side of the Country, Camp Lejeune, North Carolina. I had no idea why I chose that, it was just a random decision. I was soon to learn what the center hub for prisoners on the East Coast was going to be like.

There was little to pack. We filled the car and we were off. We were experienced endurance travelers now and made good time to North Carolina. Again we arrived early, as planned, and again I took the first place offered to us. This one was better than the mobile home, but not much. It was a row of four small apartments, built along one of the waterways. It had to have been built by transient, disgruntled, alien farm workers. Although a thin wall of stucco covered the outside, the inside walls were built with plywood. The entire apartment was little less than a large living room in size, but it was home, and we stayed there our entire tour at Camp Lejeune.

The Brig was massive in size, a four-story brick building that housed hundreds of prisoners, some for committing violations that wouldn't even have been breaking the law on the outside. Others were headed to Leavenworth for hard core crimes. Our job was to keep them in line, and some didn't want to be kept. We had to be stronger, meaner, faster, smarter, quicker, and more alert than they. Some of the Duties paid a price for a lapse in concentration. A "Duty" is a staff personnel who is on "duty" at the time. We were understaffed, and our work shifts were collapsing our motivation. Eight hours on, and eight hours off, day in and day out. After a rotation of several days we'd get two days off. That gave us enough time to sleep, catch up on training, and spend a little time with our wives, those who had one. The Marine Corps didn't care much about us having wives. It's been appropriately said that if the Marine Corps wanted us to have a wife, they'd have issued us one.

I grew to love the Marine Corps but disliked my job. I was a hard core Marine and those on both sides of the fence inside the Brig knew me as such. Other Duty Personnel saw me as Gung Ho. The prisoners saw me as one to avoid. My spit-shined brass and boots were beyond what was demanded, and I was content with that. As much as I disliked the hours spent on the job, I never wavered in my determination to be an outstanding Marine.

I was home lying in bed on a hot summer day. There was no air conditioning in our little house and the humidity was high as water evaporated off the slough next to the house. Paulette and the neighbor had been at the nearby dock trying to stay cool. I lay in my skivvies, knowing that all too soon I'd have to report back to duty. I started to doze off when Paulette ran screaming into the house. "The neighbor's baby fell in the slough," she screamed. I jumped up and ran outside. Looking over at the dock I saw the neighbor standing waist deep in the water and screaming, waving her hands. No doubt what Paulette had said was true. I dove into the water and held my breath while trying to find the baby. Up I came for air, and back down again. Then the awful feeling of a little baby, motionless underwater, hit my hand. I grabbed him and surfaced. The baby was limp and blue. I had been trained in the Marine Corps how to give mouth to mouth resuscitation and after clearing his lungs, started it right away. Paulette and the Mom stood by watching and crying. I kept it up for several minutes and could hear sirens in the background. Suddenly, the little baby flinched, and gasped for a breath of air on his own. "A miracle," I thought, and kept breathing into the baby's mouth. He took a second breath on his own, and the sirens got closer. As the ambulance arrived, the baby was breathing, and alive. I was happy I could help. I was able to watch the baby grow and play, until we left North Carolina.

The announcement came out that there was a quota for three Marines across the Nation to be assigned to the Silent Drill Team at 8th and I, in Washington D.C. This was exciting to me to hear, but only in a casual way. Three out of hundreds or thousands weren't good odds. Besides, my assignment was here, and it takes quite a Marine to go to Washington. Almost in jest, I filled out the paperwork. That was unusual in itself as the Marine Corps usually doesn't ask for paperwork. They just tell you where you're going. I left the notice at the Clerk's office and went about my way. Since then, I answered questions and willingly subjected myself to testing and research about my height, weight, facial features, mannerisms, posture, and social behavior, as well as other things that I'll never know I was tested for.

The news came by way of the Brig Warden. I was called into his office for some unknown reason. Normally this was not for a good reason, and I didn't expect this to be different. What had I done? I wasn't comfortable when reporting to the Warden. "Yes sir," I announced when I entered. "Stand at ease Lance Cpl., I have news for you." I contemplated a family death or trouble at home. "You're being transferred," he said

with a connotation of pride. "Pack your gear, you're going to 8th and I."
I could literally feel a cold chill run up my spine. "The Drill Team?"
I asked in surprise. "You're on your way, Purdue. Good luck." I can't
remember a time I was so excited. I had to report to the Clerk's office
for more paperwork. I learned then of the warnings of taking such an
assignment; tours away from home, escorting dignitary's wives, heavy
costs in housing and living, and hours spent at training. It was all
laid out in black and white, but I read little of it. I had but to sign the
papers acknowledging my acceptance, and I'd be on my way. "I'll be
in tomorrow to sign the papers," I told the Clerk. I was off to break the
news to Paulette.

It was hard for me to understand how she couldn't be as excited as
I over this duty assignment. A Marine's Marine. The only other thing
equal to it might be a Drill Instructor. Paulette's hesitation was steadfast.
She wasn't going to be left alone in a town she didn't know, all the way
across the Nation, while I was away on tour. How could I blame her for
that? But I tried. With everything that was in me I wanted to go. But
her warning that if I went to D.C., she would go back home, was the
final deterrent. I went back to the Clerk to decline the assignment, but
I'll always remember that it had been offered. I was a very lucky Marine.

Several months later, I was sent to El Toro in Southern California.
Paulette and I were happy to go back to California. It was nearer to
home and neither of us liked the eastern States very much. This would
be a welcome relief to the eight hours on and eight hours off shift that
I'd been working so long and resented so much. We drove back across
the States in the same three days that it took the first time, and with
the same stress. El Toro was near Santa Ana, Los Angeles, Disneyland,
and a lot more activities than we found out in the remote back country
of Camp Lejeune. We were both excited about this new duty station.
Again I tried to find an apartment, but this time ran into unexpected
difficulties. There weren't any available anywhere, at least, nothing that
was in our price capability. Desperate, I drove down the block of rural
residential areas asking people if they knew of anything for rent. We got
the tip that a small place was available above a photography studio. We
found it, and took it. Next, I reported to El Toro. This brig was old and

decrepit, nothing like Camp Lejeune. Security was a concern here and a prisoner could escape equipped only with dedication to the task. The brig was next to the airfield and we could hear the Marine jets taking off and landing. This would be another new experience, but at least I wouldn't be working that eight on, eight off, shift.

I was signed in and reported for duty the following morning. My assignment would be the high security segregation hall for hard-core prisoners. All duty personnel at the brig were to work 24 on, 24 off, with two days off every other week. 'Jesus', I said to myself, 'more time away from home than before.'

Paulette got a job as a beautician, something she liked very much and was good at. It kept her happy when I was gone, but we suffered our trials anyway. With stress and responsibility come grief and pain. They seem to go hand in hand. The successful people have learned how to cope with one, while controlling the other. I was working on it, but failing. Paulette was not happy, and it was my fault.

I had a year to go in the Corps, and gave hard thought to making it a career. I could be a good Marine, and loved the Corps, but in time, it would cost me my marriage. It was one or the other. I started taking correspondence courses in Law Enforcement and felt I might be able to get a job as a police officer on the outside; that is, if I didn't get into any trouble while on the inside. I had never had any opinions regarding black and white issues until I joined the Marine Corps. By far, most of the prisoners we watched were black. They weren't actually black, most were brown, or a shade of brown, but they liked to be called black for some reason, so white people complied. We weren't actually white either, kind of tan or yellow I'd say, but we've been labeled white, so I accepted that, too. It was the blacks that made me dislike many of them, not because of their skin color, but because of their character, or prejudices. Honkey, Cracker, Opie, and other names ran rampant amongst them and were always directed toward a Duty Personnel who had his back turned. Most of the hostility, rebellion and fights that broke out were started by them, and normally always against whites. They were picking us out as targets, not the other way around. In fact, our orders were not to, and we didn't, at least I didn't. Black, white, yellow, pink, or orange,

I didn't care. As long as you conducted yourself like a Marine, I'd stand behind you. If you didn't, I'd be the first to jump in the middle of your pleasure zone.

I had a personality conflict with one Marine Duty Personnel, a Corporal who was black. He wasn't really black; he was half black, half white. I didn't like that. It was really none of my business, but I didn't like it anyway. He saw me as a redneck and didn't like me, either. We avoided each other when we could. It was a casual dislike back and forth, but he was a good Marine. I watched him work, and you couldn't ask for a more professional, squared away Marine. That made me mad. I was the most squared-away Marine at the Brig. He just didn't know it.

There was a ruckus down in Segregation one afternoon. I opened the heavy metal door to find a handful of young Marine Duty Personnel standing at an open cell. All were standing outside, but the focus of the contention was clearly inside. Why was the door open I thought, and what are these Duty's doing there? The yelling was loud inside the cell but it was a familiar sound. It was a prisoner who had experienced LSD flashbacks in the past, and was going through one again. He was a hulk of a man, big, strong, and angry. One Duty was holding a strait jacket and it was clear that this prisoner was entitled to it, but also clear was his position that he wasn't as deserving as we thought, and he was focused on winning his point. He'd flipped out multiple times during his confinement and been taken to the hospital each time. He had hurt other Duty's before and no one wanted to be his next experience. As I surveyed the situation, I felt this prisoner was ordered to the hospital, and it was the hospital that he was going to see. Vertical or horizontal, it made no difference to me. I pushed past the Duties standing outside the cell and entered the cell alone. He welcomed my challenge and the fight started. I had expected some assistance shortly afterward, but it wasn't to be. The young Duty's outside the cell all elected to be Duty observers. They stayed outside the cell waiting for me to bring this prisoner under control. I was glad to have their confidence, but not sure I wanted to endure this difficulty alone. It was only seconds later when assistance came. It was a lone Marine who grabbed this prisoner with the force of genuine Marine, and together we put him to the deck. Moments later he was wearing his new coat and strapped to a Gurney waiting for transport. Now I had time to thank my teammate who saw to it that I wasn't in there alone. We nodded at each other with satisfaction and approval, and returned to our individual assignments.

On rare occasions the Marine Corps grants rank to individuals who earn it. Or at least that's the way it's supposed to be. But politics and the need to fill a position many times get in the way of better judgment, and someone is promoted early, too early. When that happens his position grows faster than his character. Once that ball starts rolling, it's hard for character to catch up. It lags behind even when needed most. Especially when needed most, even in the Marine Corps. There were a couple of Sergeants who suffered that character flaw. Both knew it, and didn't care. They were difficult people to relate to, communicate with, or even obey. To them the glass was never half full or half empty. It was just wrong, and your fault it was wrong, and you fix it, now! The Corps isn't the only place who has these kinds of people, they're out in the workforce with every major employer. Someone has already come to your mind as you read this, hasn't it? New promotions were soon coming and I hadn't been in rank long enough to be up for one. It meant I'd get out of the Corps as a Corporal instead of a Sergeant, but the only way I could change that would be re-enlist. I hadn't yet made up my mind on that subject. But as I sat in the chow hall one afternoon a well-dressed Marine sat down along side of me. He said little, and commenced his obligation of seeing that what was on his plate found a lower altitude. The chevrons (stripes for you uninformed) were new, and they made the mark of a Sergeant. "We have a new Sergeant," I thought to myself. I prepared to attach a face to an arm. This wasn't near as bad as I had envisioned. In fact, it was deserved. And in fact again, if anyone deserved it, he did. It was Griff. There was little I could say to him because we were at odds. He refused to acknowledge how good I was and I took offense to it. I think he had the same dilemma. But "right is right," I said to myself as I took a swallow of water. "It's nice to see someone wearing those stripes that really deserve it," I said. It happened to be in front of the other two Sergeants seated at the table who visibly took offense. Griff looked at me in the eyes and nodded a thank you. That was the end of our duel. From that point on, we not only became tolerant of each other, but friends; no, not friends, brothers. And to this day, 50 years later, we still stay in touch. We will always love each other as brothers until the day I die. I think he might go first though, he's older than I am. He denies it and won't tell the truth about his age.

Paulette was distressed about Tammy and Lee. She was very burdened about what had happened when we had taken them to Marriott's. She started a campaign for me to get custody of the kids, who were still at their grandparents. I hadn't thought about that as a possibility, but she encouraged me to, and even contacted her father, an attorney himself, to see if it could be done. It wasn't long before I was convinced that it could work, and Maurice filed the paperwork. I knew that Les and Edie didn't want to raise more children anyway, and didn't think they'd put up much of a fight.

It was time for Court and Paulette and I took leave and went to the trial. It was a painful thing to go through. I saw Cheri for the first time in a long time, and we were enemies. The Court listened to Cheri and me criticizing and hurting each other over who should have custody of the kids. It was a horrendous experience for both her and me. Maurice prevailed, and I got custody of Tammy and Lee. "Unbelievable," was my only thought. I was both happy and scared. Lisette was at the trial and was there for the decision. As I talked to Maurice about what was to happen next, Lisette and Paulette talked outside. It wasn't more than an hour or two later when Paulette approached me quietly. "I don't think I can do this," she said in a timid voice, but boldly stated. I don't recall the rest of the conversation, but the next day I had to tell Maurice that we may not be taking the kids. I understood how much of a shock and imposition it would have been on Paulette to take on and raise two children. As a consequence of the Judge's decision, we soon learned that Les and Edie, Grandma and Grandpa, were challenging the Court's decision and would be appealing. We were surprised that they were fighting custody and wanted to raise the kids, but were both happy and sad that they were. We allowed them to keep the kids without filing their appeal, at least until I got out of the Marine Corps.

We continued, as we always had, to send them Christmas and

birthday cards and presents. We'd fill a box at Christmas time and mail it off. Paulette always found one more thing to put in it. There was never enough. We were long on desire and very short on ability. We envisioned the kids opening the presents and being excited that Dad and Paulette had sent them things. We never heard anything from them. No phone call, no card, no thank you in any way. We later wondered whether they ever got the gifts or not. I understand that they did and were told they could call us if they wanted to. Those times were so embroiled in pain for everyone that each individual has their own recollection, even to this day. We eventually slowed down our attempting to contact the kids, and, in time, ceased it entirely. I prayed that one day they'd want to see me and would contact me. They'd have to get older and much more curious before that would happen. In years to follow, I found myself, on more than one occasion, down in Lodi where they lived. I kept track of them by putting their house under surveillance, hoping they'd come outside. I watched them grow from across the highway.

Staff /Sgt. Johnson and I stayed in touch throughout our tours and wrote while he was stationed in Hawaii. He and Mary were coming back Stateside, and were going to Camp Pendleton. That was near us at El Toro and we would surely see each other again. We did, and had a lot to talk about. The four of us visited each other when we could and we'd frequently meet somewhere in between to go to the beach, out to dinner, and occasionally a night club, where we imbibed the fruits of the stem, usually a large glass with rainbows and other such nonsense sticking out of it where we'd all stick in our separate straws. Oh, those nights brought on a lot of laughing and good times; silly times I must say as well. Too silly for us Marines, but we didn't mind. It was good to be with a good man, doing innocent things, and having a good time doing it. The four of us got along well. Gunny became Jim and Jim became my friend.

We went camping one weekend up in the mountains. I took my Yamaha 360 Enduro and Jim got his first ride on a dirt bike. Sadly it was around the pavement in a State Park and the Rangers sought more appropriate places for our source of fun. We complied, with apologies, and put it away. That was okay and I was sorry I got us into trouble.

We spent the evening playing cards and talking. Jim was a Christian and I had some questions for him. He may have thought I was bold and disrespectful, but he addressed each and every one. Quietly and deliberately he convinced me he was truthful in his commitment to God. I grew to respect him for that, but he never converted me to Christianity. I believed in God, that was it.

It grew chilly, then cold. Jim lit a heater in his tent and warmed it for Mary. We didn't have one so we covered the sleeping bags with blankets and Paulette and I snuggled in for the night, just in time, as it got very cold. Blankets and all, we huddled together in the same large sleeping bag.

Jim and I had tried to scare the girls by telling bear stories before we turned in. I may have tried too much. After an hour of feeling the cold trying to creep through our blankets, I heard a rustling at the front of our tent. Something was certainly out there and I lifted my head to get a better listen. The zipper on the sleeping bag slowly opened the door to the tent, and I wondered how a bear could do that. A hand reached in, carrying a heater. Jim set it down, zipped up the tent and went back to his own, knowing that cold was soon to take him now. *Thank you Jim.* The tent became warm and we even shed some blankets and clothes. Later that night Paulette said, "I just got pregnant." She was right.

Lisa was the first of our family. My fears of not being able to pay for her were not there, as they were when Tammy and Lee were born. The Marine Corps was going to host this campaign. Paulette wanted me in the room with her during the delivery, and that's something I could not do. No matter how I thought I could talk myself into it, I couldn't even come close to succeeding. It was close to time, and Paulette flew up to her Mom's in Orinda to have the baby there. Lisa was born October 12, 1975. She weighed 7 lbs. 9 oz. I didn't see her until I got emergency leave and flew home where Paulette presented me with the first of our family. The second child, Nichole, was only 13 months behind Lisa, a crowded pregnancy to be sure. Our family was going to be closely spaced. She was born in Orange County, on November 8, 1976. She was 8 lbs. 9 oz. and the second of our family. One of my favorite names was "Nicki," and Paulette and I gave her that name.

Time went by. I guess Paulette wanted a rest. Duane Jr. wasn't born until August 10, 1979. He was 9 lbs. 11 oz. and would be known as Dee, he was born in Sacramento, CA. after I had left the Marine Corps. He was our first boy, the one I expected to give us the most challenges as a teenager. I was going to be wrong.

My tour in the Corps was ending. I decided not to re-up; however I didn't know what I was going to do on the outside either. My correspondence classes had ended and I had earned several certificates, but it gained me no job. I applied at Contra Costa County for the Sheriff's Office there, and was on the testing list. January 5, 1975, was my last day in a Marine Corps uniform. I put it on at the house, gazed at myself in the mirror and knew I'd never see this man again. Paulette said little as I closed the door behind me. This was a difficult day, but I knew there had to be adventures ahead. That afternoon I drove out the gate and was proud just to be passing the Marine standing guard. It would be for the last time. I stared in the rear view mirror for as long as I could, until the picture faded to a blur.

A true honor for me was having a Marine Corps Crossed
Swords Wedding. Years later I'd return the honor extended
to me by participating in Honor Guard Duty myself.
Here, the second Marine back, with Griff to my left.

Marines have a cynical approach to war, they believe in three things:
liberty, payday and that when two Marines are together in a fight,
one is being wasted. Being a minority group militarily, they are proud
and sensitive in their dealings with other military organizations. A
Marine's concept of a perfect battle is to have other Marines on the
right and left flanks, Marine aircraft overhead and Marine artillery
and naval gunfire backing them up.
Ernie Pyle

A Marines Prayer:

Almighty Father, whose command is over all and whose love never fails, make me aware of Thy presence and obedient to Thy will. Keep me true to my best self, guarding me against dishonesty in purpose and deed and helping me to live so that I can face my fellow Marines, my loved ones, and Thee without shame or fear. Protect my family. Give me the will to do the work of a Marine and to accept my share of responsibilities with vigor and enthusiasm. Grant me the courage to be proficient in my daily performance. Keep me loyal and faithful to my superiors and to the duties my Country and the Marine Corps have entrusted to me. Help me to wear my uniform with dignity, and let it remind me daily of the traditions which I must uphold. If I am inclined to doubt, steady my faith; if I am tempted, make me strong to resist; if I should miss the mark, give me courage to try again. Guide me with the light of truth and grant me wisdom by which I may understand the answer to my prayer. Amen

CHAPTER 7

New Times - New Experiences

I had no idea what I was going to do for a living now that my security in the Corps was gone. I had a family to take care of and I was trying to get hired with the Sheriff's Department in Contra Costa County, but that long process hadn't seen its way to the hiring list yet. The only thing I knew before the Corps was working with Bill in the tree service, so I spent what little money I had on a used chain saw and put an ad in the newspaper. Within a couple of days, I got a call and bid the job. I got it and went down to rent a trailer to haul the brush away. I took the tree down, loaded the brush and headed to the landfill with my load. I cashed the check and placed a bigger advertisement. Within a month I had as much work as I could do. Three to four days in advance was all I dared to book. I'd wake up early in the morning and be on the job by 7:30. Starting a saw at 8:00 sometimes seemed like a long wait. By noon I usually had the tree trimmed or down. The rest of the day was spent cutting up the brush and loading it onto the trailer, as high as I could load it. I'd shove stakes down the sides and load it higher. When I couldn't throw the branches up on the load any higher, I'd climb up the sides dragging the limbs behind me. "This is probably against the law," I said to myself. After several weeks of doing the same thing, I felt more comfortable with getting by with it. Eventually I'm sure that the trailer wanted to get up and hide in the closet, but I paid no attention. I had to get the load to the dump, unload, and start all over again. I needed occasional help and the first one to offer was my old adversary, now my closest friend, Griff. He had no idea what to expect when coming out on his days off to help. Paulette tried to tell him, and he responded in the affirmative, "Yeah, I'd expect that from this guy." But I don't think he really knew what we were going to do or how hard we were going to do it. Griff worked right alongside me without saying a word. Limb for limb, branch for branch, he loaded, climbed, loaded some more, and tied down the load. "Let's go empty it and come back for another load," I suggested. Griff just shook his head and grinned. He was a great guy, and still is.

I kept the family fed with the tree service for the next year, but the more work I did, the more equipment I needed to do the work; ropes, climbing gear, bigger saws, a trailer, and the list grew. I ran into a deal from a competitor to buy a stump grinder and agreed to make payments. This would increase my business two-fold and I was excited about pressing the new stump grinder into work. I sent him his payments faithfully and had several thousand dollars paid off within the following several months.

Jim, now a Gunnery Sgt and I kept in touch. Paulette and I made a few trips down to Camp Pendleton to visit. They made some trips up to Tustin where we were, but I'd never show him our house. The little shack was just too embarrassing. We'd meet them for dinner or at a club. He never pushed God on me, but was always willing to talk about him when I was. He invited us to church one Sunday, and we drove down to go with him. I remember feeling uncomfortable when entering the church. Everyone was saying "Hi" and welcomed us with zealous enthusiasm. I found myself feeling awkward, thinking that they were overly nice to someone they didn't know. They'd never met me, but were treating me like a good friend. It was unusual and, for me, foreign. Paulette was less inclined to share my feelings. She moved right into socializing with the church group, and I stood by her without saying anything or participating. Gunny asked how we enjoyed it on the way home, and I told him how I felt. He seemed a little surprised, but never criticized my thoughts. He was politely silent.

Eventually Gunny and I lost track of each other. He stayed in the Corps until it was time to retire, and he's probably gone back to his home state of Oklahoma to buy some property and farm. He talked about that like it was what he really wanted to do. I hope he's there now, looking out over his farm with a warm heart, lots of grandkids around him, and Mary nearby to share his years and wisdom. Gunny is a good man and I miss not knowing where or how he is. How do you find a Johnson in the United States? I've resolved myself to the logical conclusion that I'll just have to remember Gunny, and hope he remembers me.

"I want to move closer to home," Paulette reiterated. I knew she was really homesick, but I was making a living in Orange County. We weren't getting ahead, but we were able to pay for our small cottage each month. Her persistence later became an ultimatum. She felt she was supposed to move north and was firm that this is what we needed to do. I disagreed that we should move to the Bay Area. It was too close to relatives to allow us to be our own family. If we were going to move, I wanted to go to Grass Valley. Instead, I had family there and she felt that what was good for her was good for me. I didn't argue the point. Well, maybe I did, but I knew she'd win. We decided that Auburn would be a good place to look, and I thought it best to visit Auburn to check things out for work, and a place to live. "Nope, we're moving," she decided. She started packing before I'd made up my mind. She'd made it up for me. She packed my things too. I was moving whether I liked it or not. I packed my tree service equipment, motorcycles, tools, and loaded the trailer. We moved everything to her mother's house in Orinda and packed it in her garage. I made a second trip to bring the stump grinder up. I hoped that it'd be my saving grace for work until I could start the business again or find something else to do.

Paulette stayed at her Mom's and I went to Auburn. I looked for an apartment or small house, but housing was difficult to find, and it was expensive. I settled for a small condo at 3783 Sapphire Drive, in the Auburn Greens. It was a small two-bedroom apartment with an open garage. I put an ad in the paper right away and hired an answering service. Trip after trip, I moved things from Lisette's garage to Auburn to our new apartment. When it was finished, Paulette came up and saw her new house for the first time. Day after day went by and I received not a single call from my ad in the paper. A month went by and no calls. I took out a larger ad and put one in the Sacramento paper too. Not a single call came in. I became despondent and worried. I owed 6 more payments on the stump grinder and couldn't make them. The owner called me several times and was very nice. Eventually he sent a man to pick it up. I lost it and the chance to get work here with it. The thousands of dollars that I already paid for it was gone and so was the stump grinder, my biggest accomplishment, and the representation of it were also gone. Life wasn't looking very good.

I answered an ad in the Sacramento paper for a salesman. I took a job selling home alarm systems. It was a small company just starting out and I was one of three employees. They gave us the leads and we went out to demo the alarm system. I sold many and seemed to be a good salesman. The income was poor. I got paid when the company got their money. The commission wasn't paying our bills and I didn't like the drive to Sacramento. I soon took a job in Auburn working as a mobile home salesman on Hwy. 49. There, too, I was a good salesman, the top salesman in the company. My commissions would have been good except, again, I didn't get paid until the company got their money. Many of the mobile homes were to be put on private property and getting them set up was a long tedious process. I took draws every week, but my commission never seemed to pay them back. It was a stressful time. We moved to 100 Mulberry Lane, off Auburn Ravine, a house owned by my boss. In fact, it was a modular home itself. It was the nicest home Paulette and I had lived in yet. It was a move up for us, and I was happy that we were progressing in life. This house had room to move around, it was clean and fairly new, and it had a garage. I was ecstatic. Selling mobile homes was not the career I had envisioned, but since the Sheriff's job at Contra Costa never panned out, I had no direction to go. Paulette was very apprehensive in being married to a police officer and during the testing process for Contra Costa, she revealed her feelings. I quit the testing and let it go, but I had an inward need to be a part of something productive, something important, and couldn't let that go.

The sales lot got sold and our house on Mulberry Lane was to come to an end. We found a house on Rancho Circle. Paulette liked it because she had always wanted a house with a swing set in the back yard for the kids. We looked at this house and it had a swing set. That was the house for her, and we took it. We were just able to put in our first, last, and deposit to move in. We've lived there ever since. The little 1,000 square foot house was small at best, but it had a garage and I felt better with that. I wondered if I'd ever be successful enough to get something that we really wanted, something that we could be proud of, something we could even buy.

Paulette had been dragging me to church lately. The pastor was a nice man, gentle, yet firm in his ways. He truly loved God and there was nothing ambiguous about his beliefs or teachings. He was down to earth and taught not only the word of God, but how to implement it into your life. He wasn't the type to have his head in the clouds teaching things that normal humans couldn't aspire to. He wouldn't compromise God's word, but instead showed you how to apply it in your life. I liked Ralph. I wasn't sure about this God thing, but I did like Ralph. He and I talked one day and he asked what I did for a living. "I'm between jobs," was a way to say I'm out of work. "What would you like to do?" he asked. "Well, I'd love to be a police officer, but Paulette is against that," was my only thought, almost wanting to blame Paulette for my work failures. "What else then?" he retorted. "I'd enjoy being a private investigator," I admitted as a second choice. "Well, why don't you then?" he responded with almost a challenge in his voice. I didn't have an answer to that. I didn't even know where to start. It got me thinking, and the next day I went through the phone book. Listing by listing, I called every private investigator in the book. Most laughed, some rejected me without the insulting undertones, but one listened. Ben, in Sacramento, said he was going on vacation, but asked me to call him in a week. I waited anxiously for that week and called him the first morning he was to be back. "Come on down and see me," he consented. I was very excited about that and hoped I'd be the type of person he needed. He worked out of his home and hadn't been working as a private investigator for very long himself. He had a contact that was feeding him work and needed someone for Workers Comp surveillance. I started working for him in 1978, and I was lucky to have gotten a job that I enjoyed very much.

Although my job was something I didn't want to trade for anything else, life with Ben was an exercise in turmoil. He was a thin, gaunt man with glasses and an exceptionally deep, low voice. Almost an oxymoron in terms. Ben was a small man in stature and with his size came the expected overcompensation that befalls many small men. Ben could be mean. That may have been because of his wanting the best from his men. No one can blame him for that, but he seemed to enjoy meanness. This wasn't the Marine Corps type of macho, mean, loud, and forceful way of accomplishing something. It was just his way of doing things that didn't need to get done in a way that would ruin someone's day or weekend. He was critical to a fault. Yes, to my faults, but also to a fault of his own. He was just overboard to a grossly unnecessary degree. As time went on, I learned that it wasn't directed just at me, but to each one who worked for him, male or female, investigator, or secretary. No one was immune. If he got you upset, he'd see the weakness and pounce on you for the kill. I learned a lot from Ben, mostly how not to be. We had our confrontations, during most of which I stood my ground if I felt I was correct or made a field decision that could have gone either way. At other times, I saw his view and agreed. Either way led to the same ending. I was upset and left analyzing myself and my actions, finding fault in my own decisions and remorseful that I had disappointed someone. As the years rolled by, and I had endured all the whippings I felt I was entitled to, I challenged him in return. He'd back down, but he didn't like it, and there would certainly be repercussions coming. I look at this as a fault of mine, not his. Ben owned the business he was operating. I was nothing more than an employee. He could treat all his employees any way that he wanted to. It was my job to take it, or find another job, not to draw a line in the sand for him to step across. I'm sorry that Ben had such a critical nature. I'm also sorry I challenged him during those years. It wasn't my position or place to do so. I didn't have to like it. My responsibility was to do what I was told or go somewhere else. I should have gone somewhere else. I offer that for the benefit of anyone else who is subjected to what they feel is unnecessary critique, criticism, or insult. You may feel you don't deserve it and that person should change. My advice, and you be your own judge of this, is to recognize and accept the authority and position of someone above you. We all have a boss to answer to or someone who has authority over us. Police Officers if no one else. It's our responsibility to accept that authority and live with it. If you want to fight it or beat it, you can try if you want to, but there will always be repercussions for those who try. Always. No one is so important that they don't have to answer to anybody. No, not even me.

But if you accept, respect, and obey that supervision, you'll wake up to a tomorrow that's awaiting new adventures.

Ben also had a generous side. It was diametrically opposed to his mean nature. He'd ask us if we wanted to go fishing and he'd charter a boat. River fishing started up and he'd take us out for a day. He bought a fishing boat and kept it at a dock at the river for us to use when we wanted. He'd give out tickets for a Kings game when he couldn't use what he had. These are things above and beyond what you'd expect of an employer, yet he did them not wanting to be thanked. I'd try and get little response. He was hard to understand. I thought many times that he just may not like me, which was too bad. I was very loyal to him and his company. During my 25-year tour with him, I never asked him for a raise. I felt that he'd give it to me when he thought I had earned it. I was frequently too patient. Others would go to him for their yearly raise and negotiate for the upcoming year. I'd let 2-3 years pass before he'd raise my salary on his own. I have to wonder whether that was fair to my family. I wonder whether Ben felt I was worth a raise, or felt guilty because everyone else was getting two or three. I won't know that answer, but I learned a lesson from that experience. It's not out of line to discuss with your employer what both of you think you're worth. I should have done that. My loyalty to him at the time dictated that I wouldn't challenge his decisions. His meanness yes, his decisions no.

One day in the late 70's, Ben asked four other investigators and me into his office. He had decided he was going to give us some money, a large amount of money, in fact, tens of thousands of dollars. The condition was that we were to invest it. If it was invested wisely, he'd fund the same amount next year, and for one more year to follow. This was a shock for all of us and came with no forewarning. What was he up to? We left the room shrugging our shoulders, looking at each other with amazement. The five of us immediately initiated our own meeting. What are we going to do with this money? Within an hour, we had decided to invest it in real estate. Using the total amount as a down payment and combining our incomes for credit, we had a realtor start looking for a fixer upper. We found one on Midnight Dr. in Carmichael and made an offer. It was accepted and we were on our way to creating a future. Alas, in came the gremlins. Roger, one of the beneficiaries of Ben's gift decided he didn't want to participate. Instead, he wanted his money in cash. That wasn't Ben's intent, or offer, but Roger was steadfast. He was determined to see Ben about it. Shortly afterward, Roger left the company. He went up the street and started his own PI business. It was clear what he wanted his money for, and I was angered that he used Ben's money to start a competing business against him. In spite of running into him occasionally, I never spoke with Roger again.

Fred and Dan were at odds with each other. Fred was a nice man, but coarse, abrupt, and although married, a player with the women. Dan was of a formal nature, very business-like, talked of little else but work, and was very married. The two different characters led to a confrontation and Dan felt it best to cease any business dealings where Fred was involved. He pulled out and asked Ben for his share of the money. By now, Ben had to be sorry for what he'd started and offered. We knew then that this would be the last funding we'd get. He never said so, but his donation promise for two more years would not come to fruition.

With as little down payment as we could make, and as much working capital in the bank as we could muster, we purchased the Midnight house. Fred was the carpenter and enjoyed it. He spent most of the time there fixing what he felt should be done. Randy and I accepted his recommendations with confidence and let the project continue. There were ups and downs in our relationships during the upgrading of the Midnight house. Neither Randy nor I had any source of income other than Ben's work. We had to make that come first. Fred had an alternate source and could afford to take more time off than we. He grew weary of it and felt he was making the biggest contribution to the business. He was, but we had discussed that at the onset, and all had agreed that this is the way it must be if it was going to work. Putting things in motion can sometimes feel different than when it's discussed over a table. There was trouble brewing and I didn't know how to address his problem.

The Midnight house was finally sold, and Fred found another in the South Sacramento area. It was a bad area as friendly neighborhood bar-be-queue's go, but we could get the house at a good price. It needed a roof, a lot of upgrading, and paint. We agreed and bought it. I tried to get down there as much as I could to avoid the problems suffered at Midnight. Working from daylight to late afternoon for Ben and spending the next several hours in South Sacramento was taking its toll. We had recently suffered a bold break-in and the robbery of all our tools. Someone should have stayed at the house, but no-one was able to.

While working on that house, Fred found another just around the corner. It, too, needed major repair. We were running very low on funds, barely enough to buy another house and still have money to repair them both, but Fred talked us into it, and we made the offer. It was accepted and we owned another house. I must admit that I never saw the inside of that one. I drove by it several times, but never stopped to look. My attention was devoted to the first one and I was giving every hour to it. So were Fred and Randy, but as it got closer to completion, they moved over to the second house. I stayed behind to finish the first.

Fred approached us with an opportunity to buy two more houses, side by side on 69th St. in Sacramento. To me, the purchase was out of the question. We were out of working capital. However, we could get them for no down payment, and just make the monthlies. This was a tempting offer but one I wasn't sure about. My sole income was all my family had to live on, and we lived month to month, hand to mouth. We never seemed to get ahead. If we did, something happened to eat up what I had made. I wasn't a private investigator because of the money, to be sure. A grocery clerk or warehouseman was making more than I. I was a private investigator because I loved the work. I thought about Fred's proposal and voted no. Randy and Fred voted yes and the purchase was made. I had my vote and I had lost, now it was time to move on to what the company wanted to do. I gave it all my support. And then trouble hit.

I had learned that Fred had refinanced the houses and paid personal loans off with the money. We had put the houses in his name for convenience sake but refinancing them for his own personal gain was far and beyond what I was going to accept. Had I not found out through a third party, I may not have found out at all. Although not as secretive, Randy needed money to purchase a dependable truck and took some from the company funds to buy it. I didn't object to that as he had asked

Fred and me before he did it. We knew he desperately needed reliable transportation to keep his job with Ben, and both Fred and I immediately said yes, but Fred had lost my trust. He had done other things while working with Ben that I was disappointed and angry with, but this was more than I would tolerate. I called a meeting and told Fred and Randy that the company must dissolve. No trust means no company. I developed an equitable division that seemed fair to all. Fred was to get one of the South area houses, Randy the other, and I the two 69th Street homes. Fred and Randy could keep the remaining monies in the bank. The math was unusually fair, the division was made, and the company dissolved. We never seemed to get along after that. It's too bad. It wasn't long ago that Fred knew I was voting against buying the 69th St. homes, yet after I was outvoted, I devoted myself to the project. I had no hard feelings. I had my say and lost. Now it was time for Fred and Randy to do the same thing, but they chose not to. Randy did come around years later. I haven't spoken to Fred since. There are many lessons to be learned here, each one is its own subject matter.

Prior to the housing development company, Fred and I were tight. He had his faults, of course, and he overlooked mine. But we worked together for years and teamed up on several cases. We were labeled as the "A Team" around the office by everyone except Ben. He didn't compliment anyone. Case after case, Fred and I teamed up, we were successful on over 90% of our assignments. Fred would do almost anything out in the field. When he reached his boundaries, I was open enough to take it a step further. I wasn't any better than Fred, I had made it through the Marine Corps and knew I could do difficult things. That was a dangerous attitude to have.

Making a living as a private investigator is thrilling, adrenaline filled, exciting, rewarding, and not the least of which, challenging. It's also tedious, boring, monotonous, dangerous, and hard on a family. You can't afford to be yourself, even when you're off duty, as you must always exercise caution against showing a weakness in your personality and character. Law enforcement officers suffer the same consequences in their job. A P.I., however, doesn't wear a uniform and is usually alone. He has to learn to fend for himself. He may find himself, and usually will at some point in his career, in an atmosphere of hate and discontent, and find a way out of it by himself. It comes with the territory and is not a profession for anyone with weak knees. Living this way 24/7 makes you the kind of person that some people don't like, even your friends or family. You learn to live with few friends, but those friends you learn to trust implicitly. You learn who in the family are going to stand by you, understand you and your moods, and learn to accept it when you need some winding down time of your own. Wives need to trust their husbands, and the other way around as well. A private investigator may have to engage in deceit or a rouse. But never with his own family. A wife has to learn to accept not knowing where her husband is or when he'll be home. He may kiss her goodbye when she hands him a cup of coffee on his way out the door, and not see him again until late at night, or even days later. It takes a special woman to be the wife of a private investigator. Most investigators will find their niche in one area or another. Criminal investigators usually represent someone who's been charged with a crime. Their attorney will hire them to close up some loose ends or find evidence that hasn't been discovered yet by the other side. They frequently deal with some sort of hostile criminal element along the way. Civil investigators are called upon to find facts or discover evidence, usually regarding lawsuits of some form or another. A person suing a company, company suing company, product liability issues, and a cornucopia of issues which would bring a Plaintiff and Defendant into court to air their grievances. Though usually less hostile in nature and usually a more structured work schedule, a civil investigator has to be awake, alert, able to ascertain deceit quickly, and frequently suffer with a poor credit rating while waiting for a check to come in from a client or attorney. Domestic investigators focus their attributes generally on family matters. A suspected cheating husband or wife, adolescents feared to be traveling down a dangerous path to adulthood. Or simply attempting to locate a lost friend or relative who hasn't been heard from for years. Most frequently domestic matters are wrought with tension, high emotion, and anger. These are some of the more difficult types of investigative work that an investigator would willingly accept. Reporting to a husband or wife that their spouse is having an affair and showing them film of it is extremely distressing to both the client and the investigator. Unless you're a cold blooded, matter of fact type person. I am not. My heart would hurt for days if I needed to make a report of that kind. There is the insurance fraud investigator who spends much of his time attempting to confirm or refute the effects to and injured person, and the degree of that injury. There's a great deal of money to be made by a person claiming to be significantly injured at work, in an auto accident, or any other way. Throughout my career the consequences for the injured person who was exaggerating that injury were almost insignificant, but the rewards were great, if they got away with it. Insurance companies pay out billions of dollars to individuals who sometimes don't deserve it. And what happens to the next injured person who does actually deserve some type of dollar recompense? They're put under suspicion, and don't deserve it. So, who loses with insurance fraud? The insurance company and the next injured person? Yes, but the rest of the public, too. The insurance company must raise their rates to make up for their loss. The public pays for that. So how does an investigator usually catch those who are exaggerating or lying about their injury? Surveillance. Covertly watch them for a period of time and attempt to determine from there whether they're legitimate, or deceitful. Then let the court and the attorneys sort it out. Of course, there are other forms of investigation, corporate espionage, surety recovery or bounty hunting as it's most commonly referred to, and executive protection. Bodyguard service as it were. I've done anywhere from a little bit to a lot of each of these. Some were exciting but uneventful. Others were unexpectedly adrenaline filled. I'll share with you a couple of stories, lessons I've learned, experiences I've had, and events that have turned into adventures. You'll find that these are not the James Bond, CIA, or FBI type of adventures. These are real life, non-TV type of experiences that many veteran investigators have had. You just never hear about them. But before I share a couple of these adventures with you I think it's important to fill you in on the type of investigator that I am. Many investigators take an assignment with the thought and goal of representing their client in the most aggressive and client biased manner that they're able. When a client has a side, position, or opinion that investigator adopts that and focuses his investigation attempting to prove his client's case. I don't fault that and have frequently done that myself. Even attorneys do it. An attorney is retained and expected to believe his client and the report he hears from that client. "The other guy ran the red light, I didn't," " It wasn't my joint, it was my passenger's," I've been alone in my room all night." A client expects his attorney to believe him. Why not, he's paying him to. Many investigators are of like mind. An attorney will frequently assign his investigator to go out and gather evidence that will support his case. You can't blame him for that. Although that was my philosophy as well for many years, consequences are generally a great teacher, and my mode of investigation changed. I found it better to be able to stand on the evidence and maintain my integrity by reaching the agreement with these attorneys that I will investigate the incident and report back my findings, period. Good, Bad, or Ugly, everyone has a right to know the truth, and that's what I would set about to find. "Just the facts, ma'am," as Joe Friday on the old show Dragnet would say. You remember that, too? Ok, what was his badge number. Right, #714. Joe was a no-nonsense integrity filled L.A. cop who didn't want to just catch "somebody." He wanted only the one who committed the crime. My philosophy became something similar. I wasn't out to prove a case, but to find the facts. Now it must be said that this doesn't mean that law enforcement or the D.A. don't care about the facts, they just want to get someone charged and convicted. Other than a rare exception I don't believe any of them do. But in reality, many law enforcement detectives have a lot on their plate, many things to do, many cases to solve, and a miniscule amount of time to do it. As a result they sometimes (or frequently) conclude their investigation when enough research has been done to reasonably suspect or prove that an individual has committed a specific crime. There might be more involved than initially learned, another person involved, another similar event that occurred, additional or exculpatory evidence found, other witnesses to interview who may have a different account of the event, or a myriad of integers that can affect and even change a jury's view. If they exist, I'll find them. If they don't, I'll report back to the attorney that he has a difficult road. The same is true about insurance issues. Insurance companies will hire an investigator to put someone under surveillance and prove they're a fraud. That violated my standards of ethics and I had to tell them no, I wouldn't do that, but what I would do is aggressively investigate this matter and report back what I find. Exactly what I find. I lost a lot of work through the years because of this approach, but I slept better at night. And even my adversaries who knew me would openly agree that I would call them as I found them. Nothing more, nothing less. I was a private investigator, a trained observer, and a professional reporter of facts.

For clarity it's important to note that the events I relay both before and a significant time after these events occurred was a substantial time from the current. It's hard to believe but during those days and times, the only popular computers used were IBM office computers used for typing. Any computer used for gaming was on an Atari or Commodore 64, with the games being no more than box drawings. No Internet to speak of, there were certainly no cell phones. And the thought of a cell phone in a car was reserved only for the rich and well to do. Correspondence and communication at the time was done by land line telephone and mail through the Post Office. Eventually, investigators were assigned pagers to let us know when the office needed to get in touch with us. Communication with another investigator in the field was done by walkie-talkie radios, if you had some. Your car was old, and you worked hard on keeping it alive for just a few more years. The average pay for a good investigator was less than the minimum wage that a worker at McDonald's gets now. To think of earning $1,000 a month was a goal, not something expected. With these in mind one can more appropriately enjoy the upcoming stories and adventures.

Fred and I drew an assignment together for a case in Portola. It was during the winter months and Portola is in the high country of Northern California. A man there was on Workers Comp, and we were asked to determine whether he was employed somewhere else while off work from an injury sustained while at his normal job. Our task was to find out. If he was employed, he wasn't entitled to Workers Comp payments. If he wasn't, and was genuinely injured, my feelings were that he was entitled to his injury payments. Ben got paid a tidy sum of money for each minute of film that was taken on a subject. He passed a small amount of that on to us, but the potential revenue to him in our taking film was an encouragement to have us get the film. I disputed that and generally took film only if a subject was violating his declared restrictions.

We arrived in Portola to find snow everywhere. Some places it was two feet deep, not bad for Portola, but certainly a deterrent for covert surveillance. Our subject's house was located, and we found there was no place to put him under surveillance. He was next to the highway, but there was no place to discreetly park. Neither Fred nor I had an answer to this, until I looked across the highway. We drove over to the opposite frontage road and across from our subject's house. I got out and bundled up, tuned my radio, put on a camouflage jacket over my other coat, and went up in a tree. At about 50', I could see the house and all that was needed to alert Fred if our subject was leaving. It was cold. The wind was piercing and blowing the tree to and fro. I was used to the height, and the swaying, but I'd never get used to the cold. After making myself a nest and getting as comfortable as I could expect, I settled in for a long tour at this outpost. Hour after hour went by. Fred was in his truck down near town waiting for me to alert him that our subject was moving. I didn't mind, we always took turns standing watch. Fred wasn't comfortable with this kind of watch, and I'd have to bear the brunt of it. He did relieve me on occasion, but soon I'd be back up in my place, watching the house, the monotony broken only by the different colors of passing cars.

The second day I was back up in my fort when, at mid-morning, our subject came into view. He walked outside to gather up some firewood and I took some film; not much, but at least we could determine what he looked like. I didn't know if his back injury precluded him from carrying an occasional armload of firewood, but it went down in a report and was documented. I was tiring of this assignment by noon and hoped a weather front didn't move in on us, making life more interesting and less tolerable. Around 2:00, our subject was again outside for more firewood, but not to pick it up, this time to split it. "Oh geeze", I thought as he swung the mall time after time, bending to pick up the split pieces and rolling the rounds into place for another soon-to-be pile of split wood.

I found myself wishing he'd stop, wishing he wouldn't do this, but my wishes weren't as predominant as his desire to put in more firewood. After an hour or so he had enough and he carried another armload in the house, and was in for the day. Before dark, I came down from my home and went to a restaurant/bar to warm up. Our hotel rooms were not quite up to the standards of being a hole in the wall, so we weren't in a hurry to get to them. Fred and I sat at a table after dinner, having coffee, talking, and trying to unwind when a couple of the locals walked up to ask us if we were new in town. "Just passing through," was Fred's response. "Want to sit down and join us?" Oh great, Fred just asked two strange women to sit with us. Within minutes I excused myself and went to my room, which looked better now than it did before. I called Paulette, turned on the TV, and fell asleep. I don't know what Fred did, or when he got in, and I didn't ask. The next morning, I was in my tree house once again, but only for a few hours this day. We called it and came home that afternoon. I'm still thawing out. We reported out findings to the insurance company and to this day know not as to whether our information was of any value to them. Investigator's rarely do unless the case goes to trial. Once we submit our report, our job is done, and we go on to other cases.

Modesto seemed to yield its share of questionable claimants and I made the trip there frequently. It was a long drive, with the goal to be there before daylight, but it needed to be done, so I looked at it that way and always left in the middle of the night to get where I needed to be.

This subject lived in a housing community where many people didn't work. That meant they were home during the day and would recognize any strange vehicles in the area. It made my job more difficult, but not impossible. I stayed away from the house and planned on picking up my subject whenever he left. The problem was, he didn't. I was there for three days and didn't see any movement at all. That afternoon I made my usual periodic pass-by of the residence when I noticed a 4-speed transmission sitting on the driveway. "Oh my", was my thought. No one was around, but I stayed close to the house waiting for my subject to come out to see what he was going to do with this 200-pound transmission. "No wonder he didn't leave," I thought. He doesn't have a transmission in his car.

An hour before dark, I called it for the day and decided I'd stay for one more. I got another room at the local sub-standard motel and went out to get some dinner. It was dark when I was finished, but as I normally do, I wanted to take advantage of one more opportunity to check the house before I went back to my room. This time the car was jacked up, a drop cord was under the car, and so was my subject. Aware of the possibility of surveillance, he was waiting for dark before he started doing his work under the car. This was many years ago, and we were still using 8mm film cameras. It was an effort to get good quality telephoto lenses. Getting a night lens or quality night film was to be an event in the future. There was no possibility of getting film of this tonight. I got out and walked by his house to make sure it was him. It was. All I could do was file a report, but I'd get this guy yet.

The following morning, I was watching his house as the sun came up. The car was off the jacks and there was no sign that anything had been done at all. Just after 8:30 a.m., a woman arrived in a car and walked to the house. She seemed comfortable with doing this, and clearly knew where she was and what she was doing. A short time later she and my subject walked out of the house to her car. She was wearing a white top and matching white pants. I asked myself if she could be a nurse???? Unknown yet, but I'll keep my eye on her, too. My subject walked to her car as a normal man would, in fact, with a little stride to his gait. "Last night must not have hurt him too much," I thought. He easily sat down on the passenger seat, and they drove off. I now knew my subject was aware of the possibility for surveillance, so I used some techniques to maintain a discreet tail. I was successful and shadowed them to a doctor's office. The female walked to the trunk of her car as I watched her through binoculars. "Yep, just as I thought, she's a nurse." After opening the trunk, she struggled to get something out of it. It was a wheelchair. She unfolded it and wheeled it to my subject who could now barely move. She helped him get out of his seat and carried most of his weight. One would think this man was severely injured. She helped him as he swung his body around to the chair, and she pushed him into the doctor's office. Yes, I filmed the entire event.

An hour or so later, they came out and repeated their show as he re-entered the car. I took the appropriate film and prepared for the tail home. They drove straight there where he got out of the car, and both walked normally to the house. Sometime later she came out and left. Months later, in Court, I confirmed what anyone would suspect. The nurse was his wife.

I worked on another case in Lincoln for several days. The woman had a knee injury and reportedly used a cane and walked with a limp. The only one who could find anything wrong with her was her own doctor, who by happenstance was Paulette's doctor too. She was sent to several other doctors however they could find nothing wrong. Surveillance was requested and I drew the assignment. There were steps to her porch leading to her front door and it would be important to see how she negotiated them. After a few days of surveillance, my subject came out and leaned heavily on the side rail to walk down the steps. She certainly looked hurt, but let's observe her for a little while longer. She drove to Auburn and made three or four stops. She didn't limp or move with any difficulty, and I took the appropriate film. It was late in the afternoon and time for her to go back home, but she didn't. She headed east bound on I-80 and made a 20-minute drive to Colfax. She exited and drove straight to a bus station where she pulled alongside of a waiting car. They spoke for only a second and the car left. She made a U-turn and followed. "Interesting," I thought. I followed them across the freeway where he took her directly to a Motel. They got out and walked across the parking lot together, into an already rented room. I had a camera at the ready with a telephoto lens, hopefully to get I.D. on the male she was with. I did; it was her doctor. It was later determined that he had also billed the insurance company for this appointment!

I was in Oroville working the case of a man who alleged he had a bad back. Doctors couldn't find any problem and we were assigned the case. He lived down a winding narrow dirt road with berry bushes growing out toward the center. They were desperately in need of being cut back. You could hear them scratching the car as you drove down the road. I got to his house, turned around and left, as is sometimes done in situations like this one. I didn't leave as uninformed as when I arrived. Alongside his house was an above ground pool full of water, and around the pool, he was building a deck. "This would be worth watching," I said to myself, because no one was with me to hear me. I found a place to park my car and suited up in full camouflage gear. Crawling on my face through the berry bushes, and not liking it, I slowly approached the house, all the time ensuring that I wasn't crossing over onto the subject's property itself. I finally found my location and got set up. My subject showed himself later that morning and I watched and filmed him working on his deck that he must have been, before this day, so proud of. The quality of the film was great. There was little chance he'd talk his way out of this deceit. He didn't.

The first day I took a new hire out to train I told him to camo-up, that we were going into the woods. I had previously found the house I was looking for, but it couldn't be seen without getting out on foot. Again, it's important to note that although covert surveillance is legal and moral in most cases, the investigator cannot cross the line by infringing on the subject's own property. I needed to research property boundaries through the County before I would go out the second time. It was still dark when we started our trek down the hillside toward the residence. The house itself sat on top of a knoll, so we climbed down the mountain to a small valley and up the knoll to the house. Looking over the edge of the knoll like two military combat soldiers peeking over their foxhole, I surveyed the surroundings and lowered my head. "He has a dog, so we've got to be quiet", I whispered to the newbie. He nodded in the affirmative. Using hand signals, I set the game plan into motion. I was to move left, around the house, he right, but stay off his property, I firmly instructed. He nodded again and we separated to our own assignments. I crawled halfway around the property looking for a place to set up surveillance. I found nothing but trees and brush, with no possibility to view his house. I crawled back to our meeting place knowing that the trainee wouldn't be there, but it was a good place to stop and re-plan anyway. I arrived to find my trainee right where I had left him. "What are you doing here?" I firmly whispered. He motioned in the direction I had sent him and shook his head, no. He held in his hand a length of piano wire and we both knew what it was used for in the woods, booby-traps. This assignment had just moved into another stage. Why were there booby-traps around this man's house? He's up to something he shouldn't be. Contemplating my next move, I heard in the distance the sound of a skill saw. An easily recognizable sound, I knew it was coming from our subject's house, in the direction where I had sent my second man. "Follow me and stay exactly in my tracks," I whispered to him. The surprised look on his face was clearly understood, but he followed me anyway. Carefully, we worked our way around the property line until just below the noise of the frequently running skill saw. I nodded in the affirmative as though it was time to ascend toward the sound, but that's where Ben's new investigator drew the line. "No," he nodded back. I was surprised that he would take such a position and directed him again to follow me. I got the same answer, so I left him behind. I climbed the hill on my hands and knees and got only halfway up when I ran into a black PVC water line. "This is what the tripwire is for," I announced to myself, and I followed the water line to a garden of marijuana. That's of little to no consequence during these days and times but back at the time of this event it was a significant occurrence and very illegal. We're all subject to the laws of the day, whether we agree with them or not. Our subject was in the "or not" crowd. There must have been 30-40 plants, all at least 5' high. Our subject's house bordered BLM property and the garden was growing on government land. And this was quite a garden. I learned quickly that I wasn't alone in his garden. Just a few rows away I could see the subject working in the garden, building something. I didn't know what it was and didn't really care. I recognized him as the subject. Camera in hand, whenever he turned his back, I squatted up to get my head and camera above the plants. I took film of the garden, his residence just a few hundred yards away, and him working in the garden that he thought was so protected. Getting what I felt would be enough film, enhanced by filming him in the garden itself, I crawled back out, picked up my cautious partner and returned to my vehicle. I didn't speak to him during my climb up the mountain. He may have thought it was because he left me to climb to the house alone, but it wasn't. I was trying to breathe.

Early on in my 25 years with Ben, I took an assignment in Ceres, below Modesto. It was a heavy Mexican population, and my subject was one of them. I didn't say Hispanics because I don't believe in that game. I call a spade a spade, but not in a derogatory sense. Some would contest too, I'm sure, that I shouldn't have used the word "spade" either. Get over it. I'm not referencing the word to a race. The house was in town and easy to watch, but my subject never left it. He wouldn't even come outside. It was reported that he used a wheelchair and I needed to see whether he was using it or not. The case stretched on for two days. No subject! I had already confirmed that he was home by a phone call to the house. I feared that I'd spend several days on this and make no determination of authenticity at all. My job isn't to prove any one thought or position, but simply to report facts, as I've said elsewhere here, but you must have some facts to report to a client. They don't particularly like to hear that they're getting billed for three days' work and have nothing to report. It doesn't make for good relations. However, I report what I see, and I hadn't seen anything at all. He lived next to a dirt alley and a wooden fence separated his property from the alley way. I stayed on the case until dark and decided I'd try one more thing before dropping the assignment. It couldn't be used in Court, but maybe I could see whether he actually used the wheelchair or not. It was time for dinner and the dining room light was on. Now was my chance. I left my car and walked to the alley. "No street lights were in it, good," I thought as I entered and walked down the alley. Directly across from the subject's kitchen was a small cottage with a door which exited onto the alley. The cottage was dark and it appeared that no one was home, but the door was open leaving only a screen door closing it off. The screen door itself was partially open as it had lost its shape long ago. I was looking for a hole in the fence that would allow me to see the subject's kitchen and dining room window. How was he moving inside his house? Yes, there is a knothole. In fact, several of them, but I couldn't stare through the fence if someone was home in the cottage. I walked slowly and carefully across the dirt alley to the cottage door and looked through the screen. Confirming that no-one was home I was more confident now as I walked back across the alley, next to a black telephone pole I looked through the fence. There he was! Seated at the kitchen table with only his face showing, I knew that when he finished with dinner, I'd have my answer.

It was only seconds later when I heard the screeching of tires, and lights lit up the alley. The car was still at the head of the alley having pulled off the main road, but I couldn't make anything out with the lights shining down my direction. I was on the opposite side of the telephone pole from the car and thankful that it partially concealed me from view. I heard a car door slam and knew someone was now on foot. A second or two later, the car backed out and left. My eyes had to get used to the dark again, but they fixed quickly to a silhouette of a large man walking down the alley toward me. As he approached, he veered off toward the cottage and opened the door to enter. Suddenly he stopped and turned around. He looked for only a second, and slowly closed the screen door and walked carefully across the alley toward me. Almost in a crouch position, he arrived on the other side of the telephone pole. He found his knothole and peered through it at the house I was watching. "That's interesting," I thought as he stared at the house. I remained motionless until he felt he'd seen enough, and he turned around to enter his cottage. When the door closed, I took one last look at my subject before abandoning my post, and returned to my car. I never worked him again nor found out whether he was really injured or not. Sadly, sometimes you never get the answers you're looking for.

It was a hot summer day when I worked a case in Stockton. The valley gets hot, and I'd rather work in the foothills or mountains, but this case needed working and I agreed to do it. The house was easy to watch. It was reported that our subject liked to work during the day, and party at night and I was to expect long hours. I went there already tired and without sleep from the last case I had worked. There is a lot of stress in this job, and it was compounded by the need to work as many days and as many cases as I could. I had learned long ago that I needed to work 6 days a week, 10 hours a day to make ends meet at home. Without that, something would go unpaid. In the 25 years I was with Ben, I never took a vacation. Other than an occasional 3 days off, which was more consequential than beneficial. I never took time away from the job. At this point in time, it was catching up to me. This wasn't going to be easy, as I was admittedly tired, both physically and mentally.

I watched the house from daylight to late afternoon. I saw my subject and filmed an occasional violation of his self-declared physical limitations. It was difficult to stay awake, so I ran up the street for a cup of coffee and came right back. Eventually just before 9:00 p.m. he came out dressed like he was on the prowl. One club after another, I followed him. He was looking for women and I was too tired to care. I didn't want to watch him anymore, but I stayed on assignment until he closed down the bar at 2:00 a.m. He went home to bed. I found a motel nearby and asked for a wakeup call in 3 hours. I hate motel telephones. They always wake me up when I'm sleeping. Again, the phone went off announcing a new day of work. I dressed again and felt rummy. "This wasn't going to be an easy day," I admitted to myself. Two coffees and a donut later, I was sitting at his house as the sun came up. He came out of the house at 8:00 a.m. and the day was starting. I tailed him throughout the day and late afternoon. Things were getting bad, and I had difficulty staying awake. Darkness fell, I coffee'd up and waited for his nightlife to begin. It did, and once again I followed him from one club to another, watching him dance and move about. I was too tired to talk to anyone and my only hope was that he'd find someone to take home and do it soon. He didn't but called it a night around midnight and went home. I didn't like the motel I was at the previous night. It felt moldy, so I drove a little farther to another one. I checked in and couldn't get my gear into the room fast enough. It was still very warm so the first thing I did was turn on the window air conditioner. Humm, tick, tick, hummmmm. The sound was enormous. I can't sleep with this thing clanging like that, so I shut it off and opened the window. The slight breeze cooled the room down enough to sleep and after a quick shower I lay my wallet, watch, and side arm down on the nightstand next to me. No TV, the lights went off and right away I started checking my eyelids for holes. Sleep is difficult for me when I'm that tired. I have dreams that are generally graphic and violent. Many times, I know I'm dreaming but can't wake myself up. We've all had that experience, I'm sure. This night was no different. I dreamed that a burglar tried the door to my room and found it locked. He saw my window open and slowly pried the screen off and climbed inside the room. "This isn't what I needed to get any sleep," I said to myself. But because I couldn't wake myself up, I kept dreaming and watched the burglar walk to the foot of the bed and reach into my overnight bag. He walked to my nightstand and found my gun. Picking it up, he cocked it and put it to my face. "I've got to go to sleep! I can't keep this up or I'll never get up in the morning," I thought to myself in my sleep. My dream continued. The burglar lowered my gun, crawled out the window, and was gone. I thanked Jesus for answering my prayer and I fell asleep. Only a short time later, the telephone rang for my wake-up call. I didn't talk to the answering system anymore, I just picked it up and set it back down. Maybe 15 more minutes could help, but I was too nervous to take the chance. I reached for my watch to see what time it was, but it must have fallen onto the floor. Reaching around the tabletop, I found my wallet in the dark, but something was wrong. Immediately, I jumped out of bed and turned on the light. My gun was gone! Looking on the floor, I saw neither my gun nor my watch. Like a science fiction movie, I walked to the window and pulled the drapes back. The screen was gone. It was on the ground in front of the window. My dream hadn't been a dream! It was real. It wasn't a good night.

I spent several days looking for a subject in Grass Valley. Once I discovered the road he lived on, I talked to neighbors until one identified the subject's house, another mile or so up the dirt road. His lane went off the dirt road and was protected by a locked gate. I had to know what vehicles he was driving so I could put him under surveillance near town. I walked to the residence to talk to any occupant and the subject came out of the house. Using a ploy, we talked for only a moment, and I announced to him that I had the wrong address. I walked back toward my car and heard him yelling at his wife, "How the hell did he find me?" I grinned, but knew I'd have to be careful during the upcoming surveillance.

I tried to approach a residence up in the mountains near Grizzly Flat. Alone and in camo gear, I dropped my car off a mile or so from the house and hiked cross country toward the residence. As usual, no one knew where I was or where to find me if I didn't come home, but that's the life of an investigator, I guess. The house sat on a hill and I hiked up the hill to get near it. I needed to identify any vehicles so, as before, I could place the subject under surveillance when they drove into town.

I discovered the most unusual thing as I found holes in the ground with pink residue poured in them. "What's this?" I asked myself. I walked further up the hill where I came across a wooded tower. It was about 10' X 10' on the ground, but stuck up two stories in the air. It had plywood siding running its entire height, from ground to roof, but no door on the ground floor. You couldn't get into it. I didn't know what this was. I walked around to the side of this tower to find a door on the second level. Nothing else, just a door. No stairs to it, no balcony, nothing but a door at the second-floor level. "How's anyone going to get in there," I asked myself, "and what's this thing for?" As I walked up the hill, the second door got lower. It was poorly fitting and had a large open space at the bottom. I put the binoculars up to my face to look through the crack and saw the bottom of drums and five-gallon buckets inside. He was cooking drugs in there and I just ran across his hiding spot. This wasn't a good place to be. Most drug cookers don't welcome strangers in camo gear. Although I admit to being a little nervous, I finished my reconnoitering and returned cross country to my vehicle. "Someday I'm going to start telling someone where I'm going."

I worked several cases in Oroville, one of which was a woman who lived down a narrow dirt road in the flat lands. I couldn't see her house from the highway, and I could get by with driving down her road only once. There was no discreet place to park for miles. She was tucked in as snug as a bug. That presented a challenge to me, but I didn't mind those. I got a local map of the area and found her house, then surveyed the surrounding area. I could come in from another road, cross country, to a location across the road from her house. That might just do it. I wouldn't be on her property, and I might just be able to see what goes on. The next morning, I hiked in from afar but the closer I got to her house the more berry bushes I encountered, massive growths of thorny berry bushes. Drawing on past experiences, I cut my way through toward her house. I knew better than to break through across the road, and in fact, had to leave the berries intact where she could see. So, I set up camp behind the wall of berries across the road from her. Cars came and went all morning into the afternoon hours. I had no idea what was going on, but knew she was a busy woman. I tried everything I could to see but each new idea met with failure. Since there was no place to park within miles of her driveway, it was useless to try to see the vehicles coming and going from there. I had only one idea left. Ben got permission from the client, and I rented an airplane. We flew over the area taking pictures looking for any area where I could get in and see what was going on. I didn't have to. We developed the photos and found a large play yard at the rear of her house with several kids on swing sets, jungle gym, sand box, and so on. She had a day care center, and the film verified her activities. That would not have been a bad thing, except she had told the insurance company that she was completely incapable of any form of gainful employment. Sadly, she made the statement while running the day care center. Her deceit was costly for her.

I normally don't work surveillance on police officers. I have an abnormally high regard for them, their position, the responsibilities they accept, and the duties they perform. Most of my friends at this time were police officers and I wouldn't compromise that friendship. If an assignment for a police officer came across my desk, I'd pass it on to someone else. Save one! This Placer County Deputy was a notorious jerk. Most of the other Deputies didn't like him, and that's a good indicator. I contacted one of my friends at the Sheriff's Office, a Captain, and told him of the possible assignment. "I'm all for it, go get him" was not only a clearance signal, but a request. With mixed emotions, I accepted. This Deputy had already told the Captain that he knew the Captain would have someone watching him and that they'd never catch him. The game is now afoot. He'd been off duty for several months and working somewhere, but no one knew where. He wasn't supposed to be. If he was well enough to work somewhere else, he should be well enough to come back to work at the Sheriff's Office. I initiated surveillance at his house one morning just to find the general direction he departed. I intentionally lost him and picked him up the next day at that spot, to tail him another mile or so. After several days, I had a good idea of where he was headed. The following day, I sat near the entrance to a gated housing development and sure enough, here he came. He passed through the guard without signing in and I knew he had a pass to the community. After giving him time to settle, I gained favor with the gate guard and entered to commence my search. Sure enough, I found him building a large, no, exceptionally large home at the back of the subdivision. I exited the community and searched for a spot to come in from behind. It was a large open field, but if I could discreetly get across it and find some cover I could watch the house. I hiked and crawled in. Finding a small oak tree near the house I was able to watch and film him throughout the day building his new home, while getting paid by the S.O. to be off work. They were very happy, and I didn't feel so bad for working a police officer. I wouldn't want to do it again.

I put a house under surveillance in South Sacramento and before long found several cars making brief stops at the house and departing. "That's not good," I warned myself, and as the day went on, it continued. I gathered numbers from over 30 license plates, as this house seemed to have a revolving door. Someone always stood outside looking up and down the street. I filmed him, too. A marked police car cruised by that afternoon and everyone at the house disappeared. Clearly it was a crack house, dealing drugs out the front door. I covertly pulled out of the area and hunted down the recent police car. I asked him about the house, and he confirmed it was a suspected crack house, admitting he'd like to bust it and anyone who visited it. "Well, this may help," I offered, as I handed him my list of license numbers. A grin came across his face. "I owe you one," he vowed. A couple of days later, I found myself sitting up the street from the crack house again. The same man was outside as a lookout. Mid-morning the traffic started. I watched for a couple of hours and knew that the lookout had seen my vehicle and was concerned. As long as he stayed there, I felt okay to sit it out, but things could get difficult here. An hour or more had gone by when I saw the marked police car enter the area and pass by the house. Everyone scattered as both he and I knew they would. Several minutes later the cruiser came past me from behind. As he came alongside, he slowed and motioned for me to come with him. "Oh geez," I thought. "I don't want to leave this spot and not be able to get back in here." But I knew it must be important, so I pulled out and followed him to a nearby shopping center. "I'm sorry to blow your surveillance," he said, "but I know the two men who were coming up behind you and they were clearly coming for you." I had been picked off by the spotter at the crack house and he made a phone call. Had it not been for the police officer, both of us think I might not be worth anything more than worm food today.

I followed another young lady one day and found her working at a shoe store on the K Street Mall. There's certainly no place to set up any discreet surveillance and instead of subpoenaing employment records, Ben was emphatic about getting film of her working. I told him I'd do it in a couple of weeks and put it on calendar. As Paulette held off from complaining, I held off on a shower and shave for several days. Finally, when I was ripe, I got some old clothes from Goodwill and went down to the mall, dressed as a bum. I lay on the bench across from the shoe store and took film through a paper bag. Again, she would probably have been fine had she told the insurance company that she was capable of working. She didn't.

I made a long drive to Shasta and arrived just before daylight. I compared the vehicles in the driveway to the information I had been given and found them to be different. I ran the plates in the drive, and all came back to the same family, the wrong family. My subject had moved. I contacted the Post Office but got no new forwarding address. County offices had no information regarding my female subject so I took a chance and called the phone number that I had. She answered. I had her on the phone but had to get her address out of her. We talked for almost 30 minutes when she said that her husband had a bad heart, and they had an "open relationship." I could see what was coming and I got nervous. I prodded her a little and she asked me over for lunch. "Sure," I replied, and she gave me her address. I hung up and laughed. That couldn't have been orchestrated any better. I found her house and confirmed it by the vehicles. I sat up the street until about 2:00, when she came out of the house, slammed the door, got in her car to slam that one too, and left. I followed her around town where she did some shopping and went back home. I was sorry to have ruined her day - but not that sorry.

There are many more stories and adventures to tell. Each one offering its own lessons in life. Some dangerous, some funny, some showing the advantages of having a 6th sense and thinking on your feet. But those adventures will have to wait. The second book will offer its own stories.

I had some good years with Ben but sadly, most of them were what I made from them, not what he made them to be for me, but that's a good lesson in life. Don't expect someone else to do for you what you should be doing for yourself. Ben didn't owe me anything, I owed him. He gave me a job and I was loyal to him for 25 years. I never lied to him, stole from him, or cheated him. I frequently told him what I thought, and that may not have set well, but I felt that my loyalty provided that privilege, but alas, the second lesson.

Ben's work slowed down and my 6 day week fell to 3 or 4. That was tough times for Paulette and me. We faced losing our home and eventually considered bankruptcy. Our credit was destroyed and the kids needed things that I couldn't provide. It went on for many months, getting worse as time grew on. I became scared and despondent. At that point in time, I received a small settlement from a car injury several years back. Paulette and I talked about it and decided I'd open my own business. I rented a small office on Maple Street and was excited, as well as worried. "Just contact the people you work for now and tell them where you're at," Paulette suggested. "We should have plenty of work." She was right, we would have. Many of Ben's clients were asking for me to handle their assignment anyway. Letting them know where I was would only be a courtesy to the client. But no, I felt that would be stealing Ben's clients, and I had seen investigators before do that. I thought it was a questionable thing to do to Ben, and decided I wouldn't do that to him now. So, I continued to be available to Ben while trying to establish my own business. Ben worked solely in the Workers Comp industry. I grew tired of that and wouldn't compete against Ben anyway, so I advertised for civil, criminal, and domestic matters. I'd get one or two a month, but between that and Ben's sparse work, we survived - not well, but survived. I was tenacious with my work and my clients were appreciative. Other clients came and the business was slowly and moderately getting on its feet. Ben learned that I had an office in Auburn and clearly didn't like it. He didn't say anything, he just cut the work assignments out entirely. Thinking that work was just slow, or that others in his office were getting their share of the assignments, I sat it out day after day, week into months, and eventually had to ask what was going on. The secretaries wouldn't answer, and Ben was never around to talk to. Eventually Ben sent a message through the girls to have me bring all his equipment back to him. Dismayed, I did it immediately. I wasn't angry, I was disappointed, and disgusted. I never came against him, I defended him to others, I allowed him to pay me what he thought I was worth, I listened to him berate me when he thought it was amusing, and then waited for work to come in. Lesson Number 2): Now that I've experienced it, I would do the same thing all over again, except tolerate the verbal abuse. My duty to an employer is to be loyal to him, I owe him that. Without him, I'd have to find another way to feed my family. I also learned how not to treat employees who are trying to do their best for a company. There's no excuse for mentally abusing a subordinate. It should never be amusing, at their expense. But the truth is that I owe Ben a thank you for that, too. He brought to my attention that I will not do that to anyone myself. So openly I say to Ben, thank you.

I brought my equipment down to the office and while in route, thought of the secretaries that had come and gone while I was there. Ben gave them a memorable send-off, a lunch with all the staff there and a verbal appreciation. I appreciated that he treated them with respect. It was good to see. I did not expect a similar parting in my case, but this was finally the time for Ben to express some degree of appreciation. I anticipated we'd have a talk in his office and maybe lunch with whoever happened to be there at the time.

I arrived at the office and took his gear in. "Ben's too busy to come out, but you can leave it over there," one of the secretaries said. I was a little taken back, but complied. I had to inventory the gear and it would take some time. Before I was done, Ben came out of his office and was pleasant in his own way. He said little more than, "It was nice having you." I didn't feel that this was the way to end a 25 year relationship so I asked him to lunch. We went up the street and he said little. I thanked him for the opportunities and the time spent, and really didn't want to address the most recent course of events that led to this day. This was going to end on a good note. Sadly, Ben had nothing noteworthy or complimentary to say. His only memorable comment was, "Well, the girls certainly won't have as much consternation now that you're gone."

He had to be kidding, but with Ben you could never tell. His coarse comment cut me to the core. I thought to myself, "this is how he wants to end this?" This cold-blooded cut after investigator after investigator has come and gone, solely because of the way he treated them? Many of them were good people. I responded to him that I knew better than that and mentioned the girls by name who would disagree with what he just said. It went over his head, and he made no comment. I paid for the lunch, and we walked back to the office. We shook hands and I left. We haven't spoken again.

Your loyalty provides you with nothing that the recipient doesn't wish to surrender. Some people are grateful for loyalty, others expect or demand it. The latter causes difficulty and conflict. Loyalty is a two-way street. When you give something that important to someone, and when you allow yourself to be that vulnerable, there has to be a return of some nature, at least recognition or appreciation. Neither came in this case and after time, I grew to resent my own loyalty to Ben. I never compromised it, as that would have been a violation of my own ethics. I knew that Ben would move me out and someone else in without a second thought if I hadn't been good at what I did. I also knew that when he learned that I had opened my own office it would be the end of our relationship. Why, I don't know. He didn't like it and paid no regard to my resistance to contacting his clients. I learned a lot of lessons from Ben. Sadly, many were lessons in how not to be.

So, you've seen stories now about the excerpts of an insurance fraud private investigator. Some may be lackluster to you. Some may be exciting. All are true and reported to you as well as I can remember them. One thing is a certainty. Each day you go to work you'll have no idea what will transpire or what to expect. You'll learn to think on your feet and your moral character will follow closely behind you, displaying for everyone what kind of person you are. Make sure that those opinions fall on the ethical side of the fence. You'll be in places and have opportunities to do things wrong, illegal, or immoral. In one word I can emphatically declare to everyone, without exception, DON'T. It'll cost you more than you want to pay, for longer than you want to pay it.

CHAPTER 8

My Spiritual Side

It's time to talk about God. This isn't going to be a sermon, a lecture, a teaching, or even preaching. This is going to be a down to earth discussion about my experiences with God. Yours may be similar, or you may have had few at all. Your beliefs might be strong, or you may be a doubter. You may have a desire to know him, or no interest at all. Irrespective, what you're going to read is fact. Both Godly, and ungodly, these are true. It'll be difficult to read about them and not have an amazement about the spirit world. Does it exist? Is it real? Is there really a God, and on the other side, demons as well? Let's take a look at my experiences, then you be the judge. You can skip this chapter if you'd like, or if you're uncomfortable talking about God, but I would suggest that you don't. These aren't stories, they are events that have happened. They will clearly reveal that there is a spirit world. Not one in the same, but good and bad. We each have a choice as to which one we want to embrace. If we don't make a choice the bad side will make one for us. They always do. The good side will not force himself on you. You have to consciously choose that side yourself. It's not possible to hug the bad side and call it good. It isn't. Bad is bad, in fact, it's really bad. And I'll say it once again, it's not possible to not make a choice at all and think because you're a good person, you're on the good side. You're not. Because you haven't made a decision to be on the good side, the bad side will take you for themselves. Note, however, that bad can put on a costume and appear to look good, even do good things. But coming from the wrong side of the spirit world, they're still bad. And they want bad things to happen to you. The more that does, the happier they are. The bad side is not godly, and they have no angels. They are demons. With that in mind, let's talk about the spirit world.

Other than here, I rarely talk about my pre-Christian days of diving down into the depths of Hell to shake and titillate the demons that have chosen to reside in this most Satanic place, however, my experience may serve as a lesson to some who choose to be wise and take heed. No one has to reinvent the wheel unless they want to. I've always thought it best to avoid learning from my own experiences if possible, but instead learn from someone else's. It's usually less painful.

I was twelve or thirteen when I started playing with the Ouija board. We all know what a Ouija board is, I don't need to belabor it here. If you don't, Google it. Just don't buy one. My brothers and I had fun playing with it for a while but I got little out of it. Cliff or Jack and I would try to get the indicator to move by having both of our hands on it, and if it did, what word was it trying to say? The indicator, or planchette, as it's formally called, is a small three-legged table with a window in the middle that sits atop the Ouija board. With our hands on the planchette, it will, should, or may move across the surface of the board to letters on the board itself. We brothers didn't have much luck with the Ouija board. We rarely got it to move. Mike and Donna tried it on occasion and were much more successful. Pen and paper in hand, I'd write down letter after letter the Planchette slowly spelled. Normally it was best just to ask a yes or no question. The purpose of it was to communicate with spirits, or ghosts. "Are you a good ghost?" "Do you know you're dead?" "Can you see us?" "Can we see you?" "Is there a Heaven?" "Is there a Hell?" Our questions were routine until the spirit, or ghost as we would refer to it, got tired. They were generally nice spirits and answered all our questions. It was titillating to get responses from something we couldn't see. At that age we didn't quite know what to make of our adventures into the spirit world, but we were learning that it may actually be real. I'd watch the hands of Mike, Donna, or anyone else who was using the board and neither of them were pushing it to a specific word or letter. In fact, on many occasions their hands would uniformly start to move one direction as if to know the answer the spirit was going to provide, only to watch the planchette itself go another direction. All of us looked at each other with shock, but it happened many times. Frequently we'd sit in the living room at home to play the Ouija board for hours. And just as frequently we noticed how nervous and fidgety the dog was. On more than one occasion neighbor's dogs would all commence barking and were clearly upset. We wondered at this phenomenon but enjoyed the control we had. We got more deeply entrenched in calling up spirits and talking to them.

What we didn't notice was how deeply troubled our own spirits became. Sleep was always difficult and distressed after using the board. Dreams and nightmares always followed, but they were no deterrent. We'd learn how someone lived, and how they died. They'd tell us what it was like where they were, and how they could see us. They could tell us things about our past and advised us of future events. They weren't always right, but often enough to be frightfully convincing that we were clearly talking to the spirit world. They never warned us of Hell, as we would know it or Heaven as we would visualize it. These places were less dramatic than we were told on earth. "Hell wasn't so bad, Heaven wasn't so good," was their representation, and we listened.

In time we started asking for things. "Can you help me with my homework?" "Can you make someone do something for us?" The encouraging part was that frequently these things would happen. The expected result was that it got us more deeply fascinated and entrenched. We shared our experiences with a handful of others, but it generally stayed in the family. Then Mom started to have sessions with us.

Mom was quite different than the rest of us when using the board. She was able to talk to no-one but Dad. She sometimes tried, but without success. She and Dad communicated so quickly that we could barely write the letters down as fast as the planchette moved. "Mom had to have been doing this herself," I thought, but I'd ask Mom to look away from the board as Dad wrote lengthy sentences to her without missing a single letter. It made no difference that she couldn't see. This was the most amazing thing we had experienced so far. Mom couldn't do it very long, it seemed to drain her energy. When she did sit down with us at the board, things were going to happen, such as the time the planchette came out from underneath her and my hands. It flew across the room and hit the wall. I didn't do it, and Mom wasn't looking. No one else had their hands on the board. I'll assure you with certainty that neither one of us moved or threw that planchette.

Generally, when Mom joined in, it was at our house in the country. Rolling hills provided plenty of grazing for cattle. Like clockwork, we could get them to start mooing by sitting down at the Ouija board with Mom. It was such a powerful thing that we were elevated to a position of control. How little did we know that we were being controlled ourselves!

Because we were so receptive and invited these spirits into our home, in time we started seeing what are called ghosts, or apparitions as one would more appropriately describe them. Each of us, without exception, saw different things moving in the house. Sometimes we'd see or feel the same thing and describe it the same way, a movement in the hall, a dark cloud in a room, a cold touch. We were familiar with these supernatural things and didn't like them. It was too much. We could invite them to talk on our Ouija board, but didn't want them haunting our house. I was to have a specific spirit torment me for years. It came in the sound of a rumbling or groaning under the house. Convincing myself that it was the house settling, I tried to ignore it. It followed me from house to house wherever I moved, for years, even after I married Paulette.

At fifteen or sixteen, I became more unnerved at the spirit world that I had invited into my life. I walked off the hill one night after dark, down the dirt path to Huston Road below our house. The trail meandered down the hill without obstruction. Small twists and turns were no obstacle, and I had only the darkness to cope with. This was always an uncomfortable walk for some reason, not because it was dark, or even lonely. I was used to that just by way of living up here, but the walk this night was unusually unnerving. Walking down the trail through the knee-high dry grass I experienced a heat going through my body and a wave through my face. I immediately felt the strong pull of something behind me. I turned quickly around to look, and there it was. An object walking only a few feet back. This couldn't be possible! I spun completely around and walked backwards, staring at this thing. I was terrified. It was really there. I wasn't sleeping, and it wasn't too dark to see. You know something is there when it's close enough to both see and feel. Although human in form, it lacked the detail of a person's form. This form was dark, black, and seemed to have no face. It wasn't aggressive, nor did it retreat. It remained there motionless, as though that's where it was supposed to be. I broke out in a run down the hill. Somehow, Huston Road was my safe haven. Once I got there, I'd be okay. I didn't know why, and I was too scared to look back to see if it was chasing me. I reached the road without incident, and I never experienced that again. For years to come I feared I would. I never told anyone about what happened. It was too unbelievable to tell, I guess, but it happened. The thing walking only a few feet behind me --- was a demon.

Although I would talk to Dad, I was always afraid that I'd see him. I didn't want that, nor to see any other ghosts or spirits. That was too much for me to take. One warm evening, Mom, Donna, Cliff, Jack, and I were at the Ouija board. It was an exceptionally powerful night and Mom was communicating with Dad. However, Dad was talking to me. "Do you want to see me?" he asked. I immediately got scared. "No," I replied. "Why?" I had no answer other than I was too scared. "Scared that I'll hurt you or scared of the unknown?" the spirit asked. "I don't know," was my only answer. "Have I ever hurt you?" he asked. I could only answer "No". "Why would I hurt you now?" Dad was persistent. Donna was encouraging the exchange and prodded me to consent to seeing Dad in the flesh. That was probably the most nervous I'd been in my life up to that point. With pressure from the family, I gave in to letting Dad appear before me. The others wanted to see him too, but this seemed to be directed at me. This night was lit by a full moon and the animals in the area were unusually noisy or upset. I knew something was going to happen tonight. I just didn't know what. I'd rather have stopped the whole thing, but peer pressure prevailed. "Get up and walk to the front door," the spirit said. Mom and my brother continued to relay his message through the Board. I did, and expected a knock from the other side. "Open the door." It really took everything I had to comply, but I very slowly opened the door, knowing that I'd find someone, or something, standing on the other side. It was like throwing the switch on your own electric chair. Could I do it? Would I cower to my own fears and surrender to my inability to reach deep enough inside me to overcome this? I was almost paralyzed as I touched the doorknob. I let my body do the rest, without my cooperation. I watched the door open. The dark air entered first. My senses were overloaded as the first crack in the door got larger. "This is no way to face this fear," I confessed to myself, and I swung the door open to meet my dead father. Nothing was there, nothing but noises from the surrounding animals. "Walk outside," he instructed through Mom. Still, with inward resistance, I continued to comply. Once out in the dirt driveway I could hear no more from inside the house. I was there alone waiting for Dad to appear. Donna ran out to me to say that Dad wanted me to walk up the dirt road out toward the highway, and she was going along too. I slowly started my trek up the lane, past the bushes and brush, to the top, where it turned right and meandered over toward the highway. I had to pass through the fruit orchard and a small canyon of oak trees before getting there, and I didn't know how far I was to go. It was the middle of the night, and all the lights were off at the neighbor's house as I passed on my way down the road. Each step was a task, but I put one foot in front of the other and complied with the instructions. Donna was more willing to go. She wanted to see what was going to happen, and maybe see Dad. I passed the neighbor's house now and their knee high yellow haired dog ran out to greet us. He was friendly and wanted attention, but this wasn't the time. The dog danced around us wagging its tail and I was annoyed. I sent it back home. We continued to walk out the road, almost to the canyon. Donna became discouraged and wanted to go back. "He'd never ask us to come up this far," she convincingly said. "Let's go back and talk to him again." Relieved, I quickly agreed, and we walked back down to the house. Mom and Jack were at the board now but not really communicating, just waiting. Donna revealed to them that nothing had happened, and Dad may have just been testing Duane or trying to scare him. "Let's find out," was the consensus. So far, we had said nothing about our adventure other than nothing happened. "Why didn't you show up?" was the question put to Dad. "I was there," he answered. "You rejected me." Donna and I thought for only a moment. It was the dog.

We spent time at Donna and Bills playing with the Ouija board, and there, too, we started seeing apparitions moving in the room. I saw a white robed object move across the hall from the bathroom into the bedroom but didn't say anything to either Bill or Donna. A week later, we were watching TV when Bill shouted out, "Did you see that?" He described what he had just seen, and it was the same apparition that I had seen a week earlier, moving the same way. I never told him I had seen it, too. I just listened.

As the years went by the Ouija Board wore off and we ceased dabbling in the occult. The visions and haunting continued for years to come, up to the time I entered the Marine Corps. Ghosts are scared to haunt Marines, but my inner spirit always remained in turmoil. I didn't know why, I just accepted it as a way of life. My first introduction to Christianity was through someone who eventually became a very good friend, Gunny Johnson, my Boot Camp Platoon Commander. I soon realized that his giving us a full-size table bible wasn't an accident or just a good gesture. It was his way of bringing me closer to God. And he'd continue to try throughout our relationship. He talked to me several times through the years that we were to know each other. On occasion he even took us to church. I was open, but not very much. Little was I to know that someday in the future I'd look back on his introduction with respect and admiration, just as I had for him.

Paulette didn't participate in the Ouija Board and when we met, I hadn't indulged for many years. Paulette had a softer spirit in her and was always seeking God. She was a strong believer in God and Jesus. I believed in both God and Jesus too, but I didn't understand any more about it, and didn't care to participate. At each town we lived in she sought out Christian people. While in L.A., she dragged me to church a handful of times, but I got little out of it. She took me to a healing revival one evening at Huntington Beach and I saw people say they were healed. I doubted it. A Marine Drill Instructor turned pastor wanted to speak to me at Paulette's prodding, but I never went. Eventually we moved to Auburn and as usual, Paulette found a Christian group. This group of people was different than others. I didn't know why, but they were. They were led by a man that I found both interesting and credible. Pastor Ralph was a good honest man, not given to drama or show, but instead preached the word of God directly from the Bible, and explained how it could be used in our everyday lives. His approach was not the overzealous TV preacher asking for donations. Instead, during the first few times Paulette took me to his church, he didn't pass around the offering plate at all. That was strange, I kind of liked Ralph.

Ralph would periodically drop by the house to see how Paulette and I were doing. We'd sit and talk for an hour or so and he was very up front, honest, and truthful. He spoke directly to problems and how to repair them and mend fences. He had a genuine concern for people. There was no mistaking his caring. I became more receptive to the church and began attending with Paulette.

It was September 17, 1977, and I was at an associate Pastor's house when Ralph stopped by. It was nice to see him, and a conversation ensued. People had spoken of being able to hear God and what he was saying, and this puzzled me. How can you hear God? "It's not through your ears," Ralph explained, "but in your spirit." This was equally confusing, and he gently outlined what God said about being Born Again. "Without being Born Again, your spirit is unable to hear the Spirit of God talking to you," was his simple answer. This was getting over my head, so he opened the bible to show me what God was saying about being Born Again. And he showed me scripture that said, "Unless ye be Born Again, ye shall never see the kingdom of Heaven." Now that scared me. I worried about that for the next round of conversation. I didn't know what had to be done to be Born Again, but I didn't have to ask. "Do you believe that Jesus is the son of God?" Ralph asked. I did. "Do you believe that he was a man who walked the face of the earth and was put to death on the cross to pay for your and my sins?" I didn't understand that one, but my spirit believed it. "Do you believe that he arose from his grave in three days and ascended to heaven?" I did. My spirit was comforted as he spoke these words, and although confused, I agreed. "Then with these confessions, and your prayer that Jesus will forgive you for your sins, and being baptized in water, you can become Born Again. If you invite Jesus into your heart, the Holy Spirit will accept your invitation and come to live inside you." Wow, this was a bit much. God was the chief of all spirits and for Him to allow me to join my spirit with Him was quite an honor. "Yes, I'd like to be Born Again." On that day I turned my life over to Jesus and became a Christian. A week later Paulette and I together were baptized in the American River.

I later revealed to Ralph my past experiences with the occult and Ouija Board, about seeing and talking to ghosts and spirits, and about communicating with Dad, and the dead. "That wasn't your Dad," Ralph cautioned with firm resolve. "Look at scripture here," and he showed me verses in the Bible to convince me that the dead do not come back to talk with the living. Nor do the dead become ghosts. There certainly is a spirit world at work, but its run by Satan and his demons. Ralph laid out scripture after scripture to show me how I had been deceived for so many years, and how I had actually invited these demonic spirits into my life, and home. He showed me how they would be forced to depart in submission to God, and that all I had to do was call on the name of Jesus to enlist his presence. I did, and Ralph and I prayed that these hauntings and apparitions would leave, and never come back. They did, and I neither saw nor heard any more ghosts, movements in the house, noises, or the moaning under the house. Jesus had returned everything to normal.

Paulette and I became committed to church and our church family. Things didn't always go well and there were spats and disputes, but that's natural among any group of people. One believes this, the other that, but nothing that went against the word of God, merely different understandings of what God might be saying in his Word, the Bible. It was good to have these differences. If all believed alike, there would be no growth or improvement. Being a robot isn't always good. Challenging a brother or the Pastor over a belief is always wrong, but it happened, and the church went through its hard times. Naysayers went away, the believers stayed. Ralph continued to preach, and more believers came. Ralph suffered deeply from those who wished to challenge his unyielding stance on the Bible. "You have to be more flexible," they'd say, talking about premarital sex, living together before marriage, gay and lesbian rights, abortion, and other things that God has spoken directly about. Ralph preached it as it was said by God, not as man would water it down for convenience's sake. He was challenged many times for this and stood his ground. Some church goers contacted others to create a disturbance and unite in confronting Ralph. I was firmly loyal to a man who had also become my friend and challenged the discontented.

What they were doing was clearly in violation of God's Word, and I let them know. If they objected to Ralph preaching the Word as he does, then their option was to go somewhere else to church, not try to change this one. Some listened, some didn't. Most who didn't eventually went away anyway. What God doesn't build, he's faithful to destroy. He was building Ralph's church and removed those who objected to his stance. I was proud of Ralph for standing with the Word of God. Some other pastors may have submitted to the pressure and altered their teachings of God's Word. Right or wrong, Ralph didn't. I learned some lessons there, too.

It was after several discussions with Pastor Ralph about my dabbling in the occult and talking with spirits that I learned how dangerous this could be. God's Word reveals that the spirit world does really exist, but He specifically commands in his Bible that you do not conjure the spirit world. There's a black and white difference between a spirit that's sent from Satan, and an angel sent from God. Don't be confused by trying to determine if the spirit sounds nice or is doing a good thing. Bad spirits do good things to deceive you. Once you get taken into their world, it separates you from God.

The bottom line is, don't toy with anything that invites or titillates the spirit world in any way. There's nothing good about it. Nor are you talking with loved ones or nice strangers. There are no dead people who become ghosts. Those ghosts are in fact real, but they were never living beings. They are demons, commanded by Satan, who would love to scare the Hell into you. But you don't have to be their prey. Don't invite them in, don't dabble or play with them, and if you do feel like you're being tormented by a spirit, call on the name of Jesus. Spirits have to submit to the power of Jesus, and with Jesus living inside you as a Born Again Christian you'll have the power to send that spirit away forever. Only a fool would doubt what I say, for it comes from experience, not from imagination.

Shortly after becoming Born Again, I went to a nighttime gathering for singing and prayer. It was a pleasant gathering, small but enthusiastic. Not long after we started worshiping and singing praises to the Lord, a cloud covered me from head to toe. It was not visible, but one I could clearly feel. I became nauseous with both hot and cold flashes that instantly took turns ravaging my body from top to bottom. My feet tingled as though they had immediately gone to sleep. Something was trying to take me over and I knew that this was decision making time. I couldn't stand but was able to make my way outside and there I felt the very real tug on my spirit, Satan pulling on me from one direction, and God inviting me from the other. I felt as though I had to vomit but couldn't. My vision was blurred, and I didn't know what to expect next. Without speaking anything out loud, I ordered the haunting spirit to leave me alone, and asked Jesus to help me. The nausea, tingling, heat and cold all immediately went away. It's never returned. I believe it was Satan's final effort to take me into his world and had I not called on Jesus for help, I may have been captured by him. What happened that night was a very real thing. Years later as I grew in God, I wanted to hear the voice of God. Not just talking to my spirit as I admit I couldn't hear or understand much of the time. I really wanted to hear the actual voice of God talk to me. Unlikely as it might be, I kept that wish for quite some time, always wondering in the back of my mind whether He would or would not.

In my mid 30's, I spent a lot of time working in the garage. I was a fair motorcycle mechanic, and many would bring their bikes to me for repair or routine maintenance. I didn't mind, as it gave me some spending money. Working with Ben didn't provide any more than just enough to get us by. A friend brought over a small Honda CT90. It was old and rugged looking from sitting outside for the last few years. I agreed to try to get it running for him and pushed it up on the rack so the bike was chest high, and I wouldn't have to bend over. The rack was a real benefit for me when working on bikes. I'd place a ramp out behind it, open the garage door, and roll a bike on or off of it. Using tie down straps I cinched the bike down to the rack by its handlebars, and everything was secure. I went on to perform any task needed for repairs. This Honda 90 needed its gas tank flushed and I had to rebuild the carburetor. It took a few hours to accomplish that, and it was getting late in the evening. Paulette was gone and I was caring for the kids as many fathers do. They were inside the house watching TV. It was a quiet summer evening, not too warm, not too cold. I wondered where Paulette was at this hour but not to the point of worrying yet. "It'd be nice to get this bike running tonight," I thought as I poured fuel into the freshly cleaned gas tank. This bike had no shutoff valve for the fuel line that fed the carburetor directly from the tank. Vacuum from the engine would either suck in fuel, or it wouldn't. The "wouldn't" part was the one I was concerned about. I really wanted this bike to start up and run. I had three other bikes waiting in line to be worked on and I couldn't spend much more time on this. I looked behind me at the three bikes that were standing directly behind the rack, and I shook my head. It was getting hard to work on all these motorcycles and work all day for Ben, too. With little choice, I continued taking in bikes. I didn't want the neighbors to hear the bike if it started up tonight, so I pulled the heavy wooden garage door down and closed it. I double checked my work and made sure the gas line from the tank was hooked up to the carburetor. "Of course it is," I laughed to myself. I just filled the gas tank. If the line wasn't hooked to the carburetor, it'd be pouring fuel all over the bike. I felt stupid for checking, but I always seem to double check everything anyway. "Oh, geez, I can't find the gas cap." The full tank of gas was up to the brim and the cap was gone. After tiring of looking, I convinced myself that it'd be okay. The bike was tied down to the rack and couldn't go anywhere. The cap would turn up.

"All is ready" I thought and pulled the kick starter down by hand. There's not much compression to a CT90 so it's not difficult to start by hand. No life yet, so I pulled the kick starter down again, still no life. Several more times I pulled the kick starter through its cycle and got only a pop from the engine. "It's trying," I said to myself as I kept pulling the starter through its cycle. "It's got to be starting to flood by now," I thought, and I opened the throttle to full open to try to suck air into the cylinder and clean out the fuel. There's a 14.7 to 1 air to fuel ratio needed to start an engine like this and I hadn't met that ratio yet. Soon, this bike will start. It kept popping like it wanted to start, and then I heard a louder, hollow and deep-throated pop come from the engine. A flame backfired out of the carburetor. That's happened before and is usually not a concern, but this time the flame found its way to some fuel residue on the frame of the bike and ignited it. The small fire immediately grew larger as the old bike had plenty of oil and gas all over it. The flame reached the seat in little more than a few seconds and I grabbed a rag to smother out the fire. It wouldn't smother and the flame was now climbing its way up around the top of the bike and gaining control. "My God," I thought, "I'm going to burn the garage down." I became very worried that I couldn't get this fire under control as I grabbed the small extinguisher and emptied it onto the bike and the base of the fire. It made no difference and the fire kept raging. I had kids in the house, and I called to them. It was then that I heard the audible spirit voice. "Pull the gas line off the carburetor!" Then the voice said it a second time, "Pull the gas line off the carburetor!!" I knew that this was a crazy thing to do. There was no shut off valve from the tank to the carburetor and gas would pour all over the bike and the garage. Louder this time, I heard the audible voice again, "Pull the gas line off the carburetor!" Almost without any control over myself, and knowing what it would do, I reached up and intentionally, but without being able to stop myself, as though I was under someone else's control, pulled the gas line from the carburetor. Gas poured out from the tank directly onto the fire. It kept feeding the fire as fast as it could pour out onto it. I couldn't stop it and the flames burst into a full-fledged fire. The kids heard me calling for them and answered the door from the house. "Call 911 and get out of the house. Out in the road." I yelled as they saw the flames shooting up into the rafters and all around the bike. I had to get this bike outside or get outside with the kids myself. The tie down straps were hooked over the handlebars, there was no ramp behind me to get the bike down off the rack. There were three motorcycles directly behind me between me and the garage door, which was now closed. I remembered there was no gas cap on the full tank of fuel, meaning I'd have to keep the bike level when getting it down and out of the garage. Getting burned wasn't as prominent a concern to me as saving the house. The fire now almost engulfed the bike. Somehow, I was able to free the tie down straps from the handlebars, back the bike off the rack without a ramp, kick the bikes behind me aside, force the garage door up with my foot, and drug the bike out onto the lawn where I dropped it and the remaining gas poured out onto the ground and immediately ignited. I couldn't tell whether I had been burned or not, yet. I started for the garden hose when the fire department, which was only a block away, arrived. They put the fire out and checked me for burns. I needed to check the garage for fire as it had reached the rafters before I could get the bike down. The kids were okay, and I took a deep breath. This was no less than miraculous. I had not been burned at all, and the house didn't catch fire. I don't know how I got the bike down and outside through all the obstacles. And the voice I heard? It was real. Loud and real, and it repeated itself until I surrendered to it, even knowing what would happen if I did. It wasn't the voice of God, as I had been hoping for so long. It was the audible voice of Satan. God stepped in to protect me after I gave in to this demonic demand. God saved me, my children, and my house, despite me. Another lesson was learned. Through the years, and even to the present, I've been haunted, hounded and hunted, much of which I brought upon myself. Occasionally I've played no part in causation. And on even a rarer occasion, something quite extraordinary, surpassing all previous experiences, will present itself.

Most recently, it was an exceptionally hard season that I had been going through for the past many months, and even years. Many long, late-night hours at the office failed to produce the hoped-for goal of making ends meet with confidence, and be assured that this advancement into financial security would not be just a rare exception. My fervent prayer was that God would bless my efforts, my hands, and my mind so I could feel productive and confident that the bills would get paid next month, too. "If I supplied the effort and the motivation," I convinced myself, "God would provide the blessings." The time would come when God would recognize my heart and provide the work so necessary to care for a family. Other issues preyed on my mind and heart but as pressures escalated, as the stress grew far beyond my means of coping, I found myself frequently seeking God and trying to understand why my life had failed, and why I'm failing my family, yet, no answers, no changes. Not even a sign from God that he knew I was there or that he understood my prayers. "Why? WHY?? What's it going to take to get God to hear me? What do I have to do to get Him to speak to me? What am I going to do? Where am I going to go if I close my office down and try to start a different career, at my age, somewhere else? Is God really telling me to do this? Is it time to move on? Has God provided an open door somewhere that I hadn't seen? Is He going to provide one in the future? God, you are confusing me, and I can't live with that right now. I need answers. I need you to show me that you love me, you hear me, and you care!" My petition to God was made under real duress. Some have made this type of plea before, so you know the feeling of desperation that accompanies the prayer. Others, without praying, have suffered the loneliness of feeling this way, alone, without turning to God. Either way, you can understand my desperation.

I had worked through the day and realized I hadn't taken time to eat. I wasn't really hungry. I was more distressed than hungry, and eating wouldn't take that away. "Well, maybe it'd help," I quietly thought to myself. I picked up my keys, turned the lights off, and locked the door behind me as I made my way slowly out to the car. Where was I going to go? I didn't know. What did I want to eat? I didn't care. How long was I to be gone? It didn't matter. I presumed that the most likely place I'd wind up was a local McHamburger drive-thru not far away. "That's alright," I thought to myself. "It really doesn't matter." Something told me to turn left up ahead and go to the "Out in No Time" burger stand. "Nope," I argued with myself. "It's Friday and that place will have skiers going up the mountain packing the door. I'm not going there," I firmly said to myself. It came to me a second time, and for the second time I logically rejected the thought. It came the third, and this time I got more firm with myself. "No, absolutely not. Not, No, Nothing, Not going to Out in No Time tonight.

A couple of minutes later I was at Out in No Time. "I don't know what I'm doing here," I argued. "And look at this, a line 20 people deep!"

I stepped up to the rear of the line, disappointed that it was backed up almost to the entrance door. My attention was broken when I found myself standing behind what appeared to be a nice-looking young man. A late teenager or in his early 20's, this man was clean-cut, strong, and although not well dressed, dressed well. His thick neck made an appropriate transition to some broad shoulders, and his short-sleeved shirt exposed arms that were accustomed to high intensity workouts. They were well formed, even in their relaxed state. For some reason this young man had my attention. His shirt was tucked in and pleated, his trousers, even though just a pair of Levi's, were freshly ironed. His shoes were clean, and he had just had a haircut. Yes, that haircut was familiar to me - High and Tight. I wore mine that way in the Marine Corps. In fact, all of this young man represented the Marine Corps. Yes, he had to be a Marine.

Only seconds later, another young man walked out from the nearby bathroom and approached my attention-getting young man in front of me. "I was right," I applauded myself. This second young man is in a Marine uniform. He's a PFC. One stripe. Probably just out of Boot Camp. I studied his uniform in detail. No Irish Pendants, his shirt was bloused perfectly, and as he turned sideways to look at his friend, I could see that his shirt, trousers, and belt buckle were in perfect military alignment. The brass buckle shined with fresh polish, and his shoes were spit shined to nothing less than a pure black mirror. He was clean shaven, as I'd expect him to be, with no day's shadow growing out. His hair short, it was easy to see he was trying to find something to comb over. "Not yet, my friend," I thought to myself. "It's going to have to grow out a little more." I studied this man, as I had the first. They were both strong, professional fighters, trained killers, the best in the world. Yet they stood in front of me so gentle.

They were respectful of each other as they quietly spoke. Not as kids do, but as men. "What are you going to order?" one asked. "Just a hamburger," the other responded, "it's a long way to payday." The first responded back, "I'm sorry, I don't have anything to loan you, and I'm short, too." "It's okay, we'll make it work" they both agreed. These two young men were Marines of the utmost kind. I stared at the back of them both, knowing that the Iraq war was well underway, and these two young heroes were most assuredly going to soon provide an Iraqi terrorist his prime opportunity to give his life for his Allah. "These two young men could soon be at war," I thought. Or maybe they already have been, and they're home on leave. If it weren't for the grace of God, these two men could be dead right now and here they are trying to get enough money together for a hamburger.

As the thought of their struggle went through my mind, I noticed an old gentleman arise from his table and jettison his trash at a nearby container. He prepared to pass by on his way out but stopped and looked over at the Marine in uniform. It was easy to see this old man was proud, as he reached out without saying anything, and offered is hand to the young warrior. "Thank you," he said with firm resolve as the Marine offered a gentle smile and a firm handshake. The old man nodded, gave one last smile, and walked out the front door. The two Marines only looked at each other to exchange manly smiles and turned toward the counter once again.

The line was shortening, and it wouldn't be long before they and I would have our turns to order. I had little time to reminisce about my time in the Marine Corps when a voice spoke to me, *"Buy their dinner."* "Oh, gee whiz", I thought. "I only have a $20.00 bill, with no money coming in. This is my last. I'm broke, and if I do, I may not be able to eat myself." *"Buy their dinner."* I heard it a second time. And a second time, I presented my argument, as I found myself reaching up to the shoulder of one Marine, interrupting his order to the cashier. "Excuse me, Marine." I turned to the cashier. "Ma'am, give these two Marines anything they want." I laid my $20.00 on the counter. No, I wouldn't eat tonight, but that was okay. Both Marines looked to me with surprise, and smiled. They both gave me a respectful, "Thank you, sir," and each reached out to shake my hand. It was a pleasure to shake theirs - warm to the touch, yet firm and friendly. They squeezed my hand tightly as they looked into my eyes. These were no sissy little men playing army, or office clerk nerds playing imaginary rolls in a computer combat game. These were real men, young, but real men.

I watched as both ordered their meals. When done, they stepped off to my left to await their order. Out in No Time doesn't pre-cook their hamburgers and on a normal day one could expect a 10-minute wait. It's normally worth it. Many pre-cooked meals have been thrown away at other stores because they got stale before they could be sold but tonight would be a longer wait. The size of the crowd meant this meal would take 15 or more minutes to be delivered to the counter in front of us. "Oh well. I'll talk to the Marines while I'm waiting."

I turned to the cashier as she reached out to hand me my change. "Oh," I thought, "I've got enough to get a hamburger myself." I was pleased and ordered a simple burger and small coke. An adequate meal under the circumstances. She handed me a few coins back and I put them in my pocket as I turned to the waiting Marines. I'll find out if they've been to Iraq yet. Out of my view for only a few seconds while I ordered, I found myself looking to speak with them again. I looked at where they had been standing only seconds earlier, and they were gone.

Gone!? Where could they have gone to? They wouldn't have had time to even step toward a table in this amount of time. I scanned the room understanding the possibility that they may have wanted to spend their time alone, without a stranger sitting down with them, but they hadn't gotten a table. In fact, all the tables were full. Two Marines in a small diner aren't hard to see. And one in uniform? This was puzzling, but as an investigator I don't let strange things take control. I look into the unusual thoroughly and that's what I did. I scanned the room again, more thoroughly this time. I hastily stepped outside considering the possibility that they might be on a cell phone or leaving in a car for some unexpected reason. Staying long enough to ensure that this wasn't the case, I checked the patio one more time before stepping back in. The only area not searched was the bathroom. One Marine had come out of there before ordering, so it wasn't likely, but I needed to check. No, they weren't there. One thing couldn't help but cause them to surface. I positioned myself at the pick-up counter and waited for our numbers to be called. They were just ahead of me, and my number was a long way off. As I stood there befuddled and in denial at the same time, I knew they had to pick up their meals. I reviewed the introduction and meeting in my mind several times to analyze whether I had embarrassed or offended them in some way. Those options were slim, and I continued to wait with confidence that this mystery would soon come to a close.

It seemed like a long wait, but eventually my number was called. A small hamburger and a drink, yes, that's what I ordered. But where are the two hamburger meals before me? Where are the two Marines?

Neither appeared. Neither the Marines nor their meals. The cashier passed right over their numbers and continued serving other patrons as if nothing was out of the ordinary. But it was. I saw them. I touched them. A pleasant old man shook their hand. They talked to a cashier as they ordered their meals. I received the change back from their order. And less than 30 seconds later they were no longer in the room, or on the premises. If that still isn't enough, the cashier skipped their order number when serving the other patrons.

Who were they? What were they? Why were they? And who sent them? Did God send a messenger to tell me He still knows I'm here, He still sees me, and He still cares? If He were going to do that, He couldn't have picked a better way than to send two Angels to me, dressed as United States Marines. I'm but a very small person, and significantly undeserving of seeing an Angel of God, however in my quiet way, I'll take comfort in my own opinion. I've loved God, trusted God, questioned God, and doubted God, but He's always been there. Facts are facts, and this experience is a fact.

CHAPTER 9

Children Have Their Own Problems Too

Our kids were getting older now. Lisa and Nicki were in High School. Dee was in Middle School. Trouble was beginning to brew with the girls. Lisa was growing from a beautiful little girl into a gorgeous young woman, but still too young to look that way. I was scared for her, big time. Fortunately, she wasn't interested in boys, but boys were zeroing in on her, older boys of course, juniors and seniors, and of course their interest wasn't in a game of checkers. Lisa was a model quality young lady. Paulette was first to recognize it and wanted to send her to modeling school. Lisa was excited about that. My job was to keep the hounds away from the door, and I let Lisa know she was too young to date. She didn't object to this much, as boys weren't the focus of her interest. That made things a little easier for me, but I was still worried and careful.

Nicki wasn't beautiful like Lisa. Instead, she was cute, very cute. She had a cute face and a cute personality. She was always laughing and finding something funny in everything. She was my joy and made me laugh, inside and out. Although younger than Lisa, she was the dominant force between the sisters. Lisa was submissive, Nicki was the planner and schemer. It was in her first year of High School that I knew the next four years were going to be difficult. Nicki liked boys, and she didn't hide it. There was no doubt in my mind that at 14, she wasn't going to be dating any boys yet, but they came around anyway. Not boys her age, but older boys, boys with cars. I said, no, no, no way. But they still persisted in coming around at Nicki's encouragement. I was having a real problem with this and needed to protect my daughters while not letting them feel like they were being treated unfairly. I soon learned that this approach would be impossible. I was hearing things about them from police officer friends, and I soon was on my guard even more than before. It would be easy for these two girls to get into trouble, big trouble. They were starting to miss the bus after school and would walk home. They'd start getting home two hours late, and then later. They were resistant, almost to defiance, and Nicki was the ringleader. We would talk to them, scold them, punish them, restrict them, deprive them, and even spank them, with no change in behavior. You have to remember that during those days and time a light spanking was not a taboo act of inhumanity as it is this day. Even at that, swatting a teenager is not and was not a socially acceptable thing to do. But desperation can bring on an extension of boundaries, and it did. Thinking back on it, however, I feel more shame than justification, even though in later years I would find myself apologizing to both girls, for a single incident. I pray they've accepted my remorse and forgiven the incident. It will probably be easier for them to forgive me, than me to forgive myself. Did any of those forms of correction change their behavior? Nope. Mom and I were doing something wrong, but we were trying everything imaginable, and suggested, to maintain control over our girls.

Then came a fateful day in school where Child Protective Services, CPS, visited and gave a class on parental abuse. I certainly would not have objected to such a class had I known about it in advance. I didn't but didn't consider it a threat after I learned about it. No child should be abused by a parent or anyone else. It would have been a good education for them. But things did not go as they should, and the kids were taught more than they should have been. CPS went way outside the boundaries of maintaining a loving and working relationship with children and parents. Within days, Nicki was educating us that parental abuse can also be a parent who said "no" too frequently, or was too firm with their children. I got firm with her and straightened her misconceptions out. Her rebellion got worse, and Lisa-the-Follower, followed. They didn't come home from school one day for hours. Paulette and I were worried to the point of calling the police when the girls walked in, scared but cocky. It was 7:00 at night and although still light outside, school had been over for a very long time. "They were just hanging out with friends," was all I could get out of them, and they had finally gone too far. Something had to be done to bring them under control. That's when the paddling event occurred. They were humiliated, and sometimes that's the result of many forms of correction. But these girls were feeling, and taught at school to feel like adults. I went quietly to my bedroom and cried myself. That was probably the most difficult thing I had ever done as a father. I knew I had to break that defiant spirit, but this was just too much even for me to handle. What had I done?

A few days later I got a call from CPS who wanted to talk to the girls. I questioned the caller as to why, and he refused to say. I, in turn, refused to allow him to talk to my children. He was an arrogant individual with a superior approach that I resented. "Why was he involved with my children and what did he want?" I insisted. I assured him that if he wanted to talk with anyone, he was invited to talk with me about any concerns he had. He declined, saying his business was with the girls and it was none of mine. He refused to reveal what had prompted his call and declined to reveal any intentions that he had. I invited him to call back when he could be more open with me. He was clearly livid that I had not recognized his authority over mine and Paulette's regarding our children. As I ended the call I knew trouble was brewing but was satisfied that I had invited him to call back when he could be more communicative.

Within two hours, he showed up at the house with two police officers, both of whom I happened to know and was friends with. They were both clearly understanding and sympathetic, however they were obligated to stand by while CPS took the two girls from the house. They left Dee behind. Paulette and I were beside ourselves, hysterical to say the least. CPS wouldn't reveal why they were taking the kids, or where they were taking them. That was a day that Paulette and I will remember to our grave. One of the children, probably Nicki, was manipulating CPS to get what she wanted with her social exploration. We later learned that the swatting wasn't the main focus for their getting involved. Nicki had reported to them that we were too strict on her in telling her "no," she couldn't "socialize" with older high school boys, and go for rides in their car. She was 14 and had that right. We were never able to confirm that for ourselves but were told that by others. Nicki was of that mindset and certainly may have done just that. Lisa-the-Follower, followed.

The girls, at 14 and 15, were put into a shelter and we were prevented from seeing or talking to them. They were given an attorney and we were advised to get one too, if we ever wanted to get our kids back. But not the same attorney for Paulette and I together. Paulette was to get her attorney, and I was to get a different one. CPS's plan was to separate Paulette and me as well, and turn one against the other. They charged me with child abuse and Paulette with failure to protect. This was emotionally more than either of us could bear. We loved our children very much. We were strict with them and maybe too strict at times, but to think we'd abuse them was so far beyond the scope of reality that it became nothing less than a nightmare. Court hearing after Court hearing, Paulette and I were put on the defensive, with CPS saying the girls were giving statements against us. I later learned that this was not true and was reported by CPS only to influence the Judge. It did, and we were barred from visits or communication with the kids. We tried to comfort Dee through this as he was very close to his sisters, yet he was seeing what they were doing to us. It was a confusing and difficult time for little Dee.

The girls were sent to separate foster homes. One in Auburn, the other in Newcastle. We pleaded that they be kept together, and put in a Christian foster home, but our request fell on deaf ears. CPS was doing exactly what they wanted to do without a modicum of concern for our family. The kids were allowed to call us while being monitored, and only when they wanted to initiate the call. Lisa did frequently and Nicki on occasion. We learned that CPS was questioning them heavily about any sexual abuse they may have suffered at my hands. They both appropriately denied any such thing ever occurred, and I became furious at such an insinuation. "Give me a polygraph, question me in any way you want, but don't compromise my relationship with my children by planting seeds like that," was my call to CPS. They paid no attention and hung up.

Lisa's foster mother was a middle-aged woman who was grossly made up like a Dolly Parton look-alike, but with heavier makeup and a less realistic wig. She drove a red Corvette and was obsessed with sex. All she talked about with Lisa and the other girls she provided foster care for was sex. Lisa spent several months there and although not interested in boys at the onset, was quickly learning about all the nuances of sexual intercourse. This foster mother eventually taught the girls how to perform oral sex using a cucumber as a model. Paulette and I were beside ourselves, yet we were helpless to do anything about it and could only listen to Lisa's report during her calls. CPS paid no attention to our complaints, and in fact denied that such a thing would occur. Lisa was given freedoms that she wasn't allowed at home, and at 15 years old, under foster care supervision, became pregnant. Not long afterward, she ran away from their home and back to us. We kept her and the Judge dismissed the case and all charges against Paulette and me, as far as Lisa was involved. Nicki was still in her foster home in Auburn. As the instigator of this devastating event, she had more reservations about coming home, until the foster mother left for the weekend, leaving only Nicki and the foster father there alone. It wasn't long before he went into her room and tried to comfort her with a back rub on her bare skin. He then asked her to give him one. He left the room for a minute and Nicki got up and ran out of the house. She wound up back in the shelter, and then ran away from there too. She ran home to us, and the Judge dismissed the case and all charges against Paulette and I. "I hope you can rebuild your family and go on with a normal life," he wished us as he dismissed the case, but that would never be. The damage was permanent and although we tried to treat the girls like nothing had ever happened, their experiences away from home would follow them the rest of their lives, and ours. We spent the rest of their teen years trying to repair things, to no avail. We sued CPS, and both of the foster homes, but they relied on their immunity status and the suit was forcibly dropped. We lost again. We encouraged the DA to file charges against the foster father who attempted to and did molest Nicki. They did but we lost the case at trial for lack of proof. His word against hers. This devastated Nicki and she cried openly in court. She would never be the same cute giggly little girl.

My knowledge or even suspicion of drug use came by way of a phone call from a police officer friend who was at our house. Paulette and I were in the Bay Area where she had a doctor appointment earlier that day. Dee was under the influence and was in an argument with Lisa. The noise brought our local cops, who discovered the reason. Our world was about to change again, and we didn't know what to do. Drugs remained an active part of their lives for the next few years. I had no knowledge about Nicki, but Paulette advised me later of her knowledge. If true, that meant all my children were into drugs. I felt so hopeless. This was so foreign as to how I felt my kids would be and I had a very hard time accepting it. You offer them discipline, you offer them guidance, you offer them counseling, you offer them rewards, you offer them encouragement, you offer them close monitoring. Nothing worked. We insisted that they go to church with us. It was an effort in futility.

It was Nicki's eighteenth birthday. She grew to be a very independent little adult. She made up her own mind and spoke her own piece. I couldn't tell how we were getting along, she ignored me most of the time. Her birthday was a chance to show her how much we loved her. Paulette and I bought her presents, a cake, and invited some of her friends over for her eighteenth celebration. She was happy and laughed and I knew she was having a good time. A little later she decided to go somewhere with her friends and got ready to leave. "Where are you going, honey?" Paulette asked. Apparently, that's what she was waiting for. I watched as Nicki turned around and with all presence and intent, looked directly at her mother and said, "I'm eighteen. I don't have to tell you anything anymore, and I'm not going to." She walked out the door and I don't remember the next time I saw her. It doesn't really matter whether we deserved it, or she was being unfair. That hasn't been straightened out to this day. We lost our daughter that night.

Lisa remained with us and had her baby. Jesie was born March 12, 1992. At 16, Lisa was clearly unable to raise a child herself, so we commenced the job of raising another child. It was difficult as my time needed to be spent working and Paulette was past her youthful child raising years. We found we were less patient than we were years earlier. We had to face this new challenge. We'd be polite by identifying it only as difficult. We were grandparents starting to raise a child all over again. We loved Jesie. It wasn't his fault he was here with us. We loved Lisa. It wasn't (all) her fault that she was a mother at 16. These were circumstances that we all had to raise to the occasion to. Throughout my adult life I've observed people who respond to miserable or devastating circumstances and display to everyone how miserable they are. Angry and complaining, they maximize every opportunity to express their anger. My advice to them, when they wanted it, was to recognize this experience as something less than desired, but turn this experience into an adventure. I would say to all, regardless of the specifics, coveted or cursed, wanted or rejected, don't just live through an experience. Turn it into an adventure. All experiences can be addressed that way. Once you focus on this adventure, the sting of the experience diminishes, you find yourself a more pleasant person, and you learn something from that adventure. We certainly loved Jesie and Lisa as well. We weren't in love with the thought of raising another child, but it was time for me to live my own words. I was reminded that when I hold my fist out and point a finger at someone who could be handling an experience in a less than admirable way, there are three more fingers pointing back at me. They're all my own. The challenge is now for me to turn this experience into an adventure. And I will.

A painful time for me was during the next few years as Dee and Lisa explored what direction they wanted to go in life. They decided the bad road wasn't the way they wanted to go only after traveling and experimenting down that road. They each got into trouble with the law, and I sat through several of their Court hearings. It was so difficult to do that I almost cried out loud. God saved me that humiliation. Seeing my children dressed in orange was almost more than I thought I could endure. Personally knowing the policemen and lawyers in town only compounded my emotional turmoil. This was a very difficult time in life for all of us. I didn't know if it would ever end. We traveled out of one trouble and into another. I didn't know which prevailed, anger and hurt or love and compassion. They were some very long years. Paulette and I supported and stayed with both of them during this long adventure. Eventually, both had experienced enough and decided to live a straight and productive life. I thank God for bringing them through it.

Lisa had her second baby, Serena, born October 29, 2002. She loved and cared for Serena up to a year old when Serena just became too much for her. We accepted another child until Lisa could finally take over, and we prayed she'd be able to soon. In the meantime, we started at ground zero once again. Nicki had chosen not to communicate with us for that last few years but we heard she had a little girl, Bonnie, but know nothing more than that. She was married by now, but we weren't invited to the wedding. In fact, we were specifically uninvited. Nor were we ever told by Nicki about little Bonnie, but the message got to us, along with Nicki's vow that we would never meet little Bonnie. Paulette is still hurt by that. I found myself indifferent, but for a different reason.

Only a couple of years earlier I was having a conversation with Paulette's father, whom I refer to as Dad. During that conversation he revealed that Nicki had been down to visit him and that he didn't believe anything she was telling him. I wondered about that and what she might have said. He went on to say that he's sure I was not the type of father that would ever do such a thing to his own daughter, and he's confident that I'm not a child molester. That had to have been the final breaking point for me. To think my own daughter would develop such a story and offer it publicly to relatives and friends everywhere was abhorrent. The audacity to concoct such a story was beyond my imagination. What hatred would make someone do such a thing? In my mind it severed my desire for a relationship with Nicki. Paulette spoke to her on occasion and attempted to address her troubled prevarication. She denied ever accusing me of such a detestable thing however we knew she had. She later told her mother that, yes it happened, and then after that, no, it didn't. What a sad thing that someone can hate so deeply. I made many mistakes while raising my children, and I pray that God and the children will forgive me, but never did I expect such retaliation for my failures. I'm so sorry that I failed her. The pain of her accusation has followed me close in my footsteps up to my now senior years. It's caused some members of family and friends, who Nicki has visited and talked to, to turn their back and close off their relationship with me. I'm sorry that they weren't able to reject the accusation as being not even a possibility. It isn't.

Dee matured after spending some time in jail. It was fortunate that he did. Substance abuse was his only crime but both the Judge and the District Attorney confided in me that he was nearing a prison term. Dee met a nice girl who cared for him very much. Michelle became pregnant with Sayde, who was born August 26, 2006, and became Dee's life. He made a 180 degree turnaround and had become the most caring and loving father one could aspire to be. I've become pleased and proud of him. To this day we talk every day, just to say hi, if for no other reason. Dee's adventures were rough, but he turned them into lessons. He has a remarkable wife who backs and supports him all the way.

Lisa followed her dreams in a different way. Hers were with an older, black ex-felon and she became pregnant by him. Deja was born on December 26, 2006. Lisa and he had their troubles together and he had his own set of individual difficulties. She left him in L.A. to come home, pregnant again. C.L. was sent back to prison and continued trying to contact Lisa. I've let him know as firmly as he wants to play that he won't see her again. He'll serve the remainder of his life there in prison. If he should get out, there'll be a brick wall guarding our door. Me. In the meantime, Lisa has come around to knowing what he really is and she's over him. Paulette and I are very thankful. She's worked hard on getting her life together. Sometimes successful, sometimes not. She focuses on her children now, and we're thankful for that. There's no doubt she loves them all. Sadly, she's burned out on men, and it'll take a lot of work for someone to capture her heart. Lisa did not have that real first love in her life that many of us can think back on with fondness and remember that warm feeling that fills the smallest corners of our being. I'm sorry about that. I wish I could somehow give that to her. Everyone is entitled to it. And as I mention it here, someone has come across your mind, too, didn't it?

Around the turn of the century, 1999 - 2000, I received a short e-mail. "I don't know if you want to talk to me or not, but I'm your son, Signed, Lee Purdue." This was my son whom I hadn't seen for over 20 years. In an effort to see him and his sister while they were young, I went to Lodi several times and quietly put their house under surveillance hoping I'd get a glimpse of them outside. During the next few years, I saw kids there but couldn't tell if they were Tammy and Lee or not. I'd take pictures just to have them with me at home. As years passed and the computer generation progressed, I signed up with several search engines so someone could publicly find me if they chose to. That was contrary to my normal safe practices, but it was important to me to make myself available to the kids should they ever want to talk to me. Lee did, and I wrote back. We talked by way of e-mail for quite some time. I wanted to be sure it was really Lee, and that he didn't have any ulterior motive for wanting to contact me. He sent me his photo and as it unfolded on the screen a chill when through me. It was a carbon copy of me when I was his age. "I couldn't deny that boy was mine, even if I wanted to," I thought. What a spitting image, with the exception that I was much better looking of course.

Lee was excited to talk to me. He wanted my phone number and address and was going to come down right away. I cautioned that we might talk on the phone first, and we did. He met Paulette on the phone and got to know me. We set a time a couple of weeks away for him to come down. He couldn't wait and the next weekend, he showed up at the house. I was glad, and Lee and I have been father and son as well as friends ever since.

Lee and his wife, Joy, were devout Christians and were raising their children, Jessica and Austin, to be the same. He was a drafter and a very accomplished artist. I was proud of his work. Eventually, he moved from Redding to Stockton and started his own business. He's become very successful. He's going to become a good man.

A week or so after Lee sent me his e-mail, I got another one. "Do you want to talk to me?" it asked. It was signed, Tammy. Of course I wanted to talk to her too, and I wrote back right away. Tammy was in Austin, TX, and our communication was initially strained, as she had many concerns. We talked through them, and she flew out to Sacramento where we met. As soon as we saw each other I knew she was my daughter. We hugged and she cried. We talked for hours at the restaurant and let our dinners get cold. Eventually, she had to leave for her drive to Redding to see Lee, and we parted. A short time later, Tammy moved out from Texas to Auburn, and we got to know her much better. She's a bright and beautiful woman with goals and ambitions. She's an accomplished singer with a strong desire to sing in a successful band. She's businesslike, yet soft and compassionate. We had many talks, and I grew a fresh new love for her. I was happy she moved to Auburn. But there was a yearning in her heart that couldn't be ignored. I wasn't sure what it was and she didn't say. I know she was torn between her mother and me. I think she saw things in me that didn't ring quite true from her mother's recollection of my mistreating her. I'm sure her mother didn't lie to her, she just had a different perspective of things. I know this caused Tammy grief. She had been, and still was, close to her mother.

Tammy contacted and became friends with Nicki. This concerned me a great deal but I'm not to dictate who she could communicate and be friends with. I understand that they talked a lot and Tammy grew farther apart from me. Sometime later, she got a boyfriend in the Bay Area and moved down with him and his two children. I don't remember her saying good-bye, or even that she was moving. I've heard little from her since she moved away but know that they later married. She's devoted to her new life and moving on with that. I hoped I hadn't done anything to disappoint her while she was here, but apparently I did. She doesn't write or call, but during a full moon, I know that both she and I can see it at the same time.

Cheri was one I didn't expect to hear from, but an e-mail came in shortly after I started talking with Lee and Tammy. Cheri had raised them from her perspective of our relationship and I'm sure she didn't want the kids put in turmoil, or her relationship with them compromised. Cheri was still bitter after 30 years, and although I thought that her marriage to Steve, and mine to Paulette, would soften each other's wounds, hers didn't seem to diminish. She wasn't contacting me for any personal reasons or gain. She wanted to monitor, the best she could, the relationship I was gaining with the kids. I didn't blame her for that either and it gave me an opportunity I hadn't had before, to express my guilt and sorrow for the pain I had caused her during our marriage. I had to be careful in doing that, as I didn't want her to get the misconception that I was accepting all the deficiencies causing our demise. But I did want her to know that I had made a lot of serious mistakes that had hurt our relationship. I hoped that she, too, had similar feelings and would get some things off her chest. It was never to be. The confessions were mine. They were difficult, but I expressed them during the next several e-mails in a genuine fashion. I was starting to feel relief and felt a monumental weight lift. A weight of guilt. She could accept my apologies or not, but they were genuine, regardless. She had some questions to ask, and I answered as honestly as I could. I set a boundary and told her I'd answer her concerns but no more than one at a time. I feared that she may have been tempted to bombard me with questions and accusations. During the next few weeks or months, we talked through the e-mail only. It was productive for her, and sometimes frustrating for me. Our relationship is over, and I love Paulette with all my heart. Cheri and I are not a threat to each other's current relationships. It was good that I could get things off my chest, and good that she forgave me for my sins when married to her. To date, she's gotten nothing off her chest as I revealed to her. Maybe there is nothing. Maybe she just doesn't want to say. During the course of time, we've occasionally chatted back and forth using e-mail, generally always about the kids. It's good that the hostilities have diminished. I'm comforted that she feels better, and I do, too. I'm saddened that she wasn't able to respond with admissions of her own that may relieve her of any guilt feelings as well. Certainly I would have forgiven her. I had already done that long ago.

Cliff and I had gone different directions some time ago and I kept track of him through third party channels. He worked nights as a bartender. During the day he was a house painter. Between the two, he made ends meet, but was never financially comfortable. He struggled as many of us did and do. I knew little about Cliff's personal life because we weren't close and in fact, we were at times hostile toward each other. I'm sorry about that. For years we weren't interested in contacting the other one- and let time pass under us. One evening I got a call in the middle of the night. It was Cliff. "I want to bury the hatchet," he said. I was glad to hear from him and glad that he wanted to get to know me and let me learn to know him. We talked for a couple of hours before hanging up. We arranged to go for a dirt bike ride together and a few weeks later he brought his bike out. I took him to Foresthill, and we had a great time. We didn't talk much, but we were together, and I liked that. Cliff called me every two or three months and we'd have a talk. He had usually been drinking and was hard to talk to, but something was bothering him terribly. He would never reveal what it was, but always said that nothing could be done to remedy his feelings. I was grieved over his sorrow, and explained to him that God would forgive ANYTHING he had ever done, but he may find it harder to forgive himself. I tried talking to him about God each time he called, but it only angered him. Eventually, he quit calling, and I didn't hear from him for a couple of years.

Mike grew weary of scratching for a living in Grass Valley. His wife, "Sam" divorced him, and he felt there was nothing to keep him in California any longer. His children, through his first wife Julie, were in Florida and they invited him to move down closer to them. He sold his house, packed up and moved to Florida. It was a strange thing for Mike to do, even though I understood his reasoning. It just didn't seem right. Something was wrong with his decision. We didn't talk enough for me to determine what that was. He got a job driving a taxi and I understand that he and his kids may have become at odds over some issues. They may have grown apart to some degree. I never pried. Mike didn't call me from Florida, nor I, him. I'm sure we thought about each other, but as our own individual lives go on, we many times put off until tomorrow what should be done today. I waited too long to call my big brother. Instead, I got a call from the local Police Department where he lived to tell me Mike had put a shotgun to his head. He was dead, and there was no note left behind. I was shocked, devastated, grieved, angered, suspicious, hurt, and a conglomeration of other emotions. I couldn't even imagine what would press him to doing this. Not just to himself, but to his family and everyone who loved him. What had happened in his life that brought him to having no hope at all? Was it loneliness, was it a drama induced accident, was it an act of only alternative? No-one knew. He had said nothing to anyone that I know of. Yet this final act was yet unsigned. What he left behind was my responsibility to go tell our mother. This was one of the hardest things I'd ever have to do. But I'll remember him as the proud Marine that he was, and that's the way he'll always be.

Cliff took Mike's death hard. He was closer to Mike than I had thought. Although Cliff and I hadn't talked for some time, I learned through Jack that he was very distraught about Mike. Six months after Mike's death, Cliff called me. "Hey brother, I understand you're trying to paint your rental house," he said. I affirmed his suspicion. I was preparing to tackle a job I couldn't put off any longer. "I've got all the equipment. I'll come down this weekend and we'll knock it out together. We'll finish it in a weekend," he offered in almost an insistent way. "Gee Cliff, I'm very grateful. This was going to be a big job for me."

We met for breakfast in Sacramento and time got past us. By mid-morning we agreed it was time to get started and went over to the rental house to prime and paint. Cliff was definitely an experienced house painter. Within hours he had the entire house primed. We started with the topcoat and got carried away talking, laughing, telling stories, and laughing some more. It was good to be with Cliff and better to have old things pass away.

Sunday, we met early and finished the topcoat of paint and completed painting the trim by that afternoon. Painting is a messy job and a miserable one to me. Cliff didn't seem to mind at all. He just went about doing what needed to be done while we talked as brothers once again. It was starting to get dark and although we'd been finished for some time now, it was time to put things away and go home. We agreed that we'd see each other again very soon, and I asked him to bring his bike out and we'd go for another memorable ride in Foresthill. He liked that and agreed. We pulled away from the house and Cliff followed me up the freeway until it split, and we were to go different directions. Before he did, he pulled up alongside of me and mouthed the words, "I love you, brother." My heart was warm and I was pleased to have my brother back again. "I love you too, Cliff," I said back so he could read my lips. He smiled and turned off for home.

After Cliff got home, he put a rifle in his mouth. It was all I could take, and I'm fortunate that Jack came out to handle the affairs. I couldn't even go to the funeral. I was angry, depressed, and hurt, at the same time. What did I fail to do or see could I have done to prevent this? What could I have done that I didn't do? Like Mike six months earlier, Cliff didn't leave a note. There was so much loss in such a short time. I never thanked Jack for stepping up to the plate and taking care of things, "Thank you Jack."

Within months, Mom had given up her will to live. She got sick and couldn't care for herself. Donna and Jim drove down from Montana, packed her things, and moved her up. Paulette and I were at her apartment when they all left. Mom was sitting in the back of Jim's car, with Donna and Jim in the front. I knew they'd take good care of her, and she'd be happy to have company rather than living alone in her apartment. As they pulled away Mom raised her hand in a slow tired wave. "Bye, Mom," I said quietly as I waved. I felt like crying as I walked to our car with Paulette. "I'll never see her again," I said just over my breath, and I didn't. Mom passed away peacefully at Donna's, knowing that her kids loved her very much. Mom loved God, and she's met Jesus now. But I miss her.

Mom no longer misses Dad.
She's laughing with him now, holding onto his
arm, with her head on his shoulder.

CHAPTER 10

Search and Rescue

I went through a long stage of loss when we moved to Auburn. I lost my business, an expensive piece of equipment with only six payments left, and friends I had in Orange County. If I hadn't found an apartment in the Auburn Greens, I may have lost Paulette and the family to her mother in Orinda. I gave up the tree service that was failing in Auburn and started selling alarms in Sacramento. The good commission was hampered by canceled sales and a struggling company. I took a job selling Mobile and Modular homes in Auburn. It's now a car sales lot near the canal. Jim was the sales manager and we got along well. We each had talents that seemed to complement each other. Paulette was home taking care of the kids. My riding had diminished. There weren't many motocross tracks in the area, and no one I knew rode or could introduce me to the Northern California woods. My bike sat, and I was distraught at not being able to ride. By now, riding had become a passion, and racing was a fire I couldn't put out. Jim was involved in the Sheriff's Search and Rescue Squad, on the 4X4 Team. I didn't have a four-wheel vehicle but he invited me to a meeting anyway. I visited and found their mission heartening. They fell under the supervision of the Sheriff's Department and were assigned to respond to any callout's the S.O. might make regarding a lost, stranded, or injured person in the woods or back country. This was something I might be adept at and enjoy, but I had no 4X4.

Timing was right as I was introduced to Buzz, a 50-year-old big barrel-chested, experienced old timer who was heading up a small off-road motorcycle club in Auburn, Trail Bike Sportsman Association, or TBSA. Buzz invited me to a meeting where a Sheriff's Officer was to talk. Marvin came to the meeting and revealed his interest in having the Bike Club head up a motorcycle division for the Sheriff's Search and

Rescue Organization. I joined forces with Buzz and we were to devise a plan, a method, a protocol, interview possible members, and ensure that our participation on motorcycles wouldn't create an injury problem for the S.O. Some in the club were apprehensive, some enthusiastic. Those of us who felt it would work joined together to create this thing called the Sheriff's Search and Rescue Motorcycle Unit.

We wanted to be something, knew we weren't, but visualized making a contribution to the community. We were on call 24 hours a day, 7 days a week, 365 days a year, day or night. We did it for free. In fact, it cost us out-of-pocket expenses to participate. Survival gear, training, upkeep, and maintenance were all our responsibility. The S.O. would pay for fuel to and from a search. We were content with the terms, and a new life opened up for many of us, including me.

Buzz had more experience with the S.O. and handled the Team Commander chores as the Team grew. He frequently included me in his planning or training, and we got to be good friends. The President of the TBSA organization changed hands each year, with both Buzz and I taking our turns at bat, along with many others, but the SAR M/C Team fell under the leadership of Buzz, with me as a material contributor. I had no complaints with that. I was young, Buzz was experienced, and I was fortunate to play an active part since the concept of the Team.

We suffered our share of growing pains, as the Mounted Unit, or Horse Team, found our motorcycles a trying experience when we were

 near them. Their horses weren't trained to be around noisy machines like that, and we were shunned by those who felt our participation unnecessary. Our feelings were that if we could demonstrate a significant usefulness, we could work on improving relations

with the naysayers. Little did we know that our goal would take years to achieve. There were times when we had to force ourselves to enjoy our own participation, but we felt that by hanging in there, we would become valued and appreciated. We were, but mostly by Marvin, the Deputy who enlisted us years earlier at Scotts Corner during one of our meetings, and eventually by other Deputies at the S.O. who saw a void in the overall program that we could fill. When searching for a victim, we could travel farther and quicker and search at night where some Teams yielded less success. We recognized our assets and drawbacks. Noise prevented us from hearing a victim's call for help, and certainly a motorcycle injury could be somewhere in the horizon causing insurance problems for the S.O. Weighing the pros and cons, we proceeded cautiously with the Team. We grew in size and quality but what we needed was more training. Buzz campaigned for that, but never saw it come to fruition before he passed away while riding his motorcycle in a dirt bike race. He pulled over to the side of the track, laid it down, and went to sleep. Those first on scene say he was smiling. I believe he was.

We were left without a Team Commander now, and the majority of the Team asked me to step up to the plate. With trepidation, I agreed. No one had ever thought of Buzz not being involved or heading up the Team. Filling his shoes would be a task for sure. I'd be happy if I could just make him pleased in how his Team was coming. I surveyed the loyalty of the other Team members and set about on a trek to make this the best Team in the County. So far, it was the only known off-road motorcycle search and rescue team in the State. I wanted to ensure our place in history when folks looked at what Teams were successful and what assets to use on a search. With respect to Buzz, and feeling his approval, I moved forward to improve the Team.

"We're going to be organized, disciplined, uniformed, of one mind set, and heavily trained," I announced at a following meeting. "Those who can rise to the occasion are invited to stay. Those who cannot, are thanked for their past efforts and will have to move on." I made friends and enemies that night. I'd have to wait to see which would prevail. I talked to several Deputies and found them encouraging and supportive. That being done, I had to see about training. Timing was again on my side. Dennis M., an enthusiastic young Deputy, was making his mark in Search and Rescue. We talked about a SAR Training Program and setting minimal standards for prospective new members. Dennis started putting a lot of work into what was to become a SAR Tech training program and I into techniques specific to the Motorcycle Team. The wheels of progress turn slowly, and it took years to perfect the SAR Tech program, as well as my own standards for our Team. But as we progressed, we impressed. As we impressed, we were given more respect and leeway to venture into new avenues of training. I moved forward to the limits of what freedom was given to me from the S.O. Dennis had developed 5 areas of training for the overall organization. Search and Rescue Fundamentals, Map and Compass, Man tracking, Wilderness Survival, and Rough Terrain Evacuation techniques. We added to that the minimum of Basic First Aid, then monthly training specific to each individual Team, which had grown now to include all areas that would benefit a search. Mounted Team, Ground Team, Four Wheel Drive Team, Dog Team, High Angle Rescue Team, Communications Team, and the Motorcycle Team. We were becoming an all-encompassing, very effective, highly trained Search and Rescue Organization that other Counties had heard of and were emulating.

Being at the forefront of change, evolution, and improvement can also bring its challenges and challengers. It grieved me immensely when someone, Deputy or member of another Team, would question or criticize. My true devotion was to the Search and Rescue Organization and making it better. Rarely did I stand up to declare that "*I*" had done something, but appropriately replaced it with "we," yet to little avail. Those who resented my standing out continued to resent, while those who appreciated it always let me know they did. By the tenth year of heading up the Team, I was dedicating 20 or more hours a week volunteering something to Search and Rescue. It was creating conflict at home and at work. If my Team were to be called out, I'd leave work, day or night. The loss of income took its toll between actual searches and the other time volunteered. If any of my teammates were to take a class, either as a first or a review, I'd make sure I was there alongside of them. I took many classes over and over without objection. I was able to see how my teammate was doing, supporting him while he was learning, and always learned something new myself. Eventually, I moved into teaching some of the classes and again, didn't object. I was privileged that I was felt worthy to do so. I vowed never to be caught with less knowledge than a student taking a class I was teaching, so that meant more study and time dedicated. By year 15, I was all consumed by Search and Rescue, and my family knew it. I continued to push the envelope with regard to learning, improving, and qualifying the Team, and sometimes other Teams. With the exception of my own Team, the resistance was noticeable. In came Deputy Dennis H. Unlike Dennis M., Dennis H. was a hardcore, take it or leave it, old school Deputy who never, ever hesitated to speak his mind. He was tactless and had few social graces. He was a great guy. If he liked you, you earned it. If he didn't, he pulled no punches in telling you why. It didn't matter whether you were a volunteer or another Deputy. It didn't even matter if you were his superior. You were never left in the dark as to where Dennis H. stood. Most of the time he was right. I was fortunate. Dennis liked me, and I liked him, very much. When Dennis took over as Liaison Deputy between our Team and the S.O., I knew I would have my back covered, as long as I was right in what I was doing. If I wasn't, Dennis would always cover me, but let me know where he thought I was in error. Dennis had the same goals I did, to make the Motorcycle Team the best that it could be, not better than anyone else, but the best that we were capable of being. Dennis firmly believed that it would result in us being better than anyone else. I was encouraged by his outlook but had a deep appreciation for some others and their Teams. The "Best that We Could Be" was my goal, and I soon wouldn't settle for anything less, and the Team rose to that standard. Within a couple of years, we stood out as one of the top-notch Search and Rescue Teams in the area. We were called upon by other Counties and asked to train those who wanted to follow. I was immensely proud of what we had accomplished, and I frequently looked back to make sure that we didn't step on any toes to get where we were. It had been suggested that we incorporate a bicycle Team into our Motorcycle Unit and significant consideration went into the concept. Dennis' thought was that if the Sheriff's Department wanted a bicycle Team, it would be best to start their own unit. Later, it was suggested that we consider 4X4 quad runners or ATV's and that thought deserved much more consideration. There were prospective members standing in the wings, and an ATV might prove to be quite an asset. We cautiously opened the door to ATV's and found them very beneficial. The Team was expanding, and with it, more duties on my part. I had to take on help that had the same goals and projections that I had, and Mark stepped up. Mark was another Dennis H. who was very supportive and demanding of himself and others. Together, we developed an ATV or quad-qualifying class that was unmistakably taxing, severe, and all encompassing. If we were going to have ATV riders, they'd have to be good. If they weren't, we'd make them that way. Those who wanted it badly enough would always succeed. Those who fell short were never scoffed. They were just excused. Our final phase of ATV training was comprised of an obstacle course that surprised even the most die-hard riders. "Not possible," was the comment of the day, during every class we held. "Watch and see," was our retort. "When this day's over, you'll do things on an ATV that you didn't know were possible." Both the participants and the S.O. were amazed at what could be done. Eventually, S.O. middle management mandated that any Deputy who was to ride a Sheriff's ATV would have to qualify in our class first. Many Deputies went through it, and we qualified each one, not for any other reason than that they genuinely qualified. Grins always abounded when an obstacle course was completed. We never failed to impress someone as to what an ATV could do and what they could do on an ATV. It took days to build an obstacle course, and much time to dismantle it when we were through, only hoping that someday we'd have a permanent course to offer. For now, we built, tore down, and built again for the next class, all out in the woods somewhere where we could train in real life situations.

Within a short time, we were asked to offer our class at a yearly SAREX where Counties from all over the State would gather. We agreed but had it not been for the reliable people on the Team, it would surely have failed. There were days of preparation work to do, and always an obstacle course to build. Lowell, a Deputy, was one I never held a class without.

Lowell was always there to help. Two new members of the Team were going to prove to be an invaluable asset through thick and thin. Mike and his wife, Judy, were as loyal as any FBI Field Agent. No matter what was planned, what went on, what we did, or how many searches we were called out for, Mike and Judy were always there, without complaint. Middle management of a business of any kind could only wish to have such people working for them. I was fortunate, and then Mike brought his son, J.R, aboard. Had it not been for these anchor Teammates, accompanied by all the others who willingly gave their time to participate, our goals would have fallen short, and we would have failed. They were incredibly dedicated and loyal people, coupled with the Deputies who made this Team what it was. I'll always thank them and hope I didn't fail to do that when I was their Team Commander.

Year after year, each County who hosted the SAREX that year asked us to teach our ATV class and, year after year we did. It was tiring, even to the point of fatigue, and it was costly. We got no compensation for it other than a genuine "Thank You" when it was done. We'd come back to our County satisfied, but wondering if we'd have the energy to do it again the following year.

We were in for a surprise when we were asked to attend the Nationwide

SAREX at Stead Air Force Base outside Reno, NV. The invitation was a prelude to asking us to teach another one of our classes. "A nationwide class would have to be good", I thought. Are we up to it? The usual loyalists all said yes, and I agreed. We went to Reno a couple months before the event to survey our options for a course and found little there but desert terrain. This would be difficult, we agreed, but somehow, we'll succeed. We made our preparation trip several days before the event to commence our build and were aided by local inmates from the County Jail. That was fortunate as we were profoundly in need of modifying the desert for our training.

The weekend of the event came, and we gave our usual pre-ride training and academic portion of the class. I could tell there were experienced riders here and some were growing weary of the basics that we felt were necessary before seeing any action out in the saddle. The entire Team came up for the exercise and we had enough to ensure the safety of the riders. The press came out to take pictures and film highlights of the class for the evening news. One by one, each pilot rode the course, feeling the boredom of basic elemental initiation to the more complex "Blue" course, as we referred to it. Some were surprised at what lay in store for them and upon completing the "Blue" section thanked us for what they had learned. "You're welcome," was the natural answer, "but don't plan on going home yet. We still have the RED course for you to finish." This is where riders could get hurt if we didn't have enough spotters. My major concern was injury and made each pilot pledge that they wouldn't go any farther than they felt their own capabilities would allow. One by one, they each progressed through the Red course and the news media found this the best place to take their film. I missed the nighttime broadcast, as did everyone else on the Team. There was just too much fatigue for us to stay up to see the news. Talk abounded the next day of the SAREX at STEAD and the classes that were taught. It'd be unfair to suggest that it was just our class, but we certainly were a focus of attention. Critique sheets went out to all participants at the SAREX, and months later we got the return comments. "Best class I've ever had, of any kind," was one I was proud to see. "Amazing." was another. "Should be a mandatory part of training." was yet another. The entire class, without exception, offered positive feedback and we had built a Team that could make a contribution to the Search and Rescue community. As the Team Commander, I unjustifiably enjoyed the respect and admiration of the Sheriff's Office, Deputies, and other Counties. We were looked upon by other Teams in the County as an equal and reputable contributing factor to the Organization, and I was fortunate in knowing that we had built not just a Team, but a tight-knit family of Team members. We'd do anything for each other, and each Team member knew it. We could be on a search that presented a life-threatening situation for any member, and we were confident that the other teammates would be there for us. This was a great Team. After 20+ years of building, it was paying off as a Team to respect. Not one better than any other, unless you asked Dennis H.

Paulette tired of doing without me time after time, week after week, and found a way where she didn't have to. She joined the Team as a Support Member. Although she didn't ride, she trained with us and was to ensure we had equipment and supplies on hand. We got to spend some time together and she grew to admire me and the Search and Rescue organization in general. Ultimately, she transferred from my Team to the Dog Team where she really felt at home, and was an active participating member in lieu of Support. She enjoyed that very much, learned a lot, and has many memories as a result. I'm glad she did that, and we have much to talk about in the future.

Mike was adept at Map and Compass, and we exchanged thoughts and ideas together. One of them was to set up a thorough GPS class for those who had trouble mastering the concept and system. GPS's were a new thing at the time but becoming very popular, and as time went on they would get easier to read and more user friendly, however, at this point in time they were not. Their direction manual was of little consequence other than to convince you the writers were very pre-occupied with impressing you with their advanced knowledge, and seemed to forget that some weren't at their level yet. We've all read those types of manuals before. They seem to start in the middle, instead of the beginning. Mike and I devoted ourselves to remedying that, and commenced a long term study of GPS's, their use, their strengths and weaknesses, and how to make them work. After months of preparation, we had our class ready and gave it to the Motorcycle Team. They were ecstatic and the GPS now seemed to be something useable. It's critical in the woods to always know where you are, and more so, when you locate your victim. A GPS was going to give you that information if you knew how to read it. Soon after the Motorcycle Team, other Teams were asking for classes. Mike and I got involved in teaching one after another, improving our format each time, and giving another class. Each time it got better and in time we were giving classes not only to Search and Rescue, but the Deputies, the Forest Service, Parks and Recreation, and the Highway Patrol. We never failed to get commendations and accolades. Mike, Judy, and I were always pleased that the efforts were successful.

Dee was 18 now and for years I had envisioned having him by my side on a search or a training mission. It was a secret intense desire of mine to share this with him. My two girls were just as important, but I had no delusions that Search and Rescue wasn't for them. Dee grew from 14 to 15, 16, 17 and finally 18. I waited for him to bring it up, hoping that he'd have that desire too. He was a teenager with thoughts and temptations going in many directions. I hoped I could create the same attachment and commitment in him when he approached me in his mid-18th year. "I'd be proud to have you on board, son," was my response. "You'll have to go through the same rigorous training that everyone else does, but I know you can make it, and I'll be right there going through it with you myself." I looked forward to what was coming, and I even bought him his Search and Rescue bike. I dreamed of taking him on his first search, or riding with him on a search for someone badly in need of help. He was on board for about a year and responded to several searches with me, but Search and Rescue was not as enticing as other aspects of life for an 18 year old and Dee later realized it wasn't for him. Without making him feel guilty, I kept my disappointment inside. It wasn't his fault. Few would dedicate the kind of time needed to do this when there are girls and other things in life to offer an 18-year-old. But I'd always miss him and will remember the time that we did this together.

Paulette and I responded to the same calls for our respective Teams. We'd frequently run into each other out in the woods, but we were very business-like. We were there to find someone lost, evacuate them, and hopefully do both before they succumbed to injury or death. Paulette trained her dog several times a week, while I spent hours attending to SAR academia and developing training exercises. It was a productive time in our lives, at the expense of not seeing each other very often. The end result was to give us memories and a sense of accomplishment that may be unequaled by any other experience. Giving oneself to the good of another in an unselfish manner renders a sense of satisfaction that's enjoyed only by the giver. The cost of doing what we were doing, in every sense of the word, was far too great to make the commitment worthwhile without the inward satisfaction in knowing that we've done good for someone somewhere. Although we needed it, and appreciated it, no "Thank you" or other form of appreciation was up to the task of making the commitment rise to the level of the cost. Every time we assisted in a search where we saved a life, we knew why we were there, and we wouldn't have traded it for anything else.

The nature of a search differs according to the time of year it occurs.

Summer brings out its own enthusiasts while winter sees a different breed of recreational chance-taker. The woods or high country can be a dangerous place under the best of circumstances. Regardless of how experienced or careful you are, things just sometimes go wrong. Other times, due to their own miscalculations or neglect, trouble sets in. It takes only minutes to think back on memorable searches.

On Thanksgiving Day, we were called out to a suspected airplane down somewhere in the French Meadows and Hell Hole area. Heavy snow created difficulty in mobility, but several Teams responded and dozens of trained searchers gave up their holiday to help. Deputies had conducted a preliminary search of the area to no avail and Search and Rescue was asked to extend the perimeter to whatever degree necessary to bring the victim back to civilization. A white, single engine airplane in the snow was a task to be reckoned with. Our Team responded with quads and motorcycles. No-one mumbled a complaint as the going got tough. We searched miles of back country looking for a clue as to where the plane went down. Days passed and we searched from daylight to dusk. Darkness and cold prevented even the most dedicated to continue the search effort after nightfall. No clues were found for the small aircraft, and our search widened. Eventually, we were advised that a "Medium" had foreseen the airplane in the Foresthill area. Knowing that public opinion was a strategic factor in enlisting the aid of public support, several of us were assigned to search the Foresthill area. There was no snow there, but the rainstorm was cold and brutal. For hours, we searched an area we were confident was barren of our victim. Beale Air Force Base had tracked the Bonanza V-Tail to French Meadows before it went off the scale. After two days in Foresthill, we reported back to the snow for additional assignments. The Snowcat was manned by Lowell and some others and was able to negotiate cross country movement. On the fifth day, Lowell discovered an unusual mound of snow and had the Snowcat turn around. He had located our aircraft, which had gone in upside down with snow piling up over the top of it. Only a few tree branches were broken, which suggested it had gone in on a steep descent. Our rescue moved to a Recovery, as the pilot was deceased, but the days of searching provided closure for a loving family.

Two elderly motorcycle riders ventured up into the high country during questionable weather. Without realizing what they might be in for, they were too far in when the snow started. They were trapped and couldn't get back to their truck. The family called the S.O. that night worried about their overdue husbands, and we responded to Foresthill to attempt to locate their truck. Once found, I was confident of the direction they headed and the route they might have taken. I was, by now, very familiar with Foresthill and their trail system. Where these two went was not only dangerous during inclement weather but intended for expert riders only during even the best of conditions. Using a military helicopter to search Trail #6 area, the two riders were located within hours. They appeared to be alert but we knew that exposure overnight in the cold and snow would take their toll on the mental and physical prowess of these two adventurers. They knew the helicopter had seen them and that would give them encouragement, but with no landing zone nearby, we had to get in and get to these victims before night fell again. Tom, a very qualified Forest Service Law Enforcement Officer, and accomplished motorcycle rider for even the more difficult demands, loaded up in the helicopter with me and we were in route to the search site. Landing a distance away, we hiked in to the victims to arrive mid-noon. One victim was okay, the other had been injured on the bike and his buddy elected to stay with his friend. A wise decision, we agreed. We were able to evacuate the two back to the helicopter, which then transported the lost and injured victims back to safety. That was all the helicopter could carry. Tom and I headed back for the campsite they had made to endure the weather the previous evening. We arrived to find both bikes were there in the snow, and both ran. Tom and I knew the trail back and with little discussion, started out using what daylight we had left. Trail #6 was a test of wits as it was replete with hairpin switchbacks one after the other on a cliff side, where a simple mistake would never be forgiven. The unfamiliar bike that I was on was annoying, but it was providing us with the opportunity to evacuate ourselves. Hours later, we found the main road, and my Team was there to pick us up. Cold, tired but satisfied, we went home knowing these victims would not have to spend another night out in the wilderness.

Sometimes we were called out with little in the way of a search, but rather a Recovery to begin with. China Wall outside of Colfax is a beautiful place to see, but dangerous to explore. A vertical drop for several hundred feet to a valley floor was awaiting anyone who didn't appreciate the narrow space between the edge and the railroad tracks traversing its slope. A young teen couple visited the area for quiet and solitude to set up a makeshift camp spot and spend the night. After a night of drinking and fun, they crawled into their sleeping bags until morning. Morning came, but the young man found himself alone. Not being able to bring himself to imagine the possibilities, he called the Sheriff's Department who dispatched their helicopter. The young woman was found almost at the bottom, but the recovery was difficult. Ropes and several searchers from all Teams were required to bring this young woman down with the appropriate dignity. The loss was sad, tragic, and probably didn't need to occur, but how many of us have done things that we later felt was careless? Sadly, she didn't find the mercy for her mistake as we sometimes have in ours.

Dennis H. was the Search Coordinator for a call out in El Dorado Canyon. He had always placed a lot of faith in our Team and called us, as well as others. This call-out was for a miner down at the bottom of the Canyon who was using a dredge to suck sand out from underneath a boulder. Using a mask to see his progress, he pulled out as much sand as he could for his partner to sift through for the inevitable gold reward. His focus on the booty outweighed good judgment, and as he continued to reach under the boulder to siphon more black sand, the boulder came loose from its mooring and fell on his arm. Pinned, his partner tried in vain to move the boulder, but the miner drowned. His partner walked out to get help and we were dispatched. I had been developing a method of transporting victims in a Stokes Basket behind a quad so the available Rescuers could save their energy and not have to lift, push, carry, and manipulate a victim during the transport. The method employed a wheel under the basket with a harness attached to the rear of the quad. The pilot could negotiate the terrain under supervision of a Rescue Captain and the ATV was able to pull the weight of the basket, its contents, and all the Rescuers, at a pace comfortable for them to walk. An entirely new system was being offered to these weary Rescuers, and all of them appreciated not having to hike out of the deep canyon under their own power. We had tested our system over and over before pressing it into service and it served flawlessly. Again, we were able to offer something to the Search and Rescue Organization that aided everyone involved. I was proud of my invention and was pleased that it was well accepted by others. "Well of course," was all that Dennis H. had to say.

I had established friendships with many of the Officers at the Auburn Police Department. Most of my friends were Sheriff's Deputies, Police Officers or SAR Volunteers. I got a call from one of the Auburn Officers one night needing help with an Alzheimer patient who had walked away from home and his family on the outskirts of town. "Sure, we'll help," I assured him, "I'll notify the S.O. and we'll bring as many people as needed." Soon we set up a Command Center at the end of the Court and were briefed by the Officer as to what he knew. The senior citizen was a man who had walked away from his family's home before but was never out of sight or gone so long. Darkness was setting in and I was asked for my approval of the Officer's plan. It was sound, but I wasn't the one to make that call. A Search Coordinator was in route. In the meantime, I dispatched my Team for a cursory search.

The SAR truck arrived and the communications van, several SAR personnel from various Teams, the local Fire Department, and Auburn P.D. were on site. We searched high and low for our victim. He wasn't to be found. Darkness fell and we searched well into the night. My Team was searching the nearby railroad tracks to cover as much ground as we could before the freight trains rumbled by, as was their routine custom. One of my Team members ventured off the tracks to check a brushy area that might conceal our victim and was jumped by a local resident with a shotgun. Explaining who he was and what he was doing was of little value to the resident as he pushed the shotgun up to the rider's face. "Sheriff" written all over the motorcycle, his uniform, and his helmet didn't deter the hostile resident and all I heard over the radio was a call for help. I knew where he was but didn't know whether I'd get there in time. When I arrived, the resident had already retreated into his house, but my teammate would never get over the close call he had with a hostile neighbor who declared himself a foe.

We eventually moved the search to another area while two more of my teammates were busy putting out a fire that the last train had started on the trestle over the Auburn freeway. "All in a day's work," they reported. Several of us had worked our way down into a wooded, brushy draw leading down into the canyon. Berry bushes slowed movement to a crawl, but it had to be searched. There were five searchers in the draw all calling for "Bob," the name of the victim. "Bob, Bob," was heard frequently, and many times in unison. All five were worried that Bob had worked his way down through these berries and into the canyon. If he had the search area was about to widen dramatically. All five again called out, "Bob," and all at the same time heard six voices calling for "Bob." Calling again, they confirmed six, and zeroed in on its source. Bob was prone in the berry bushes, not knowing where or who he was, but if others were going to call for Bob, then so would he. We returned him to his family unhurt but for scratches and scrapes from the thick berries. His family cried with thankfulness. We were happy to have helped.

Summertime brings out the hunters and we were on our guard for those who would get turned around or chase their trophies too far. Our call-out was for the back country area deep past French Meadows, where a young adult hunter had not returned to camp. Dad was beside himself when he called the Sheriff's Department, and we knew this would take an all-out response from the major Teams. The direction of travel was searched and the nearby lake, with no results. The steeper canyon walls were climbed in search of our victim, with no sign of him at all. Hours went by and we discovered no clues to his whereabouts. The Deputy was convinced that we had covered all the area that could be covered from this side of the gorge, and we packed up to move to the opposite wall. It was a long drive going around the deep canyon. Several hours later we established a new Command Center in El Dorado County. Explaining our presence and inviting their SAR Teams to join us, we continued our search. It was disappointing to discover that the little store and restaurant where we had set up didn't welcome us there. We never learned why, but we complied with their request to conduct business outside. We spent the remainder of the night and most of the next day searching for Dad's son. Eventually, "We have a confirmed find," came over the radio. "No medical needed," was a welcome sound. The Team who located our lost hunter evacuated him to our Command Center where he could be debriefed by the Deputies. It must have been a bad day for him. He was rude and uncooperative, declaring that he needed no help and was about to venture out to hunt again. Fatigued, we packed up and came home.

Two off-road bicycle riders didn't make it back to their cars just above Cisco Grove and we were called out to run the motorcycles up to try and locate them. The night was cold and we didn't know what to expect. A contingent of Search and Rescue personnel prepared for the trek into the wilderness mountains while we started off ahead of them on the bikes. Several miles in, the trail split and I sent part of the Team one way while I took the other route with the remainder. For hours we searched and found trail after trail leading off from the main one. "There's no way to search this entire area at one time," I concluded, and reported back to the Command Center by radio. "Continue on," was the Search Coordinator's orders and we followed. As daylight arose, one Team found the bicyclists and escorted them back. "We knew what we were doing and had no need for you people," was the nicest thing they had to say. I'll never know why they felt that way, but we packed up and returned home for some much-needed rest.

Mike and his son, J.R, had a rescue of the utmost success when a husband and wife took their horses down into the depths of a Manzanita and rock strewn canyon off I-80 near Signal Peak. They had gone into the deep canyon for a horseback ride. The husband had come out alone to get help in getting his wife and her horse out. The terrain was far too rugged to continue on and the husband was beside himself when having to leave his wife behind to get help. Several of the Teams responded. Mike and JR. took an insistent husband to the area where he had last seen his wife and the search started just before dark. I remained behind at the Command Center with some asthma problems but listened attentively to all radio traffic. It wasn't long before Mike reported the terrain too tough to negotiate the motorcycles in a timely fashion and they were leaving them behind to set out on foot. We received their last location before they descended into the gorge and lost radio contact. I was sure of Mike and JR, but they were responsible for a third person, the husband who was frantic over leaving his wife alone out here. As night fell, the husband was unsure of himself, and started leading Mike and JR into areas they knew were not as he had originally described. They climbed one hill and dropped down from another, going deeper into the Manzanita filled canyon. By now, no one could follow or find them, and they were on their own. Trying to decipher sense out of what the husband was saying, Mike took charge and established an isolated search area on the map. GPS coverage was unreliable or nonexistent, and Mike navigated by a compass, the stars, and his map. He was able to ascertain what the husband was looking at when he saw his wife last, if a highway was visible, and whether he could hear a train or see any tracks. Question after question, the husband answered, and Mike zeroed in on his probable area for the search. Fatigue had set in hours before. Mike and J.R. were watching each other for signs of confusion or weakness, and both were present. They had pressed themselves far beyond normal acceptance but continued to try to find this man's wife. Finally, as the husband was more of a liability than asset, Mike forced everyone to rest. It was long needed, and they laid down in the dirt just before daylight.

The sound of a nearby plane stirred them to their feet in preparation for a continued descent, chopping brush out of the way as they did. The CHP plane flew over and immediately spotted Mike and J.R.'s orange shirts. "Search and Rescue personnel," they radioed, "we've spotted you on the canyon wall below." "Affirmative," Mike radioed back, "please search the area to our front most direction. That's the most likely location for our victim." Moments later the radio coughed and broke the silence again. "Search and Rescue personnel, we've located your victim, as you stated, directly in front of you, several hundred yards away." The husband shouted and called for his wife. Mike and J.R. prepared for the hike to her location. Using all of his resources and assets, Mike had successfully homed in on our victim and would have located her within hours had the plane not saved them the time. It was a remarkable feat of training, resourcefulness, and tenacity. The trip out was as difficult as the trip in, and it, too, took hours. Mike and J.R. had brought in food and water for the victim, as well as a large amount of water for the horses. Chopping their way out to the road, they completed another successful rescue. This family looked at Search and Rescue like heroes. No, we weren't heroes, but it made us feel good to be appreciated. Whether you're a part of the actual find, or playing another role, everyone on a search is equally elated when a successful find is made. As for my thoughts, I think Mike and J.R. were heroes.

Mike and J.R. again were integral parts of a search in Weimar when a small boy walked away from his cabin home out in the woods. His parents were hysterical as we were called out. All Teams responded to this callout knowing that wildlife may play a part in significant consequences should the boy not be found early. The parents had tried to find the boy on their own for hours before calling the S.O. Having failed, they called before dark and we knew that time was of the essence. We expedited our response to the search area and the Team unloaded my bike and equipment while I got our briefing and assignment. We were ready as soon as I was briefed, and the search commenced. Teams going different directions, Mike and JR were sent to one local. Darkness had fallen and we had no clues or signs of where this boy might be. We called, we whistled, we searched for tracks, to no avail. The helicopter was responding with its FLIR, an infrared method of detecting a heat source from a human or animal. It's normally used when the ambient temperature has dropped to below that of a human signature. It seemed like only a short time went by when the crew chief radioed in to report he had found the boy, on the edge of a cliff. He was radioing a Team on the ground, showing them how to get into the search area. Mike and J.R. were on the same road and followed the pilot's commands as a secondary backup Team going in for the rescue. They reached the end of the road and the pilot told them they were on site. It was only then that Mike realized the Pilot was talking to him. He and J.R. became the primary rescuers and abandoned their motorcycles as the road ended and the cliff got steeper. They went in on foot and arrived to find the boy hanging onto a Manzanita branch overlooking a drop over the side.

They grabbed him, hugged him, and brought him home. The news media again played a part in broadcasting our successful find and Mike was interviewed only to give credit to all Search and Rescue personnel. He was right, but he was humble. Mike's a good man.

The middle of the night brought another reason for a callout at Mumford Bar. A Boy Scout leader had arrived late for his Scout Troop's planned camping trip down at the bottom of the gorge, and another Leader took the boys in by himself. The late arrival set off by himself over the side, but didn't make it to the bottom, as we learned by way of communication with the front Scout Leader. No one knew where he might be or how he would have gotten off the trail until we arrived on scene. There was no moon that night and we learned that the Scout Leader went in without a flashlight. Veering off the trail in the pitch-black woods was a real possibility, if not a certainty. Three of us rode in on motorcycles, stopping at every turn to hunt for signs of a departure from the trail. Mumford Bar is an exceptionally long and steep descent with the trail winding back and forth along the cliff side for miles. Each turn presented a new search, and the switchbacks were continual. Shutting the bikes down to get off and searching for track or sign became tiring at best, but the search went on. Halfway in, we discovered how dark the canyon really was as all the lights were turned off to gain a perspective of our victim's environment. "There's no way he'll make it to the bottom or stay on this trail," was our firm consensus. Our hope was that he wouldn't be hurt when leaving the trail, and could hear us calling for him. Almost all the way down, and several hours after we commenced our descent from the top, we heard a response to our calls for the Scout Leader. "I'm here," he returned with a clear relief in his voice. He had veered off the trail and over the side of the mountain as we expected. Fortunately, he was astute enough to stay put until daylight, but fatigue and hypothermia were setting in and his ability to make it to daylight was in question. He was completely disoriented and the direction where he thought the trail lay was wrong. After daylight had come, he'd have headed deeper off the trail, possibly lost forever. He was a lucky Boy Scout Leader who got a ride out of that mess on a motorcycle - - -Mine.

Lowell was the Search Coordinator when he activated us to an area up the mountain, off I-80. This mountainous area is an attraction to campers who want to enjoy the outdoors. Grandma and Grandpa had taken their seven-year-old grandson camping while trying to reassure the parents that it would be okay. The boy was very fearful of people and the family was trying to get him comfortable with his ailment. The motor home was parked, and the grandparents walked down to show their grandson the stream. In no time at all, they turned around to find the boy was gone, vanished within seconds it seemed, and the grandparents were frantic. They checked the stream and each camp spot to no avail before calling the Sheriff's Department. This part of the country was in a different County than ours and they responded as soon as they could. But that County, at that time, had little in the way of a Search and Rescue Unit and they asked for help from our County. Lowell was given the assignment and activated us right away. All were concerned that if not found in short order, the boy would not make it through the night. The high country cold, the wildlife, and his age and frame of mind were too many things against him to expect that he might survive. We arrived a half hour before dark and I reported to Lowell. The Team was getting my equipment ready as I received the assignment. "I don't care what you have to do Duane, find this boy," was Lowell's firm and concerned instructions. "Yes sir," was the only reply I could offer, when radio traffic came in from a helicopter that had been sent out earlier from Fallon, NV. "Command Center, we've located the Subject on the top of a hill about a mile west of your location." We wanted to cheer and cry at the same time. But the job wasn't over. Lowell cautioned the military helicopter about the boy's fear of people and asked that the helicopter keep him in view from a distance. It was a smart thing to ask. "Duane, find that boy and bring him home," was Lowell's final instructions. My bike had already been warmed up and my survival pack and helmet hung on the bars. Each minute was important, and I was thankful the Team was so well disciplined. We had a general location for the boy, but no knowledge as to which of the several hilltops he could be on. We could get no more specific information from the pilot other than direction and distance. We rode in that direction listening for Lowell's radio traffic as he conversed with the helicopter pilot . We could see the chopper hovering in the distance but couldn't tell which of the hilltops he was over. "That's the hill", Lowell announced as the chopper relayed to him that we were there. "Turn right and go to the top." As if in one parade motion, all of us spun right while riding at speed, jumped up the road embankment, and started our climb. It was well after dark now and our headlights were the only thing lighting our way to the top. As the hill got steeper, and pine needles more prevalent, traction left us. Even at the momentum we were ascending, we were not going to make it to the top. Laying the motorcycles down, we immediately split up, with some of us going straight up the hillside, some going to the left, while others to the right. This little boy wasn't going to escape in another direction off the side of the hill. As we got closer to the top, the sound of spinning rotors was deafening. The helicopter was near and had his eye on the boy. We had no communication with it but knew that this boy wasn't going to get away from them, or us either. We crested the hill to look up through the treetops to see our helicopter hovering overhead, all lights on, shining to the ground and rotating in the air. It looked like an enormous spaceship. Its huge lights illuminated below as I watched the rope fall from above and seconds later the Crew Chief slid down like the well trained professional that he was, to reach the boy, who was mesmerized by what he was looking at. He was too scared to be scared and the Crew Chief took advantage of his opportunity to capture the boy and hold him. He had hardly gotten his arms around the boy when I reached them both. "You're a hero," I complemented him with genuine feeling. "Take him home," was the only thing the Crew Chief could say, and we did just that. We knew that the news media was back at the Command Center, and it would be proper to have the media see personnel from the County we were in bring the boy back in. So just outside of the Command Post I turned him over to someone from the other County and my Team and I rode in alone. It was okay. The boy had been found, and he was safe. Family, friends, grandparents, and the media were congratulating the personnel from this County who brought the boy back in. My Team and I stood back out of the way, at a distance, and quietly smiled. Lowell smiled back.

Mike and I were dispatched to Mumford Bar in search of two

horseback riders who had gone in a day earlier for a short day ride, but didn't come out. Their wives called the S.O., looking for help to find them and we, in turn, were sent down into the gorge to make friends with these adventurers. Our job was to locate them, determine their condition and medical needs, if any, and radio the information back to the I.C. where the Command Center had been set up. The I.C. had other Teams on standby until we located the riders and determined a proper course of action.

We arrived at the top of the mountain after dark and the Search Coordinator briefed us. It was cold, and the fresh snow was over a foot deep. "This wasn't going to be a good night," I thought. We started down and soon reached our first obstacle. We were on the windward side and the recent storm pummeled the mountain. Instead of getting thinner, the snow quickly got deeper, and we were trying to ride through two feet of snow. I got off and walked back to Mike. "We'd better leave them here and go in on foot," I suggested. "The snow's pretty deep," I concluded as I pointed back to my bike. We noticed the snow was holding the bike up without the kickstand being down.

A 40-pound survival pack gets a lot heavier when wet and it had been raining for the last few hours, only a mist, so the snow was still present, but still wet enough to soak us and our survival equipment. Mike and I worked our way down the mountain following the trail. We had been in here before and knew where the trail was and where it led. The snow eventually subsided, leaving horse tracks clearly visible in the soft mud in front of us. "These two sets of prints had to be our horses," Mike and I logically assumed, and we continued down the mountainside, deeper into the gorge. It would be a long and steep descent down into this gorge. Half way down, we rounded a switchback corner and heard a thunderous crashing through the brush and trees in front of us. A bear directly to our front crossed the trail at a full run and descended vertically down the mountain side. A pleasure to see, we knew it was a concern to encounter. We continued on.

It was just before daylight when we finally made it to the bottom. I knew from previous trips down into this area that there was a makeshift cabin alongside the river at the bottom of the trail. Maybe our horse riders were there and didn't want to try this long and very steep climb out. It would take several hours under the best of conditions. My hope was abated as we searched the area near the cabin. There was no sign of the riders. We radioed our position and informed the I.C. that we would need some help and suggested he dispatch the Mounted Unit with some horses that could assist in the search. We needed two extra horses to carry us out. "Ten Four," was all we needed to hear, acknowledging our request, and we continued following the trail as it paralleled the river. The mist had been persistent for hours and we were wet and cold. Our packs were twice their weight. We had a long way to go and then the trip out. Mike never murmured a complaint. I didn't bother to ask him if he wanted to stop for a while. I already knew his answer.

Mile after mile, we paralleled the river, calling for our targets, and checking each side trail for track or sign that they may have veered off the main trail, but the over-growth cushioned any prints that would normally have been left and we had to search as though we had no tracks of any kind. The Mounted Unit caught us about 11:00 a.m. There were five of them, but only five horses. I was too tired to ask why. Mike and I had gone as far as we could go. We were both at a point of collapse. We took our packs off and handed them to the riders. "You've been carrying these?" I nodded in the affirmative and let the horse pass so I could grab its tail. As the horse walked on, it pulled me along with it. Normally this benefit is all it takes for a second wind, but it wasn't to be here. We were having trouble just standing up. Tailing the horse meant we were only going deeper down the trail and further into this massive gorge. Mike and I were quiet for the next hour or so. We were hoping for our expected second wind to come.

We arrived at a narrow part of the trail where it crossed a creek that was descending the hillside at a steep angle toward the river. The embankment was almost vertical on the right, and the drop-off was severe on the left. Walking through the creek was slippery. Mike and I checked it first, and then called for the horses. One by one the riders dismounted and carefully walked their horses past this hazard. Pat was the last one with her horse, Reno. As Reno got into the creek, his feet slipped, and he floundered, losing all control over his balance. Pat could only watch as the horse fell over the side of the embankment, out of view, to a shallow pond below. The horse landed on its back and the rocks and boulders took their toll to shock and injure Reno. Pat was paralyzed with shock and fear. We couldn't blame her after what she saw. Mike and I immediately climbed down the embankment to the pond and knew we'd have to wade into the ice water to get to Reno. "Don't get any wetter than you have to, Mike," I warned. Hypothermia has taken many lives in the past, it's no respecter of persons, and it would not ignore us. We took the reins of the horse and tried to help it to its feet. As soon as it got up, it slipped on the wet moss and fell back down. It got up, slipped and fell, again and again, over and over. Each time it fell back into the water we were in fear that Reno would unavoidably fall on either of us. Tired, fatigued and injured from his initial fall from the trail above, Reno couldn't get up any longer. He tried, but his head was the only thing he could move, but only barely. He was unable to catch his breath, and lying in the icy water, Reno was fading fast. Mike and I had both gotten fully immersed trying to keep his head above water. Most of Reno's body was underwater getting colder from the snow runoff each minute. Soon he'd be unable to move at all. Mike and I both knew we'd have only one more chance to get him to his feet. Before we could encourage him to make one more effort, Reno looked directly at my face with his big, beautiful eye only inches from my face, as if to say thank you, and slowly closed his eye. He had given up and was preparing to surrender. "RENO! RENO!" I yelled in his ear as Mike slapped him on the neck. Reno opened his eye as if to say, "One more time." I stood up and using the reins, turned his head around toward me while Mike got under his back to help lift this massive and almost paralyzed animal. Pleading with the horse for one more effort, not knowing what would be different this time than any of the previous ones, I forced him to turn his head far enough to where he had to try to stand up. As he did, Mike got under his back and lifted with all the strength he had. Reno resisted for a moment, and then got the idea. Making the slightest movement was clearly a struggle for him, but you could see the determination as his shaking body fought for life. With one last push, Reno jumped to his feet. His legs slipping and sliding on the rocks below, his hoofs were reminiscent of his previous efforts, but going down this time would mean he wouldn't get up again. Simultaneously, Mike and I closed in on the horse, one on each side, and using all our weight, pinned him upright. He was up and standing. Searchers watching and wanting to get down into the creek with us were cheering. The pond we were in was only big enough for Mike and I. Reno had maximized all additional space. There was little chance that anyone else would be able to get down there with us. Mike and I pinned Reno between us for almost 20 minutes before we let him try to move on his own. His breathing returned to normal, and he quit shaking. We had taken his saddle off in the water. Now we needed something to warm him up. Another horseman took a blanket off his horse, and we covered Reno the best we could. Pat was sobbing with relief and happiness, but our job wasn't over yet.

Someone had called the I.C. (Incident Command or Command Center) up on top of the mountain and advised them what was happening. A more recent call had gone up to advise that we had the horse up and on its feet. Armed with that information, the CHP helicopter picked up a veterinarian in Auburn and was flying him to the site. There was no place to land so he was lowered down to a small open area about a ½ mile away. He hiked in and arrived to give Reno a shot and check him for the extent of his injuries. Using a folding military shovel, Mike and I had been digging a trail in the embankment to get the horse out. It was far too steep for a normal climb. We were almost finished when the Vet arrived. We outlined our plan and he agreed. After the shot took effect, he led the horse up the new and marginally adequate trail to safety. It was a good day, but even now, it was still not over. The effect of the incident was taking its toll on Mike and me. We wouldn't be able to get out of the gorge and with only an hour left before dark, we'd be fortunate to find a place to set up a survival shelter on the side of this mountain. We were two horses short to begin with, and now three. Pat would double up with another rider to get out, but neither Mike nor I were even remotely up to the trip. "There's a small flat spot under the trees next to the river about a mile back", I recalled and passed the information on to Mike. "Let's try to make it back there before dark." There was enough gear in our survival packs to keep us safe and warm for the night. We'd sleep on the ground, in the mud, but that's acceptable. A few rations would give us something to eat, and we had plenty of methods for starting a fire, even in the rain and with wet wood. "Sounds like a good plan," Mike commented, and we started slowly in that direction with the horse riders carrying our gear once again. Search and Rescue horsemen are good people. We were beyond tired at this point and weren't looking forward to the energy it was going to take to set up a survival camp. The Horse Team had their own challenges, and I hadn't thought about them helping us get things set up, but I'm sure they would have. None of us had forgotten why we were there. There were a couple of unaccounted for horse people out here somewhere and we needed to refocus on locating them. We soon learned that there was no need. While Mike and I were devoting our attention to Reno, the two horse people arrived on their own heading back out and were not looking forward to making this climb back up out of the gorge. Cold and fatigue had set in on them earlier and instead of taking the chance on trying to climb out, they, too, set up a temporary camp site, rested their horses, tried to stay warm and dry, and prepared to make the trip out today. They were both ok and were surprised to see a whole contingent of Search and Rescue personnel out looking for them. They were both impressed, and thankful.

As we all now traversed the side of the mountain headed back to Mike and my planned destination camp spot, we heard the rotors of the CHP helicopter. It got closer and we could eventually see it at our own height as it paced us along the cliff side trail. He was looking for a place to land, but I knew that would be an effort in futility. This gorge was very unforgiving. Suddenly we heard the sputter of radio traffic. It was the Crew Chief on the helicopter. He was directing us to a specific location just up ahead. We followed his directions only to find that there was nothing there. No landing zone, no place to set down. The trees, however, were spaced farther apart. We stood in awe as the pilot slowly slid his chopper closer to the cliff wall. Watching his rotors as he crept closer to the brush and trees, ever so slowly he edged as close as he could and reached his target, a boulder sticking slightly out of the ground at the edge of a drop off. We were several feet away watching the Crew Chief guide the pilot as he set just the front tip of one skid down on the edge of the boulder. That's all he needed to stabilize the craft a little. His rotors were only feet from the brush, the mountain, and the trees. He had set his ship down for us. Maintaining balance, the Crew Chief slowly climbed out of the aircraft and ducked down low to avoid the spinning rotors, and walked to us. "We can only take one at a time," he said, revealing that the Pilot would have to do this a second time. "Who's the lightest?" Well, looking at Mike, we recognized that I was by 100 lbs., no fooling anybody there. and the Crew Chief wanted to take me first. I objected to that, but he was adamant. He was very concerned about getting into the aircraft and shaking it or moving it off balance and causing the rotors to catch the side of the mountain. It was clear that this wasn't open for discussion, and I consented to going first. "You have any experience in aircraft like this?" he asked. I knew he was referring to how unstable it can be when floating on a skid like he was. "Yes, sir," I answered, and that was enough. "When you climb in, be very slow and don't shake the aircraft", he said. "Be VERY slow and careful climbing in," he reiterated, and we ducked down low to approach. The helicopter hovering loudly, the Crew Chief opened the rear door, and I watched the chopper shake with that little movement. Stepping up inside would be a challenge for the pilot to control the craft, and I did so while displacing my weight over a larger area of the craft. Slowly I crawled in and buckled up. The Crew Chief followed, and the chopper backed away from the mountainside. On the way to the I.C. the Crew Chief asked me if my partner had any experience in helicopters. "You bet he does. You've got to go back and get him," I responded. "We'll get him if there's enough daylight left," he assured. Landing at the I.C. I crawled out and the chopper took off after Mike. They had to have been concerned doing the same thing again, and with a lot heavier man, but Mike was acutely aware of the concerns and crawled inside in a similar fashion, giving the Crew Chief and Pilot confidence that this would work a second time. Mike was shortly reunited with the I.C.

Cold, tired, hungry, and with hypothermia setting in, we had some recovering to do. The Mounted Team would be coming out sometime during the middle of the night. Some that had remained at the top had already brought our bikes back up to the I.C. Others helped load them, and Mike and I were done for this search.

Sierra County was the site of a massive multi-County search callout. We didn't know any particulars when we loaded up. "No bikes," was the recommendation, "the terrain is too rugged." We'd heard that many times before and never failed to surprise those who felt that way. Eventually we'd run into an area that we couldn't actually ride, but I hadn't found it yet. We loaded up the ATV's and motorcycles and headed up. Many hours later we arrived at their Incident Command center. The I.C. was swarming with search personnel and family. They had been there three days looking for a six-year-old boy. He and his Dad were hiking and playing. The little boy chased his Dad, and then Dad chased the boy. It was good-natured fun until the little boy didn't come around the next corner in the trail. Dad went back, called, and looked for his son, but he wasn't to be found. Dad found a small trail leading off from the main one and took it. Within a short distance, it took him alongside a precipice that dropped a thousand feet down to a lake. Dad looked frantically for his son, but he was nowhere to be found. Sierra County search personnel responded, as it was their District, but they were unable to locate the 6-year-old. The following day they called for additional help, and each day thereafter, until we were called on the third day. It was a long drive from our own County, but we all responded without hesitation. The Search Coordinator was very helpful and cooperative with the new Teams that were arriving. "I don't think you can ride this area," he said, "But if you can, you may be able to cover a lot more ground than others can on foot." I agreed, and as it was well into dark when we arrived, we decided to push the ATVs into service. Ralph, another dedicated Team member, and I started out to cover our assigned area. It was near the precipice, and we were to cover ground already searched. This isn't unusual. If the boy was alive and moving, he could work his way back into a recently searched area.

The trail was rugged to say the least, but passable. The ATV's worked flawlessly. The accessory lights that we'd mounted on them were working up to their task. To one side of us a brush covered hillside, a narrow trail only wide enough for the tires of the quad lay in front and to our left was deep black darkness. As if an entrance to a huge black cave we saw nothing to our left at all. We could see the trail up ahead traversed this hostile area for 300 yards or more before making a switchback turn to the right, away from the precipice. "I'll go first," I told Ralph, and drove out to traverse the trail. The quad jumped and shook on the rocky trail and the tires wanted to go in their own direction. Force from the handlebars brought them back under control before the tires tried to go another direction of their own choosing. A lose or narrow spot under the left tire would send me on trip that would allow me to review my entire life within seconds. In short order I made the right-hand switchback, pulled up a distance, and parked. I walked back to the corner, but Ralph's headlights were still a distance away and not moving. I walked back to him, and he took the opportunity to ask me if I'd take the ATV through here instead. Ralph was new on the Team and very motivated. He was training every weekend, but hadn't gotten to the ATV training yet, and I was glad that he didn't try to do something that he wasn't confident in. If it were a year in the future, Ralph would have taken the bike across himself. Instead, I made the second trip. Ralph and I were on our way again.

We searched all night in that rugged terrain, stopping only for water before getting immediately underway again. There was no sign of our little victim. We called for him with high powered whistles, shouted his name, and whistled some more. The rocks, boulders, brush, and trees were taking their toll on our endurance. By daylight we had completed our search assignment and two tired searchers found their way back to the I.C. I reported in and they promised to have another assignment for us soon. We surveyed the quads for damage, refueled, and prepared to go out again. Night-time provides the best opportunities to search using sound. Your victim can hear you at night much farther than in the daytime, and you can hear him calling for help. Daytime provides the best opportunity for visual searching. We weren't about to lose any daylight just sitting back at the Command Center. We got our next assignment and took the motorcycles this time. They're quicker, less brutal on the body in rough areas, and we were very much at home on them. Ralph and I meticulously searched our large assigned area, calling in on a regular basis to update our coordinator.

Night fell and the search went on. Ralph and I made it back to the I.C. and were growing weary. "We need another assignment," I reported to the Search Coordinator. He gave us a small area to cover, and we fired up the quads. Several hours later we were back, with no results. It was around 3:00 a.m. and we must have exemplified fatigue. But that little boy was still out there. Divers determined that he probably was not in the lake below, so that was being ruled out. A helicopter was sweeping the cliff side with his FLIR to determine whether the boy had gotten hung up during a fall to the bottom. The search coordinator ruled out a fall, so he had to be somewhere up here, but where? We had been searching for a day and two nights. We were ordered to, "Get a couple hours sleep," and I couldn't argue. We lay down on the ground and guilty sleep overtook us. Three hours later we were being shaken awake with a new assignment. "We're on it," I acknowledged, and Ralph and I were out on the trail again. We were in our second day of searching for this little boy, and no-one on any search Team had found so much as a footprint or any other clue as to where he had been or might be. I wondered whether the divers may have missed him at the bottom of the lake, but it wasn't my call, and I did what I was asked. All day Ralph and I searched new and old areas. The search perimeter was widened, and we searched the newly assigned areas. No clues surfaced. Night-time fell and the search coordinator was running out of ideas. I knew we'd start all over again, if need be, but help came in the form of one of our own deputies who had arrived on scene. "You're not going out until you get some rest," was his order to Ralph and me. Our objections fell on deaf ears, so we complied. Four hours later we woke with renewed energy. The search perimeter had been widened again and we headed off for our new assignment. As daylight increased, we returned to the I.C. for the motorcycles and headed out yet again.

Late morning, we were consulting our maps and felt that one small area understandably may not have been searched yet. It was a steep narrow canyon-type draw to our west. We decided to check it before progressing any further in front of us. As we approached, we could see that it was exactly as it appeared on the topographic map. Little more than a grass and brush covered slit in the earth, it started at the top of the hill and cut into the hillside all the way down to the bottom where we were. This wasn't going to be easy. It couldn't even be walked. You had to ascend it on your hands and knees. Whatever needed to be done, we were there to do it. Ralph on one side of the slit, me on the other, we started to crawl up the mountain through the grass and brush. Halfway up, I saw it.

"Ralph, come here." I had found shine in the grass. Shine is the result of someone stepping on a plant or foliage and bending it over. The moisture extruded from the plant shines from the sun's rays during certain parts of the day. When approached from the right angle, during the right time of day, a trained tracker can pick up this shine and its story. "Yes, I see it," Ralph concurred. I pulled a tape measure from my pack and determined that this was too small a print for even a woman to make. This was the sixth day the little boy had been alone in the wilderness, and so far, we had no clues as to where he might be. I didn't want to alarm the entire search contingent unless I was sure. I radioed back to the I.C. and asked for my own deputy from our County. He responded and I asked to go on a private channel. He complied and I asked him to check to see if the search coordinator could determine with reasonable certainty whether he'd sent anyone into the area where Ralph and I were. The deputy complied and reviewed the question with the I.C. "Negative, M/C-1, no one has yet been assigned to that area. What've you got?" I was then confident we had something, and I reported it. Ralph had already started trying to track the next print to determine course and direction. I followed up and came alongside, agreeing with his findings. We tracked the prints, step by step, for several hundred yards when we came to a mound of dirt overlooking a descent down the mountain. The prints came to a stop on top of the mound, but careful review revealed that the boy backed up off the mound, turned right, and went down the hillside. I plotted his travel on the map and studied it. "Of course," I excitedly said to Ralph, "Look at the map. Town is down here. He was here last night and saw the lights in town. He's attracted to the town lights," I excitedly acknowledged. We notified the I.C. and they reported back that they were sending scent dogs in to verify our findings. Within an hour, the bloodhounds arrived. They had been given the boy's clothing to isolate their objective. Their handler took them over to the first print I had found some distance behind us, and the howling started. Yes, it was his print! The dogs got onto his trail, and I watched the handler as she followed her dogs on exactly the same path as we had been earlier, including up to the mound of dirt where the boy stopped. The dogs sniffed some, found his sent to the right, and continued tracking him. At the same time a helicopter swooped in to hover overhead. He was taking a GPS reading and getting his bearings. The crew chief motioned down to us asking which way the boy had gone, and I pointed my message back to him. He nodded and offered a thumbs up as the pilot swung the chopper around and crawled off in the direction the boy had walked. Was he still alive? Admittedly, we had to doubt it, but God sometimes does miraculous things, and we all had our hopes up. The dogs and chopper were out of sight making progress as Ralph and I saddled up and rode the bikes back to the I.C. No need for us to add to the crowd of searchers now on this young boy's trail.

A couple of hours later, radio traffic sputtered through my hand-held. The helicopter was calling to the I.C. "We've got him," was their only traffic, before silence. Everyone and everything came to a stop. Silence reigned for several minutes. Not even the I.C. tried to re-contact the pilot. Did he have him alive or dead? No one knew. An eternity later the pilot radioed back again that he had picked up the victim, and he was alive. They were in route back to the I.C. He had been found on the edge of the mountain that dropped off to the town below. He was following the lights but couldn't have made the last vertical descent down to the town. A remote and unpopulated area, he would, in all likelihood, have perished where he was. He was in no condition to travel any further and badly in need of medical attention. The combined efforts of dozens of searchers for days at a time paid off and this little life was saved. Months later we were invited to a celebration in the Bay Area where we got to meet our little friend, now as a healthy 7-year-old. It was a good day.

All in all, during my tour with the Sheriff's Search and Rescue I've learned to have an unusually high regard for police officers, and a law enforcement uniform in general. To this day, I have that same high regard. I was very privileged to have been allowed to be a part of this. If there is any such thing as a hero in our community, it's clearly a police officer. Regardless of what Department they work for, it's definitely a cop. Thanks, guys, for letting me be a part of that.

Search and Rescue was my life for over 25 years. It provided me with a sense of accomplishment and worth that couldn't be equaled anywhere else. Moreover, the people that I got to know there were genuine caring people. The Deputies were a breed of their own. The largest majority of my friends, by far, were Deputies or people in Search and Rescue. I wouldn't have traded it for anything else that I could imagine, then or now. My sorrow is that it cost me time from my family and a very large amount of lost income. We were next to broke for the most part of that 25 years and gave almost as much time to Search and Rescue on a voluntary basis as I did as a private investigator. It was a value judgment that I made on my own volition, and I made it several times through those years. Each time we couldn't pay a bill, or make a payment for the utilities, I re-evaluated my commitment to Search and Rescue. "I'll stick with it just a little while longer," I'd always say. Then a successful search would follow, and my commitment was set in stone again. Then I asked myself, "When I go to meet Jesus will this long adventure be the mark that I leave behind me?" Maybe. Would that be a good or bad mark? It depends on which perspective you look at it, and who's doing the looking. And therein lies the lesson. The cost factor in doing this to the degree that I did, and for the amount of time that I did it, extracted its own very high price to pay. All of us in similar situations have also had to evaluate and re-evaluate the cost factor in doing what you feel you've been called to do. Make sure, and be convinced, that you're called to do it, whatever it is, and that it's not just your own personal desires driving you. Remember that your decisions and commitment are your own choosing, but that choice will also call you to be accountable to those who you love, and who love you. It may also affect your work and subsequently your income. Each of us has a passion of some kind. Mine was not only this but in the chapters ahead you'll see other obsessions that seemed to control my life. What I didn't recognize at that time, but do and readily expose now, is that in my older years when my wife and I have to pay the price for the decisions I made back then, is that this price or cost factor can be more than I want to pay, and for a longer period than I want to pay it. In simpler terms, I couldn't devote my full attention to Search and Rescue, as I was being asked to do, and earn a living at the same time. I sacrificed the living and income for the reward of following my passion(s). In this case, Search and Rescue. So, what's the cost factor? You can't help but ask. Getting down to the most personal, candid, and embarrassing answer, because you deserve that, is that I was never able to build a retirement program or savings account. We lived month to month in the simplest meaning of the phrase, literally. And we still do, and it's my doing that did this to us. We live in an old, small home badly in need of repair that I can't do or have done. We have no insurance other than what's mandatory for our vehicles. We ration our groceries, and during my life as an adult I've never taken my wife on a vacation. There's more, but that's enough for you to see that there's a cost factor, sometimes significant and long term, for anyone who chooses to follow their passions instead of their logic. You may be in a similar situation. If so, it's your job to consider and caution others of this cost factor. Once you're aware of it, you're more able to wear the responsibility of your decision. If I had known back then the manner of life that we'd be living in our senior years, would I have made the same decisions? In my case, yes. I say that with caution and don't want to influence you to make the same decision, or mistake. Each individual has to evaluate this under their own set of values. But do it knowing, after reading this, that nothing is free. There's a cost factor to everything you do and every decision you make. No exceptions. And that decision will affect the ones you love the most, as well. Choose wisely but do it after reading the high cost of payment I've uncomfortably revealed to you here. Your travels will never isolate themselves just to you. You and your family will live happier lives if they're happy to follow your trail.

"If you can walk it, we can ride it," became a mantra.
Sometimes it was a challenge, but we never let anyone down
because we couldn't get in or out of a search area.

At every search we envisioned the victim as not only lost and can't
find their way out, but possibly injured or clinging to life, praying
that someone, anyone, would come out and get them out of this.
We did many times, and every one of us would do it again.

<u>Rough Terrain Evacuation Required Endurance</u>

Training encompassed a vast array of subjects. It
was necessary to fine tune each one so we wouldn't
become a victim out in the wilderness ourselves.
We train, trained, and re-trained.

When not training, we'd put on demonstrations and teach others how to care for themselves. Middle school kids were always mesmerized by the motorcycles, and the guys who rode them.

And then there were the Parades.

More parades

And yet more parades

And of course, the photo ops

When not taking care of teaching or training, we'd venture out
to study the mountains, learning all their trails and nuances.

This was a great Team.

CHAPTER 11

Racing: A Passion for the Love of Life

In each character lies a flaw. I, too, was blessed with character, but plagued with many flaws. One of which, it's agreed by some, is my addiction to adrenalin. I suppose it started as a teenager back in the "Bill" days when I went with him to a couple of speed boat races. He'd wonder around the pit area talking with as many boat pilots as he could. I could see the future in his eyes. He was going to wind up buying one of these race boats. Donna didn't often go with us to these races. I don't know why. Perhaps she wasn't interested, or maybe it was because of the brood of children she was raising. Bill's tree service gave him access to some significant amounts of money at times and he was waiting for the next opportunity. It came, and he didn't pass it by. We went to Lake Berryessa to watch a race one weekend, and came home with a race boat, a two-seater, flat-bottom outboard hydro. There was no doubt this boat was fast. It had taken first place in races past, but the pilot and co-pilot would make the difference between winning or losing. I was the official co-pilot for the boat and my job was to watch the other boats, set up strategies, and jump from the co-pilot's seat up to a cockpit opening in the bow and lean over the side down to the water as we approached and negotiated each turn. In these races the turns were always to the left. The boat did not turn right. Well, it did, but not without skipping across the water and looking for its submarine relatives. The sensation of speed while flying across the water, only inches above the surface, is unmatched. The engine screaming in your ear, the boat slapping each undulation in the water as it skips over it, and the sudden launch into the air as it porpoises over the surface looking for another wave to challenge, is thrilling to say the least, fearful at best, and usually terrifying during the experience. But as soon as you're done, you want more. Bill and I would go out to the sloughs around Concord and

214

practice for hours - turn, accelerate, top speed, last minute slow down, and turn again. If we could get the boat to lean over on its side going around the pin, we'd maximize our ability to dig the chine in the water for the quickest turn we could make. If you miss the timing, the boat comes off a plane and settles into the water. Miss it the other direction and it won't lean at all. It'll skip sideways, the opposite direction of the turn until the edge catches a wave and over the boat goes, pilot and co-pilot with it. We experienced one such launch out of the boat when Bill missed his timing and started the turn before I did my lean to get my head down to the water. Instantly, we felt the boat slide sideways and pitch us out. Many thoughts passed through my mind before I hit the water. None of them were wondering what was for dinner. We were alone, and there was no-one around to give us a #10 for style. Normally when a boat goes over like this, it's done. If it doesn't come apart or destabilize, it's probably going to land on top of you as you all hit the concrete surface of the water together. It's not a pleasant way to check the temperature of the water. As the chine, or edge of the boat, dug into the water, there's less than a second for all of your thoughts to come to a conclusion. I remember skipping across the water until the edge of my helmet caught it and slowed me like a parachute, pulling my head away from my shoulders for what felt like a 6' stretch. For a few moments everything was black. When I got my senses and equilibrium back, I determined I was afloat, my head was above water and survived my imagined 6' stretch, and I hadn't been crushed by the boat. I looked for Bill right away and saw him bobbing several yards away. There are no atheists in a foxhole, and although I had not been introduced to God as a Christian yet, I was thanking him profusely for saving Bill and me. What about the boat? It had done a complete 360-degree roll-over and was upright in the water. Bill failed to attach the kill switch to his life vest and the engine was still running. Boat in gear, and steering wheel turned at just the right angle, the boat was circling us, unmanned. We were alone on a practice run. Had we flipped it during a race, the concern would turn to avoid being run over by other adrenalin addicts. Here, we had to determine a way to get to shore, or more immediate, how to get the boat back without getting run over by the propeller. Bill was farther away than I, and I might be the only chance to save the boat. It came around again, and I swam toward it, leading the bow like a hunter leads his target. It slammed into my shoulder as we met and I reached in to grab the side rail of the cockpit. I had it and swung my leg up to get inside and cut the engine. There was no more practice that day. Bill and I took the boat home to survey and repair the damage. A week later, we were practicing again.

Mom never saw us race, but I think Donna did. Racing isn't really racing unless someone you care about is watching you. Cheri came out to watch on occasion, but most of the time it was Bill and me, alone. He finally sold the boat to his brother, Johnny, and I continued as co-pilot. It was after Johnny took over that we started winning races. We were a good Team. Johnny and I will always remember our boat racing days.

My life with Bill fortunately ended with Donna's divorce. She eventually moved on to a boyfriend, but it was years later. Jim would prove to be her future husband. We became good friends. Jim was a car mechanic, and you can see the writing on the wall from there.

Jim bought a 1950 Ford pickup truck and put a Cadillac 365 cubic inch engine in it with 3 deuces and a four-speed hydro transmission. In today's standards this marriage would be a ho-hummer. A barely impressive sleeper truck. But we weren't in today's standards. This was back many decades ago, and this truck was fast. Brutally fast. It would burn the tires off, but a byproduct was that it broke axle after axle as it twisted them in half. Frustrated, Jim finally sold the truck to me and built a '57 Chevy with a 327, two 4's and 4 speed transmission. That car would lift the front end off the ground and we enjoyed taking it to Fremont raceway to pit it against others in its class. I took the truck down and raced it on the 1/4-mile track where it clocked in the low 13's, a fast time for days of old, now not much more than a traffic light sprint. This type of racing was different. A good crowd was nearby, and you could hear them while feeling their enthusiasm. There was no one in my class so I raced the next step up to achieve my own clocked time. I was pleased that I was able to race at all. Track safety was strict and it took a long time to prepare the truck to qualify for racing. I won my class, of course. I came in both first and last place. I took the first-place trophy as a preference.

Then back home to tinker, test, and toy with our race cars some more. Jim, Donna, and I lived at the same address together, with me living in a cottage behind their house in Concord. We had a lot of time to work on cars and enjoyed each of the frustrating minutes. My truck was street legal. Jim's race car was not. His was more race focused and we zeroed in on his for any improvements we could make, no matter how minor. In this case there was a problem with it at mid-range and we spent days trying to sort it out. Finally, we figured that it was a fuel problem. There was no fuel injection back then, or we certainly didn't have it on this race car. Jim studied this dilemma and eventually came up with a possible solution and once the adjustments were made, we looked at each other and grinned. With nothing being said between us, we both got in and fired it up. The roar of straight pipes could be heard for blocks. We certainly didn't want to disrupt the neighbors, so it was best to take the car for a test drive around the block, away from our house. Jim pulled it out onto the roadway and up to the next intersection where we stopped for a red light. I don't know why, there wasn't anything else legal about a full-on race car rumbling down our city highway. The car loped and rocked back and forth as the engine struggled to stay alive at such an embarrassing slow RPM. This was good we both thought, but really no place to test it. Jim solved this problem, too. Instead of turning right to go back to the house and conceal the car from irritated neighbors, Jim drove up one more block, to the freeway on ramp. Turning right at little more than an idle and looking at the nice straight, vacant on-ramp in front of us, Jim dropped the hammer. The car came to life and screamed with joy as it lifted its front end in celebration. "This isn't something you see every day," I thought as I looked out the side window to look for any semblance of ground. The car tracked straight and true as it climbed the short on-ramp onto the freeway. Whether Jim decided to put it down, or whether the car peaked out in its power band isn't as important as the timing that occurred as this incredible piece of machinery settled back down to earth. Directly in front of us, nearly bumper on bumper was a sweet little old lady probably on her way to church. Our speed didn't match hers and Jim went around her while trying to scrub off speed himself. As we went by her at warp speed she looked over at us in a calm and collected fashion, as though she had sons herself. I'll always wonder what she thought when she saw the underside of a '57 Chevy in her rear-view mirror. She'll have something to tell her great grandkids, too.

We quickly took the next off-ramp, and as unobtrusive as a race car can be on a public road, we sneaked back to the house and put the car in the garage. Seconds later, the local police cruised by, not one, but several. I don't know what they were looking for.

I later built a corvette engine to put in a '67 Chevy Impala. It, too, had three deuces and was a lot of grief to keep tuned. That street legal car got me into a lot of trouble. I was driving a '67 Pontiac GTO before I went into the Marine Corps. Paulette liked that car a lot. It was very fast.

My most favored racing was yet to come. In North Carolina, I bought a Yamaha DT360 dirt bike. You don't even hear of that bike anymore, it goes a long way back, but back then it was known as a death trap. All engine and no suspension, it had either already gotten you into trouble, or was trying to. This one was a basket case and I took a chance that I could put it back together. All the pieces were in a cardboard box except the frame. It was cold outside so, of course, my work had to take place inside the house. Paulette wasn't happy about sharing our one-room apartment with a dirt bike, but I promised her it wouldn't take her place. Piece by piece, it went together as I had the occasional time off to work on it. Finally, the night came when all I had left was the exhaust pipe to put back on. The expansion chamber fit like a glove and it was only 2:00 a.m. I didn't want to disturb the neighbors by starting it up outside, and naturally it'd be quieter inside the apartment. It started on the second kick. It was louder than I expected and I'm afraid it woke people up ---- for miles! I shut it down and went to bed thinking back on the days of a '57 Chevy.

North Carolina is flat, loamy farmland, but I soon became adept at riding a bike with an engine whose speed far exceeded the suspension's ability to handle it. The Yamaha DT360 kicked, bucked, and jumped around like a rodeo horse on PCP. I quickly got the feel for balance and throttle control. Sometime later, I was stationed at El Toro in Southern

California and discovered a nearby motocross track. Others went there to practice too, and of course we pitted our bikes against each other. It was my first experience with motorcycle racing, and I was hooked again. Over time, I bought another bike, then another, and another, and went through several while trying to find a match for me. Paulette shook her head each time I brought one home, and she'd go back into the house. A year or so later, the local Yamaha shop talked me into going out to a famous (but now gone) motocross track, Saddleback. I raced against other hard-core enthusiasts and my adrenalin was addictive. I rode every time I had a day off, sometimes alone, sometimes with friends. It didn't matter as long as I was able to ride. I'd never had any lessons and there were no such thing as VCR tapes to view and learn, so I'd watch others closely. I'd go to the track on practice days without the bike just to watch the amateurs and the pros. Every move, every adjustment, every technique that I could observe, I logged into the memory banks. On my next ride, I'd try it. If it didn't work, I'd have to try it again. If I fell down, I'd get up and try it again, then again, then again. I was going to keep at it until I got it right. With no-one to teach me, I had to experiment. For a long time, my biggest experiment was which lotion to use on the bruises. Paulette never saw me race at Saddleback or Carlsbad. Perhaps I was fortunate. She'd have made me quit riding. I got to know every inch of the track, either by rolling over it, sliding across it, or scooping it up with my helmet. Those were good times!

Paulette expressed sincere feelings that I was going to get hurt and naturally I didn't listen. She was just my wife you know. One of her motivations for moving to Northern California was the hope that I wouldn't be around the racetrack anymore. I outsmarted her and found a new form of racing; Cross Country, Hare Scrambles, and Enduros. Yep, these were fun. The Cross Country and Hare Scrambles races started out with a hundred motorcycles side by side. When the gun went off you started your motorcycle and raced for the first turn. All hundreds of you can't get into a two-lane wide turn at the same time. Physics prevailed over enthusiasm, so the first ones there gain victory over the remaining pack. The less nerve, the more catch-up you play. There's nothing like having handlebars all around you when you're trying to fight for your spot in the first turn. The dust coming out of that turn normally isn't from the motorcycles. It's from everyone trying to catch their breath all at once. From the moment your foot lights that engine to life, you trust and depend on your fellow pilots, as they do you. Yes, motorcycle racing is dangerous, and very, very fun.

It was the late summer of 1976. I was riding my new '77 Yamaha TT500 four stroke. The bike was very fast, but four stroke suspension was not up to par on a two-stroke level and the four stroke riders suffered while trying to find that sweet spot where the bike would perform as fast as the engine would push it. Trial and error found us exchanging secrets and experimenting with exotic theories. I was no different, and a race was coming. I made some last-minute changes to the bike and needed to test it before race day this upcoming weekend. I told Paulette I'd be back soon, and I drove down to Mammoth Bar, just outside Auburn where some fire roads and trails would surely test this new setup. I unloaded the bike and fired it up. The deep throat exhaust and pulse of the engine was familiar to me, and I felt the adrenaline rush from my loins all the up to my throat. I tested the suspension around the pit area and was unsure of the results. I picked up speed and tested some more. "Ok, but there's more to test yet, not much time though, it'll be getting dark in an hour or so". I rode out the dirt fire road toward the back of the Park and was alone with my thoughts. There were no trailers at the staging area, and I knew I wouldn't run into any head-on traffic if I turned the speed up a notch. The bike was acting appropriately as I dove into each turn in the road. Rolling the throttle on, I could slide the rear end around until it was alongside me and a short chop of the throttle would bring it back behind where it belonged. Things were looking better, and it was time to add another log to the fire. Fortunately, the sun was right, and I caught the reflection of light in the next corner. Downshift, break, and downshift again. The open class four stroke engine pulled the bike down from speed as I approached the corner. Yep, a car had made its way back here somehow where it shouldn't be. "That's strange, and dangerous", I thought as I passed the young driver with another young man and girl aboard. Two guys and a girl, they can't be out here to park, but I'll have to be careful of them when I'm on the way back out. I immediately throttled up as I went by, and the front wheel lifted high as I expected. I hoped I hadn't thrown rocks on their car but motorcycle riders hate riding slow. Some say it's impossible and I have cause to believe they're right. I made it to the end of the Park in short order and was disappointed in the ride. Things weren't right. The bike was stiff and not doing what it was told quickly enough at high speeds. I'd have to make some changes when I get back, even if it's to return to the old setup for the next race. Nope, this wouldn't work.

Sliding around the next few corners I knew I was to meet my car friend soon, but this time head-on if I wasn't careful. I slowed to what I felt was irritating but cautious and looked around each corner. He wasn't there. I eventually ran across him going the same direction I was, again. He had turned around too. Probably after finding out that not even a 4X4 truck should be down in here. I met him at a good spot and went around him on the inside, climbing the embankment up higher than the roof of his car and when alongside, blipped the throttle enough to lift the front end and drop down in front of him on the rear wheel "That was safe enough," I thought as I was convinced that no one was in danger of that pass, I waved and again throttled up and was on my way back to the pits. It was getting darker and I wanted to get loaded up before the sun set and I couldn't see. "Only a mile or two left so let's see if this thing's going to cooperate or not." I rolled the throttle up to race speed and made the next few corners in an acceptable but not a very comfortable fashion. Diving into a left turn, I used the mountain side on the right of the turn as a berm to stop my slide and straighten the bike out, a common practice and usually the fastest way to make a direction change in loose dirt. I felt the bike lay over on its side as I crushed the suspension against the hillside. "That's okay," I quickly thought and I was paying particular attention to how the suspension rebounded to its static position. With a massive force, the suspension snapped back as I came out of the turn and momentum took me all the way across the road. I was able to make the direction change, but I wasn't in the line I wanted to be. I wasn't even in the road any longer. I was on the shoulder of the road, in the grass and gravel, inches from the edge of a 300' drop to the canyon bottom. The lean of the bike was taking me over the side, and this wasn't amusing. Split seconds make yards of difference at speeds of 70 plus miles an hour and I didn't have yards to play with. The bike was winning, and I knew we were going over the side. Contrary to what a devout racer would do, I leaned up toward the road and pushed the bike away from me, over the side. We were just separating when I saw the two-foot-thick pine tree straight ahead. I tried but didn't have time to get my hands up to my face for protection and my head hit the tree at full race speed. My body wrapped around the tree like a horse's rein on a hitching post. The speed of the impact distorted my head to a point where my helmet came off with the strap still fastened. Most of which I don't remember at all. And who witnessed the entire incident but the car that was behind me? The one I passed only minutes earlier. They watched it happen from across the canyon and were sure I'd be dead when they got to me.

I woke up with emergency room doctors all around me and doing things to my face. "What happened?" was my natural question, and I remember someone saying I was in a motorcycle accident. He was sewing my face and I knew I was hurt this time. I couldn't stay awake any longer and thought of Paulette and the kids as everything went dark again.

Some say I was in a coma for several days but I'm not sure of that. I wasn't around. It may or may not have been so. I do remember waking before I opened my eyes. The pain was extensive and indescribable. I could barely breathe and couldn't turn my head or move any part of my body. I could feel the flesh on my face was far beyond its normal state, and even while closed, my eyes burned as though they'd been punctured. I lay motionless, drowsy, but miserably conscious. I didn't know where I was, and I didn't care. This all-encompassing trauma was about to take my life. Although I couldn't remember what had happened, I lay there with my eyes closed and knew I was bordering death. All I had to do was give up and let go. I knew I'd have to fight to stay alive and I consciously thought about whether I should or not. "It'd be so easy to let go." I thought. "Just let go." Resolved to give in, I started letting go of my consciousness. Some strength I'll never be able to explain forced me to open my eyes. Through the cracks in my swollen eyelids, I looked down at the foot of my bed. There was Pastor Ralph, quietly praying for me. As I looked, warmth came over me and my mind flashed back to a Drill Instructor standing at parade rest at the head of a squad bay. Somehow, I knew Ralph had been there for a while, and I knew he'd be there a while more, until I woke up. I decided to live. The doctors said I was the first person who had been crushed that bad and lived. I don't know how true that is - they could have been given to exaggeration. Several doctors came in to visit me and discuss what to do with this mess. I wasn't looking forward to them doing surgery, but I couldn't do it myself. They rebuilt my face and supported the bones, with Teflon as

I understand it in my simplistic mind. My face was a project for them and tackle it they did. I'm much better looking now than I used to be. I woke up in Recovery with the usual moaning and displeasure at being where I was. I felt the ice bag on my face, and I flinched as I took its weight. "You have to leave this on." the nurse said, and I fell back to sleep.

Home from the hospital and in bed for weeks, Paulette faithfully nursed me back to health. My pumpkin head slowly diminished to half its size, but my eye would not heal. Swollen, black and blue, and generally shut, I could see blurred objects, but with double vision. I could see two of everything. Now I have two wives. As I progressed in healing, things slowly returned to normal, except my double vision. It persisted beyond tolerable, and I was going to ask the doctor what could be done, even if it meant removing my eye. Using tweezers, he forced my eye back into place, but once he let go, my eye exercised a mind of its own. "It'll be okay in time," he said. He didn't tell me how many hours that would be.

My post-surgery checkup was looming and Paulette drove me back to the hospital. The doctors were less than happy, surprised to say the least. "Why, what have I done?" I asked in fear. "Your face has collapsed, and we'll have to do the surgery all over again." Oh my. I had to decide whether I wanted to go through that again or not. What if I just left it? What if I let it heal on its own? What if we wait a while and do it sometime later? Paulette became the decision maker and didn't want to look at an old collapsed puffy guy the rest of her life. Surgery was scheduled. This surgery was tougher than the first. By now I had contended with all the pain I felt capable of enduring and I wanted no more. Every movement I made was still painful, each touch to my face, and certainly every doctor's examination. And there were many. Each of them wanted to learn what he could from my injury and the subsequent treatment. I was a lab rat disguised as a human. "Dad was in surgery and never woke up," I thought as I looked up at the surgery lights above my head and the masked doctors looking down at me. The anesthesiologist was kind to put me out of that misery quickly. I guess they were all in a hurry to get started.

I recall waking up in recovery after this surgery as well, and again I felt the weight of the ice bag as the nurse placed it on my newly constructed face. "What are you doing?" I heard Paulette yell. "The doctor ordered ice," the nurse defended. "He just had his face operated on. The doctor meant ice PADS, not a BAG." Paulette's voice stood out as I lay still. I went back to sleep to wait for the long process of recovery once again. But from then on, we'll know how it was that the first surgery collapsed all that reconstruction. Three months later, I was not yet on the bike, as I still suffered with double vision. With one eye I could see the trail, but two gave me multiple choices and one would always be wrong. It was difficult to endure. Months later it slowly faded away, for which I'm thankful. It's said, "If you fall off a horse, you get back up and ride it again." I believed that and with respect to the horsemen, I knew I would ride again. With a full-face helmet from now on, I started out riding slowly, balancing the fear of injury with the addicting pull of adrenalin. By the following year, I was back in form and challenging my competitors for their best. I won my share of events in my class. Hare Scrambles, Endurance Racing, Grand Prix's, Stadium Motocross, etc. I was accomplished but humble. I never have, nor ever will call myself a good rider. I will say that I love to ride. With all the passion that's in me, I love to ride. My forte was Enduro riding. Timed events where you're told how long it must take to get from A to B to C to D, etc. It always sounded easy when explaining it to others. What I couldn't explain was that A to B was generally as fast as a pro rider could ride it without traffic. The course was set up based on that premise, with a slow area deliberately set somewhere inside the 100-mile event. You just never knew where that slow area was. The promoters tried to fool you into riding fast through it. You tried to outsmart the promoters by figuring out where it was and riding just as the promoters intended, slower. Most of the riders were far behind their scheduled times anyway and the slow part was a moot point. You used that slower section to catch up to where you're supposed to be, up ahead. I developed a time keeping method and enjoyed pitting my talent against the competition, but most of the time, the Enduros turned out to be a 100 mile race through the forest as fast as you could ride with a pit stop for fuel somewhere in the middle. Always an unsettling experience to ride at high speed over unfamiliar country where you have no idea what's ahead in the next turn, I found myself comfortable with the challenge. Winning some, I generally always found myself in the top 10%. Yep, I loved to ride.

Racers begin to recognize each other even through the helmets and riding gear, even when there were a hundred or more at an event. But Endurance racing is a lonely sport. Once the pack breaks up, most of your riding is by yourself unless you catch a dust cloud. You know that's a rider up ahead and you reel in that cloud until it gets thick enough for you to see the rider in it. It was time to pass and most of your competition didn't like that. Once you find a safe place to put the pass on him, he'll eat your dust until your cloud thins out after you put distance between him and you.

Occasionally, you run across a rider whom you recognize by his frequency at the races but have never really met. I caught one at such an event and followed him for miles. He was fast, and a good rider. I watched him as he seemed to have a sixth sense about what lies ahead. He seemed to know which way the trail was going to turn and how to set up for it. It's a pleasure to follow a good rider. As the miles passed under our tires and the hours went by, fatigue is always the enemy of endurance racing. My pilot friend, who I had enjoyed watching, was fading and I found myself starting to slow with him. That's not good, as my plan of attack has always been that the race doesn't start until the 70-mile mark. We weren't at the 50-mile gas check yet. I passed him with respect and moved on ahead in search of our pit stop for fuel. He must have found a second wind. After I passed him, he picked up his pace and stayed behind me. Not so fast that he could pass, but not slow enough for me to put any distance between him. "This is a good race," I thought.

We rode into the pit stop for fuel and I jumped off. My crew, who volunteered to come out and pit for me, refueled my bike while I refueled my own self. After something to drink and something sweet for energy, I fired the bike up again and pulled out of the pits ready for the second half. "This is the half that counts." Within a half mile, I came across my riding partner again. We settled into a pace and waited for one of us to make a mistake in a turn, throttle control, an unexpected boulder or branch, then the other would move in for the kill. Mile after mile I followed him. His bike danced back and forth, and it was well dialed in. I appreciated his talent and didn't mind riding behind him. I wasn't up to the pass, and might have to resolve myself to finishing in this order. The 70 mile marker was long behind us and my friend was still in good form. I didn't know whether he was amused or frustrated at seeing me behind him at every turn and corner, mile after mile. I knew he was trying to shake me, but didn't know how he'd feel that he wasn't able to. "Maybe we'll talk at the end," I thought. Finally, coming around the last corner, and finding it a surprise, as is the custom, we crossed the finish line. Our helmets were marked, and he pulled up ahead to get out of the way and stopped to look back. I pulled alongside and we both smiled. "Great ride!" he said with pleasure and pride. "Yes, it was," I agreed. "I tried to pass you and I couldn't," I said with regret, then added, "But I've had a flat front tire since before the pit stop." He looked at my front tire, shook his head in recognition, patted my shoulder, and rode off. I hope I didn't offend him.

The national event in Carson City, Nevada was an experience. Starting at the casino, the bikes left the starting line for some exceptionally high-speed riding over rocks, sand, and sagebrush in an effort to gain points to represent the United States in its bid for another world championship in Europe. Another timed event, you could arrive early, but you couldn't arrive late at any secret checkpoint along the 126 mile event. Arriving early was a comedy in terms. This event had all the best and fastest desert riders in the country riding for points for their European seat. The heat and rugged terrain took its toll on many of the riders. Broken bikes and broken bodies were to be expected but would never happen to you - always someone else, of course. Paulette was there to pit for me, and she was a gift from

God. Too fatigued to do it myself, I hoped she'd take longer to fill the tank. She didn't, and I rode out again for the second loop. One particularly rough section was for the expert riders only and we had to go through twice. Boulders the side of office desks, through a creek bed two miles long, found riders stacked up one behind the other. I'd been through here a few weeks before and had sorted out the best line to take. Passing several riders at a time, I took advantage of my pre-ride experience and pushed on toward the end. No time for water at any of the check points, I passed on the offer and continued to push. That afternoon the end was in sight, and I crossed it with nothing left. My energy at zero, my strength depleted, I had forgotten that we had a motocross race that must be started within 5 minutes. I pulled up to the start line wondering how I was going to do this. I couldn't hold on to the bars any longer and couldn't catch my breath. "It isn't possible", I thought until I looked to my left and then at my competition over to my right. Each of the riders on line had their heads down and chests were heaving, some with their eyes closed. I knew I wasn't the only one on the line who felt like this. "But I'm going to handle it better than they do." I vowed to myself. The gun went off and bikes raced to the first turn, three in front of me, and a whole herd behind me. I would be sitting in a good overall position if I could keep it. Sliding through the sand and making jumps that took everything to land, I passed number three. A trench in front of us had to be jumped or ridden into and back out of. Number one jumped it, number two rode through it. I jumped it to pass number 2, and was in chase of number one. Three more turns, a large jump and sprint to the end, I couldn't catch number one, and he couldn't lose me.

It's comforting to know that when you've done your best, someone you love is there to see it. But Paulette had gotten a flat tire coming back from the pit stop and wasn't around. She'd arrive later. In the meantime, I laid down alongside the truck and hoped to stay there for a very long time. I took home a Silver Medal for the event and was pleased I could accomplish that. With no excuses for not doing better, I was content that I had been competitive, and given it my best. But next time I'd do better.

Once a year, a club hosts a family Enduro out in Foresthill. This is a great event and I always loved to see the wives and kids come out to ride as a family. I had a bike for each of my three kids and they had looked forward to riding this for months. "We're a Team and we all ride together," I cautioned. They agreed and when the race started, Paulette was on the starting line to see her family take off. She had to have been worried, but this event was a slow methodical ride where it's seldom that anyone gets hurt. It was a job for me to ride back and forth keeping the kids together and checking on each one. They'd get several hundred yards apart and I'd hurry one up while slowing the other down. They didn't object and our goal was to have the entire family finish the race. That's a chore in itself, but we were dedicated to that end. A few hours later, we rode up to the pit stop and everyone had 20 minutes to rest and refuel. Paulette and I refueled the bikes and made sure the kids got something to eat and drink. Dee was the youngest, but the most anxious. Lisa and Nicki walked to the bathroom and talked to Mom. Dee was on his bike, helmet on, waiting for the time to start out again. He didn't move. He stayed there motionless, looking straight ahead, fixated on the second half of this race. "I wouldn't have any problem with him getting ready", I said to myself and yelled to the girls to helmet up. They fixed their hair; put their helmets on, their gloves and finally their goggles. They fired their bikes up and were ready to go to the start line for the second half. Dee had been ready for 15 minutes and was still fixated on the trail in front of us where the second half of the race was to start. I motioned for all to head to the start line and the girls started out. Dee was still looking straight ahead. I lifted his helmet to look into his face. He was sound asleep.

All three of the kids not only finished the event, but with respectable finishes. They rode well, stayed together, looked out for each other, and pushed themselves to do the best they could. I went home a proud Papa. I unloaded the bikes after getting home and put them away in the garage. I went into the house to tell them how proud I was but would have to wait for another time. All three were in bed, reliving their day in their dreams. I hope they remember it as I do.

The following year, the family ride was in Grizzly Flat. We took the old travel trailer out the day before and got things set up for tomorrow's ride. Mountain weather is changeable, however, and that night it rained. Morning came and the promoters were deciding whether to hold the event or not. The rain had stopped but they didn't want anyone hurt on the course. I was reluctant to vote "yes", but all three kids enthusiastically did. The yeses prevailed and the event was held.

"Go out easy, and see how slippery the course is," I said as my final caution before the flag dropped. All three complied and I'm sure they were nervous about what may lie ahead in the mud and slush. We had no rain to contend with, but the aftermath would take a riding style of its own - nothing new to the kids, but they'd have to be careful anyway. They were, and the two girls got ahead of Dee and I. Dee was having some problems with the bike and I stopped to make a minor adjustment. On our way again, Dee wanted to catch the girls. I knew they weren't far ahead but that wasn't satisfying to Dee. I saw a flash of the girls as they rounded a corner and Dee did too. He sped up for the final catch and made the same turn. The bike slid out from under him, and he put his foot down before the bike landed on it. "Dad, it hurts," he said as he lay there. I pulled the bike off and checked his foot. His boot didn't look scarred or damaged and he said he could move his foot inside his boot. "Are you able to ride, son, so we can get the girls?" I asked. "Sure Pop, it's okay." I started the bike for him, and he carried his foot on the peg with caution. We eventually caught the girls and I explained that we'd be stopping at the gas check this year. Sometime later we rolled into the pit stop and I prepared to cease the ride. "No Dad, I'm okay, really," Dee insisted. Maybe he was, I thought. Sometimes we can shake it off and we're okay after a while. Dee seemed to be okay. We didn't have time to take his boot off to check, but he wanted to do that later, at the end. It was a difficult decision to make, but again, I yielded to consensus, and we finished the rest of the race. Dee guarded his foot but rode it out. Finally, we reached the trailer and I was able to pull off his boot. The bruise told me he had hurt it. He sat down while we cleaned up the camp and we went home to take him to the doctor. A "broken foot" was the

Doctor's diagnosis. Dee had ridden and finished the race, but at the expense of my guilt and failure to insist that we stop. I wanted to cry at my failure. I'm very sorry, son.

I can't remember taking them to any more races. I felt so bad about my last decision, and although boys will be boys, I didn't want my girls hurt that way. I was just afraid to take them anymore. I, on the other hand, continued my racing with full vigor. I traveled all over Northern

California and even to Oregon for a race. This was something I seemed to need to do. It was a part of my life that I couldn't put away. The adrenalin before and during a race was more than I could ignore. We raced in the summer heat, fall rain, and even through winter storms back then. A hundred miles can be a long trip out in the woods during a cold rainstorm. It was said that only the strong would survive. I preferred to believe that it was the strength of mind they were talking about. You could quit at any of the checkpoints along the way, but I never did. During my 20 years of racing, I never quit a race, and had only one DNF (Did Not Finish) when an ignition coil went bad. I was a respectable rider and there were those who grimaced when I arrived at a race. Rarely were there any hard feelings and many of us would help each other on last minute prep. It was good camaraderie and good competition. There was an unspoken code that you never did anything to endanger your fellow pilot, and that code brought us all together. The race was dangerous enough and didn't need the added factor of a careless rider.

I was running in the top 5 when I reached the gas stop in Foresthill during their Fools Gold Enduro. My pit crew refueled me while I sat aboard the bike, and I went out at warp speed. A mile down the trail, I dove into a hard left-hand turn and center punched a boulder in the middle of the trail. In less than an instant, I was in the air flying over the handlebars. Both hands got caught in the bark busters and pinned my hands to the bars. Unable to let go, I flipped over and slapped the front wheel between my legs, upside down, with my arms at full stretch behind me. I could feel both hands and arms pulled back behind my head, down to my shoulders, with nothing left to give. Another inch of movement and I'd break them both. The bike fell over and I was pinned to the front wheel, upside down, in a blind turn, with many other bikes racing down the trail behind me. Unable to release myself and pinned motionless, I waited for the inevitable to come. I heard the bike coming down the trail and struggled to free myself one last time. No good - get ready for impact! The bike downshifted from speed to prepare for the corner and entered it slower than I had. He saw the reflection of my bike as he entered the corner and slid to a stop. Running back up the trail, he flagged other racers to stop, and then he came back to me. We carefully peeled my arms out and released me from my bondage. I told him to throw my bike to the side and get back underway, letting the other riders through too. It took me a couple of minutes to unwind myself, but thanks to adrenaline, I was back underway in a matter of minutes. I had a painful remainder of the race for the next several days, but I made a respectable finish, and was glad I finished at all.

I was in Nevada racing a cross country event when, during the motocross portion of the track, I came across a slower lapped rider in front of me. He was in the middle of the steeply banked right hand turn and I came on him so fast that there was no chance to change lines and make a safe pass. I was going to either hit him or sacrifice the bike. I chose the latter and straightened the turn out to miss him, to intentionally fly over a 10' high banked berm. The bike was out of control at that speed and with such a severe directional change. It landed upside down, and so did I, slamming my shoulder into the hard pack. There was no doubt about it, it immediately broke. I rolled over and tried to get up. That was tough. Spectators picked up my bike and gave me a #10 for the step-off. I don't know what they were thinking when they picked me up, too. I got back on the bike and was able to get it started, but my throttle arm wasn't cooperating very well. I picked it up with my left and placed it on the bars. My grip was still there, but my shoulder was telling me "NO, NO, NO!" I listened to my grip and rode the remaining hour of the race. The ambulance crew was waiting when I finshed and just shook their head. I agreed that I had no sense. They wrapped me up and I came home to sit out the next six weeks of racing with a broken shoulder.

Coalinga was an area where I avoided racing. It was notorious for having asbestos dust in the air and I didn't know if I'd be able to finish a race with asthma or not. Finally, as one of the only races I hadn't done, I went down to Central California with my racing partner, Wayne. Not only did the officials recommend wearing a mask for this race, but even prescribed the type of mask needed to filter out the asbestos. I didn't think I was going to enjoy this race. Halfway through I had an asthmatic episode, but continued on as best as I could. I wasn't going to give in to it but wanted this all day race to end. I knew I was finally close to the finish line, and weaving through the Manzanita bushes, I was counting down the miles. My throat was on fire, my lungs burned, and I felt like a snake had wrapped itself around my chest again. Spectators had started to gather along the trail denoting the tell-tale sign that we were within walking distance of the finish line. Trying to avoid some enthusiastic spectators on the outside of the turn, I dove too tight into a right-hander and caught my helmet in the Manzanita. It grabbed my full-face helmet and jerked me off the bike by my head, slamming me to the ground. Fortunately, my body weight and momentum pulled the helmet free of the Manzanita, or I'd be taller today than I used to be. I got back up after amusing the crowd with the thought that, "You shouldn't camp in the Manzanita," and finished the last mile or two of the Coalinga race. Pulling the helmet off, I found that it had cracked the full-face portion of the helmet at both jawbones. Manzanita is very strong stuff.

The Sawmill near Clear Lake was a great ride. Many didn't like it because of the time of year and terrain conditions. It was very cold and sometimes rained during the event. The country was exceptionally steep and very fatiguing. The danger element was heightened by the frost and ice on the mountainside during the morning portion of the ride. Traversing the side of a steep mountain could end in a slip off the side for even the more experienced rider. If it rained, it took the ice away, but you then had a whole new set of problems. I liked this race. It was filled with adventure. I always placed well and won it in my class at times. I didn't want to miss the Sawmill whenever it came around. Wayne usually went out with me, but Wayne was more relaxed than I. He was there to have fun. I was there to do the best I could possibly do. Wayne and I got along well and enjoyed traveling to the races with each other. This year was no different. The ice and cold took their toll on many riders, and the rest rode in their own comfort zones. I like the tough rides. I set my mind to handle it better than the rest, and I looked at it that way when I rode. On the way down the mountain toward the end of the event, the clouds moved in, and rain was imminent. I hoped to get in before it started. Wayne was behind me and by the look of things, he had a lesser chance. However, Wayne had a motivator this year. He caught me halfway down the mountain riding like I hadn't seen him do before. I let him pull alongside and he yelled over to me that the rain was coming. Yes, I knew that, but what I didn't know until I looked back was the wall of rain that was chasing us down the mountain. Only a quarter mile back, this sheet of rain was a motivator to keep going. We beat it in by only a couple of minutes. It was a good race.

Other times we weren't so lucky. I started a race in Georgetown during the morning hours. The rain had been pummeling the area all night. Nowadays, the Forest Service will call the event in such conditions, but back then you rode rain or shine. This was rain, sheets of it and I was uncomfortable, but really didn't mind. I'll handle it better than the rest who were looking around wondering what they were doing there. Riding behind a rider in the rain is difficult. Mud, slush, water, and debris inhabit your goggles, if you're able to wear any. A turn of the throttle by the rider in front and you're wearing a whole new wardrobe. Riding in the rain was fun. Breaking and cornering took a whole new technique, but I adapted to that just fine. The worrisome part was always descending down into a canyon, knowing you'd have to come back up the other side. Lack of traction, coupled by other riders before you who were facing the same conditions and having the same problems, sometimes made the terrain impossible to negotiate. If you couldn't make it back up the other side of the mountain, you had only three choices. Turn around and go back, into head-on race traffic if that route hadn't been destroyed by other retreating riders, find an alternate route down a creek bed if it wasn't too swollen and access was allowed, or spend the night. The drag riders always swept the course after the last rider went through to pick up any stragglers or broken-down riders, but they wouldn't bring your bike out. That was your responsibility after the rain stopped. Most riders wouldn't leave their bikes behind, and although I never had to make that decision, I wouldn't have left mine behind either. I was always prepared to spend the night if I had to during events like this one, but never actually did. I always found a way up the mountain, one way or the other. I was fortunate. Some of the other riders got to hear the owls. This Georgetown event may have broken my string of good fortune with regard to making it up the next mountainside. After trying near a dozen times and failing in the slippery mud, now turned to grease, I vowed to make one more try before parking to set up a camp and prepare for a cold rainy night. My final attempt was my best, and I crested the hill onto the dirt road with no energy left to spare. They called the event at the next check station and the ride was over. I was disappointed after the difficulty in getting out of the last canyon. But they didn't want any more of a mess to clean up, and they set about to look for stranded riders.

My first race on a 250 machine was memorable. I normally rode in the open class or unlimited class but manufacturers had put a lot of R&D work in their quarter liter bikes and the improvements were significant. Riding a motocross bike in the woods had its own difficulties. They had such an explosive power band that you could be in a tight area or weaving through the trees only to find that the bike wouldn't take just a small amount of throttle. It was almost full on, or full off, with little in the form of mid-range control. A collision was looming somewhere down the trail. On the other hand, their suspension was so far advanced that it lent to a monumental step ahead, if you could control the bike's engine. Most woods riders at that time didn't care for the tradeoff, but I found it an advantage. Like those who made the same decision, we would lug the bike down and slip the clutch through the tight woods. It was a chore, but when mastered, a motocross bike was a very fast weapon of choice.

The 49er Enduro was my first race on this ultra-light and fast machine. Right from the start line I was happy I was aboard this bike. I could flick it back and forth between the trees with little effort and on the single-track trails it was phenomenal. Here, it fell into its power band, waiting to bark. I felt like I was riding a zealous dog with cabin fever, pulling on the leash with his neck and jumping out in front. I could tell this bike had much more to offer and she was just waiting to show me. We hit some two-track trails and off we went. I gave my dog the leash and it exploded to life. Pulling it down from speed was a graceful thing as it made little effort to scrub off momentum for the upcoming corner. I grinned as I enjoyed this bike. A blip of the throttle and it would stand on its rear to lighten the front, and away we'd go to the next obstacle.

"Give me more," the bike yelled, and I went along with anything it asked. I was flying faster, slowing quicker, turning tighter, and accelerating with confidence. This nimble bike was going to do its job.

I dropped down onto a fire road and I knew from races past that this road was going to take us at a high rate of speed for 3-4 miles. My aftermarket digital speedometer and odometer said 72 mph between turns and that's all my CR250 could produce. I wanted more here, but I was still passing riders who didn't. I could contend with this but found myself still checking to see if I had another gear somewhere down there. "Nope, that was it. Get used to it," I said to myself, but I never did. Coming around a right-hand sweeping corner I was in a two-wheel drift and grabbed a handful of throttle to straighten it out. A straightaway lay ahead and I was looking for my 72-mph peak again. Up ahead was a row of race officials standing across the dirt road. "This was unusual," I thought, "normally we'd go down here another mile or so." I downshifted and scrubbed off speed as I approached, and they waved me to my left, showing me that the trail was turning here. We follow arrows on these races, and you learn to pick them up out of the corner of your eye. Yep, I see it, an arrow pointing up the embankment, and another at the top turning right. I slid sideways to make my turn to the left in front of the officials, and realized why they were there. It wasn't to direct the racers, they were there to watch them crash. They like entertainment too, you know. Alongside the road, between the road and the embankment was a drainage ditch. We had to drop into the ditch and make a vertical climb up the ten-foot embankment, and an immediate right at the top to avoid hitting the trees that happily chose to grow up there. I saw the ditch and decided my new motocross bike wouldn't tolerate such an indignant insult. I blipped the throttle to bring the front wheel up and slammed both wheels into the embankment. Body weight forward over the bars, the bike climbed the embankment with little effort. I needed speed at the top and throttled up to gain some air after cresting. The bike seemed to defy the laws of physics after going over the top and I shifted weight, pulling the bars hard to the right. As if alive and knowing what I wanted it to do, the bike made a mid-air directional change and settled both tires down on the new trail at the same time. A small blip of the throttle led me down a trail I hadn't gotten to see before. "This bike likes me," I thought as I flipped it easily through the trees at incredibly fast speeds. All to soon, coming around a right-hand dusty turn, I found the end, and all the spectators waiting for their own riders to come in. I locked it up and slid across the finish line to a stop. The official logged in my time and wrote it on my helmet. Two other officials quickly jogged up and while pointing at me and my number plate on the front of the bike, yelled to the timekeeper, "This guy is a heck of a rider!" He was one of the officials back on the fire road looking for amusement. I appreciated his compliment and went to get my trophy. This was a good bike.

My racing career went on and I suffered the usual bruises, breaks, and tears. I enjoyed the admiration of my peers as I sought to be the best that I could be. I had successes and accomplishments that others didn't enjoy, and I consider myself a very lucky man. The memories I take with me to my senior years will give me pleasure each time I relive them. I close my eyes and have years of memories. God granted me a talent. Not too much, not too little. I enjoyed what He loaned me, and I hope I didn't disappoint Him. Thank you for those memories, Lord.

CHAPTER 12

Run For Your Life

My asthma was never under control to a point where I wasn't concerned about getting an attack during any unexpected moment. It generally started with my throat closing down, followed quickly by a feeling of suffocation. It's difficult to explain to anyone who doesn't have it, and embarrassing to describe to someone who doesn't understand. The best way I found was to suggest to someone that they tape their nose shut, put a straw in their mouth and breathe through it. Difficult at best, you can always remove that straw to catch your breath. With asthma, you can't. Now try running around the block with the straw. If you make it back, it's likely you'll have panic running right behind you. With asthma you don't need to run to experience it. You can be sitting in a chair or doing anything else and it's like a band strapped tight around your chest. Similar to a boa constrictor taking its prey. They don't squeeze their prey to death. Rather they wait until their prey exhales, and they squeeze tighter. The prey struggles for his next breath. He may succeed, but his fate is scheduled by the boa. Asthma has been my snake since I was a boy. With no medication then, my only solace was to sit quietly and struggle until it passed on its own. Many trips to the hospital suggested that it didn't pass quickly. Odors, pollen, foods, dust, animal hair, cigarettes, temperatures, exercise, stress, there seemed to be an endless list of causes. What was a boy to do? I grew weary of the ailment as it controlled my life. Everything I did and every place I went, asthma was at the door in front of me. There was no avoiding it, no relief from it, and no cure for it. My job was to live with it, and I did my best. Odors, foods, dust, and pollens I could avoid. Other things I couldn't. In those days there was no such thing as a "No Smoking" room in public, and both Mom and Dad smoked in the house. Smoking was prevalent everywhere and it would immediately bring on breathing problems when I inhaled. I learned to walk away from smokers, but I knew the nicotine left in the room was a demon in disguise. Sometimes it wouldn't bother me. Other times my lungs could feel it and my snake was coming.

As I grew older, one of the things I couldn't avoid was exercise. I loved it. Whether cutting trees with Bill, loading brush, or working out at school, exercise was something I enjoyed. I loved the outdoors. Asthma was a real source of grief. I learned to ignore it much of the time so I could enjoy its cause. Many times, after exercise I'd go off by myself to reap my "reward", but it never deterred me. I was too in love with exercise. The end result was that during Intermediate School and High School I saw the doctor less, and maybe even built a small resistance to asthma. We battled each other like opposing military forces, and I was winning some battles. As long as I was able to hide it, I was winning.

High School presented its own problems as I was strong enough to excel in their activities, but weak enough to succumb to my nemesis. Concealment was the name of the game, and I grew proficient. My next obstacle was the Marine Corps and I succeeded there, too. Life was getting better as I was winning more. I felt it was the running I was doing in the Corps, and I continued after getting out. Every other day I'd run a mile around the block near the house. Summer, winter, it didn't matter. I was able to fight this demon and I would continue to win.

Our move to Auburn brought on new triggers for asthma and new opportunities for me to gain control. I continued to run until the accident in '76 when I was down for months. The shock had taken its toll and running after that was difficult. I tried, but it was too draining to continue as I had been doing. As time went on, my exercise took a second seat to work. Salesmen don't run to work. Asthma got worse and I grew more depressed. It was only in 1978 that I learned through a church member with asthma about an inhaler that helped. Yes, it did, and it was like a new opportunity for life for me. I carried a canister with me all the time. Normally it would help, never would it cure, but it was always comforting. I needed more exercise, and maybe this would open that door. I wasn't going to put Paulette through the first stages of my inevitable suffering so I couldn't do it when she was home. Finally, she went down to see her mother for a couple of weeks, and it was time for me to put up or shut up. This would be a deciding factor of how I would live the rest of my life, and I put on some shorts.

I jogged slowly up the sidewalk but by the time I reached the nearby stop sign, my snake caught me. I could feel my chest tighten and my throat close down. I rounded the block, taking a few more strides, and the air I needed wasn't there. I fought to suck it in, and the snake squeezed tighter. A few more strides and my head hurt, my vision blurred, and my lungs burned with fire. I couldn't suck in any air and forced the effort with all I had in me. I set a goal for the stop sign down at the nearby grocery store, and vowed I'd make it that far. Each stride was a desperate effort to reach a goal, but as a voice told me I wasn't going to make it, my inner force pushed me on. The stop sign was in sight and I looked at the distance in the strides it would take to get there. How many left? I counted them out in my head, and then counted them down as I moved. Grabbing the pole as I reached it, I went to my knees. Embarrassed or not, I was to stay there a moment. It wasn't getting better even with the inhaler, and I got worried. I wasn't going to suffocate there in front of everyone, so I rose to my feet and started the block-long walk home. I made it to the front door and collapsed in the hallway. Unable to get up for a while, I overdosed on the inhaler hoping for some relief. It did come, but sometime later. As I started to breathe better, I arose to take a steam shower. That sometimes helped.

I was determined to do it again the next day. I wasn't looking forward to it, but was determined, and I did it, with the same results. The next day, then the next, I donned my shorts and went out for my painful and suffocating run. I had no idea whether I was going to be able to beat this thing or not, until almost two weeks later, when I was able to round the corner at the second stop sign and run a few yards further. "I'm winning!" I thought as I turned to walk home. Still fighting asthma but with more success.

Paulette came home and I had to be more careful with hiding the effects of my new running regime. It took months before I could jog a mile again, but I did. On good days, I could do a mile and a half. I wasn't going to let my improvement fall into oblivion if I had any control over my resolve, and I did. Winters were cold and tough on my lungs. Using a ski mask, I'd cover my mouth to warm the air before it went down to visit my lungs. I continued jogging for the next couple of years and felt a lot better about myself.

In 1980, the Search and Rescue Motorcycle Team was asked to patrol a section of trail for some runners coming through at a yearly event. We went out to Sliger Mine, in El Dorado County, down to Ruck-a-Chucky rapids on the American River. "They'll cross here," the Deputy said, "Then two miles up this mountain, they'll pick up the trail to Auburn Lake Trails, then on to Highway 49, down to No Hands Bridge, then the climb up to the High School in Auburn." Wow, I said to myself, these have to be incredible athletes. "How far are they running," I asked Marvin. "This is the 78-mile mark. Auburn will complete their 100-mile trek." 'You've got to be kidding me!' was my only thought. "How many days do they have to make this run?" Marvin shook his head as though it were hard to say, "24 hours" was all he got out. After shaking his head again in disbelief, he explained that this was the Western States 100 Mile Run, from Squaw Valley up in the high country near Lake Tahoe, to Auburn. He didn't know a great deal about it himself. Later, I learned that it wasn't just the run that was impossible, but it was made worse as the trail never hit a flat area. Its length stretched up over the top of the Sierra Mountains, down into two massive gorges, and back out to Foresthill, then into another gorge to Ruck-a-Chucky and out again until the final 20 miles to Auburn. Temperatures at the 5:00 a.m. start line at the Squaw Valley parking lot were generally around 32 degrees. Four hours later, the runners would be in the deep canyons facing the sun's 90 degree heat, and by that afternoon the canyons would be baking their intruders at 105 degrees. There were no stops to rest, and the athletes would carry their own water and food, with supplies replenished only at the Check Points. There are some incredibly steep mountains and gorges between Squaw Valley and Auburn. These runners would climb and drop over 37,000 feet during their 100-mile quest. Yet each year the best ultra-long-distance runners come from all over the world to challenge this event. A silver belt buckle to be awarded, and earned, by all those who complete it in under 24 hours. From 24.01 to the 30-hour mark they earned a beautiful and coveted wall plaque. Anyone completing it at 30.01 hours or later goes home as empty as they came out, but with a lot more memories.

During the run, the runners will each generally drink over 5 gallons of water, at 8.34 lbs. per gallon, they'd withstand a weight gain of over 41 lbs. during those 24 hours. But that will never be. It's been figured by the lead physician for the race that a runner must drink at least 1/3 of their own body weight during the 24-hour period to stand a chance of surviving the event. Yet at the end, they all will have lost weight before making the lap around the football field at Placer High School. If they were found to have lost too much weight at a check point, they were pulled. If they lost too much between checkpoints, they could die. That's where we came in. The same event, called the Tevis Cup, is run by horses a month later, and horses have died trying to complete this test. Race officials vowed that a person would never die in this event. I was awestruck beyond belief. I was going to see what had been determined to be the most difficult endurance event in the world, right here in Auburn.

We went out a month before the event and pre-rode the assigned trail where we were to work. Only inches wide in places, and drop-off's reminiscent of my accident site, I looked at this as amazing. Many of these runners were going to come through this section at night. They were allowed a pacer to join them at the Foresthill mark to keep them awake and alert as they continued their trek through the forested woods. The pacer was there to protect and guide them the best they could. I was soon going to see the value of those pacers.

The news media gave a blurb about the run but nothing more than a courtesy release. I was saddened by their lack of interest but made up for it myself. I took the Team out to the event several hours before the first runners were to come through and we set up camp at an Aid Station where the runners were to get checked before being allowed to go on. We familiarized ourselves with the trail one last time and prepared for our adventure. Equipped with only 2-way radios from the Sheriff's Office, it was state of the art, at the time. But with reference to that day and time, there were no handheld cell phones, no pocket radios for runners to communicate, no headband flashlights, no GPS's, or any of the other amenities or needs that are common today. When one references "remote," these runners were remote to the very definition of the word. A medical emergency out in this country is a very serious thing.

It wasn't long before the leader came through, Mike Catlin, a local man, who looked good as he passed. His feet firmly directed to the forest floor, he ran with purpose and direction, but he had a gaze on his face that made me wonder if he knew where he was, or what he was doing. My doubts passed as he did. He was quickly checked and allowed to go on. "Remarkable" was the only word that I could muster. This man has run through this rugged mountain range for 80 miles and will run another 20 before stopping. Is this humanly possible?

Other runners were soon to follow. Jim Howard was close behind Catlin. Jim was also a local boy. Gaunt, and of small stature, he made it through the Aid Station and pressed on almost immediately, but not soon enough for Howard to offer a verbal concern. Out on the trail, "How far ahead?" was the only thing he'd occasionally ask his pacer, referring to Catlin's place. "Not to worry" was the tired pacer's response as he matched stride for stride with the superman next to him. The pacer was usually right. We left Howard to turn back and check on whoever was behind and found that these gladiators had a sixth sense as to where their competition was. Rarely were they off by a minute.

Darkness grew close and soon gained control. The forest offered a whole new world in the dark, but it was something my Team and I were used to. Many of our searches were during the night, and we were comfortable with the environment. The runners coming through were not so comfortable. Flashlights in one hand, a water bottle in the other, over 200 runners attempted this impossible task, relying on their pacers to keep them on the trail. As time ticked by, the condition of the runners passing through got significantly worse. Although running slower, they'd been out on the trail longer than the front runners, and it was taking its toll. Most were disoriented. Some were confused and irrational. Others didn't even know their own name. But all pressed on as though being driven by a force planted in them during past history and now being unleashed. What they couldn't speak or remember was inconsequential as long as their inward drive didn't fail. Unbelievable, was my only thought hour after hour. Daylight pushed the darkness aside as the sun yawned when it looked over the distant mountain. One more runner left, the last runner before being forced to stop at the Aid Station. Everyone's goal at the start line at Squaw was to complete this event in less than 24 hours. If so, you went home with a belt buckle that would have your name on it forever. A hundred miles in twenty-four hours was a goal that only the best of the best ultra long-distance runners in the world had accomplished. Many more had tried and failed. Their consolation was a second chance. Their name engraved forever in a piece of wood that would become a remarkable lifetime treasure. Anything over thirty hours, and one minute, they may as well never have started the run. The runners coming through our area after the new morning light would not see a belt buckle this year. There just wasn't enough time to make it to the finish line. They were running for a plaque, and knew it was getting farther away. With rare exception, these runners were unconscious on their feet. They could answer no questions or barely talk. Their pacers assured us they were okay, but we knew they weren't. Our goal was to get them to the Aid Station where they could be checked. Many would be pulled from the race there. Some would argue but most would comply with the look of death covering their face. It was an incredible night for me. I had witnessed the impossible and couldn't believe what I had seen.

We packed and loaded up. Pulling out, we were all fatigued, but embarrassed to confess it. We drove back to Auburn to clean up and sleep, but as I drove up the canyon, I pulled over to get out and look over the side down at No Hands Bridge. In the distance I could see these last runners, barely able to move one foot in front of the other, shuffling along with determination that I could only envy. Who they were, I'll never know. What part of the country or world they came from I couldn't tell. But they were all human beings accomplishing a superhuman feat. I turned to get back in my truck, only to look back one more time. "I could never do this," I quietly said to myself. And I went home.

Mike Catlin did win the race that year. Jim Howard tied it with Doug Latimer the following year, came in behind Jim King in '82, and won it himself in 1983. Jim King came back to reclaim his title in '84 and again in '85. I knew both Howard and King to be nice people, and both were locals.

My passion has always been racing, of one kind or the other. I excelled in and enjoyed my motorcycle racing most. There has never been any feeling to take the place of flying through the woods, weaving in and out of trees, throwing your bike to and fro, accelerating then braking only seconds apart, and controlling a machine that has been equated to a Double AA fuel Dragster when compared to weight vs. horsepower ratio. Good riders make it look easy. Aspiring riders get hurt. When the day is done, and you've mastered your bike and the course, you go home feeling thankful, lucky, and tired. Oh, what a great feeling it is to ride a dirt bike at speed. I got a double blessing from it, as I spent a lot of time talking to God, and thanking him for getting me out of the last bit of trouble a couple of turns back. God and I got close when I rode. I was pleased that he took the time to ride with me. Or better put, let me ride with him. I thanked him for it on my jersey, "One Way, God's way." It's been said that motorcycle racing is the second most physically demanding sport in the world, second only to soccer. I never played soccer, but I can attest for motorcycle racing.

Climbing back into the truck, I heard God speak to me. Unless you're already a Spirit filled Christian this sentence will probably raise red flags all across your chalkboard of logic. Hear God speaking to you? Really? Sure. What in the world are you talking about? Are you saying that God, if he exists, could or would take the time to speak to some small, single individual? That's pretty hard to believe. Before accepting Jesus into my heart, I would agree with these naysayers emphatically. Why would God take the time to say something to anyone who isn't a pastor, priest, clergyman, or someone higher up than just a Christian man? The answer is simple, my friend. When you accept Jesus into your heart you also invite his Holy Spirit to come into your life and dwell within you. It's the spirit of Jesus that speaks to the Holy Spirit inside you that you hear and feel. Although you can't see him there is no doubt in your heart that he's spoken to you. Each time he does it's an event that you will always remember. This one, I remember. "You're going to run this," he said. Now there's a shock I never expected. I hadn't even thought of it. In fact, when I did think of it I got scared. "Impossible," I said to myself while sitting down in the truck. On the way home I ran it through my head over and over. "Did God really say that to me," I asked myself. I had to quickly answer in the affirmative. I knew he had. Now I had to digest the magnitude of his declaration. I kept going back to, impossible." One thing I did know was that God never lies or speaks a falsehood. But if he was to set this challenge in my path, he'd also set the stage for it to come to pass. He's not going to set the stage for me to do something and turn around and just leave it to me to get it done. No, he'll guide and direct me. All I'd have to do is put one step in front of the other, so to speak. But the first thing I had to do was redirect my heart and mind. That was my job, so I did.

I first had to recognize that this insane idea wasn't mine, it was God's. That being true, it will work. If I could put into practice the talents that God gave me to ride dirt bikes, as I have, then he may just extend that talent to something like this. He'd have to, I sure wouldn't be able to do it on my own. Shaking my head in amazement and confusion, I set up and commenced a training program.

My mile and a half runs soon got pushed to two miles, slow in pace, but two, nonetheless. I was tired after two and pushed myself to do it 3-4 times a week. Paulette was quiet about watching me go out. I hadn't told her about my dream, nor that God had spoken to me. As I ran, it became more than that. There was a fire kindled inside me, his Spirit was talking to me. He was saying that I could do it. I certainly didn't believe in myself, something greater than my own drive to push myself was at hand.

My first 5-mile run was a triumph over asthma and fatigue. It took me back to my Marine Corps days and I was pleased. I ran a couple more 5 milers that month and thought back about my initial attempts to make it to the stop sign around the corner. A neighbor saw me running and introduced himself. Dennis would soon become a reliable friend and runner. He was heavier than I and not suited to running, but he tried, and I admired him for it. He was enthusiastic and reliable. Three times a week, like clockwork, he'd knock on my door with his running shoes on. He never challenged me to run faster or push harder. He encouraged me, and I him, but the roads and sidewalks were tough to run on, and boring. We introduced ourselves to the dirt trails near the house, which also happened to be a part of the Western States 100, and we were hooked. There was nothing like running on the trails. Seeing things that you never saw before, no matter how many times you ran the same trail. Climbing, turning, descending, and climbing again, you set a goal for a destination and worked for that end. I liked the trails, and hated the mile run from the house to where my heart was, the start of the off-road trail.

Each breath was a chore for me as I could never get into a glide or aerobic state. I'd gasp for air on the up hills, try to catch my breath on the flats, and rest during the short down hills before the next climb. Dennis had a slower pace but was able to run aerobically. I didn't know whether I'd rather have his style or mine. We both learned to contend with our own thorns and help the other.

No Hands bridge was our goal for months, but getting there and back without stopping was no easy chore. There was a steep climb coming back out of the canyon, and neither of us was to admit we'd have to walk it out. So, week by week, we ventured just a little farther down into the canyon before turning back for home. Months later, No Hands Bridge was in sight. A ten-mile, out-and-back run, this was our first unimaginable accomplishment. Dennis and I did it together, and we considered ourselves canyon runners.

At least once a week we tested ourselves to the No Hands run, always trying to make it back out without walking, even if it were a slow run. Sometimes we made it, sometimes we didn't, but we always felt good at the end. Now Dennis had another goal in mind. He wanted to run up the railroad tracks to Colfax. He was more ambitious than I to tackle that so soon, but we talked about it frequently. We set a date, and now had another objective.

I worked late that day and got home an hour after our planned time to leave. "Dennis left just a little while ago," I heard when I called his house. I threw my shoes on, filled a bottle of water, and headed out for my friend whom I had disappointed. He shouldn't be too far ahead, and I paced myself faster than I normally would. This was about a 15-mile run up the railroad tracks, and one of our wives would have to pick us up in Colfax. "Dennis wasn't going to run alone," I vowed. Each turn in the tracks I expected to find him. Each turn let me down. I wasn't running fast enough. I wasn't sure how to tackle this long-term pain, so I thought of one short goal before the other. I had ridden this route on my bike many times and knew what was ahead. This run wasn't going to be fun.

Halfway up, darkness fell. I continued running but hadn't brought a flashlight. I just didn't think about it. It was dark now and I had no idea what lay ahead of my feet. Rocks and gravel were a sure bet. Twisting an ankle out here may mean spending the night. And where was Dennis? Was he hurt somewhere? I called for him every mile or so, but no answer. I resolved to finish this adventure alone. Nearing Colfax, there were two options to take. One was the high side over the hills, continuing along the tracks. The other was a drop down on the road to finish the trek on hard pavement. I wondered which way Dennis may have taken and knew myself that the tracks were the only successful way to say you ran them up to Colfax. But if Dennis had his choice, not knowing I was behind him, this late at night, he probably took the road. I'll take the road and maybe catch him before he enters town.

We were going to end our run at the Police Station in Lower Colfax, so I knew where to stop, but as I got closer, and found no Dennis, I worried he was still out on the trail somewhere. I'd have to find him, but I'd have to call for help to do it. I ran the plan through my mind as I approached the Police Station and deduced that I'd start there. I would alert the Officers, and then build a plan from there.

I walked off the last mile of the run to cool down and drive the lactic acid from my muscles, a caustic waste product as a result of exercise. Not doing so will surely lead to pain for the next couple of days. As I walked toward the train station and got closer, there was my friend Dennis, trying to catch his breath, walking out the lactic acid and as happy to see me, as I was him. It was a great day.

Mom lived in Foresthill, and I set my next goal. This 25-miler was something Dennis didn't want to tackle, and I was scared to set it for myself, but I was going to try it for my 31st birthday. I didn't say anything to Paulette or anyone else as I said goodbye in the morning for a run she expected me to normally take. Running across town to the top before dropping down to the Foresthill Bridge was tough, annoying, and tiring. I didn't like the pavement or running through town. When I made the turn to drop down the hill toward the Bridge, I knew I had made a commitment that I couldn't back out from.

Across the highest bridge in California, I looked over the side and thought of the bodies I had helped recover, those who had lost their dreams. I looked out over the mountains in the far distance and couldn't imagine how someone could start on the back side of those, and run here. Impossible, but true, was my only consolation. The miles slowly passed under my feet as I taught myself to run as a trail runner, not a road runner. Slide your feet forward, don't pick them up high for momentum. Stay level from your waist up. Don't waste energy trying to gain momentum there either. Arms held loose at your side, don't use strength to hold them up. And drink water every ten minutes, lots of water. I tried to quiet the sound of my feet hitting the pavement. The louder it was, the more energy I was wasting. Quiet down, think of other things, plan your run up the next hill then think about being on top of it, not climbing it, and don't stop.

"Everyone's Inn" was my goal to get more water. I got some strange but admirable looks from patrons who asked where I had come from. "Auburn," was my humble answer, and I prepared for a tough climb up the mountainside to Foresthill.

I shuffled into Mom's mobile home park to find her outside in her garden. She looked up with surprise to see me, and then looked behind me for the car. "You're kidding me," she said with a tone in her voice suggesting she knew of course it was true. "Hi Mom" was my agreement that it was true. It was a good birthday.

Dennis introduced me to Cardiac Hill near our house. A steep 1-mile descent with 36 switchbacks, it was a monumental task to run down it, let alone up. Your quads burned as you held your body back from gaining speed on the way down. This was a beautiful place to run. Once you got to the bottom the trail meandered along the American River. The next stop from there was Rattlesnake Bar. This was a tough

15 miler, with the nightmare climb back up Cardiac even though it was a given that it was a walker. "No one could run this," I thought. In time someone would -- Me! It took years to accomplish the first time, but as I progressively made it farther up the mountain, I knew that someday I'd make it without walking. It was my goal, and I wouldn't quit until I made it.

Dennis and I had other goals. Running all the way to the town of Cool was one that took many months to slowly achieve. Getting there was one thing. Getting back was twice the run, and far too much to ponder. We made it to Cool for the first time after almost two years of running. Paulette picked us up for a very proud ride home.

We ran all the way to Rattlesnake Bar, then later to Granite Bay. The one-way runs became out-and-backs. And I ran Cardiac for the first time. We set our goal to run Cool, out-and-back, and within a couple of years had succeeded. We were feeling like legitimate trail runners before I got the visit.

The knock at the door came as a surprise. Rex introduced himself as a trail runner and said he had heard that I could run. He had run Western States before and this was my first chance to talk to one of those insane heroes who had. I looked at him like a true warrior and soaked in every comment or suggestion he had to make. We ran Cardiac together for the first time at night. And ran the trails that he knew: Stagecoach, the back way to Cool, and down in the canyon over the foundation for the Auburn Dam. This was new running to me. I would never leave Dennis behind, but sometimes he just passed on the offer to go.

Rex introduced me to other runners who were planning a long out-and-back. One of them was Jim Howard, the winner of the Western States. Jim lived in Foresthill and ran every day - fast, hard, and long. This was over my head. "Come on, there's eight or ten of us going out. It's about a 20 miler. You'll enjoy it," Rex said. Dennis was more aspiring than I and he said yes first. I was leery because of the quality of runners going out. Their talent far exceeded mine, or more appropriately said, my lack thereof.

We met in Michigan Bluff, behind Foresthill and each wore their day packs around their waist and carried two bottles of water. We were anxious to head out. I didn't know what a day pack was, but did have two bottles for water, and a sandwich tucked in my shorts. Without a word, all turned to the mountains, and jogged out of town, over the side, down into El Dorado Canyon. I was in awe of these runners who could talk and carry on a conversation while running. I tried to answer their hospitable questions without letting on that I was fighting for breath, and only hoped they wouldn't ask me too many more.

It was the most beautiful run I had ventured out on. Jim Howard had taken a place behind some other runners and was casually keeping their slower pace without getting annoyed. I, quite by chance, fell in behind him. I stared at his feet while they pushed the ground beneath them out of the way. He stepped in the rain puddles and sloshed through the mud from the last downpour and thought nothing of it. I, on the other hand, was running behind Jim Howard, a hero.

As the miles grew, each runner settled into their own pace. Distance grew between each one. No-one was with anyone else now, and we were essentially alone in the woods by ourselves. Many runners ahead of me, there were some behind. I didn't know why, but there were. Dennis was back there somewhere. I hoped he would make it as far as I intended to.

We crossed the footbridge at the bottom of the canyon where it was well known that rattlesnakes abound, and started our several miles climb up the other side to Deadwood and then on to Devils Thumb. It'd be a few more hours before we'd reach the old ghost town that barely existed anymore. I walked some but ran the climb when I could. I wasn't going to give up or turn back until I got there. In fact, shortly after we headed out that morning, I forgot even the possibility that I could fail. My mind had Devils Thumb as my turn-around spot, and I thought of nothing else but that.

We stopped at Devils Thumb as each of us arrived at our own time. A few of the elite took me over to look at its namesake and I admit I was impressed. In the background, just behind the protruding rock outcropping was a gorge. The bottom couldn't be seen. "That's part of the Western States," one of the runners said. "The other side, over there, is Last Chance. You'll be coming from over there, to here, and on to Michigan Bluff where we started," he explained as though he were talking to a real competitor for the event. I appreciated his complement as I ate my squished sandwich and waited for the others to arrive. Dennis was one, and I was very happy.

The trip back started with the long multi-mile drop back down into the Canyon. My body was tired, my muscles ached, I was out of breath, and didn't know whether I had asthma or not. I didn't care. I was going to finish this miraculous event. I was ahead of many of the more casual runners as I hit the footbridge. Not because I was a better runner, but because they were just as described, casual, and I was not. I was focused, driven, and determined. The climb out was the only thing left. It would take a couple of hours, but I would not fail. I would not fail.

I jogged into Michigan Bluff with only one runner ahead of me. Bruce, a Highway Patrolman. I was glad he was a cop, and he was a nice one. We talked for a couple of hours as others filtered in. And just as I had become to expect, Dennis made the round trip too. Jim Howard and a couple others decided to go farther than Devils Thumb, so we didn't wait. Dennis and I rode home together with memories that will never be taken away. It was a great day.

I met Gordon Ainsleigh out on a run one day. He was a chiropractor in town and offered to help me with my back. I had Spondylolisthesis, a slipped vertebra, and no doctor could help without surgery. It offered me much pain at times and prevented me from running, riding, or doing other things when it decided to dominate my attention. In 1974 Gordon was also the first man to ever run the Western States, when his horse took ill before the Tevis Cup. He walked to the start line without it. At times all of the horse racers got off to run alongside their horse during this grueling event with the intent of giving their horse a rest. Gordy decided he'd do it from the start line, but without his horse. No-one believed it possible, but 100 miles later Gordon crossed the finish line in under 24 hours, and beat many of the horses in. The Western States Run was started. Only a couple other fools stepped up to the start line the following year. News traveled fast, and in 1981, world class ultra long-distance competitors were arriving to challenge the most difficult run in the world. So many had signed up for the superman test of all tests that a lottery had been formed to select the lucky participants and only pre-qualified athletes were allowed to be put in the lottery for a possible seat. No one came to the event thinking they could enter. Anyone who was chosen to compete were all for the next upcoming year.

Gordy was polite and cordial. We enjoyed talking and he took a fancy to my job as a Private Investigator. It gave us something to talk about, and I soon became his patient. He helped my back, and my mind. He gave me ideas, suggestions, pointers, and ran with me at times. Over the next year Gordy and I became friends. He had much more confidence in me than I. I needed that, as I didn't know how far I could really go.

He called me one Friday night and said let's go for a ride. "Where?" I asked, quite surprised he suggested it. "Cow Mountain," was his answer, and he went on to explain. Cow Mountain was near Ukiah, and tomorrow they're having a 50-mile run. The horses will go out first, and the runners a ½ hour behind them. It's a great race, and you have to qualify in a 50 before you can enter Western States, he explained. There's no way I can run 50 miles, but he talked me into driving him over there, and yes, I took my shoes.

The next morning, I found myself on the starting line wondering what and how I got into this. The horses left at the signal when the clock hit the top of the hour. The runners stood quietly by, some talking, others staring ahead into the darkness. The horses were to have a head start. It was barely light when we started out. I took a pace slower than I usually do, but there was a long way to go. Gordy had run this before and laid out the course for me while we drove out the night before, "Just in case I wanted to do it myself." I listened intently as I knew I wouldn't be left in camp when the runners were all taking on this challenge. Gordy was right. I slowed in the areas he cautioned me and picked up the pace at the top of the mountain. Gordy was ahead of me somewhere, but I was content that I had made it this far. Coming into the 25-mile marker, horses and runners were passing me on the way back. "It's okay," I consoled myself; I've made it halfway, as I turned around at the marker. Gordy wasn't too far ahead, I noted as he passed me on his way back. I knew where we had been, and what to expect ahead. I was going to complete this run, either running or walking, I wasn't going to quit.

Ten hours after I started, I crossed the finish line. Many were ahead of me, horses, and runners alike, and many were behind me. I took selfish pleasure in knowing that many of those behind me were horses. I had outrun half of the horses. I was becoming a long-distance runner.

Saturday night was a barbeque feed before a band came in to set up on a flatbed truck. My private opinion was that this wasn't the time for a dance party. I learned that the runners always challenged the horse riders to see who the last person standing would be. I don't know who won. I was asleep in the back of my truck.

Gordy explained on the way home that I also had to qualify doing a 26-mile marathon to get into Western States. Actually the 26 miler wasn't the qualification for W.S. It was a qualification to do a 50. I had just done that on Gordy's vouch that I had run a marathon. I hadn't, but Gordy really wanted me to do this 50. There was so much in store for me.

My first marathon was also with Gordy. We decided to do the California International Marathon from Folsom to the State Capitol in Sacramento. This would be a faster run than I liked, yet I didn't want to be left behind. As we started down near the Folsom Dam, this marathon would be entirely on pavement. The pounding on my back was taking its toll before the event even warmed up. This was a new thing to me as spectators lined the streets and sidewalks through most of the 26.2-mile news-making event. It meant I couldn't slow or surrender to any effects of asthma. Running at this pace, on this pavement, for this long, was not in my pleasure zone. By the tenth mile I was miserable, thinking only of the next mile to come. By mile 18, I experienced hitting the wall. Men usually feel it before women do. The body uses up all its fuel sources and turns to burning fat as energy. This is a poor source of fuel and the change-over is an experience equal to a full body root canal. Making that changeover takes you through a wall where you can't move another foot, you become angry and disoriented, your vision blurs, your headache is pounding, and you try to press on akin to having a nightmare where the monster is chasing you and you're trying to run away from it but can't. Women usually have a higher fat content than men and can push the wall out farther than mile 18. Many times, in a marathon, they'll run through the wall gracefully and not hit it at all. I had my price to pay and was having a difficult time. So was Gordy. He was behind me. This was different than the 50. You run faster here and suffer more when your body energy is used up. During a 50, you're taking in nourishment, and because your speeds are slower, you hit the wall slower and become more adjusted to it. You know you're miserable, but you expect a 50 to do that to you anyway. You, or I, seem to ignore the pains of a 50 more than a 26 miler.

By mile 21, I was starting to run through my wall, but with five miles left, I wanted this to end. It became one step at a time as I passed Sac State College and went into town. The Capitol was getting closer, but I more weary. Some athletes were good at this, and they were far ahead. Some weekend warriors were behind me, but I wasn't satisfied as the Capitol came into sight and the finish line took so long to close in on me. Gordy came in later and we got a ride back to Folsom for our cars. I had finished my first marathon in 4 hours 16 minutes, a slow time for competitors, an accomplishment for me.

I ran a couple more marathons during the next years of training, only to prove myself right. This wasn't my forte, and I'd have to leave it alone. As I ran more 50's, I found that I did better, felt better, and accomplished more. The American River 50 was one I enjoyed the most, from Sac. State over to Folsom, then up to Auburn, finishing at the Western States Trail near my house. I was familiar with these trails and couldn't wait to work my way down the bike trails from Sacramento to Folsom to get on the dirt where I learned so long ago to be comfortable. Other runners hated this part of the trail. Rocky, narrow, and easy to turn an ankle, the last 20 were demanding, as 50's go. This was my area to catch up to those marathon runners pushing the bike trails under their feet so effortlessly. Carrying food and water with me, I was prepared for the climb to Auburn. Nine to ten hours were my entry zones to the finish lines. I was pleased whenever I finished. Dennis tried twice to complete a 50. It wasn't his specialty, and he settled into 10 to 20 milers. I always admired Dennis's drive. He wasn't a born runner but tried very hard.

My training seemed to leave Dennis behind some. He'd go with me on some runs. I'd go alone on others. Many times, Dennis and I'd go out, and later that night I'd go do a second run. By 1984, I was running 100 miles a week. It was all consuming. Anything I did was either work or run. There was no time for Paulette or the family, certainly no time for home chores. Any spare hour I had, I spent running somewhere, resting, and getting ready for work. I was training with the experienced runners now, Bruce, Rex, and the Club we had started a couple of years earlier, Sierra Express. 1985 was the year I was to decide whether I wanted to challenge the Western States or not. My training regime was more than a marriage could take and Paulette and I were very distant. She no longer supported my running or my lack of attention to the family, and our marriage was very weak. We had little interest in each other and were clearly going our own ways. My training wouldn't survive another year while leaving from the same house and it was time for a decision. I filled out the application with trepidation and sent it in with my entry fee. That's not enough for the Western States. All entries are thrown into a hat and the lottery will decide which 300 will be accepted. I got a pass on the lottery for the many years I had worked the event on the motorcycles. My acceptance came in the mail, and I opened the letter like a high school grad looking to see if he got accepted for college. I was in, and now the serious training was to begin.

Heat, rain, cold, day, night, none of it mattered. We were on the trail pushing ourselves. Could I have run that last section better? Should I rest during this next stage? Should I run this hill, or take it slower and save energy? Everything was a decision. When a run was through after work that day, frequently I'd get up in the middle of the night to do another 10 miler to No Hands and up Stagecoach. My drive had become all-consuming and self-induced. Paulette had given up on me by now and hated the thought of the Western States Run. Who could blame her? She was a married widow.

Sometimes when the fatigue and despair were too much to put the shoes on that day, one of my running buddies would call to ensure I was coming out. Ten to fifteen miles a day were enough, if you had a rest day somewhere along the week. But to get the 100-mile week, I'd have to go long on the weekend. As the event grew nearer, I'd back up a long Saturday run with another long Sunday run.

"Where you want to run to today?" was the question posed after a few miles out. "I don't know, how about that far mountain over there?" a buddy would say, and we'd start in that direction. Not knowing how far it was, or how to get there, we'd go out for the hours on the trail. Even now I was unable to talk while trying to breathe, but I listened as others told me their stories. Nothing said on the trail ever leaves the trail, an unspoken fact that had never been broken. I was probably fortunate I couldn't talk and run at the same time. Most of the runners didn't mind talking to me. Not because I was a good listener, or even a thoughtful participant in their solo conversation. Probably more so because they didn't have to look at me while they revealed their secrets. I wore a face mask when I ran. A white one with a rubber band wrapped around my head. It staved off the pollen the others were breathing without concern. I only had to look at the mask at the end of the day to see what I had avoided. Embarrassed most of the time at needing to wear the mask, I explained that I was just too ugly to look at.

A month before the event, Paulette had suffered enough. She couldn't take it anymore, nor could I. Devastated, I told her I was going to quit. I wasn't going to train or run next month. I was through, and I genuinely gave up. I hated her for it but wouldn't fight her any longer. It was a wonder she hadn't left me long ago. My forfeiture was more of a psychological surrender to the pressure of the impending and most challenging event of my life. Through our contempt for each other's views, Paulette found it within her to visit our Pastor. Ralph and Sandy spoke frankly to Paulette and told her that whether my focus was right or wrong, I truly felt it was directed from God, and I had to see it out. They were right, but I too was wrong. I failed to realize that God had spoken to me, not her. I was expecting her to have the same enthusiasm. What I was willing to do to see this through was more than I should have expected Paulette to put up with. "One more month and this will climax," they offered Paulette, and she listened. She came back to me with a vow that she'd support me to the end and made every effort to do just that. Sandy, a recreational runner herself, offered to help me if she could, and I put together a team of pacers who could run with me from Foresthill on. Sandy from Foresthill to White Oak Flat, John E. from White Oak to Rucky Chuck, and Dennis would take me in the final 20. Dennis knew me well, my strengths and weaknesses, my tolerances, and failures. He learned on his own when asthma was about to visit. My left elbow would go numb. Shortly afterward my snake was coming. How he learned this I'll never know, but I always knew Dennis was watching when I'd hear, "How's your elbow, Duane?"

A week before the Run, we taper off and carbo load. Our bodies starve for exercise and the accustomed run. Carb loading is in preparation for overfilling your body with fuel that turns to energy. First you starve yourself of any carbohydrates. After your body is screaming for a fix, you cram as much as you can in, to culminate the day of the event where it's to be used up in the upcoming hours. This takes its toll on the body, and many can't do it at all. I didn't care about my body complaining to me and didn't mind making it suffer.

Something caught me a week before the Event. Whether pollen, the food change, stress, I'll never know, but I did know that I was in a full-blown asthma attack. Unable to breathe or recover, Paulette rushed me to the hospital. I was in the best condition of my life, preparing to tackle the toughest test of my life, and I was rendered impotent by the snake that followed me through my life. This training, dedication, focus, drive, and fixation I had on this event was about to take me into a chasm of failure. The doctor looked me over, diagnosed the need for strong treatment, and left the room to prepare for a shot, inhalers, and a possible admission and undetermined stay. It was difficult to hide from Paulette the stream of tears as I turned my head to avoid her seeing. I wondered how I had been so mistaken. I had come so far yet grown so little.

Doctors are professional miracle makers, and after a few hours I was able to leave the hospital with Paulette. I felt better the next day, but wasn't up to par. It was time to taper off from running and start the starving process. It took little effort for me to comply with my own strategy. What I didn't know was whether I should go to the Start Line or not. Paulette was the deciding factor when she clearly convinced me there was no choice. If God had set me on this path, he would see me through it. "Was I about to test God?" I wondered. I didn't know. I hoped he'd forgive me if I was.

I got a call from the Western States' official doctor during the final week before the event. He wanted to see me at his office in Roseville. I was sure it was about my asthma. Out of caution was he going to pull me from the event? I drove to Roseville entangled in a myriad of mixed emotions and thoughts. Arriving there I was soon to learn the reason for his request. Paulette accompanied me as we met with a team of doctors who had flown out from Sweden. They were studying muscle death and hoped I would cooperate as one of their test creatures. Muscle death was believed to be caused when one pushes themselves past the point of no return yet keeps pushing. The body eats up all its fuel sources in carbs and sugars, and then relies on the poorer source of body fat for fuel to turn to energy, and when that's no more possible, the body will start to eat its own muscle tissue for fuel. This muscle tissue is permanently destroyed and cannot re-heal itself. The study was focused on observing how much muscle death actually occurred during an event like this. Many doctors firmly maintained even after seeing this event that it was physically impossible for the human body to run 100 miles. They were right then and are even today. It is impossible. The only way it's done is through the mind. The strong-willed ones might make it. Anything less has guaranteed results. The doctors found amusement in seeing the type of people that were going to challenge this inconceivable objective. I agreed to a pre- and post-scan of my legs along with some other poking and prodding, and the doctors started their tests.

I was about to face another challenge that I hadn't expected. For the last six years, I had thought of running the Western States every day, several times a day, and sometimes for hours through the day. Not a day passed that I didn't envision trying to run the W.S. As the months grew closer to June 1985, I was so focused on it that it was all consuming. All I thought about was the event. All I planned for was the Run. All that kept me going was the preparation. It was about to arrive. My life was about to peak - and I didn't know how to handle it.

I drove up to Tahoe every day for a week before the Event to try to acclimate myself to the high elevation. It was more psychological than practical, as you have to spend more time than an hour or so to acclimate to the altitude, but some runners succumbed to altitude sickness, and I wasn't about to let that happen to me. Ben, at work, rented a condo for our family for the week and I gave it to Pastor Ralph and Sandy until Friday, when I was to come up to prepare for the run Saturday at 5:00 a.m. They were both encouraging when we exchanged places at the condo. They were headed back to Auburn. We were to stay the evening and hope to get some rest.

I checked in as a participant, carried a gallon of water with me, and forced as much down as I could before refilling and forcing again. I was tanking up and wouldn't fail to fill my body with as much water as it would hold. That night we went to dinner in Tahoe City where I carbo loaded on spaghetti until I couldn't force feed it any longer. I was as prepped as I was going to be, and the bed was waiting for my restless turnings.

4:00 a.m. found me wide awake and wondering what I was actually doing here. Paulette seemed to take it as another day but shared my excitement as well. We drove to the parking lot at Squaw Valley where 300 other insomniacs had gathered, and we waited for the inevitable. Paulette and the kids were on a mound next to me as I let the real runner's step up ahead toward the start line. I was in a daze as the noise from the helicopter swooped in and hovered just feet overhead. A familiar noise to me, but I hadn't expected the camera man to be hanging over the side trusting that his harness would keep him from visiting us up close and personal. ABC's Wide World of Sports came out to film the event. Some waved at the cameraman as the helicopter hovered. I preferred to remain anonymous. The countdown commenced and my life was about to change in one direction or the other. I hadn't had time to question my sensibilities when the mass of runners left the parking lot at Squaw at the 6,200-foot level and commenced their move up the 2500-foot climb in the next four miles. Normal people take the ski lift during the winter months. Once at the top we would travel west, climbing another 15,540 feet and descending 22,970 feet before reaching Auburn. Over 37,000 feet in elevation change, with temperatures between 32 and 105 within hours. The onset of our run over the top of the mountain and down into the wilderness and deep canyons had begun. Many expected the downhills to be their saving grace. Those would be the ones who would soon learn of the fire that would burn in their quads before the run was half through.

Last year, the mountainside we were to run up at the start was covered with snow. It was snow that plagued many of the runners for over 20 miles afterwards. You never knew what to expect each year and I had planned and conducted several tests to determine the best way to negotiate the snow during this first section. Our snow fears were put to rest as this year brought little in the form of sticking snow, causing an added difficulty for the runners. Instead, we were treated with a different surprise. Unknown to us by no other means than a forecast, the temperatures were to soar at 114 degrees in the canyons. I knew that out of the 415 runners who started the race, many had not honed their heat training to a level that would have them survive the next 24 hours. Many runners would be forced to drop due to hyperthermia, dehydration, exhaustion, and an environment just too hostile to endure.

We found the Emigrant Pass Monument at the end of our 4-mile climb and took little notice of the altitude revealed at 8,750 feet. I felt remarkably good after cresting the ski slopes to the top. This is where my lungs would scream the most but veins full of adrenaline seemed to scare my snake away. I'd always run in oxygen debt. I'd become used to the starvation, but this was better than I had feared it might be, and I was looking onward toward the next target. We were to turn toward the wilderness area. Our next stop would be Hodgkin's Cabin, only a short way out. From there the Lyon Ridge area, still at altitude where my biggest weaknesses were. I focused on not catching any other runners, nor allowing them to catch me. I'd learned long ago that misery loves company. When two runners meet, they tend to run together for a while, normally at the slower runner's pace. I wasn't going to let another runner dictate my pace, or my strategy. I'd do this one alone.

Lyon Ridge, at 10 miles out, is a beautiful run along the high mountain ridge. You'll run for as far as you can see, then pick a new distant target. The miles slid between my feet as I practiced what I had learned, to lift them only inches off the ground, yet over rocks and debris. Those less educated would suffer consequences for their errors. Today, this day, a stone in your shoe or slightly twisted ankle could prey on your mind, breaking concentration that your body would demand, and you're no longer the master of your fate. As fatigue takes over, any annoyance you give leave to ponder will become your destroyer. Every step, every movement, every breath, everything you drink, everything you eat will all demand their reward or consequences 12 hours from now. Six years of training culminated in this day. There would never be another chance, no more opportunities. Today I would win or lose, but I knew I'd never be back. Neither my marriage nor my job would make their sacrifice again. I had never given any thought to finishing over the 24-hour mark. It wasn't even a consideration. Under 24 or run myself into the ground, the latter acceptable if it accomplished the first. Up to this point in time fewer than 2000 of the best ultra long-distance runners in the world had finished this Event in less than 24 hours. I wasn't even in their class. I had no business being here, but somehow God was going to run with me, if he had really spoken to me six years ago. I had plenty of time to lose my focus. Alone on a trail, miles from anywhere, is a lonely place to be, and solitude becomes your friend.

Drink, drink, and drink some more. Eat a candy bar, a banana, or crunch bar smashed in my fanny pack, near the snake bite kit and asthma spray. No cell phones, no radios, nothing to bring me back to civilization, I had only one thing to focus on - the next aid station.

I was looking forward to climbing Cougar Rock at 13 miles out. It's a famous photo opportunity for enthusiasts who want to venture into the high country. There would certainly be spectators there encouraging us as we climbed the massive outcropping. It'd be a way to break the isolation and steal some energy from those appreciating us. Cougar Rock came and passed. I was refreshed and ran on.

At 16 miles, it was up on Red Star Ridge that I caught and passed Gordy while climbing a hill. "Looking good, Gordy," I offered as I passed on his left. "You too, Duane." Passing another runner was a common occurrence as they fade in and out during the day and into the night. Long distance runs were a place where a pass was never a final standing. I didn't care

whether Gordy passed me miles ahead or not. I was racing a ticking clock, not my old friend.

Duncan Canyon was a major Aid Station at 23 miles, where doctors would weigh and check you for weight loss or other signs of failure. It was wise to get in and get out of there as soon as I could. I could re-supply my pack once away from the station. I left Duncan Canyon without concern from the doctors and left for the push down into the canyon, across the river, and the long steep climb up to Robinson Flat. It was time for the weather forecast to prove its message. The heat in the canyon was morbid, and you could see the distorted air rising from the canyon walls and floor. Deeper we went, knowing that stagnant heat awaits our arrival.

Shoes get wet and feet blister. Sweat was enemy enough. I carried a second pair of socks to change between Check Points. I had planned on taking my shoes off and carrying them across the river between Duncan and Robinson. I almost failed that test for fear of stopping too long to take them off and put them back on, on the other side. But I still had my judgment and forced myself to comply with my own pre-race strategy. Shoes back on now, tightly secured, I commenced the unwelcome climb up the mountain to Robinson Flat.

Robinson greeted us at 30 miles. It meant we had been down inside the gorge and back out the first time. We had two more trips down in before Auburn became a closer reality. I checked out good at Robinson and was happy to see Paulette, Mom, and the others there to crew for me. They changed my shoes and socks while I sat to catch my breath. They refilled my bottles and pack and sent me on my way before allowing me to relax. Each extra minute you spend at a Pit Stop is multiplied tenfold later down the trail.

Just after Robinson Flat, Cavanaugh Ridge meandered across the top of the mountains before dropping down into Deep Canyon One, then Deep Canyon Two. Cavanaugh was famous for bees and rattlesnakes. As we got closer to Foresthill, bears were a bigger concern. I passed a hive that was swarming on the trail and ran through it as though unconcerned. I was neither stung nor chased. I was neither surprised nor relieved. I just didn't have time to be bothered by either. There was a lot of Manzanita and brush on Cavanaugh. It lent little relief to the scorching heat. Mom had built a hat for me, a ball cap with a white drape down my back to keep the sun off my neck. I had her sew a zippered fish net pouch on top that replaced the normal cloth. At each Aid Station my crew would refill my hat with ice. I carried it on my head until it melted down my back, cooing my spine. It was a welcome relief to feel the chill in my hair then on my back, even though I was to feel that relief for only the next few minutes before the ice melted.

Dusty Corners at 38 miles was properly named, and it presented its hampering characteristics after the climb out of Deep Canyon Two. We had come so far yet had so far to go. Dusty Corners was neither a goal nor an accomplishment. It was just Dusty Corners, a place to arrive at and put behind you as soon as you could. The climb up Deep Canyon Two was long and deceiving. Many felt it should be run at a good pace. Others saw the folly in implementing a plan that way for themselves. If you ran out of Deep Canyon Two, you'd have to recover in time to make the horrendous climb up to Devils Thumb. This was a difficult decision for me, as I knew I could run out of D.C. Two. What I wasn't confident of was the toll it'd take when trying to make the upcoming climb out of the second gorge coming up. I chose to take the chance of falling behind and jog more slowly out of D.C. Two. I recognized that I was nervous as I hit Dusty Corners sometime back. My second pit crew fueled me up and sent me on my way. Last Chance was ahead, and just past it, the massive drop down into the gorge once again, then up to Devils Thumb. I tried to psych myself up for this. It's where many runners go down and can't make it back up. Walking up to the Thumb was commonplace and a good plan, but just getting out of this gorge was an accomplishment under any condition.

I arrived at Last Chance at 43 miles out and detoured into the Aid Station for food and water. Leaving at the same time as some other runners, we ran the next couple miles of trail together. I was in front, but they were right behind. I didn't like that. I was enjoying the companionship too much. I had to break away somehow. Maybe the gorge would do it. The two runners behind me were German, and likely here specifically for the Run. They spoke German to each other, and I couldn't understand a word. I didn't know if they were just being comfortable talking amongst themselves, or still mad about the war. I didn't ask, but their conversation was labored, and their voices fatigued. I could tell by the sound of their conversation and demeanor that they weren't doing well. One of them spoke up to me in a heavy accent, "Hey, do you know if there are many more mountains up ahead?" he said in a labored voice. My heart fell when I heard his question. We were barely halfway, and I couldn't bring myself to telling them. "A few," I said while thinking of the arriving deep gorge we were about to enter, "Hang in there, you guys are looking good." In a heavy German accent and broken English, I knew what he meant when he said, "Ohhhhhhh." I never saw them again.

I learned after years of training that my strength was the up hills. The downhills were used to make up time or rest. The up hills were an obstacle to conquer. I had the strength to climb the hills if my lungs would give me oxygen. My long-injured back wouldn't take the pounding of a downhill pace. It was no advantage for me to try to run the down hills faster. I maintained my pace during the steep downhill switchbacks that descended past The Slide, and to the bottom where the Swinging Bridge marked our change over from descent to ascent. A force walk was as good as it gets for all but the best, climbing up to Devils Thumb at 48 miles. Those that could still force walk out were in good shape. Those that couldn't, forgave themselves and reset their goals to the 30-hour mark. It was two miles up the far face of the gorge. Each step was an effort that didn't want to be duplicated. Forty-Six tight switchbacks came and went slowly. The 114 degree heat caused nausea that wouldn't go away until you got respite from it, and that relief was slow in coming with such a climb challenging our determination. I force walked out, knowing where I was at all times. I've been here before. It was a gift from God when I saw Jim, from my pit crew, standing alongside the trail. As part of my crew, he could walk down so far, but couldn't aid me in getting out, nor carry anything out for me. He didn't ask - neither did I. He radioed up to the rest of the crew how I looked and what I needed. They had everything at the ready when I crested the top, but what I needed most was rest. They made no such offer.

The run along the top of Deadwood was another familiar trail to me and I found relief in knowing what was up ahead. The next drop down into El Dorado Canyon was another multi-miler, but not as tough as that behind me. I was much more tired now, and even the less tiring trail ahead would seem worse than what lay behind. Past the Cemetery and over the side, I prepared to drop down into the next gorge. The foot bridge at the bottom was at 53 miles and familiar to me. A few spectators had gathered down there to see the stupid people in running shoes. The climb out was unbelievably long and torturous. It was nothing spectacular when compared to miles past, but I wasn't feeling good, and I wasn't able to tackle this climb with enthusiasm. I was ashamed of myself as I crested the Canyon and entered the little town of Michigan Bluff, 55 miles out.

Another popular Aid Station, it was more than tempting to spend an extra minute there to answer questions from friends or others. The next section was commonly known to be one of the hottest, and I was hitting it during the hottest time of the day. I arose from my lawn chair after my shoes and socks were changed for me and started to walk out of town. "That would never be", I said to myself as I picked it up to a jog. The upcoming dirt road would guide me through the Manzanita and rolling mountains. I had but to follow it, turn after turn. The next canyon was smaller in size, but my nausea hadn't subsided, and my lungs needed air. I made the drop and passed a couple of runners who were also not doing so well either. "I can handle this better than they", I said to myself while thinking back to dirt bike days. I continued down, across the stream with no bridge, and started the climb up to Bath Road. I found that closing my eyes for 3-4 seconds at a time was a way to get some rest. I had to check the trail before doing it, and I got too accustomed to it. I liked the rest and my mind started to give in to the fatigue. Waking myself up in fear, I pushed on toward the top of Bath Road. Once there, it was a 2 mile soft descent down into town.

It was late afternoon when I hit Foresthill and the 62 mile marker. Two hours ahead of my schedule to reach Placer High in under 24. I don't know how I did it, but the clock told me I was doing something right. I took an extra minute at Foresthill and picked up my first pacer, Sandy. Kissing Paulette good-bye, Sandy  and I headed out through Todd Valley toward White Oak Flat. Sandy was more of a blessing than she knew. Not only had she talked Paulette into accepting this day, but she was Pastor Ralph's wife, and we exchanged scripture verses for my own encouragement. Sandy had a good pace as she neither pushed me ahead nor dragged me behind. I knew with certainty that if a runner didn't look good going into White Oak Flat at 74 miles, the doctors would keep him there until he either recovered or was pulled from the race. My two crews had performed flawlessly, and White Oak was no exception. I was beginning to think that they really expected me to finish this run. Well, I wasn't going to let them down. I entered the Aid Station with an old familiar Marine Corps

OooooooRaaaaaa, and stepped up on the scales. "How do you feel?" she asked. "Fine Ma'am, just waiting to get released so I can get back underway." "You're good to go," I heard with relief. Vomiting and diarrhea were commonplace by now and it was expected that all would suffer these familiar formalities. Other ailments were tolerated, but weighing in and out of the White Oak Flat Aid Station meant I was

maintaining fluids, and it was encouraging that I hadn't been questioned any farther. I quickly gathered my things and, saying good-bye to Sandy, went out with my second pacer, John E. It would normally be considered a leisurely descent down to Ruck-a-Chucky from White Oak, but this was no leisurely event. I ran when I could. The four miles down to the river crossing were challenging only by way of my goal to reach the river before dark. It wasn't an arbitrary goal set without

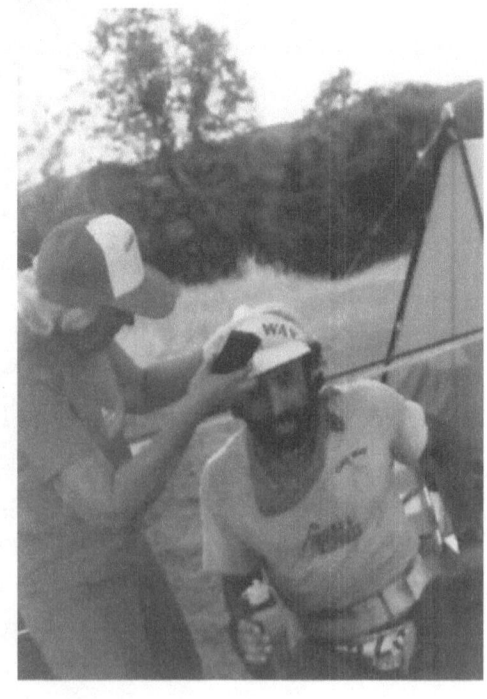

thought. I knew that the river by dark was necessary due to the known delay there, the helpful aid station with ample food and other invitations that lured you to stay for a minute, and my SAR Team would be there as part of their sweep of the trail. I pulled down onto the river embankment at Ruck-a-Chucky on time. This was a major location at 78 miles from the onset of this contest several hours ago. Outdoor lights were coming on, but I hadn't used my flashlight yet. I was still on time, and still two hours ahead of schedule for Placer High School. Getting across the river was an event that was looked forward to, feared, and much publicized. Many photos were taken at the River Crossing, where the water was lowered by the Dam above on the day of the Event so runners could wade across. A cable was stretched from bank to bank to catch falling runners before being swept downstream. The runners and pacers could be determined by the color of the number patch each wore. The runners could be helped across; the pacers were on their own. The shock noticeably took over your body as you stepped into the icy water and waded deeper, up to your shorts. If it weren't for the cable, the instant seizing of your hot leg muscles would send 9 out of 10 downstream in a swim for life. The race organization had tried in the past to ferry runners across in small boats but found that not only was it logistically challenging and unfair to some waiting longer than others, but against the natural environment of the event itself. The runners were to do it themselves. Step by step over the slippery boulders underfoot meant some would get more than their legs wet. "Do you wear shoes or don't you?" was the decision each had to make for himself. If not, you waded barefoot through the rocks and sand. If yes, you came out with wet shoes and certain blisters a short distance away. I said, yes, when I planned this portion of the race. I'd wade with my shoes on for safety, and change them with a fresh pair, brought down by my SAR Team. It was the best choice, and I saw Buzz for the first time since my world started many hours before. I sat in the lawn chair as he rubbed my shoulders, clearly with pride. I was proud to have him there, too. Dennis picked me up as the pacer from here, and we passed the sweep bikes as I arose and started my climb up the mountain to the Green Gate. Only yards out of the Aid Station, I knew something was wrong. My lungs had given out. Twenty two miles left from the River to Home, and I could no longer breathe. Dennis had picked me up as my final pacer from the river, and he knew me well. I'd never given up a run in the past, either in practice or an actual event. He didn't consider it even a possibility here either. But the climb up to the Green Gate was the longest I'd taken in the race to date. I stopped, turned around to walk downhill for a time, turned to return back up, stopped to step aside, and let others pass, tried to move one foot forward, and found myself in a nightmare that I couldn't shake. Again, I was running from a monster and making no headway. The monster drew nearer and my efforts to run were in slow motion only. I was back in my dream that I'd had so many times before, and the snake had arrived.

The burning in my lungs was different than the usual onset of asthma. As my lungs constricted, I could feel the snake tighten to prevent another breath. This time there was no second half to my breathing at all. I couldn't force enough air in past the midpoint by inhaling. It was like I had no control over my lungs, and the inhaler was no improvement. I continued to climb, and Dennis encouraged each step, but this was really wrong. I'd never experienced this type of asthma before, and I didn't know how to deal with it.

I was intimate with this part of the trail as I'd swept it all night during times past and wanted my SAR Team to think well of me. "Rest a minute" was the only solution Dennis finally resolved us to, and at the Green Gate, I had no choice. I walked around, tried sitting, tanked up again, ate some food offerings, and tried to walk off the asthma that had found a home in my lungs once again. "It's time, we have to go, Duane," Dennis cautioned. Sicker than I'd been before, we headed out into the darkness with flashlights in hand.

When you're fatigued, monsters abound in the woods at night. My flashlight attested to each one as it reflected off the pine and oak trees lining the narrow trail along the ridge. A lion here, a bear there, a ghost over there, I was dodging nemeses at each turn. I was truly fighting for air now and each breath became an event of its own. "How you are doing, Duane?" Dennis called out from behind me. "Okay," was all I could muster, and I hoped that he'd believe me. "How's your elbow?"

I heard it so many times in the past. "Okay," was my monotone brief reply. I knew he was watching me, and I knew I was in need of it now. I couldn't focus on the trail and my foot frequently slipped over the soft edge, a significant drop in some places. Dennis had considered a slower pace in this heavily wooded area after dark and was watching me closely. I pulled into Auburn Lake Trails Aid Station at 85 miles, and I was struggling for something to hang onto for the long trip in.

Medical Staff from the National Guard were there for the first time this year. I got weighed and checked. The doctors seemed concerned, but I didn't know why. My weight was up, and I was hydrated. I hadn't told them about my breathing so what's the concern? A National Guard woman gently took me over to a lawn chair and pulled my legs up to a stool. She started messaging them and in seconds I had given up the effort to resist and move on. It was only seconds later when Dennis said we had to move on. "Give me just a minute, Dennis," I pled. "We've been here too long, Duane, WAY too long." I didn't put together what he was saying. My seconds turned into many minutes, and I lost them in the darkness. "It's time to go," was Dennis' prodding again, and I knew the tone. It was time to go.

Setting out from here was almost a whole new run, not in distance, but in drive. My mind had me far ahead and pushing for the goal line. By body was giving up and at midnight, one or the other was going to win. Making it in from here on a training day took four hours. I had only five to cross the line. I had lost all my two hour cushion somewhere back on the trail, or under a therapist's hands, I didn't know which. I cursed myself for forgiving my over-stay at A.L.T. I had to push hard now, but my lungs were not going to allow it. Each breath was only half taken in before the burning and inability to draw any harder took hold. Dennis no longer asked about my elbow. He was driving me on with the firmness of a gentle man.

We continued on, across the bottom of the quarry, to a climb Dennis and I had appropriately named, Ankle Alley. It had caught on and was now well named as such. The erosion, rocks, boulders, and debris in the trail claimed many victims as they drove themselves either up or down this path. Dennis watched me closely as I wove my way through this mile long minefield of dream stoppers. At the top, we entered the Highway 49 crossing at 91 miles. We were near Cool, where Dennis and I had run so many times. The trip in was intimately familiar, but my vision was bad, and I didn't recognize some things, even my pit crew. I heard them talking but couldn't understand what they were saying. I relied on Dennis to tell me when to get up. He did, all too soon, and I heard him yell back to camp as we struggled out, "No, he'll make it."

I had to force walk the climbs now; my right knee had given out for some reason. Making the turn at Pointed Rocks to drop down into the canyon again was mentally comfortable as I knew home was closer for me than for others. I knew where we were. Gordy caught me at Pointed Rocks from the pass I had put on him way up in the high country and tried to talk a little. Dennis told him something. Gordy followed me for a mile or more before passing on a downhill. "I've got to go, Duane, you're not going to make it," he mumbled as he passed. It was a shock to me to hear that. Was I losing everything and not knowing it? Were they seeing things I couldn't? I couldn't read my watch, and Dennis wouldn't tell me what time it was. He just said we had to push harder.

Each step became a more pronounced shuffle, but I pushed onward toward No Hands below. I arrived and stepped onto the dirt surface of the Bridge. We had made it to 95 miles. Mom and Paulette were there, and they bandaged my knee. It gave me a break from the 2-mile climb out of the canyon ahead, a trip I had made several days a week for the last six years. I knew each step but was afraid this time I couldn't run it out. Could I even walk out? How long would it take?

Dennis pushed me to run when I could and let me walk the steeper parts. We made it to Robie Point where the trail had normally turned onto the paved road for the final leg home to the High School. This year the Event was extended in length to make it an official 100+ miles and we had to run along the side of the canyon to the Auburn Dam overlook, and in from there. It was a long miserable trip filled with self-inflicted torture. Dennis tried to keep me distracted from the suffocation and pain each part of my body was screaming about. It took so long to reach the staging area for the Trail where I'd seen so many horse trailers each weekend for years past. We turned away from the High School and

Dennis pulled alongside as we hit the pavement. There were flashlights ahead of me. I didn't turn around to see what was behind. "We've got to push, Duane, no more walking." A girl and her pacer passed me as I picked up the speed. It was okay, it was Jan. I knew her and we had run together before. We spoke no words that I can recall, but she was a familiar face. "You're not going to let her beat you in, are you?" was Dennis' challenge. I understood, and shuffled a wider stride, around to Auburn Folsom Road and down to High Street where, quite by accident, my business office is today. As I passed the fairgrounds, I knew there was yet another hill up to the High School. "How's he doing?" I heard from a dark figure next to Dennis now. I looked to see my old friend, Pastor Ralph. We had less than a mile to go, I didn't know what time it was, and I was digging for the last bit. Dennis and Ralph easily ran along side of me as we turned onto Finley and could see the entrance to the football field several blocks up. A flashlight was flickering in front of me, and I knew another runner was finishing his drive for another episode in life. I was always convinced that you don't deplete everything during a training run, but in a race if you have anything left at the end, you didn't try hard enough. I could smell the crowd at the High School, and I knew Mom and Paulette, the two most important women in my life, were there waiting for me to round the corner and step onto the track for the last few hundred yards around to the finish line. I passed the runner ahead of me and found it to be Jan, the same woman who passed me a couple of miles earlier. "You're looking good," was all I could muster, I still didn't know what time it was, or if I was over or under my 24 hour belt buckle. Dennis and Ralph deliberately faded back as I hit the track for one lap around to the finish line. My stride picked up, I took as deep a breath as I could, and vowed I'd go in like a Marine. Fifty yards later I was in a dead sprint to the finish, listening to the crowd cheer. I didn't know who it was for, but I soaked in the sound as I rounded the curve and looked at the banner across the track. *Don't stop early. Finish this at a run* was my promise to myself, and I saw it through. My crew grabbed me as I fell and held me up to usher me over to the scales. "Doctors weren't going to pull me now," I thought. After I stepped off, someone shuffled me to some cots where more doctors were checking, and one commenced a massage that I prayed would never end. It did soon enough, and I was helped to my feet. All of my pit crew was there, many from the church, personal friends, the TV crew, and some from work, even Ben. It was a proud day for me, and they allowed me to enjoy it while sharing it with me. I still didn't know whether my time was good enough, or second best in this test. I looked at Dennis and he read my mind. "23:38" was all he had to say. Under 24 hours.

Wide World of Sports was still at the High School, and I must have caught the eye of Diana Nyad somehow. She was the greatest long distant swimmer in the World at that time, and an announcer for Wide World of Sports. She came up to give me a hug and an offer of appreciation. I was flattered but unable to appreciate it. I had just experienced both, the "Thrill of Victory, and the Agony of --- Da Feet". The two-mile trip home was filled with thoughts. Some of which were in sympathy for those who had to drive to the airport. My trek would end in minutes. Theirs wouldn't begin until after the Ceremonies that afternoon.

I remember little being said during the short ride home. I struggled into the house and found the front steps had grown to an amazing size. Paulette ran the water, and I knew how comforting a shower would be. Getting my clothes off was another story, but eventually I stepped into the old fashion shower closet and slid the door closed. It was difficult to accept what I had done. *"It was a tough day"*, I thought as I looked at my body knowing I had to wash each part of it yet. My arm seemed to have grown much bigger than I remembered it to be, and it took so much time to wash it. "I didn't know my arm was so long", I thought, "And look at all these other parts that need washing. There are so many!" I counted each one as I lathered up. I didn't think I'd ever get it all done. I was thankful when I finally stepped out of the shower only feet from the bed. I was done, I thought, I could lie down. But I was wrong. I had to get back in the shower and rinse off all that soap!

This experience became a 6-year adventure. Some would ask why? What would drive you to do such a thing? A simple answer awaits the question. God. This was not my doing, not my choice, not my desire, and certainly not within my ability. My forte was racing motorcycles.

I put that to sleep to follow God's direction and trained 6 years before the day that he spoke of came to pass. Many of us have heard God, whether it's in your ears, your heart, or your mind. God speaks to all of us, and in different ways. He spoke to me about this mind boggling adventure. Had I not listened and obeyed, he would not have said it again. At least to me. Following his guidance, he showed me that the impossible is possible. It must be said that there is nothing special about me. Nothing about my abilities, talents, or natural abilities that isn't in the same person standing next to me. You. You may not be called to run 100 miles, but God has spoken to you and will speak to you again, if you promise to listen. He enjoys listeners and blesses those who move as he directs. You'll have your opportunities in the future. You might be having one now. Not sure? Ask him. No, I don't mean question him, just ask him, "God, is that you and are you telling me -----------?" He doesn't mind. God is very polite and doesn't want you confused about anything. In fact, if he talks to you and gives you a word, as he did me at No Hands Bridge, if you ask him to he'll confirm what he said to you. Look for that confirmation if you're unsure. It could be through another person, a Pastor, friend, Godly man or woman, or an event or experience. Once you know it's God who has spoken to you it's your job to move on it and follow it through. God won't speak to you and then abandon you. Wait a minute. Did I just say that? Well, the book hasn't concluded yet. You'd better keep reading.

The goal of every participant in this event, previously declared as being impossible, was to reach the Finish banner before daylight. At this point in time only 2,000 of the best ultra-long-distance runners in the world were reported to have accomplished that goal.

God's voice was real 6 years earlier when standing over the canyon looking at the last line of runners crossing No Hands Bridge. "You're going to run this," was all he spoke.

Diana Nyad, long distance swimmer, worked for Wild World of Sports at the time. She took time to briefly talk with me about the run. I was honored that she did.

And we close the page on the infamous clock where everyone who started this crazy event prayed they'd arrive here to read it before it turned to 24:00:

CHAPTER 13

My Fall From Grace

This is the most difficult chapter to write. I've been lamenting even the thought of putting this to a written page. Honesty and integrity prevail, and all must be told, as it happened. That, in itself, is an elementary recognition. The difficult part is walking your talk. As you have seen, some of my life has been accompanied by glorious adventures. On the flip side, some of those adventures were less than admirable. Yet they, too, are accompanied by lessons. These lessons are revealed for those who wish to learn from someone else's bad experiences rather than experiencing it on their own. Those that don't might be self-assigned to duplicate an unenjoyable lesson that may have otherwise been avoided. As God directs my hand at revealing the lessons I've learned from all my experiences, I find there to be no coincidence that this experience falls under #13. So, here we go.

The next few weeks after Western States were filled with pride and accolades. I enjoyed that but wanted to get back to health as soon as I could. Out of 294 starters, only 163 had finished, and only half of the finishers did it in under 24 hours. I was one of the lucky ones. My 81st place finish brought me a silver belt buckle.

My walk was more of a hobble, and encountering stair steps was a chore. I revisited my Swedish doctor friends, and they scanned my legs again. The dark masses were areas of muscle death and were prevalent from thigh to foot. I was amazed at what I was looking at, but not as alarmed as I probably should have been. I seemed to know I'd be okay. Three months later the doctors came back out for another re-exam. To all of our astonishment, the black masses were dramatically healing, and they now said muscle death was reversible. I'm sure they didn't conclude that based on my examination alone, but they did reassure me that I would continue to heal.

I was unable or unwilling to run for many months to come. I just couldn't put a pair of shoes on. I awoke to all that had passed me by during the last six years and had so much to catch up on. I had no goals for running now and Paulette wasn't going to tolerate me setting another one.

So, what do I do now? I was haunted by the vacancy, the voice, the void. I was, up to now, a driven obsessed man focused on a goal that I had doubts that I could achieve. My focus was all encompassing. Not a waking hour went by for 6 years that I didn't think about running Western States. When I slept, I dreamt about it. I found myself falling deeper and deeper into depression. The thing that commanded so much of my life for the last half decade was complete. The thing that pushed me, drove me, and fueled me was done. Work was routine with no notable accomplishments, and home life was getting tough. This was an emotional downhill slide and I could see I was on the edge of a precipice. I didn't know what to do, and it wasn't getting any better. Suddenly I went from an obsessed and driven man to someone who had no goals, no dreams, an no vision of future accomplishments. A vision for a future goal may not be a problem for some. For others it's a necessity of life, food for the sole, I had lost that and somehow felt like a useless shell wasting good air. I couldn't share that with anyone. I was still getting the occasional admiration and complements over Western States some months back. I imagined I must have been like a man addicted to drugs and had to immediately stop with nothing to help him through the withdrawals. I was so depressed and disillusioned that I could see my personality change, and the new traits didn't seem to be good ones. What was happening to me, and what can I do about it prayed on my mind. Yes, I was aware of how fortunate I was. Not only in hearing God speak to me, but in accomplishing such a task as W.S. where so many athletes better than I had failed. If I were smart I would have seen a mental health doctor, but I wasn't, and I didn't. Paulette seemed to be reaping the most concentrated consequences for my depression. Not deliberately, but because she was closest. We lived together, so she was able to see me at my worst, and she did. Complicating matters, she wasn't the type of person who would let my behavior go unchecked, or unquestioned. She frequently challenged me and I, in turn, responded to that challenge. Our relationship felt the strain and was about to break. Not because I wanted it to, I didn't, and hoped she didn't either. But more so because each of us was looking at this from our own perspective. I was desperate, she was fed up.

No answers came, but the depression got worse. Paulette was strongly against my going back to racing, but racing was all I had to turn to now, and I revisited my old friend, the dirt bike.

I met new friends out on the trail, and we'd ride together as in day's past. We'd share stories when stopping for lunch or packing up and I'd sometimes tell them about Western States, sometimes not. I soon became reacquainted with my talent on the motorcycle and was enjoying what I had missed. Foresthill was a playground, the rest of Northern California a race schedule. Top 10% was hoped for and often achieved. Sometimes I placed higher or won. Other times not as well, but always somewhere in the respectable finishing roster. I was admired as a good rider but thought of myself as less. You never heard me say I was good, but I always said, "I was someone who loved to ride." It was my routine humble but honest response.

Races came and went, each one a weekend event with a month to prepare. Finish one and prepare for the next. Preparation meant practicing and I did all I could. I was an accomplished rider, with a massive void.

Paulette and I seemed to argue on an everyday basis now. We stayed married because we loved each other, not because we were in love with each other. She couldn't see my position, nor I, hers. We went to counseling, and it helped each of us a little, until the next session. We spoke little to each other that wasn't a snap or a bark. I hated pulling into the driveway and frequently would sit in the car in front of the house before going in. I'm sure Paulette was grateful for that and dreaded hearing me pull up as well. I was lost, with no place to turn, and nothing to do. Life wasn't good. I knew it was my fault, but I couldn't change it, or change me. Paulette and I talked of and threatened divorce. Our past love was the catalyst keeping us together. The kids saw us argue and it was clearly affecting them and their schoolwork. We became emotionally very separated and if I wanted to say anything to her at all, I passed the message through the kids. Neither of us looked for an argument, nor did we pass one by. We had our mean words for each other every day. Loneliness was a prevailing factor in life for both of us, and mine was fueled by the massive loss of goals and direction after Western States was over.

We staged our motorcycles one morning in Foresthill and went out for our first ride of the morning. Back around 10:00 we rested a moment, refueled, and talked about where we'd go next. A pickup had arrived, and she was unloading her motorcycle. She looked over at us with a, "hello" greeting and we thought it strange a young girl out here. She came over to the group of us and introduced herself. She had brought her sister up to ride Foresthill but didn't know the area. She asked if she could go along with us. I was annoyed by her request. I was there to ride, not coast behind a couple of girls insuring they were okay. I caught myself feeling selfish for that, and agreed with the others she could come along.

Her young teenage sister, Shelly, was average at best, Pam was an accomplished rider on a sub-standard bike. I rode behind them to make up for my selfish first thoughts, and did what I originally objected to doing, ride drag. I helped Shelley through difficult areas. Pam had no such problems. That afternoon we returned to camp and the group of us offered our appreciation for her attempts to keep up.

We talked more as a group, and she invited herself to our next outing next week. She came without her sister. I came with the group I usually rode with.

That afternoon she talked about a bike she had for sale and by chance only, it was what I was looking for, for my kids, so I agreed to come look at it. She lived with her mother and several days later I drove down to see it. I liked it and bought it for Dee.

We talked some more during our deal, and as it was evening, she asked me to stay for dinner. I was uncomfortable, but excused it in the vein of harmless, and accepted. She was a nice girl, not pretty by my senses, and she had a terrible posture. She walked like a man. I like a female's posture and was attracted to Paulette's. Pam had no such attribute.

Cell phones were not a common everyday item then as they are today, but I needed one for my work and had it installed in the car. Pam called to ask some motorcycle questions and I felt guilty, but innocent. Her calls became more frequent, and we talked more often. She was only 22 years old, and I, 36. Our generations alone would protect us, however I found myself talking to her far too frequently.

She was a well-figured woman, but I found fault in her shape. Too this, or too that, was my unnatural but common way of protecting myself from being attracted to others. In this case, I really wasn't attracted to Pam, not sexually. Our conversations were comforting, and the companionship filled a portion of a void, but created another one. We saw each other more, and I was getting scared. I didn't like what was happening, and the guilt that I felt was sickening. Yet, the pull was still there. I had no intentions of leaving Paulette for this Pam, but I had no idea how to cease or end this relationship with her. She had become attached, and I was too weak or unwilling to sever the attachment.

She wanted to learn how to race, and I showed her some techniques and explained how the races took place. She had a true admiration for me, and it filled a void I discovered some time back. Even though that need was being fulfilled, I didn't know why I was really there, or what I really wanted to do. I knew what I was doing was wrong, and I knew that if no one else knew about it, God did. But I was trapped. I was in it, and I couldn't get out without hurting Pam. I didn't want to do that either. I allowed her to lead in the aggressive pursuer roll.

It was quite a while before we had our first sexual encounter. I had never pursued or tried. As out-of-the-ordinary as it sounds, I really wasn't trapped because of a sexual attraction. In fact, I was so disappointed and guilty, I didn't complete the act. "I've gone over the edge," was my thought the next day. "That's it; I'll never talk to her again." I refused to answer her incoming calls the next day, and hoped she'd get the message. She didn't, and I found my own weakness in not being able to tell her or call the relationship off. I didn't like myself for that either and we saw each other for months. I had all I could of the guilt, the pulling away from my home and family, the distance from God and my friends, and things were about to get worse.

Paulette called to let me know she had learned about Pam. She was hysterical, as could be expected, and wanted me out of the house. Pam, of course, took advantage of the opportunity and had me move in with her in a cottage behind Ben's, where she had previously rented. I was unhappy to the point of miserable. I didn't want to lose my marriage, as troubled as it was. I didn't want Pam, as young as she was, and I didn't want this life I had created for myself after falling prey to my own weaknesses.

I buried myself in work and racing. Work I could do alone, and I wanted it that way. I needed the solitude to talk to myself, and to God. Day after day went by while I sat for hours lamenting the position I had created for myself. I didn't blame Paulette. I didn't even blame Pam. This was my doing. I allowed it to happen. Whether caught at a weak time, or whether I aggressively pursued Pam, it didn't matter. I was wrong, and it was costing me my marriage. Oh yes, a rocky marriage to be sure, but after weeks of sitting alone, praying and reflecting on what had happened, I knew that the trials of our marriage were far better than the anguish of being with a woman that God did not place me with. A woman who clearly didn't care that I was married when she set her sights on me. A woman who was clearly more focused on her own happiness than anyone else's. A woman who would hurt whoever was necessary to accomplish her goals. None of these traits were in Paulette, and I wasn't used to them. No, this wasn't Pam's fault, but her character traits were the onset to the snowball as it started rolling. It was now at high speed, careening down a mountain that had no bottom in sight. I was a miserable man. I had hurt my wife and children, and I didn't know where to turn or how to get out of this. Church didn't seem to be the answer as my guilt frequently kept me away from there. When I did go, I snuck in and snuck back out. I didn't want anybody to see me. I certainly didn't want to talk to anyone, especially Pastor Ralph. He wasn't only our Pastor, but one of my closest friends. I knew I wasn't man enough to look at the disappointment in his face. No, it was better if I stay away from church. Those words were spoken to my heart many times. But it wasn't God talking to me. It was the enemy who was enjoying his romp through the valleys of my guilt with complete freedom. I was allowing him to do it. I deserved it, didn't I? It was a just consequence to lose my friends and my family, wasn't it? My own character mutilation was caused by no-one else but me, wasn't it? I could expect no tolerance or understanding, could I? There was no such thing as "the best of both worlds," and I deserved the newfound life of, "worst of both worlds," didn't I? I could expect nothing less than Paulette realizing I was not the man she married and go on to someone else, couldn't I? God had no choice but to turn aside and allow life's demons to have control over me. Life wasn't good. It was my own fault. I couldn't make it right. I had to learn to live with it.

Pam went along to my chosen races, and she also raced. She listened to my instructions and followed them closely. She had a talent that needed training, and she was getting it. Even I was amazed at her continued first place finishes. I was proud of her, but I resented her. Not for her success, but her demands. My racing, my preparation, my experiences, and my life became secondary to hers. If we were married, or even if I loved her, that would be okay. But we weren't and I didn't. I repaired her bike first, got her equipment first, got her entered in the races first, and insured she had all she needed first. I found her wanting and expecting it that way. Our give-and-take relationship was becoming a lot of give, and even more take, but we never argued, and that was a blessing beyond description. To live a peaceful life was the carrot dangling in front of me. Even if that peaceful carrot had not been there, I'd still be stuck in this life with Pam, but without any consolations at all. I had to find solace in this morbid peace.

The racing season ended, and scores were tallied. I had finished in my usual respectable top few percent. I was surprised this year as so much of my time was invested in Pam's racing. And how did she do? First place. She was appreciative of my teaching, and I was grateful that she recognized it. She was scheduled to attend a District awards ceremony and I drove her down for the evening event. I had my next lesson in store for me. No doubt she would be recognized for winning every race she entered, and rightfully so. But it seemed to present her with opportunities to "mingle" and join conversations with other groups of male racers that I didn't expect. She spent the evening enjoying this male companionship, and I had my wake-up call. This was just not what I wanted in life and the snowball continued to roll downhill. We spoke little on the way home, but at least we didn't argue. I wasn't going to, and I hoped she didn't want to. She didn't.

It was a large formal function on the far side of town. Her employer was hosting their yearly event and all employees were expected to attend. A suit and tie were the minimum attire, and I could expect this to be an expensive evening. My heart wasn't in it, and this snowball was at a full downhill run. I didn't know how to get out of where I was or where to go if I did. Only a few friends stuck this out with me. Paulette was too hurt to talk to, I couldn't turn to the Pastor after what I had done, and I needed a sign from God. Any sign. God, just talk to me and let me know you're there. Are you still around after what I've done? Do you still care after what I'm doing? Have you rightfully turned your back on me completely? Do you hear the prayers I send or have you closed your ears to me? I had so many troubles. If God would just speak to me and tell me what to do, I'd listen - or at least try.

I appreciate and enjoy anything that's well done, except meat. I don't care whether it's a football game or an opera, a completed work project or a fine original painting. If it's done well, I enjoy the opportunity to appreciate it. Normally I'll study it or watch it intently. Distractions from it are an annoyance. I find myself studying details of anything that's finely done. This was no exception. The banquet room that Pam's employer rented was the best I'd seen. The tables were not production type, but heavy, wooden and although identical, appeared individually made. White tablecloths weren't the restaurant or hotel type, but clearly fine Linen. The ornate silverware appeared to be real. The hardwood floor was massive and very detailed. Even the walls were covered in what could easily be determined to be a very expensive velvet covering. The dance floor was more of a presentation than it was an area to be used. The band members rose to the caliber of the event, both in their music and their attire. Overhead were massive chandeliers, numbering a dozen or more. Heavy brass and crystal, they had to be 10' or more in diameter. Each one identical to the others, they were a sight to see. They were about 20' in the air, yet still massive in size. Pam and I sat with two other couples whom neither of us knew. We were at the far rear of the banquet room, near a wall and only feet from a side door leading out into the hallway. It was closed and no-one seemed to use it. It was almost a perfect place for me to hide. We sat through a long multi-course dinner. It rose to the occasion, but my appreciation waned as guilt overwhelmed me, knowing I was someplace I shouldn't be, with someone I shouldn't be with. I quietly spoke to God asking Him how this going to end? Where is all this going? What should I do? How can I do it? I thought again about God and doubted that he'd care about me after becoming the kind of person I'd turned into. I spoke little to Pam, but I didn't want to be rude. There were others at the table, but we spoke only briefly with each other before they could tell I wasn't up to the task of socializing. Pam wanted to dance, but I found an excuse to decline. She was annoyed that I was killing the good time she expected to have this evening and I was sorry for that. It wasn't long after dessert that one couple decided to leave. I hoped I wasn't the cause of it. The remaining couple at our table rose to dance a few times, each time returning to the back of the banquet hall and the table we were assigned. Eventually, they laid claim to a new table up near the dance floor and Pam and I were left to ourselves. We sat quietly for an hour or so watching people, sipping coffee. I was miserable and guilty and hoped to leave soon. I'd occasionally send a prayer up to God about leaving, but more so over the situation I had created and was living in. I looked up at the massive ceiling and the giant chandeliers, hoping my prayers would make it up through them, up to God. If only He'd show me He could hear me, and He still cared. "I guess it's time to go," Pam said with disappointment. I agreed, knowing she was blaming me for the buzzkill. I felt so alone and abandoned, even though it was my own doing. There's no feeling like being separated from God, even if it's at your own hands, and I just didn't feel Him around anymore.

We rose and Pam put on her coat. I looked around as she did and absorbed the beauty of this room one more time. My eye caught the chandelier's a last time, and I concluded my thoughts with the recognition that I didn't belong or deserve to be in such a place.

Pam turned toward the main entrance across the room, and I motioned to her, pointing in a manly fashion toward the side door only a few feet away. She accepted my suggestion without comment, and we turned together toward the nearby door. Taking five to six steps, we reached the side door and it opened easily, exposing the hallway leading to the parking lot. Pam stepped through the door first, and as I started to step through it behind her, when the explosion came. The sound was deafening, almost overpowering. Its intensity was far more than anything else I'd encountered since my military days. Without thinking, it caused me to bend over in a protective posture. Pam was in front of me, and the explosion was behind me. Instinctively I felt that Pam was out of danger. I was frozen in position in the doorway and immediately mentally surveyed myself to see if I was alright. I seemed to be. Looking at Pam I could see she was ok. I looked behind me for what had happened. What I saw was no less than amazing. Hanging directly above the table where we were seated was one of those beautiful chandeliers. It had given way to unknown pressures and fallen from the ceiling, 20' above, directly onto our table. The massive fixture that I had been enjoying had completely disintegrated the table and chairs we were assigned to and the size of it covered the area where both Pam and I were seated. Without question, anyone seated at this table would have been crushed. God had protected us and held that chandelier in place until we left the table. God had been hearing me. I didn't deserve it, but he wanted me to know he was still there.

The following day I contemplated how to re-introduce myself to church, and my friend. The problem was solved when the phone rang. It was Ralph, who hoped I'd come and see him to talk. I was grateful and immediately agreed to meet with him. I sought help with Pastor Ralph, and in doing so he was gentle in his responses. He seemed to understand without condoning. We had multiple conversations, and each helped, but I still didn't know where life was going. I certainly didn't want it to be with Pam. We had little in common other than our love for motorcycles. She had become the taking partner, I the giving. I got little from the relationship, yet I was deep in a place I didn't want to be. I spent time fixing her truck or bike or working late. Paulette would call occasionally, and we'd talk. We never really agreed on how our relationship went bad but at least we were talking. We sought Pastor Ralph together and knew that we should make our marriage work. I knew I was in this place because of the voids I had in my life. Some I caused myself, some were created by Paulette. Regardless, these voids didn't justify what I had done, or where I'd been. My guilt was overwhelming, but Paulette wanted me back and I wanted to go. I had but to break it to Pam.

She apparently knew something had been wrong between us when she walked into the cottage after work. She'd been crying and said only, "You'd better go back to your wife." Her tone of voice was begging for me to deny her suggestion and commit to her, but I couldn't. This was my chance to turn around and go home and I agreed with her. Shocked, she accepted it, and I went out to continue working on her car. Later, she came out and asked me not to leave her stranded without a car and her motorcycle needed repair. I agreed to complete those tasks, but I'd move out at the end of the month. It was a struggle to keep my time commitment as the repairs took more time and money than I had. I finished the projects barely in time, packed my clothes, and after she went to work, I went home. The past year was a nasty guilt-laden trip to Hell, and I had no idea what lay ahead.

Lisa and Dee were happy to have me home. Nicki was not. "Why don't you go back to her?" was frequently said by Nicki and I knew she had a dislike for me. It hurt me deeply, but she had a right. Lisa and Dee had forgiven, Nicki had not. Paulette was trying, so was I, but the road to healing would be long, dark, with many ruts, and would take much work. The damage was permanent, the forgiveness slow. Life wasn't instantly good at home, although Paulette and I tried hard to find common ground and be at peace with each other. This was difficult, both having our own reasons, but we were trying.

I had worked late in the Bay Area one day and tried to make the drive home. Falling asleep at the wheel I called Paulette around midnight to say I was pulling over to rest in Vacaville. I lay back in the seat and immediately succumbed to the pull for sleep. I awoke just after daylight and headed toward Sacramento, and eventually home. I stopped in Sacramento for something to eat and was at the restaurant when Pam called. "I have to talk to you," she said. I became concerned by the tone of her voice. "I'm not trying to get you back or start up again," she reassured, "but I do have to talk." I thought a moment before telling her where I was, and she came down. We sat at the booth after not seeing each other for a few weeks and she commenced to tell me how hard things had been. I was compassionate but had no intention in returning. She hadn't been there for 15 minutes when Paulette walked in. I had been set up, I thought. But neither Paulette nor Pam fell into that role. Yelling ensued and I was again where I didn't want to be. Paulette had believed that my stay away from the house was to be with Pam, and she felt led to drive to Sacramento to find us together. She did, but not in the sense that she had felt. Pam's call was coincidental to my overnight stay. Paulette being able to locate me in a restaurant beside the freeway was a coincidental but factual accomplishment. To find me there with Pam was no less than a plan from Satan himself. It was a miserable day and led to significant regression between Paulette and me. I shouldn't have told Pam where I was. I should have said no, but I didn't. I fell asleep that night with such trepidation that I wanted to cry. In the middle of the night, I was dreaming of what happened that day when I was shaken awake. It wasn't Paulette, and I awoke in alarm and shock. I opened my eyes fully and heard a voice. It wasn't an audible voice, but one very strong and loud inside my head. There was no mistaking it. This was real, and the voice was talking to me. I shook my head to clear my senses and get hold of myself. Paulette was next to me and deep asleep. The dogs were beside her and not barking as they would if someone were near. My eyes were wide open, and I checked myself to see if I was sleeping or actually awake. Yes, I was awake. It was a brief message, one with authority, firm yet with gentle resolve. The effect of the voice seemed to fill the room. Its' vibrations went through me, and I knew this wasn't my sleepless imagination playing a game. There was no doubt that I had been awakened and was hearing God himself. I listened, and answered, "Ok, God." What He said to me, I will never repeat. But I had heard.

This shameful experience could be a lesson to many. It was to me. Being in a state of despair gives reason for someone to do the wrong thing, but it doesn't justify or condone it. There's a difference. We still shouldn't do it. Right is right. Wrong is wrong. It's also wrong for someone to feel that because their spouse does something, or acts some particular way that violates your standards, you're justified in your violations as well. You're not. Nor was I with Pam. You read about how I got into something deeper than I wanted to be, for longer than I wanted to be there. That's what sin is, and that's what it costs. But in finding myself in a place where I couldn't even talk to God because of my shame, God chose to talk to me. "I still love you," was what he wanted to say. Fortunately, I heard him. You'll hear him too if you have the need. All you have to do is ask, and he'll be there. Far too many of us have been in a place where there was NO way out, except God. Don't let him be your last resort.

CHAPTER 14

Striking Out on My Own

Ben's work had died down at the office. It had been dry for quite some time and he was overstaffed for the work that came in. My reduced hourly rate from what could be expected in the industry was considered a trade-off for having enough work each week to make up the loss. Ben didn't pay well and he demanded a lot. He wasn't friendly or pleasant to work for and my enthusiasm waned. My loyalty to him remained as it always had, but Paulette and I were far behind in our house payments, the car payment was behind, the utility bills were mounting, and threats were coming to turn them off. Even the food in the house was slim, and I had little vision of how to make things better. This pressure was yet another stain reminding me of my failures. Paulette and I talked about filing for bankruptcy, but neither of us wanted to do that. I was depressed and had no idea how to get through this. Ben either had the work or he didn't. If he had it, I needed it, but so did others. He paid no favors to me, and I knew I'd wait my turn for a case to come in. I began calling other firms looking for work. It was an uncomfortable thing to do, and I had to convince myself that I shouldn't feel guilty about it, but I did. No work was offered by anyone else. Paulette and I went in to see my attorney about a settlement conference regarding an injury I had years earlier. The timing was right. The small settlement came in and we caught our house payment up. Paulette and I talked and decided to rent a small office downtown and try to generate some work for ourselves. I had always said I'd never steal any of Ben's clients if I ever left to strike out on my own, and my vow was firm. Instead of contacting any of Ben's insurance clients, as many others had done during their departure, I commenced trying to advertise and create work for myself.

Cases filtered in slowly and none were the traditional Workers Comp that I had done for so many years. I continued to hope that some of Ben's cases would come in and they periodically did. The office was breaking even and paying for itself but not generating any money to live on. I relied on Ben's periodic work and the rest of the settlement for that. Ben didn't know about the office. Experience told me he'd end our relationship once he learned.

An attorney in the office building brought a matter to me he was working on, a man who may have killed his wife for the insurance money. She died as a result of a snow mobile accident, and he wanted me to look at the papers. I sifted through volumes of paperwork looking for a clue to make the accusation or conclude that it was as the man reported. Something caught my eye. The accident occurred on a roadway appropriately covered with snow. The machine was still upright when the couple were found by others riding snowmobiles. They pulled her out of a pool of ice water behind the snowmobile and commenced artificial respiration. She was blue and unconscious. The man was up against the rear of the snowmobile also unconscious. But there was something different about one of the reports a witness gave. The man's coat was slightly open, and he still had steam coming from his chest. Drawing on my Search and Rescue experience I could see a glaring misrepresentation of the facts. They were in the same snowmobile accident together. They were in the same pool of water behind the snowmobile. She was dead, and blue in color. His body was still cooling down and turning to steam. I read the scenario a second time and returned to the attorney. "I think there's something that deserves more investigation here," I reported, and we spent the next two years on the case. As a result of our research and investigation, the man was eventually charged and found guilty by a jury.

I worked on some criminal matters for local attorneys, as well as some civil and domestic matters, and an occasional surveillance. Work was gradually building, and I was gaining a good reputation. Still, we were barely getting by. Then Ben learned of my office in Auburn through other investigators and he cut the work off entirely. I expected he'd do that but couldn't understand why. I wasn't competing with him and I was supplementing what income I was losing from him due to his lack of work. I had little choice other than to try to make a living somewhere, but he was unyielding in his past history and current decision. No work came in for several weeks. I called his office everyday but got the same answers. "No, nothing's come in." With over 25 years with Ben and never a cheated day or inflated timecard, I couldn't understand why he didn't see this objectively and understandably. I didn't want to leave Ben. He was a source of income and someone I'd been with for over two decades, but his message, delivered by office staff, to have me bring in any equipment that belonged to him was a sign that the end had come. I hoped it would be congenial and mutually appreciative. Like each other or not, we had a 25+ year bond and he knew I was honest, dedicated, and loyal. Never did I violate those standards. But our good-byes came in the order of a quick nearby lunch between us, and at my invitation. I knew this wasn't going to be pleasant. His comment during lunch about the girls suffering less consternation now that I was gone was intended as a jab rather than a humorous consolation. We were done. Ben had cut the ties without remorse. He shook off our relationship that had started so many lifetimes ago and felt no kinship whatsoever. He turned to offer a gratuitous handshake as he walked up the steps to his office and turned around to enter as if I had betrayed him. I stood there a moment looking at the door close in front of me and stared. There were so many things that could have been done today, so many ways to say goodbye, but this wasn't one I expected, nor did I feel I deserved it. My heart was hurt over this. I didn't know I had meant so little to him through the years. I thought I had earned more respect from him than this. Three months later was his annual Christmas party and I heard from others of his normal plans. If Ben had suffered a bad day during our parting, he'd try to make it right now. Paulette and I never received an invitation to his party. I've turned away to try to kick the dust off my heels.

I met an attorney when he called identifying himself as a criminal defense attorney in town who needed some investigation done. For reasons known to myself, we'll call him Zorro. He needed to find someone to interview and asked if I could locate them. I agreed to try and entered the investigation. Ultimately, I found the person he sought, and he admitted his prior investigator had failed. I was pleased I could produce some results for him, and we promised to work with each other again. We did.

Sometime later he had some additional work. Nothing big and I had to cut my fees in half, as Zorro worked mainly on behalf of the County, who had set rates for payment. There was nothing enticing about working at that rate, but we agreed that when he got a private client, he'd pass the full paying clients on to me, as well. I looked at it as possibly another step toward building the business and agreed. More cases came in from Zorro, but they were a time consuming annoyance. Not because of the nature of the case, but because a lot of work went into one, with little reward from the County's set funding program. I still committed all my efforts to a case once I accepted it, so the same energy went into it as any other, but Zorro and I learned we had a difference of philosophy. He was working on the criminal defense side. He felt his job was to get people off, whether guilty or not. That meant he had to win against law enforcement and the D.A. He searched for laws and methods to reach that goal, whether he believed his client to be guilty or not. I found this out on an attempted homicide case I investigated for him. I discovered some facts that were angering to him, and he was annoyed with me for finding them. It took me back. My job was to learn the truth, nothing more, certainly nothing less. Everyone is entitled to the truth, no matter which side, and that was what I was paid to find out. I rarely felt that someone in law enforcement or the D.A.'s office had failed to do their job and, thus, failed to learn the truth. I did know that cops are given a reasonable amount of time to do something before they're forced by other crimes to move on. It's a disappointing fact of life. When there's more crime than cops, each will be allotted only so much time to resolve. Sometimes that means a case goes to the D.A. that could use more work. There are unanswered questions that could change the outcome of a trial. Other times, a new witness changes the light, or an old witness remembers something more, or differently. Sometimes the D.A. just doesn't reveal some things to the Defense side. My job was to learn these things and report it to the attorney. I was good at it. I could communicate with people and had the sixth sense necessary to evaluate the unseen. I liked my job very much. I had to. I wasn't getting paid enough to be doing it for the money.

Other cases came in and I attended to them. The business was growing. I was spending days and nights at the office, but other than being tired, I didn't seem to mind. I was productive, gaining respect in the community, and in time, maybe I'd be able to say I was successful. I learned long ago a philosophy that I never intended to compromise. I would never do something wherein if I met an  adversary on the street, I couldn't look him in the eye. I had to be an honest man. Zorro was sometimes aggravated at my outlook on things. He apparently wanted me to share his burning desire to win. I didn't. To me, winning was finding the truth.

I had the impression that the D.A.'s office looked at me as an honest person as well. They certainly read my reports in their entirety, and by the time an attorney handed them one of mine, it was because it would probably change the outcome of their charges against the Defendant. I always wanted whichever side who read it to think it was a good and complete report. If so, I was satisfied. I may have been giving myself too much credit, as I learned from another attorney over lunch one day. "You're too naive, Duane," Dean said. "Some of those guys make mistakes and hide them. Some will lie in Court. Some attorneys will manipulate the truth to win their case. To think any less is just naive." I had a hard time with his outlook, but Dean had been around a long time and was a very good lawyer himself. He had a different personality though. Dean was very outspoken, bold, and often challenging. He said things as he thought them to be. Some people liked him, some didn't. I liked Dean. Maybe I was naive to think others thought the way I did, or maybe I was even more naive to think that I wasn't an enemy of the D.A.'s office because of my work for the Defense side. Maybe I was making enemies out of some cops who didn't understand the way I approached my work, and maybe I had a lot of lessons in life ahead.

My goal was to make a client glad that they had hired me. I worked hard on that. If I thought they weren't, I'd find out why. If I felt they wanted more in an investigation, I'd go out and do it, usually at no charge. If I exceeded the limits of the retainer, I'd continue to work the case to its conclusion, hoping I could get paid for it in the end. Sometimes I did, sometimes I didn't. I ran an informal office that didn't bill for every hour. I billed for what I felt was fair. I took a lot of losses, and in some cases I worked for free just because the client really needed help and had no money. Sadly, neither did I. The office was surviving, but I wasn't able to take a paycheck home. I paid the bills from the office hoping everything would come out at the end of the month.

A couple of friends had retired from the Sheriff's Office and when I needed occasional help, they offered. I was pleased with that. I didn't want to lose my friends, and they had accepted my approach to the truth as I had. It was good to have them around, even though only on a rare occasion. My reputation was good, my work was good, my office was good, and all I needed now was an acceptable income to meet the bills there and at home.

The Remington case was well known in Auburn. A transient in Roseville used a knife to stab another transient several times in a fight over a girl. The victim lived, but that wasn't Remington's fault. Afterward, he and the girl went to have a sandwich at a local drive-up. He was caught that night by a cop I knew. A good cop, who was alert and observant. Remington was locked up and Zorro was assigned to defend him. I came into the case trying to gather evidence that hadn't been seen or researched. I confirmed statements and looked for new witnesses. Zorro was exceptionally focused on this case. Remington was hostile towards him and threatened him through me. I accompanied Zorro for any further visits and watched him carefully craft his questions to Remington so Remington wouldn't reveal too much, just in case he was guilty. It's amazing to see some people work. You can admire their technique and disdain their goals. Zorro wanted just enough, but not too much from Remington. Remington was uncooperative and challenged Zorro. I think both knew that Remington was going to prison.

Zorro asked me one day to take a trip to Oroville and interview Remington's girlfriend in jail there. During her interview she denied seeing her boyfriend stab the victim. It was generally an uninformative encounter but needed to be done. She gave me a report from her viewpoint, and I looked for more information. She provided little, but some things were learned.

Zorro and Remington must have talked afterward. Zorro called me to say that some of the things the girl was reporting couldn't have happened. Zorro normally kept a lot from me with any case I worked for him and I had no idea what he was talking about. If it didn't make sense, what did Zorro know that I didn't, and why? He needed to tell me everything he knew about a case before I went out on it. He never came around to my way of thinking.

I visited the girl a second time and got quite a surprise after questioning her. She had something to say but couldn't get it out. I talked more with her, and she confessed to doing the stabbing herself. She said it wasn't Remington, it was her. I was surprised to hear this and although I had my doubts, I took the information back to Zorro. He was excited but not surprised. He seemed to know this was coming. I was a little annoyed that he may have been privy to something he should have shared with me before I went to see the girl, but nonetheless, I reported what I had learned. Apparently, my questioning of the girl may have been too detailed though. Zorro got back to me in a couple of days to say, "It wouldn't work." "Wouldn't work" was a strange way of addressing something, and I got another taste of Zorro's outlook on his work.

Remington eventually tired of Zorro and fired him. Another attorney in town picked up the case and I continued my work from there. Remington was eventually found guilty and sent to prison, rightfully so in my opinion. I, too, thought he was guilty. But I didn't work the case to set him free. I worked on it to find the truth.

The next couple of years taught me some new sensitivities in life. People were coming to me with problems. Not just incidental problems, but life changing difficulties and they really needed help. Cheating husbands and wives were the most common. Husbands seemed to cheat more frequently, or at least more wives wanted to find out than the husbands did. It was an emotional time, and a strict businesslike approach was a cold way to handle their distress. I'd try to talk and console them. If I could say something that made their day better when they left the office, I would feel I made a contribution to improving their comfort level. Some interviews took a couple of hours to complete, but a client never left my office thinking I didn't care. I really did. I took on and genuinely absorbed each new problem. It became draining and I certainly wasn't a counselor, nor did I want to represent one. But a kind word to a distressed person wasn't inappropriate, and I felt better if I could help.

A high dollar marriage break-up was impending for a middle-aged wife when she believed her long time husband was having an affair. I took the specifics and reviewed the possibility in my mind. "Yes, it was possible," I thought, and took the case. After a few days of surveillance, I learned that he was indeed having an affair, and with whom he was having it with. It hurt me to see it and I knew I'd have to tell the wife. I play no part in enjoying that and wouldn't take part in the TV program, "Cheaters" if asked. To each their own, but the TV program has to hope an affair is taking place for them to be successful. I don't want it to happen.

I filmed the affection between the two and it was clearly a sexual relationship. After I had developed enough to compile a complete report for the wife, I presented it to her. Needless to say, she was overwhelmed with grief, but she went home to confront her long time husband. I heard nothing from her for several months, but wondered how it turned out.

She walked back into my office one day with a bounce to her step. She smiled and wanted to report something to me. After confronting her husband, he broke down and admitted everything. He was sorry and very remorseful. Sometimes a man is a man is a man, and in this case, he took advantage of an opportunity to experience a different sexual encounter, but he didn't want it to cost him his marriage. His wife still loved him, he realized his love for her, and a counselor put the two back together again. I was glad she came by. It made my day, too.

Zorro called one day to ask me to drop what I was doing and go to Roseville to check out a car in an impound yard. He wanted to know if it had a license plate on the front of the vehicle or not. If it did, I was to take a picture of it and bring it back. As usual, he told me little more, except the driver of the car was in jail and the police officer pulled the car over because it had no front plate. It seemed simple enough and I called the tow yard to announce my intent on coming down. I learned I'd have to be in and out by 4:30 or I'd have to pay overtime fees to the tow yard. The fees were more than I was going to get paid by Zorro and he certainly wouldn't have paid the fees himself. He wanted me to go down today, and this was a very last minute request. "This case is going to cost me," I worried on the trip down. I had to identify the car, verify a license plate, photograph it, and leave the premises, all within minutes from now.

I reached the yard, identified myself to the clerk and was escorted back to its storage spot. Looking down I saw what looked like a license plate on the front of the car, but I couldn't tell. It was bent and folded back out of view. I saw the top strip of plate where it was bent but couldn't read the numbers. I quickly leaned down to confirm that there really was a plate on the car. There was, but I couldn't read the numbers. I pulled the plate forward to where I could read it, confirmed that it was the same numbers as the rear plate, and the same ones that were supposed to be on the car and I took a photograph of it for Zorro. As soon as I did, I felt a cold chill run through me. I had inadvertently or carelessly moved that plate from its bent position to a more visible one without taking a picture of it first. That was wrong. I either shouldn't have moved it, or I should have taken a photo of it in its original position before I pulled it down. "What a stupid mistake," I said to myself. In my rush to complete the assignment before closing I got careless. Now embarrassed, I have to explain what I did to Zorro and went outside to call him. I was worried about the thoughtless mistake I had just made, but minutes later, I had him on the phone with both the good and the bad news. "There was a bent plate up under the car, but I had pulled it down to get a photo of the numbers." Zorro was elated. He acknowledged the bending by saying that was all right as long as there was actually a plate on the car. Yes, there was, and I was relieved I had only done something reckless, and not a further concern to the case. Zorro asked me not to put anything in writing. If I did he'd have to send it over to the D.A. My verbal report was sufficient, just send the photo's over. I had them developed, as you had to do in those days, and sent them over to Zorro. Complying with his request, there was no report to go with it. This wasn't really unusual. Zorro didn't want a written report to go with many of his cases. He didn't want a paper trail that the D.A. might get a hold of. That was his decision, and I had no input to that. I always gave him a verbal report unless asked otherwise. This time, again, it was verbal.

Sometime later I got a call from Zorro. He was questioning me as to bending the plate. I explained again that I pulled the plate down to read the numbers and take a photograph. He was aggravated about bending the plate. I was shocked that he was now upset over something that he had not been previously concerned about. I found myself very defensive and I certainly didn't want to create a problem for he or his client. I foolishly responded by telling the first lie I ever uttered as an investigator. "I didn't do it on purpose, Zorro. I slipped while crouching down and pulled it out with my foot when I fell backwards." It was a stupid thing to say, unbelievable, and for the first time, I compromised my integrity and myself. He seemed to accept the answer and we hung up. I was beside myself over what I had just said, but maybe it would pass. I didn't deny moving it, just the way it was moved. A small lie, but a lie, nonetheless. I lived in shame for the next few days. Eventually I went on to think about other things. Sometimes an incident of some sort will occur where other people just need a reason to enter a checkmark in the proper box. It doesn't matter what that reason is, they just need the question answered before they can move on. Even if they know the answer isn't accurate, they don't care, they just need to fill in the box. I naively hoped that this incident would fall into that category. After all, I never denied moving the plate to take the photograph. I told Zorro about it immediately and made sure he was doubly aware of it when I sent him the photographs. The question he was asking was, "Was there a front plate on that car?" The answer was undeniably, yes. I hoped I could save the embarrassment of my careless mistake by providing a reason it was pulled down rather than just my being in a hurry and didn't first take a photograph of the way I found it. "It looked like someone had hit a parking bumper," I described. I hoped we could just focus on the plate being there, not how it got moved.

A few weeks later I got another call from Zorro. He had fear in his voice this time and asked again about the license plate. I explained again and relived the embarrassment. He wanted a memo regarding the event, and I could tell he was worried about something. He wasn't the type to worry about anyone but himself, so his worry had to have been for him. It certainly wasn't for me. However, I had always felt it was my duty to step in front of a bullet for a client, if the need arose, and Zorro was certainly a client. If he was in trouble for something, I'd do what I could to mitigate that. I wrote the memo to him outlining what had happened, but again stupidly tried to save my reputation by saying I moved the plate by accident. In an effort to try to provide him with some sort of positive position should he be in any difficulty over the incident, I further indicated in my memo that although I had told him on the phone right afterward, it could have been that he didn't hear me. I was trying to give him a way to excuse himself to someone else who may be questioning him. I said what I could in the memo to absolve him of anything that might embarrass or compromise him and I sent it over. Shortly thereafter, Zorro called to thank me and directed me not to talk about this to anyone unless I contacted him first. That was a serious thing to say to me. I questioned myself as to what might be going on. Zorro wasn't going to tell me, so I filed it in a compartment in my mind and let it pass for now.

Months later, I got a call from a D.A. investigator who wanted to talk about the plate. I was surprised but certainly agreed. He was going to want to know if I moved that plate or not. I was sure by the focus of his concern, and I had already confessed that I did move it. I wouldn't deny that. I hoped I could save myself some humiliation by saying I did it accidentally. I called Zorro that day and it was unusual that I got no return call from him. Twice more I tried with no return. Finally, after hours, I got a long pause before he got on the phone. I explained I was about to be visited by the D.A. investigator regarding the plate and he had asked me not to talk to anyone without his knowledge. He interrupted me in mid-sentence. "I can't talk to you about this any longer, and all I have to say to you is, I'd get a lawyer if I were you." I asked what he was talking about and why. What had happened? What was going on? He hung up. Clearly, something was going on and I was in the middle of some trouble. By what Zorro said, he was clearly throwing me under a bus, leaving me to handle this alone. And there was a D.A. investigator on the way over.

He was pleasant but firm when he arrived and asked me to review the incident. I told him what had happened and admitted moving the plate, but with my foot. His focus of questioning was not on how the plate got moved, and I was enthusiastically thankful for that. If I could get away with the little story of how it got moved, it would save me some humiliation for being so stupid as to pull it out without taking a picture of it first. The investigator seemed to pass on any further questions regarding how the plate got bent but was zeroing in on whether I told Zorro about it or not. Of course I told Zorro, and we discussed it afterward as well. I was learning what the problem really was. Zorro had apparently gone to Court and in an effort to get his client released and at the same time successfully compromise a police officer that he intensely disliked, reported to the Court and to the D.A. that the photos were how I found the car and the license plate when I arrived. More so, he later admitted that many defense attorneys wanted to be the first to get this Officer. I had no idea of the magnitude this problem would grow. Zorro wanted to win so badly that he crossed the line. I don't know why he didn't think that the D.A.'s office would check out his misrepresentation. The issue was that when seeing no front plate on the vehicle the Officer had probable cause to make the traffic stop. Zorro said the car, in fact, had a plate and the officer had no right to stop the car in the first place. So that there's no confusion here, Zorro's client didn't get arrested because there was no front plate on his car. Had that been all he would have just gotten a traffic ticket. He was arrested because subsequent to the stop the Officer saw drugs sitting in plain view and arrested the driver, as he should have done. In my view, and that of most others, the Officer fulfilled his duties in an appropriate fashion. But that wasn't Zorro's view. He intently disliked this cop and his aggressive style and enthusiastically wanted to take him down. We'll high profile the word "enthusiastically" here as that is what motivated Zorro to misrepresent my photographs in Court. He knew better, and he lied to the Court. Not knowing Zorro was lying, the Judge released Zorro's client, who immediately fled.

The D.A. started their investigation and found me. Now it became a question of whether a bent plate or a straight plate would have gotten his client released. I didn't know and didn't care. I had tried to step in front of a social bullet for Zorro and he took advantage of it. I didn't know until talking with the D.A. investigator that Zorro had broken the law or misrepresented the evidence I had given him. Zorro had represented the photographs as being what I had found when I arrived on scene. This was so contrary to the truth that I couldn't believe Zorro had done that. Why was he overplaying his hand? I didn't have the answer and the D.A. investigator was concerned as well. His final question was with regard to whether I had told Zorro or not. Zorro had said, no. In fact, Zorro apparently stated that I hadn't spoken to him at all the afternoon of the incident. I challenged that and produced my cell phone records to show the time and date of my call to Zorro's office that afternoon. The investigator took note of it and left. I was so disappointed with Zorro that I was almost more ashamed of him, than I was of myself. I tried to cover how I had moved a plate, I was wrong. He intentionally tried to misrepresent the evidence, and then lied about what he was told so as to cover himself. I was taken back with his apparent feeling that I could take the fall for what he did. I had no knowledge that he was going to go into Court the way he did, and he apparently didn't think he was going to get caught. He did, and he was looking for a way out. I never spoke to Zorro again and didn't want to. I was ashamed of what I had done and didn't want to see him. Moreover, I was angry and disappointed at what he had done, both in Court and to me. It was best that Zorro and I didn't see each other again. Word gets around in a small town and I was getting feedback from the others. People wanted to know whether I had told Zorro about moving the plate, or whether he was lying. I attempted to answer without laying any more blame on Zorro than needed. I had no reason or obligation to protect him, other than it just seemed to be my nature to do it that way. Zorro could go his way, and I would mine.

Months later I got a letter in the mail. The D.A.'s office was prosecuting me for submitting false evidence to a Court. There are no words that could explain the effect of opening that letter. This couldn't be happening, I thought. It just couldn't be happening. I was inwardly confident it would get cleared up before Court, but to be charged with a crime was more than I had ever expected to happen in my life. The D.A.'s office thought I was dishonest, a criminal, and should go to jail. What in the name of God would my friends in the Sheriff's Office or Auburn P.D. think? What would my friends on the outside think? What about Paulette? What about the rest of my family? How had this come to be? I was being charged with a criminal act. I read the charges again and just couldn't bring myself to a conscious state of mind. It was like a bad dream, and I looked again. If they were going to charge me with moving the plate, I'd have called them on the phone to plead guilty. I did that. It wasn't done as a crime, but I did it regardless. Charge me with that if you must. But supplying false evidence to the Court was far beyond what I had done. Apparently, Zorro did, and the D.A. as extracting blood for it. I wondered if he had been charged as well. I wasn't about to call him, but I wanted this to get cleared up, and I prayed it'd go away.

I was arraigned in open Court, as I should have been. I had sat in this Courtroom many times before on behalf of attorneys or clients, but never in preparation for being charged for a crime myself. The Judge was a nice man, and a good Judge. My name was called, and he looked twice at the file before glancing over to his clerk with an expression of, "Is this right?" Other attorneys in the room saw me step up to be charged with a crime. If there had ever been a time when I feared I couldn't stand on my feet, this was it. I wanted to vomit. The formalities were short and brief. I was released on O.R. (without having to post a bail) but had to report to the jail to get booked a few days later. I wouldn't have to stay, but I would from there on out have a mug shot and a record of arrest.

The day came for me to report to the jail, and I dressed in a suit. I would present myself to them as best I could. The shame of this was almost greater than I was able to bear. I was fortunate though, as two old friends came by, specifically to see that I didn't go there alone. Andy, a retired Captain from the Sheriff's Department, and Bob, a retired Major from the Army. Both were there to keep my legs under me as I walked to the jail. I rode over with them and was very thankful. I'll always remember they were there.

I hired Dean to represent me, and I thought back to a previous conversation when he reminded me how naive I was. I guess he was right. There are people who would cut your throat to win. Certainly they'd do the same to save themselves from trouble. And what about the D.A., did they really believe I had done such a thing, or were they using me as a tool to get to Zorro, who they knew really did it? I didn't know.

The D.A. investigator continued investigating the matter. Dean and I prepared for a Preliminary Hearing, where evidence is heard, and the Judge decides whether I should be brought to a full trial. A week before the Prelim, Dean called Zorro to talk about the case. Zorro was willing to talk, and during their conversation told Dean that I was not lying. It had happened as I said. Dean was happy that Zorro was coming to reality and admitting things as they were. It meant that in the Prelim I'd be released from the charges and set free.

The District Attorney presented his case to the Judge, and I listened as the accusations were levied against me. It was unbelievable that someone could think that I'd do such a thing. But I sat there realizing that clearly, I thought more of myself than others did of me. I wanted to burst out, "It's not true," but I knew it'd be self-defeating.

Zorro was subpoenaed and we passed in the hallway during recess. He raised his hand to say Hi and flashed the hippie peace sign at me. I thought he was trying to tell me things would be okay. He got on the stand to testify, and I could tell he was nervous. His speech was quiet and shaking while is hands were damp as he rubbed them together. He was asked some questions leading up to the inevitable important one, "Had I called him to let him know I had moved the plate." He answered all the questions put to him. When the final determining question was posed, "Did Mr. Purdue tell you on the phone that he had moved the license plate before taking a picture of it," Zorro thought a minute, then said, "No." I was floored. He had admitted it a week earlier but was now losing his nerve. Dean asked him two or three different ways and each answer was the same. "Duane didn't tell me the pictures were any different than what he saw on the car when he arrived." I was staring at him during his lie. He was under oath and perjuring himself, at my expense. He must have known Dean was going to question him. He had to have known that the prior week's conversation with Dean was going to come up. But he stood his ground. "Duane didn't tell me he moved the plate. I showed the pictures as I thought Duane had found it." Zorro was excused and Dean made a statement to the Court. He advised the Judge that he was resigning as my lawyer so as to become my witness and explained the conversation with Zorro the prior week. The Judge agreed to let him do that and said it would come out in trial. I was held over to answer at a full blown felony criminal trial.

My new attorney and I thought it might be best if we were to have a meeting with the D.A. and report everything to him, step by step regarding what had happened, and get this cleared up. Once he knew what I did and didn't do, and I could show him I did report the movement of the plate to Zorro, he'd redirect his focus in the right direction. I was no longer sorry that Zorro was going to get into trouble after what he said in Court, and I had no intention in trying to protect him any longer. I had written a memo to Zorro accepting blame for not making it clear to him that I moved the plate, but I'd explain it all to the D.A.

The meeting was long and formal. The D.A. had his investigator there whom I had spoken with before. I answered each of the D.A.'s questions honestly and completely. I could tell from communication between the D.A. and his investigator that the investigator had caught on. He knew that what I was saying was true, and it apparently coincided with his independent findings. Then I got hit with a surprise question. "Tell me about the conspiracy between you and Zorro regarding how you planned on deceiving the Court," the D.A. said. I was shocked by his question. I hadn't even considered they'd think something like that.

I explained that there wasn't any, and I had no idea what Zorro was doing until after it was done.

The meeting concluded and the D.A. passed some paperwork over to me. I looked at it only briefly to see what it was. He had already amended his Complaint and was also charging me with Conspiracy. As painfully honest as I had been with him, was for naught. It did nothing but give him a chance to charge me with another crime. This couldn't be happening.

My attorney came to me a month later with an offer from the D.A. If I'd confess and testify that there was a conspiracy between Zorro and I to defraud the Court, they'd dismiss all charges against me. "What a dastardly thing to do," I thought. What a temptation they were laying before me. All I had to do was testify against Zorro, and I'd be set free. All I had to do was confess the sin of Conspiracy, and this would be over. All I had to do was lie. It didn't take long to send my answer back. Give me something that's truthful, and I'll do it, but I can't lie to get out of this thing. No other offers came, but it told me what I wanted to know. They were after Zorro, and afraid they couldn't get him. They needed me and were angry that I wouldn't help. They would get me instead.

I knew my other option to stay out of Court would be to plea to the sheet. If I plead guilty to the charges levied against me, I could go straight to the Judge for sentencing and avoid a trial. I thought about doing it, even though I hadn't committed either crime I was being charged with. I didn't have any good reasons to consider accepting their offer to plea to the sheet. I knew it would be wrong, yet the temptation was there. I just wanted to wake up from this nightmare. Then, one evening while standing in my office looking out the window, praying about what the right thing to do was, I felt God. It was a clear strong feeling. I didn't hear his voice, I felt it. It was just as strong and intense as he spoke to me years ago while looking down at the runners crossing No Hands bridge and telling me I was going to run this one day. God said to me this evening, "Trust me. Take this to trial." I asked him to repeat it. He did. I felt it the second time. Paulette and others had already encouraged me to do the same thing. This word from God was enough. I assured myself that things were going to turn out okay and concluded that as painful as it was going to be, this would go to trial.

The call came in from Lt. Strongarm at the Sheriff's Office. He wanted to see me. Of course I knew what it was about, but going in to see people whom I looked at as friends and face them with these accusations that were made against me was one of the most difficult things I could think of. These were friends of mine for many years. In fact, the Sheriff's Office was all I knew outside my own world of work. Search and Rescue had been my passion for almost 25 years, and we had come a long way together. I was proud of my contributions and hoped that the Sheriff's Office was equally pleased with what I'd been able to accomplish. Their confidence in me was significant enough that I had keys to several of the Sheriff buildings and lockers. I had been, "one of them," for decades and we were both comfortable in that. But this was going to be incredibly difficult, but I knew Strongarm, and we'd be able to talk.

Normally I'd go in the back door and of the building, but this was formal, and I went in the front and waited for him to come out and get me. He said little as we walked to his office. He closed the door and sat at his desk. His next words permeated my soul. "I know the trouble you're in, and I've read the entire file from the D.A.'s office. I've reviewed this with the Undersheriff, and we want you to know that we can only use people with integrity around here, and you're not one of them. Turn in your ID." That was it. He didn't ask me what happened, he didn't ask for any defense, he offered no support, and offered nothing to suggest that he knew me well enough to know I couldn't do such a thing. He had me guilty and gutted, even before a trial. I saw 25 years and tens of thousands of hours get flushed down the drain there in his office. Without the slightest tone of sorrow or appreciation, he escorted me out of his office. I've never been back. I can only hope that someday, he and they learn that I didn't commit the crimes for which I was accused. But only now do I understand that they don't really care. My history there was wiped clean with a sweep of his hand and without a second thought.

The trial came and the D.A. presented his case. My attorney was less aggressive than the D.A. was and wound up playing catch-up to his accusations. We were falling behind in our defense, not because we couldn't defend ourselves, but because my attorney was trying not to rock the boat. "Rock the Boat?" I objected. This boat needs to be turned over. He told me he had learned the D.A.'s strategy. If Zorro shows up to testify under the subpoena that he's been served, as he's supposed to, and doesn't take the 5th, as suspected he will, the D.A. will get the jury so angry with Zorro that they'll convict me as his associate. Of course that concerned me. It was common knowledge that Zorro and the D.A. didn't like each other. This encounter could accomplish exactly what the D.A. intends with the jury. Once they're upset, I could be their outlet. But I had one ace that was a hands down winner, Dean. Zorro confessed to Dean that I was telling the truth and Dean would clear this up. Dean waited day by day to be called as a witness, wanting to testify and asking me each day why he hadn't been called. I didn't learn until the last day that the D.A. and my attorney reached an agreement to read into the record what Dean said at the Prelim but not call him to testify here. Why my attorney would agree to that, and not tell me, to this day I don't know. And he hasn't provided an answer. But I knew that this was emphatically the wrong thing to do, but I wasn't the attorney. The D.A. didn't want Dean there, and my attorney didn't want to make the D.A. mad. The result was my key defense witness didn't testify. Who knew whether the jury heard or took into consideration the mundane readings of a previous statement? There was nothing extraordinary when the Judge read it into the record, and it seemed to carry little impact. This major confession of Zorro's to Dean may go completely unnoticed to the jury. My freedom may depend on Dean's testimony, but it wasn't to be. My attorney let it pass, apparently feeling he could win this without Dean.

Zorro did show up in Court and just from his demeanor you could tell he was prepared for a fight. The question and answer period between he and the D.A. was fierce and hostile. Zorro was cocky, knowing that he hadn't been charged with any crime. All he had to do was place the blame on me and he was free. He did just that, but the D.A. wasn't satisfied. He was going after Zorro as a co-participant. The D.A. charged me with Conspiracy to Defraud the Court, but hadn't charged Zorro, the alleged co-conspirator. Obviously, they didn't believe there was a conspiracy, or they would have charged both of us, but they were set on inundating me with criminal charges, and they did. Now if they could trap Zorro into admitting he was a part of it, they'd get him, too.

Zorro's focus was on the cop who made the vehicle stop to begin with. Not only did he not like that cop but reported that several other defense attorneys were trying to bring him down, too. His own words were more decorated, but the heart of his intent was to discredit the cop that was disliked by so many other defense attorneys. I was hearing this for the first time from the horse's mouth. It was amazing to me that someone would have such a vendetta. The cop was aggressive, resourceful, and shrewd. So what, that's just doing good cop work in my book. I certainly didn't share in Zorro's zeal to get that cop. In fact, I rather admire cops of that nature. Two with that character are still good friends of mine. But the D.A. was trying to put Zorro and me inside the same barrel. We were both trying to discredit that cop and ruin his reputation and career. The D.A. couldn't have been more wrong.

The atmosphere between my attorney and Zorro was far less challenging than with the D.A. and Zorro. I didn't know why my attorney was being as gracious as he was. The man up on the witness stand was destroying my life. I wanted my attorney to go for his throat. The cell phone record of my talking to Zorro the evening of the event was presented, but in an unremarkable way. Zorro challenged both the D.A. and me as being his enemies and the hostility was loud between him and the D.A. Clearly the jury didn't like Zorro, and he didn't care. Everyone in the room knew the jury would have convicted Zorro at that moment, had they the option. They didn't, so all they could do was dislike him. Then he trapped himself.

The D.A. asked him when he learned of "my" deceit, would Zorro then have been duty bound to notify the D.A.'s office? "Yes," was his obvious answer. "And when did you learn of his deceit?" the D.A. asked Zorro. He spit out his prepared answer. "And when did you actually notify the D.A.'s office?" was the D.A.'s follow up question. Zorro spit out his next prepared answer with a date and time. "What D.A. did you talk to," was next. Zorro spit out his answer. The D.A. followed up with similar questions locking Zorro into his answer until he got angry and pounded on the witness stand. "I'm telling you under oath that this is the day and time I reported it, and this is who I talked to," he yelled, "I made notes of it then, I'm testifying to it and there's no other answer." His words are paraphrased here and recalled from memory. I was in shock with what I was hearing. Regardless, he locked himself in with no escape.

The following morning we were surprised with an appearance from the same D.A. that Zorro was referring to. He denied being told at all by Zorro about his proclaimed knowledge of my "deceit," and was asked about the day and time that Zorro was alleging he informed him. The D.A. brought his calendar to Court and reported with certainty that he wasn't working that day. He was off. Zorro had been caught lying. "Oh my God," I thought, "They caught him. They caught him". I took a breath of air thanking God. All my attorney had to do now was separate me from Zorro. Show that I wasn't a part of his deceit, and I'd be free. The D.A. gave his closing argument and concentrated on tying Zorro and I together as a couple who conspired to destroy the reputation of a good police officer. He went to great lengths to do it and closed by labeling Zorro as a perjurer. In this he was correct. Zorro perjured himself on the stand, and the jury saw it. I hoped their anger would be limited to him.

The jury went out for what was expected to be a few hours. Mike and Judy had come to sit through the entire trial. We had become close friends in the last few years, and both were very caring people. Lowell, my retired Deputy friend also sat through the entire trial. They had seen me at my worst yet were still there. Of course Paulette was there. The Bailiff outside checking people in was a good cop and a good friend. Wayne had retired some time ago and had come back for part time work. He was a nice guy and went out of his way to talk to me when he could. He was clearly convinced I had not done what I was charged with. I was most surprised by the D.A.'s investigator. I learned through other sources and by way of his conduct with me that he, too, knew the truth. He objected to my being charged with a crime and knew that it was Zorro who had committed it. He never told me that himself, but the information came back to me from multiple sources. I was glad that he realized that. He investigated the case, reached a logical conclusion, and reported it to the D.A. That's the job of any investigator, and he did this properly. The D.A. was wrong to charge me, and now I found myself sitting to await my fate.

The hours we expected the jury to be out turned into a day, then another, and yet then another. They finally reached a decision and the Court was called back into session.

I awaited the reading from the Foreman. "As to count #1, Conspiracy, we find the Defendant NOT guilty." I took a breath. "As to count #2, Submitting False Evidence to the Court, we find the Defendant GUILTY." ------------------ I had just become a convicted felon.

I left the Courtroom in a daze. It's impossible for this to have happened. They convicted someone who didn't commit the crime. I lied about how I moved the plate so I wasn't innocent and wouldn't label myself that way, but I did not deliberately commit a crime, and certainly didn't do what they had just convicted me of. My world, my confidence, my reputation, and credibility had just reversed, forever. I was a common criminal, nothing more. Worse yet, I was a man who spent his life wanting to do what was right, and I'd forever be a man who lost the most important thing there was to him, my reputation.

I couldn't go home. I didn't know where to go, and I didn't want to live any longer than today. I was a criminal, a convicted criminal, a criminal, a criminal. My consciousness was in a daze, almost like being in a dark tunnel but with no light at the end. I had left Paulette to ride home with someone else and I was alone in the car. Only moments later I found myself sitting at the end of the Foresthill Bridge, looking at the catwalk. Everything I was as a human being was just erased by a single word. "Guilty" kept screaming through my mind. And there was no doubt in my mind, with 100% certainty, God told me to take this to trial. How had I let him down? Why had he left me? Why would he want this to happen to me? What value do I have in life now? None. I had no hope, no vision, and couldn't even pray now. If this is what God wanted for me, he certainly isn't going to hear my prayers of desperation now. I was alone, trapped now in a world I fought for most of my life. Labeled as being the exact person I never looked at myself as being. Every step I had made through life to be a good man, do the right thing, recognize the importance of other people, take an active part in helping to make their lives better, to be an example to my wife and children, and to earn the respect offered by my friends, had all fallen asunder. And at the most desperate hour of my life I can't even turn to God any longer. I prepared myself for the walk to the catwalk when I was distracted by a vehicle that arrived at speed and slid to a stop. The driver quickly got out and revealed himself as being my old friend, Lowell. The Deputy who had spent so much time with me through Search and Rescue and sat through the entire trial. I don't know how he knew to come here, just his instinct I suppose, but he intended to interfere with my immediate goal. Our conversation progressed for what seemed like a couple of hours, and he talked me into going home, at least for now.

Paulette was home and obviously she had been crying. There wasn't much we could say to each other and little comfort we could offer the other one, but we tried. She made sure to tell me that Wayne, the Deputy who was working the front door during the trial, and who had been a friend for a long period, came by. He was very distraught and because he worked at the trial while it was in session, he was acutely aware of each phase of it. He was so grieved when the verdict came in that when I left the parking lot he, too, arranged for a replacement and left behind me. Paulette had barely got home when he arrived, hoping to find me. I could only thank Wayne in my mind. I'd probably never see him again. As a convicted felon I'll probably be going to prison.

I lay in bed for the most part of 10 days, getting up only to go to the bathroom. I'd have urinated in bed had I slept there alone. I didn't or couldn't eat or drink. I wanted to die there and prayed God would take me, and if He didn't, tell me why? Yet every prayer, it came to mind that God wasn't listening to me anymore. Everything I had lived for, represented, and taught my children was gone, and I represented the antithesis of that. "God, I wish I hadn't moved that plate." An act of thoughtless stupidity, but not intended as a crime.

After a week and a half Paulette drug me to the doctor. There was little he could do but offer a tranquilizer. I declined and knew there was nothing that could be done to help this. If God would just let me die, he'd allow me some relief. The bridge came back to mind, but I reminded myself that this life wasn't mine to decide when it was to die. God would have to make that decision. I just wanted him to make it my way.

I reported to Probation as ordered for my pre-sentencing interview. They were to decide what kind of candidate I'd make for probation instead of prison. I really didn't care either way. They could lock me away; it wouldn't make things better or worse. The Probation Officer was a woman who had a reputation for being nasty and arrogant. She presented herself to me that way as well. Flaunting her knowledge of my conviction she said I should go to jail for what I'd done. She used similar phrases that the D.A. used in his closing argument, and I knew they'd been talking. I had little to say to her other than to do what she thinks best. "I will," she assured me in her bite back.

In the meantime Paulette had contacted friends in the community. Letters started coming in supporting me, and the character I thought I used to have. Seeing what those people thought of me probably saved my life. They were signed by attorneys, a judge pro tem, several police officers, my retired Major friend, and others, including one from an attorney at the State Attorney General's Office. Paulette insisted that these letters be included with the probation report and the Probation Officer scoffed. "They won't do him any good," she assured her. In the meantime we hired an outside independent probation review at our own expense. Their report came back in exactly the way it really was. It was honest, direct, objective, and made recommendations of no prison time.

Sentencing day came and we appeared in Court once again. The courtroom was packed with standing room only. My constant desire to vomit had not left me since I was convicted. I sat at the table listening to the D.A. recommend the maximum penalty, prison time, and referred to the County Probation Report as confirmation. The Judge had little to say, except to turn to the D.A. to announce he had but one question for him. Where was Zorro? Why wasn't he here? The D.A. just stared at the Judge with no response. The Judge referred to the many letters that had been sent in, and the independent Probation Report. Turning to me, he sentenced me to what he said he felt was right. The minimum sentence that could be imposed, with a 90 day suspended jail term. The suspension meant I wouldn't be required to spend time in jail. He dismissed the Court and the D.A. got up to storm out. He was wrong to begin with, and the Judge saw it. No, I wasn't innocent of all culpability, but I didn't commit the crime I had been convicted of. None-the-less, I was a fully-fledged convicted felon, and the Auburn Journal saw to it that the public knew. Within a year, the D.A. who prosecuted me became a local Judge. I understand that he used my case as part of his campaign platform, but I never bothered to confirm that.

Shortly after the conviction my license was suspended by the State. I had an opportunity to request a hearing, and did. The matter was studied by State representatives and their impression was that I may have been convicted of something I didn't do. I agreed. They ordered 3 years' probation and let the matter drop. Many were amazed they hadn't taken my license. I was too.

Each hour of each day of each week and month I grieve over my conviction. I'll never be the same person. I suppose some would say that's good. I'm so far unable to determine if I was deserving of this sort of demise. I'm not refuting that I lied about how I moved a license plate, with my hand or my foot, but I'm a man who's always looked at intent as a contributing factor. My intent and the resulting consequences don't seem to coincide. I don't have any temptation to feel sorry for myself. Self-pity isn't a part of recognizing any problem. It's only a means of putting a band-aid on it. None-the-less, calling a spade a spade, looking at what really happened, this was a miscarriage of justice. Since then my business has barely survived, and my family suffered with the humiliation. It's a chore to make ends meet after this highly publicized event. And I don't blame the public or others for their disassociation. Even those who want to do business with me can't. Instead of looking ahead at a prosperous reputable firm, I'll take cases from those who for some reason don't know or care about what happened. Those options were rare. Life as I knew it has permanently changed. Even trying to find a job somewhere else was handcuffed by my felony conviction. With no place to turn or options to exercise, I tried desperately to keep the office open, with only the rare attorney displaying a lot of guts to do business with me. The job I loved so much and the reputation I tried so hard to earn was over.

Losing my reputation, and becoming a convicted felon was only a part of the loss. My deepest despair was in losing God. Where had He gone? Why did He want me to take this to trial? Did He want me to become a convicted felon? Didn't He love me more than that? What had I done to deserve this from Him? Why did He dislike me so much? And now that I'm alone, who do I turn to? My Lord had given me up. He's either chosen to ignore me, or He intentionally caused this fate to happen to me. Either way, He had control over it. Why did He do it this way? I thought He loved me. I'm helpless without Him in my life. He hasn't told me what I've done to deserve this. If God is going to turn His back on me, it can only mean that I've done something so egregious that He separated himself from me. What had I done? This abandonment means that I'm really alone now. Since I accepted Jesus into my life, I had never envisioned being without Him. I have a whole new world to face tomorrow, and I'll be doing it alone. The one I sought for guidance, direction, instruction, counseling, support, encouragement, protection, provision, strength, and my very salvation has given up on me. The one that I counted on is no longer there. What's tomorrow going to bring as I face it alone?

This is the condition and state of mind of a broken man. Not just one who lost everything he stood for but lost all that he turned to and depended on as well. "God will never leave you nor forsake you," kept playing its song through my mind. Yet he had. For the next 10 years there was no more church, no more association with God or Godly people, no more praying, no more reading. I was alone and on my own to live what life there was without him. It was a miserable, turmoil filled, guilt laden, painful existence. It affected my character, my personality, my marriage, my social contacts, and my friends. I never envisioned there to be so much confusion in God's word to us. My confusion has met head on with anger. If God doesn't want me anymore, I don't want him. I hope you've never felt this way, but many have. If one of them is you, or might be you in the future, you'd better continue to read on. There's more to come, and yes, an answer to it all.

CHAPTER 15

Paulette Loses Too

No one in a family can suffer a loss or devastating blow without it affecting the rest of the family. Paulette stuck with me through the toughest times I'd ever experienced, not knowing that she'd go through her own trials soon to come.

She and her mother were close - very close. Unlike a mother/daughter relationship, Paulette and Lisette had a girlfriend/girlfriend friendship. It was annoying at times, but I understood it and accepted it as their way of life. Lisette, or Mom as I came to call her after my own Mom died, was a feisty woman who had lived alone for many years. She acquired many of the traits that a single person takes on. She took care of herself, and thought of herself, generally, first. We learned to accept her as she was. No one was going to change her. A steadfast German woman who suffered the ravages of WWII, she'd seen many things. She and her long time husband, Paulette's father, Maurice, divorced and she never got over the insult or hurt. Although remarried herself years later, she frequently thought back to her first marriage and how she had been mistreated. It was sad to see her live in a world so far back, but no one was going to bring her forward except her. She had many good traits, depending on whether she wanted to show them to you that day. Paulette grew accustomed to it without complaint.

Mom moved to Colfax around the year 2000 to be closer to her family. She was getting on in years and her health was starting to show the signs. She had breast cancer and I'm sure it scared her. This was expected to be her last move. Nicki found the house for her, and Mom bought it. It was a strange choice for Mom. Upstairs and downstairs for a 75 year old woman had its challenges, but it seemed to be what Nicki wanted. Paulette offered little input into the choice, as long as Mom was happy with it. After she moved in, Nicki seemed to disappear, with the exception of an occasional call or visit to Mom. Nicki still carried her unnatural aggression toward us so of course there was no attempt at communication there.

Sometime after moving to Colfax, Mom got sick. She was diagnosed with additional cancer, and it was spreading. She was spry for quite some time and got regular treatments at the doctor to control it. What she really needed, in her book, was attention and care. Paulette stepped in to provide that. She devoted herself to Mom, day in and day out, all day, and many times all night. She'd take Mom where she needed to go, stay with her at the house for company, clean for her, shop for her, or just be Mom's companion. Mom liked that. She was the Matriarch. Everyone would go to her. She hated going to anyone, except Paulette. As her condition got worse, her needs multiplied and she became very dependent upon Paulette, who would make doctors' appointments, hospital visits, and anything else that needed to be done. Mom got regular blood transfusions and coupled with her other treatment, with Paulette's help, she was extending her years. Mom hated the thought of dying and set aside a lot of money for treatment should her insurance company fall short.

Paulette needed a calendar to keep track of everything; everything, that is, except her family at home. There was only so much time in a day, and most of it was spent caring for Mom. As time passed, Paulette spent less time at home during the day, and I didn't know whether she'd be home at night or not. The house grew lonely, and trouble brewed, however there was little choice for a solution. Mom offered Paulette $1,000 a week, but Paulette rightfully refused. This was taking its toll on the family, and Mom could see it. "Instead", Mom said, "I'll take care of you in my Will." Paulette was satisfied with that, and happy that Mom would remember her that way. Paulette wanted to care for her mother, and wasn't doing it for the money, but at the same time, we were struggling each month to pay our bills. We weren't living extravagantly, or even comfortably. I had no retirement or visions of ever quitting work. Social security wouldn't pay our expenses at the end of the month, and I hadn't been able to establish a retirement program to look forward to. Paulette needed to be at the office to help with paperwork and communicate with the public for new clients but couldn't because of her devotion to Mom. Mom was offering something that gave us some confidence that life wouldn't end in a VA hospital or care facility somewhere. Paulette and I talked about Mom's promise and checked ourselves to see that we weren't after a selfish gain sometime in the future. An inheritance was in Paulette's destiny, just as the other kids were entitled to, but she'd also be compensated for what she was giving to Mom now and taking from us. Talking about Mom's Will was a very sensitive subject, but there was always the utmost respect even when talking about it without her being present.

When she was there, Mom outlined what she had, what was important to her, and what was to go to which specific child. That was probably the most difficult thing for Paulette to listen to, but she did gracefully, and remembered each item to insure it would go where intended. Paulette was trying to make Mom feel comfortable and at peace. She'd talk about the future when Mom brought it up, and passed on asking questions when Mom wasn't up to it. "I want you to have the house, honey," was something Mom said many times. It wasn't our kind of house, and not designed for a family like ours, but Paulette thanked Mom each time she promised to leave it to her. There were so many things that Paulette wanted to know to insure Mom's wishes were carried out, but it took so long to hear Mom outline it. She just didn't like talking about her final wishes. Mom clearly hoped to live forever. She was maybe even demanding it.

Sometime later, Mom had her Will changed. We didn't know what it previously said, or said after her change, and didn't care. We weren't wishing for Mom to die, and trying to find out what was in a Will was a morbid thought. She promised to take care of Paulette and we knew she had. The only thing we asked of her was to draft her Will in a way that would make her comfortable and happy.

As her condition deteriorated, Mom's mind grew weary. She'd forget things, do things wrong, or not at all. The demand on Paulette rose to a point where she really needed help taking care of Mom, but no one was around to offer. Paulette bore up under the strain each day and moved on without complaining. When she'd come home that night, either she'd have to call Mom to make sure she was alright, or Mom would call Paulette. What she really wanted was for Paulette to move in with her, but that couldn't be. Paulette had a family at home, and all of us couldn't move to Mom's, nor would she have wanted us to.

Mom's sickness got worse, and she fell at the house injuring her leg. It took a hospital stay to stabilize her, but she wasn't well enough to go home. Paulette couldn't lift and move her, so we all agreed to put her in a nearby convalescent hospital for therapy until we could move her home again. Mom seemed to understand and be happy with that plan. Paulette visited every day, generally to find Mom sleeping. But her pain was significant, and the doctors had her on high doses of very strong medication. We could tell when talking to her that it clearly clouded her mind. She began not to recognize Paulette or some of the kids when they went to see her. Her deterioration was sad. She was biting and fighting the nurses and demanding attention that had already been given. She wanted to go home but couldn't. Once she was able to get back on her feet, we'd see that she got home, and even get some paid help if we needed to. But Mom wasn't doing well now. She needed medical treatment and therapy for the broken leg that got her here in the first place. Yet all she would do is fight the nurses. Her biting was creating a significant problem for them.

In stepped Nicki, who had visited Mom in the hospital. Within days, she and Mom checked Mom out of the hospital and Nicki took control of her. From that point on, Paulette wasn't allowed to see or talk to her mother again. She was cut off from communication and refused access. Attempts to force her way into the house to see Mom met with a roadblock from Nicki, or her calling the Sheriff's Department. Both times, Paulette was escorted off the property. She was devastated but knew that the Deputy had no choice.

We learned that Mom had been told that Paulette was stealing things out of her home, had stolen her jewelry, pilfered her bank account, was planning on keeping her in the hospital until she died, and was listing her house for sale. None of these abominable things were remotely true in any sense. Paulette was so loyal to Mom she wouldn't take gas money unless Mom insisted. The atrocity was in that she was being accused of these kinds of things. It hurt Paulette to her core. It came from someone in the family who disliked Paulette and had something to gain from Paulette's separation from Mom.

Shortly after getting her home, Nicki took Mom down to an attorney where a new Will was drafted. Mom's signature on the Will was unreadable, less than a scribble, completely unlike her normal signature. We immediately assigned a significant degree of concern to the apparent probability that Mom never really signed it. We learned later by her own admission that shortly after Mom changed her Will, Nicki ceased giving her all her medications and taking her for her blood transfusions, stating that the doctors said it may kill her. That was proven inaccurate by the doctors themselves who denied stating such a thing, but to no avail. Paulette learned of what Nicki was doing and begged to see her mother. "I don't think it's a good idea," was the only response Nicki would give, emphasizing the "I". Within weeks, Mom was dead. We didn't learn about it for several hours, and Paulette was forbidden to see her at the mortuary. She couldn't even say her last goodbyes to Mom, who had been her best friend all her life. Paulette was made so uncomfortable at the funeral that she had to leave. Only after Mom died did Paulette learn that a new Will was "voluntarily" made by Mom, giving Nicki almost everything. A token amount was given to Paulette at Nicki's discretion. Paulette had lost her entire inheritance.

Nicki flaunted her power over Paulette and openly refused to offer even the most common of decencies. This was her way of gaining power and paying Paulette back for every failure as a mother that this daughter felt had been perpetrated on her. Paulette was so devastated by the loss of her mother, the way she was lost, her inability to see her or say goodbye, and the loss of her inheritance that we had no alternative but to hear the matter in Probate Court. Certainly the truth would come out there.

The trial lasted a couple of days. A new Judge on the bench only three months heard the case. But trouble may be looming here, too. This was the attorney who refused to even talk to Paulette about an appeal for me when I was convicted. I sat in the Courtroom with Paulette looking up at a judge who already didn't like me. The trial progressed and we showed clearly what had happened, and the influence that had been imposed on Mom to change her Will. We concluded our evidence with her signature, which was less than scratches of unparalleled lines similar to a 3-year old on a pre-school tablet of paper. Our expert witness was not only the Chief of Staff for the convalescent hospital where Mom was being cared for but was also a qualified hand-writing expert as well. "Whoever accepted the signature on this Will as being authentic and without scrutinizing the author's mental capacity should go to jail," was his paraphrased conclusion. "The Will should be thrown out." (The term Will being common verbiage for the document in question). The Judge came back with his decision. "It wasn't the Court's responsibility to try to determine the wishes of a dying woman." Nicki's Will would stand. We lost everything Mom had promised and more. There was a no-contest clause in the Will that said if anyone contested the Will, they'd lose their portion of the inheritance, no matter how small. The Judge was gracious enough to allow Paulette to keep her token inheritance, stating that the law allows a contest for good cause, and he thought she had good cause. However, after allowing her to keep her inheritance, he awarded Nicki her attorney's fees. Paulette would spend her inheritance paying for Nicki's attorney. Blow after blow, Paulette took the punches, but it was wearing her down, and her health deteriorated as well. And it wasn't over yet. Nicki had won the estate she had stolen from the family, but she was in it for one more attack. She won, yet she appealed the Judge's decision. She wanted the Appeals Court to take away Paulette's inheritance too. We had initially filed an appeal ourselves, but for Paulette's health, and for the sake of her brother and sisters who were waiting for their inheritance, Paulette cancelled the appeal before it got started. Nicki had no such concerns. She was after Paulette's small inheritance, leaving her to her own resources to pay for both attorneys. The Court of Appeal denied Nicki's vicious attack against Paulette. I can only thank them for that.

Paulette lost everything. Her mother, her best friend, her confidant, the $1,000 week income she was offered, and later her entire inheritance. This event occurred only a short time after I was convicted, and Paulette had endured just about all the stress and heartache she could handle. Her health started to take that downhill slide, and she still cries at night or lays awake unable to sleep. Her sufferings with Fibromyalgia have been compounded by the undeserving acts that were perpetrated on her. A good woman, who dedicated herself to her mother for many years, giving up her own life to do it, was stabbed in the back. Sound familiar? But whom did this to her? Her mother? Her daughter? You decide. Nonetheless, with the inheritance gone so was our hope for a comfortable retirement and anything else that was hoped for. Paulette's family were also at odds with each other, and some were angry with Paulette for tying up Mom's estate in Court. They couldn't get their portion of the inheritance until that was settled. I looked at what was happening with disgust. We had stood up to Right vs Wrong in court, risking what little Paulette was to receive from her mother, representing not only herself, but the family, who would each gain more if Paulette won, at a risk of getting nothing at all herself, and she did it under criticism from some of those she was trying to represent, as well as herself. It was such an injustice that it was hard to conceive as being real. We had just gone through my own inequity, only to face hers. I did wrong, she did not. She hasn't been the same since the day she discovered her mom had been taken from the Convalescent Hospital with Nicki's help and encouragement. Without God, she will never return to the Paulette I knew. I hope that no-one mentioned here would take satisfaction in that.

There's a lesson here in this adventure as well. It took me a while to learn it. I was engulfed in questions and resentment. Emotions can cloud your mind and compromise logic. They certainly did with Paulette and me. My life had been taken over and destroyed by a dishonest attorney and an overzealous D.A.. Only a short time later Paulette lost everything that was dedicated to her by an ageing mother who was dependent on a narcissistic immoral granddaughter. Life was not good for either my wife or me. And we couldn't get answers as to why. Although I had given up my thoughts about the Foresthill bridge, both Paulette and I went on living almost in a stupor. A daze, a dream, a vacancy, and very lethargic. This went on for me not just for days, or weeks, or even months, but for the following 10 years. I couldn't push aside anger and bitterness, and I excused myself for those emotions as being justified. Wouldn't anyone else be? The lesson I was to learn was at this time far out of my reach. And I was angry at God. I didn't care whether he did this to us deliberately or whether he just didn't protect us when we needed it. The end result was the same. So what's it like to depend on God so vehemently, and then turn around and live without him? How many of you have been so violated in life that you no longer have any hope, no dreams, no vision, or no future? Ten years is a long time to live without those things. God gives these things to you so as to give you life. Without them you feel, and might as well be, dead. Oh, during the next decade I occasionally heard God trying to speak to me, but I wasn't going to listen. I turned to let him see the heels of my shoes. Yes, I agree that I'm not the only man who'd been through problems, been accused of something they didn't do, lost an income or family inheritance, or had friends turn their back on them. But I wasn't living inside the body of other men. I was inside me. I had no future, and I was just waiting to die. But there's more.

CHAPTER 16

What's Next

I'm going to talk about God here. If you're not interested you can close the cover and go on about the business that's important to you. But I suggest you don't do that. God seems to have used me to give an opportunity to some to learn a lesson about many varied subjects without having to go through the grief of learning them on your own. Take advantage of that and read what I've learned. If you can apply it to your own life, OoooRaaaa for you, as we'd say in the Marine Corps. But realize that I don't preach or evangelize. I don't rise to the caliber of person who God has called to do that. I will, however, share the God that I know with anyone interested in lending an ear to listen. I pray you'll respond to an invitation and not feel you're being force fed by an opponent. In sharing my life with you on the pages you've just allowed your eyes to roam over, I've mentioned God in most every chapter. I'll dedicate a little more time here before I close. You see, we have some unfinished business, you and I. I've taken you through the steps of my life being controlled and altered by other individuals. I offered you the facts, from my perspective. Something I have no choice in as it's me who's writing this book. However, as you've perused these pages you've seen that I don't attempt to flatter myself or present to you some above normal super principled, moral human being who was victimized by people with fewer scruples. In fact, I've shamefully admitted to you things that I certainly would rather have kept very private, forever. The bottom line in these stories is that they are true. By in large, each chapter carried within it a lesson. One that only I may have learned if I kept it to myself. Or share it with others and let them pick up on whatever they find to be the lesson to them. Remember one of my original philosophies that I shared with you earlier. Never learn from your own mistakes if you can learn from somebody else's, first. That wisdom didn't just come along and take a ride with me. It was earned through turmoil, and many adventures.

You've seen the best and the worst of me. It all comes in one package. I haven't eliminated anything, skirted anything, high or low profiled anything, avoided anything, or said anything that wasn't true. You've seen me through my adolescent years, my military days, marriages, racing adventures, and you've read and evaluated my own values and moral character, and in some instances, a lack of it. I've presented to you issues and problems that you may have already experienced yourself, might in the future, or may avoid because you've read and learned from mine. I hope the latter is the case. But I'm not going to leave you in the last chapter being upset, angry, disappointed, annoyed, or sympathetic. You see there's a lesson here that I'm trying to share to all who take the time to read and pick up on it. Although that lesson has multiple avenues and alleys to wonder down, it starts with this.

We all have had experiences in our lives. Those experiences assist in making up our character and personality. We allow them to do just that. It's the easiest way of self-development. Just let it happen and we'll deal with it, laugh about it, or complain about it in an effort to get some attention. To do that you're doing a major disservice to yourself and to those that love you. You see those experiences are there for a reason. You may know the reason while you're in the middle of your experience, or you may never know why you were put through it. Either a good or bad experience, you may go around that mountain again if you don't go through the lesson carefully in your mind and determine what you did to cause it, what you could have done better or differently, and how you're going to allow that experience to help you grow in life. That means we don't complain about our experiences, we don't belabor it or overly talk about it to others, and we don't use it for a source of attention. When we're able to do that, we have successfully turned that experience into an adventure. And we're all up for adventures. Granted, some adventures may not be as enjoyable as others, but an adventure means that something new is happening. New, in this case, is spelled L-E-A-R-N. After we have a few of those, and learn something from each one, we're going to gain something that can only be gotten from experiences, wisdom. Many, albeit most, of the adventures I've had are good ones. I've been an active man leading an active life, accomplishing things that others, too, could accomplish if they were dizzy enough to accept the challenge. And I've had some bad ones, devastating ones. Adventures that have altered and changed my life. What of those bad ones, were they necessary for me to build my character. I would now answer, yes, absolutely. I admit, those bad ones are a little like Marine Corps Boot Camp. I wouldn't trade it for any other adventure imaginable, but at the same time, I wouldn't do it again for the same offer of trade.

But a couple of adventures were left unanswered, weren't they. Why did God have me experience the result of a criminal conviction? And why did God allow Nicki to steel Paulette's mother away and have the Will changed, (in my opinion of course), leaving Paulette (and I) without her deserved inheritance? These life altering events were permanent and didn't seem to be justified or warranted. So why did God allow, or arrange, for them to happen? That's going to take another story.

He walked into my life in a perplexing way. Happy, humble, and hungry for God, he couldn't be for real. This tall good looking man had a personality unique to most and exposed himself as a target for critique by those more miserable in life than he. His wife reminded me of Sandra many years ago, Pastor Ralph's long term bride. An attractive but quiet woman, she spoke when she was spoken to but listened to everything around her. Kim loved the Lord and listened when her husband spoke about him. But I had seen this before, ships that sail in a calm sea, but quickly break apart as the open water challenges their structure. Yet, there was something different about Jerry. Something in his spirit told me that what you see is what he is. I accepted it, and why not? I wasn't going to his church. We were only brushing shoulders in life. But Jerry wasn't going to allow things to be that way.

Sitting at my office, as I generally was, Jerry and Kim would drop by to say hello. He was always the same Jerry, and always willing to talk about God. However I noted that his willingness was consistently regulated by invitation. He could converse about anything but had a lot of difficulty keeping his enthusiasm for God hidden. His multiple visits to the office caused me to recognize his consistency, and the genuine love he had for life, and our Savior. He started to remind me of Ralph when he and I were younger. I found myself looking at Jerry as a special person.

I sat in on my first church gathering and Jerry was clearly excited. I felt welcome and listened as he and Kim openly worshiped the Lord. They were charismatic to say the least and it was good to be a part of it. I absorbed the euphoric worship. I listened to his sermon and appreciated his wisdom, sensitivity to the Spirit, and his excitement. Yes, he did seem to be for real. He preached to the small congregation as though it were a crowd of thousands. And he focused on the Bible as his source. It was good to see that. Yes, Jerry was a devoted man of God. "I'll go more often," I thought, but alas, that wasn't good enough for Jerry. He continued to come by the office. Lunch, coffee, or just to chat, it didn't matter. The more I learned of him, the more I realized that this was a good man. We seemed to have built a special friendship, both spiritual and social. I found myself enjoying him. But I still carry the load of my felony conviction, thinking of it daily. "Should-a, would-a, and could-a" were ongoing common evaluations in my mind and my conclusion turned down the same road. Life is a result of what I've done, not the fault of someone else. Although its consequences have a firm grasp on Paulette and my future, it's my job to insure that I don't get mired in the caustic mud of shifting blame and responsibility to someone else, while excusing myself for my own conduct. It's easy to surrender to that temptation, but if we do, we're headed back around the same mountain. And we'll go around that mountain again and again, until we get it right. It should clearly be said that the difficulty in losing my credibility and reputation to a criminal conviction, yet not getting mired in the event, but instead look and evaluate myself, isn't the conundrum that it may appear to be. The first is recognition, the second an admission, the third a goal.

Jerry seemed to find good in everyone. I was no exception and he made known things that he saw or appreciated in me. That's a far cry from the life of an investigator. Normally people find reasons not to like you. More fear than knowledge, I guess. I've grown to live with it. But Jerry always had something nice or complementary to say. I felt guilty hearing it. "It's time you knew more about me," I said one day. "You're not talking to the man you think you are," I continued. This was going to be a painful admission. "I'm a convicted felon, for a very bad crime." I held back the choking on my words, but hearing myself reveal such painful truth to a decent man like this was like vomiting a stomach full of acid. It hurt coming out as much as it did going in. I expected him to stop in his footsteps and ask me to explain myself, but it wasn't to be. "I know all about it," he responded. "And the man I know isn't the kind of man who would do something like that." "I didn't," was my surprised response. How did he know this? What did he know? And who had told him? No doubt it was Paulette and Lisa, my defenders. Jerry was already convinced that I was a good man. I wasn't going to continue talking and cause him reason to rethink his position. What he didn't know was the tormenting pain that haunts me daily. He's the type that would join my suffering. I didn't want that.

Jerry and I were becoming good friends. He was new in town and may not have had anyone else to choose from, but I found his character and personality genuine, and he exemplified high moral values. He was wise beyond his years. We both enjoyed draining pots of restaurant coffee over discussions of interest. Sometimes God, other times a different subject matter. Rarely did we talk about my issues with Zorro or Nicki, but he always had something encouraging to say about life, and the way we look at it. Or the way it looks at us. My 10 year hiatus away from God was a lifetime in itself, but I was listening more to the voice inside me, attending church again, and absorbing the messages that Jerry preached. Messages I had certainly heard from others in the past, but new words can sometimes bring fresh light to old subjects. Jerry was making a contribution to my life. I hoped I was offering something that he valued, in return. He was the type of man who didn't normally say directly what was on his mind or offer pastoral guidance in a direct fashion. Instead, he'd throw out tidbits of information to get you to think for yourself. His job, he felt, was to keep you on the right track so we didn't wonder away from God's word. This worked most of the time, but it annoyed me when I was too lazy to think for myself. Normally, however, that morsal of information would get me to thinking, and frequently down a different avenue than I might have been heading before our conversation. I was starting to listen to and accept God's direction and decisions once again. I was still confused and upset with the way things had gone in the past, and bewildered as to why they went that way, but I found myself more willing to accept it than I had for the last decade.

It was early a.m. and I found myself at Starbucks not enjoying a cup of coffee that I didn't like and more focused on completing a report that I had been working on for a client. My laptop was in front of me, and I had long ago grown insistent on not having my back to a door when in public. I adhered to that rule this morning as well. I glanced up briefly when a customer would walk in and went back to my task at hand. Glancing up once again I felt the adrenaline rush through my body and into my throat where the remains of that last sip of coffee still resided. A double take to be sure, and yes, 10 years of growth hadn't changed the weasel's face. It was Zorro. He saw me as well and made a partial brief turn to head back out. Stopping, he changed his mind and continued on in to stand in line behind the other bad coffee lovers. Brief case in hand it appeared that he, too, had plans on working at this sub-station for a while instead of his office. He paid no acknowledgement or offered any gestures as we exchanged glares. "Here we go," I thought almost out loud. I'm getting ready to go to jail. He was several feet away from me as I stood up and had his back to me. I'm going to knock him out, but I won't sucker punch him from behind. I stood up with 10 years of resolve in me as to what he would experience should I experience this experience. We were about to experience this event together. As I stood up it hit me as strong as any other time and I was certain it was God talking to me. It was his Spirit speaking to mine for the first time in a decade, so I thought. I heard what he said and couldn't believe what I was hearing. Putting it aside I started my walk across the room. Each step God was whispering in my ear. He spoke as the gentleman that he is, but I heard him. As I reached my target I put my hand on his shoulder to pull him around. As we turned face to face with each other he appeared to have the common problem of not knowing which coffee to order. His bottom lip was shaking, badly. I was convinced that he was genuinely concerned about something. No-one can deliberately make their lip shake like that. He said nothing but stared at my face. It was now my turn. "You have to have been living in a Hell of your own after what you did to me 10 years ago," I said. "I want you to know that I forgive you." Sure it was difficult to say, but I obeyed God, and I felt good that I had done that. In fact, I felt good that I said that out loud, and to him. The weight that had been crushing me for a decade was just released. Something had just happened, and I was free. "Oh, that was a long time ago and I've forgotten about it," was his only response. I wasn't completely satisfied with his answer but never mind. This event is between God and me. "Even so, I forgive you," and I returned to my laptop a different person. But the adventure isn't over yet.

Months squeezed themselves in between now and the encounter with Zorro at Starbucks. My outlook on life was noticeably better and occasionally even some good things would happen that I previously may not have recognized or appreciated. The Zorro event faded into only an occasional thought or discussion. I was doing some shopping for the house one day and parked away from the store as I was towing a trailer loaded with firewood. Fatigued by the day of splitting it up I was hurried to get home and sit down. It was dark when I pushed my cart out of the store and directed it toward my truck. Someone parked alongside my trailer appeared to be looking at the wood. As I approached I heard her say, "Can I talk to you a minute?" "Of course," I responded without looking and I turned to address her. It was Nicki. "Oh my," I thought, "There's a lot I'd like to say to this one." I allowed discretion to be the better part of valor and I closed my mouth so as to open my ears. Her children, who I had never met, were in the back seat leaning toward the driver's window to hear what was going to be said. Nicki started in with a challenging tone and commenced her interrogation of my treatment of her when growing up. She had a lot on her plate, and I let her air her many grievances without interruption. She paused only when she felt she had me backed into a corner of guilt. It was time for my interjection and whatever I was to say here would be remembered for a very long time in the future. There was no shaking of my lower lip as I commenced responding to her charges and accusations. Some of the things she was saying were true. Others I have to believe were true only in her own mind, from her own perspective or recollection. Yet others certainly weren't and had to have come from a dream or her own imagination. I was trying to sort out which was which as I formulated my response. First, I had to genuinely apologize to her for the mistakes I made in raising her. There was no Marine Corps manual on this. Relying only on my own experiences meant I was referring back to values that were a generation old. That wasn't to offer an excuse for my mistakes, but it did present a reason. It's important to note the difference. It was most important for her to know that I was sorry for those mistakes. I told her that many times during our 45 minute conversation and meant each one of them. I was hoping that from this point on, she might feel better about life and herself. She won't live in this miserable state of mind she's been suffering with since her teen years. I suppose I caught her off guard when making these confessions, but it was important for her to know that I wasn't living through life thinking I always did right with my child rearing. I didn't. I was careful, though, not to bring up something that I knew she was wrong about. This wasn't going to be a contest. Yet neither was I going to offer a remorseful admission for something I hadn't done. And she brought up several things that never occurred. Where she got them or how she envisioned them, I'll never know. It's possible that when you tell a story enough times, that story becomes real to you. I was starting to feel nauseous over all the accusations she was making, and in front of her kids as well. She was angry but comfortable in spewing them out. I avoided correcting her where I could, but then she asked how sorry I was about molesting her. That was over the top and I told her I knew she had gone to friends and family as well as businesspeople

I knew that she had made this abominable accusation against me to many others, but she wasn't going to make them to me. She challenged me over this but didn't take it too far. Things quieted down and saying all I could say, it was time to go. I looked at her a final time and told her once again that I was sorry for the mistakes I had made as a father, I was sorry for the way she remembers other things in her heart, and I was sorry that I had earned no fond memories of me. I concluded by telling her that we were both aware that she had handled some things wrong toward me in the last several years and that I forgive her for all that she has said. She reached out to put her hand on my arm and I turned to my truck. Maybe this encounter would give her peace through the rest of her life, I don't know, but I hoped to give it to her. My apology and my forgiveness were what I had to offer. As with Zorro, I felt I had done the right thing. Difficult? You bet, but it needed to be done. I needed to do the Godly thing, and I did. I was stressed out to the max but at the same time, relieved. I had fulfilled my repentance and my forgiveness. These were the lessons God had for me. I suppose he was saddened I had to learn in such a difficult way, but fault for that has to reside on me. Had I learned earlier I may have avoided the very difficult experiences. I pray that you, the reader, don't have to go through life changing experiences in order to learn something that could be learned in an easier fashion. You've heard me say it earlier. Learn from someone else's mistakes, so you don't have to learn from your own.

Because it's important to learn from someone else's lesson rather than have to learn from your own (where have I heard that before?) let's look again at some that I frequently learned the hard way, so you don't have to. Whether you're a believer in God and dependent upon him or rely on yourself for your own conclusions and answers it has to be recognized that there's a fine line between self-pity and self-recognition. It's a disservice to confuse one with the other. There is certainly a temptation to feel sorry for yourself after enduring a situation that has been unfairly imposed, but doing so will clearly be self-defeating. It is, however, appropriate to recognize the problem or issue and evaluate it, to include your part in it, so you can commence formulating a solution or a method of working your way through the situation. The real problem is determining whether you're recognizing or pitying yourself, and only by searching deep within your soul can you self-evaluate. Professionals can analyze the difference better than I, but the best diagnosis comes from your own heart. A "poor me" advancement on life, even as a result of your experiences, condemns you to become a slave to your problems. We all have them, with some having more than others. Recognize your problem, evaluate the answers to it, and don't pity yourself for having to go through it. The one to admire is the one who handles their difficulties and experiences with grace and fortitude. As if climbing a mountain, you remedy your problems when you envision your goal, the summit, and you work to reach it, step by step. Here, sometimes the commonly known is not the commonly practiced. You don't just wind up on top of the mountain, or on top of your difficulties. You reach that crest one step at a time, and with a plan. No one starts their climb by simply looking ahead and moving in that direction. It's a start, but it will never get you to your end. You look at your goal, decipher the best way to reach it, and then put one foot in front of the other in your selected path. Difficulties are no less stringent in their demands upon you. If you want to conquer those challenges, develop a plan, and put it into motion. You climb a mountain that way, you solve your problems that way. Moreover, you don't whine about it on the way up. You're having an experience. Learn from it and teach others so they don't have to climb the same mountain. Wouldn't you be grateful if they climbed a mountain for you? The figurative comparison between a mountain and our own problems in life can be taken to any degree you wish, but there's one denominator that never changes. If God isn't in it, you'll go it alone. There's nothing lonelier than God going one direction, while you go another. Does he want you up that mountain? Does he want you to take that path to reach the top? Does he want you to solve your problems the same way you want to? It often takes a lot of energy to learn which way God wants to do something, and that's where many of us fall short. We see the intensity sometimes required to learn what he wants, and we sometimes mentally tire before gaining his insight. It's not easy to follow God. He's quicker and smarter than we are, and we're always playing catch up. Get used to it, it's not going to change, unless he lets you know in advance what he wants you to do. Many times he'll do that, but you have to ask, and then listen. He'll speak to you in your spirit. At other times, he won't tell you at all, He'll simply ask you to obey. Do it. Sometimes you won't understand it, and you'll be tempted to question whether it was God talking to you or not. If you believed it was at the beginning, stay your course. You'll be much more content being "wrong" with God, than right on your own. I promise.

Many of the adventures God gave me were pleasurable. You'll recall in chapters back I outlined how and when I felt I had heard God directing me. Time and time again he watched over me while performing my duties and obligations as a private investigator. It's an "A" type personality occupation and there's going to be risk involved. To this day there are still bad people who'd like to find me, but I wouldn't have traded my occupation for any other that I could imagine. God directed me to Ben's phone number one day, and my life changed. I dedicated 20 years to working the Western States, sweeping the trail for them each year during the run because God directed me to take the Team out and do this. A memorable experience that certainly became an adventure. God told me to get ready to run the Western States 100 myself, an impossible event for any human being, but with my physical limitations I couldn't have survived the training, let alone the run, without him. God rode with me on a dirt bike, protecting me from things that only he could. I was immune to fear, and I didn't have enough sense to slow down. God put a burning burden in my heart to avail any talent he had loaned me to help others in need. I obeyed that by dedicating myself to Search and Rescue for 25 years. The experiences there were certainly adventures. If I were to know the future in advance, without hesitation I'd follow God's direction and do it again. Those adventures offer memories that I can, and will, live over many times between now and when I go to meet Jesus. I have only God to thank for them and I would own none of them without his guidance, direction, and wisdom. He has, and will do again, the same for you. So what do you have to do to create memories that you can enjoy during your solitude? Ask. Ask him, and he'll lead you down your path, as he did mine.

We also have to recognize and come to terms with other facts. Not all adventures come with a wedding cake. There are bad ones, terrible ones, devastating ones that you'll also focus on and relive for an eternity. These are the adventures you have to be careful of. They can destroy your life, or put it in better terms, you can destroy your own life by the way you handle these extremely harmful experiences. Many of us will turn our backs on life, and on God, as I did with the Zorro experience. We voluntarily become the enemy's playground. Self-pity and, "Why me," or "What did I do?" enters the picture and in short order someone is feeling sorry for us. "That's what I needed." "See, I was right." We become locked into our own misery because we allowed ourselves to put us there. Don't do that. It's a formula for disaster and it'll ruin your life for as many years as it takes for you to change. Learn from my experience, not your own.

Don't misunderstand me to say that by turning to God you'll have experiences like these. That's not the case. God waits, and he wants to show you his power and his love. He enjoys blessing those who love him. My experiences are not the norm, neither the good ones nor the bad. We all have our trials and tribulations in life. A "thorn in our side" so to speak. God doesn't say he's going to shield us from those, although he does, has, and will. No, we can expect that we're still going to experience uncomfortable, terrible, or even evil things. We live in a world that will do that to us. Sometimes God will protect us from worldly experiences that we might deserve to have. Sometimes he won't. But rest assured and with confidence that once you make God first in your life, he's going to recognize that you have, and he'll pay special attention to you. Truth being told as honestly as I've tried here, I may have had more experiences than these, had I not been dedicated to God. What I would not have had was God to lean on, or to seek comfort and answers from. That's the lifesaving benefit that God grants all of us who turn to him. No, He sometimes doesn't protect us from bad experiences, but he'll always lead us through them if we listen. Remember, he never allows you to go through an experience of any kind unless he wants you, or someone else, to learn something from that experience. You may never know what that lesson is. It could be that someone else learned something from it instead of you. Is that fair? Sure it is. We've all learned something from someone else in the past haven't we? From my perspective the people that I've talked about here didn't need to do what they did. Maybe they didn't have the experiences in life to teach them differently. Maybe that experience taught them something as well as me. I don't know, but God does. I did some bad things in life that I wish I could amend or take back. I was fortunate that Cheri gave me the opportunity to repent for the way I treated her. However there are many more things I've done elsewhere that were not right. Some I've revealed here, some I've kept to myself. Small things like eating a stranger's breakfast, to monumental things like the mistakes I made while raising our children. Or the way I treated Paulette at times. Or the affair I had so many years ago. The consequences could be considered karma, but I don't believe in that. If karma were a predominate force, there would be no forgiveness, and that's not what God teaches. He forgives us and wants us to forgive others. I confess that in some cases, I still need God's help to live up to some of my obligations. It's compounded by having so little time left, and so many dreams and goals now untouchable.

I frequently find myself evaluating my ambitions and my failures, and the first seem to have merged into the latter. I have wishes that'll never come to pass, but rather remain in my impossible wish box all the same. I wish I could tell my father that I love him. I wish I could hear him whisper in my ear. I wish I could see his grin. I wish I could feel his hand on top of my head. I wish I could hug him one more time. I wish he could tell me right from wrong. I wish he could tell me to stop or go. I wish before he walked out the door knowing he may not come back, that I had been old enough to tell him all the things I want to tell him now. I wish he'd play baseball with me again. Because I can't have those things I miss, I want to give them to my sons, while I can. I enjoy the times I spend with them and occasionally get to spend it with both of them together. Whether we're riding motorcycles in the dirt, sliding around corners side by side each other, or spending some time on the computer playing a game together, those times are special to me and, not often enough, I thank God for giving each of us these memory makers. At 73 my riding days will eventually come to an end.

I hope not too soon, but if they do, I'll live on memories that were truly adventures, blessed by the one who gave them to us.

I sometimes struggle to differentiate between vision and logical conclusion. One being a hope, the other expected. As I outlined at the onset of this story, each will gain some insight to life as I knew it to be, the Good, the Bad, and the Ugly. There are lessons to be learned in life. In each chapter you've either learned a lesson from my adventure or observed me as I learned it. Is there a lesson to be learned in learning lessons? You bet there is. Each one we learn makes us a better person. No, I'm not referring the old adage, "I've learned I'm too good for them," or "boy I'll never trust them again," type lessons. Those are cautions and although we all have them, the negative seed that it plants when you have such an attitude can, and will, do each of us more harm that the lesson is intended. We can allow an experience to make us bitter, angry, vengeful, spiteful, upset, hateful, retaliatory, obnoxious, insufferable, overbearing, offensive, challenging, defiant, disobedient, rebellious, unforgiving, self-absorbed, narcissistic, conceited, self-loving, selfish, egotistical, and a host of other things that many of us have experienced at one time or another. Hopefully in the past. I hope even more that being that way made you so miserable that you've vowed not to become, "one of those, again." Instead, we look at those experiences and evaluate what "positive" lessons we can learn from them. When we do that, those experiences will turn into adventures. I'm a lucky man to have been allowed so many adventures. God tested me in many areas. Some of which I passed, some I didn't. But each adventure carried with it a lesson of do's or don'ts. It was my job to find out which one. You read how miserable I was after the conviction and again when our inheritance was unscrupulously taken. I would have remained in that state of despair to my end had not God intervened to show me the lesson that was to be learned this way, and by no other way. He used Jerry to help me see it. Have you seen it yet? That lesson was Forgiveness.

Prior to the experience of being convicted of a crime I hadn't done, or prior to friends, family, business associates and others being told I was a child molester, I had not been in a situation where I was to learn the true nature of forgiveness. It was something I did because it was the right thing. And I did it my way. It usually had strings attached to the "forgiveness." I'd remind them at a later date or wouldn't forget the offense myself. I'd still hold the offender accountable. I failed to realize that this, in God's view, wasn't forgiveness at all. It took these lessons, that God orchestrated, for me to evaluate and accept God's meaning of forgiveness, not my own.

Forgiveness is a very important thing to God, and for us if we have any hope or vision of leading a peaceful life. Most all of us have somebody in mind that we hold accountable for something they did. Frequently that something is a significant issue, at least to you it is. When you think about it your blood seems to boil. Your heart rate speeds up, and you take a deeper breath. You can feel the heat rise from your stomach all the way to your head. You look away in another direction. No, that was no help. Because you have such strong feelings about this, and because your emotions are now in overdrive, you start thinking about the issue again. Your thoughts may go on for minutes or even hours, but the adrenaline is flowing and you're angry. All of this has occurred because of a thought. Your thought. Yes, you may be justified in your anger but right now no-one is feeling it accept you. It has control over you right now. You know that it has and that makes you even more upset. It has just ruined your day. Sadly and unjustly, possibly the day of those around you as well. You become even more upset when confessing to yourself that this could happen all over again in a few days or even hours. What a miserable thing to be a slave to, yet you are. We all have been. What's the solution? Our first thought is that the offender needs to come to you with a sorrowful admission of guilt, and work very hard on convincing you that it'll never happen again. As you demonstrate your disappointment and disbelief in their sincerity the distance between the two of you grows wider. "Maybe," with a capitol "M," they can convince you, and the matter can be put to rest. However if that happens, you'll always remember the past and what they did. You'll always have doubts and there will always be a speed bump between you and the offender. Is there a solution to this human response to being unjustifiably treated? Yes there is. I'm a stubborn man. It took me 10 years to learn it. Jesus was unjustly treated over and over again, and he forgave over and over again. He teaches us to do the same thing and places a monumental level of importance to it. You see our invitation to reside with Jesus when our time clock runs out is dependent upon God's forgiveness of our sins. He's not going to let sin or sinful people contaminate Heaven. To cleanse us of that we have to turn away from our habitual sin and he has to forgive us of what we've committed. That's pretty reasonable when he's offering us the most precious gift a human could receive. When we ask him to forgive us God walks up to his blackboard with our sins listed on it and erases every one of them. All of them, without exception. Gone, forgotten, over, and God responds with a kind and gentle, "I love you." That's what forgiveness is and what it does. And that's how important it is. Does an offender have to recognize and be sorry for the offense he imposed on another to be forgiven? It's reasonable to answer, yes, but wait. Can God forgive those who won't or haven't recognized they've offended? Sure he can, and so should we. As Jesus was being tortured to death on the cross, in all the excruciating pain and agony he was in, knowing he had done nothing do deserve this, spoke out loud to his Father, "Forgive them, Father, for they know not what they do." Jesus was telling us how important forgiveness is. Not "was," but "is." Now give this some thought. The most important prayer that God gave us is the Lord's Prayer, "Our Father, who art in Heaven------," you know the one. In those sacred words we pray through God's direction, that God forgives us in the same fashion and manner in which we forgive others. That is to say if we forgive, God forgives, if we forgive a little, God forgives us in the same way, if we don't forgive, God treats us in kind, as per our own request. Remember what was said earlier and can hardly be disputed, God doesn't let people reside with him in Heaven unless he's forgiven them of their sins. That's a part of being Born Again. By the way, that does not suggest that we will never sin again, that would be an impossible task for a human. Only Jesus had never sinned. But by praying that God judges us as we do others screams clearly that we are to forgive others of what they've done to offend or hurt us. No, you can't skirt around this by not praying the Lord's Prayer. His prayer is to teach us, not direct God on what to do. Whether we pray it or not, God will adhere to his proclamations. We should all see now how important forgiveness is. That remaining concern is "what" is forgiveness? Therein lies the rub, so has been said. "I forgive them, but I'll never talk to them again," "I forgive them but I'm still going to tell everyone what they did," "I forgive them, but I'll never forget," "I'll forgive them, but I'll bring it up again in the future if I think it's appropriate." This is not forgiveness. This is little more than delayed consequences. You wouldn't want God forgiving you in the same manner. No, it's not acceptable to declare that you're only human. Clearly God doesn't look at it that way. He's asked you to forgive, completely. And how can you define what forgiveness really is? To each has their own definition but if it differs from God's, then we need to readjust ours. I'm not the official authority on definitions, however I would believe that God would accept it as true forgiveness if at some point in time he came to me and asked me to report a complaint against someone who had offended me, and I was able to say, "I'm sorry, Lord, I have nothing bad to say about that person. If you need a complaint filed you'll have to look somewhere else. It's my prayer that you'll bless them beyond their dreams and expectations." Now that could be a hard prayer for many, including me, but when we're able to pray that I'm sure God will consider it true forgiveness. What happens to us when we're able to truly forgive? The answer is easy and it's what God wants for us. An enormous weight is lifted off our shoulders and heart. We find ourselves free of the turmoil we were carrying because we hadn't had fair vengeance yet. We find ourselves at peace, a pleasant and restful countenance, attractive to others, an example to those still living in anger, and you've put a smile on God's face. Instead of marginally forgiving or fake forgiveness where you obligate God to go back to the blackboard and rewrite your sins down, God looks down at you with a glow in his eye saying, "Well done." This was the lesson God had for me when Zorro used me to escape his own criminal activity. This was the lesson God had for me when he allowed Nicki to do what she did to Paulette and I. Could I have learned this some other less harsh way? Maybe, but that was God's decision. In the past I've found it easier to forgive someone if I had done something to them and they, in return, offended me. I probably deserved it and felt a mutual treaty would resolve the issue. It's much more difficult to forgive when you've done nothing to cause the offense and someone violates you. God felt I was deserving of the latter lesson. It took 10 years for me to pick up on it. Don't let that happen to you. There's a lesson here. One to be learned from my experiences, not yours. Don't let this happen to you. You don't need to go around the mountain that I trekked across. All you need to do is see my mountain and avoid it. Forgive those who have offended you and ask forgiveness from those who you've offended. You're going to live a much happier and content life, I promise.

Through a hard lesson I learned that God doesn't leave you or turn his back on you. Sometimes he allows you to experience things that you need to experience. Sometimes you know why, sometimes you don't. The "don't" part doesn't mean that God is wrong. It means that we're elementary in our understanding of God and he'll sometimes carry out his wishes without our approval. This wasn't a new revelation to me. I had heard it before under prior Pastor's tutelage. This new Pastor and his contagious enthusiasm for God made me check my own conviction. God didn't abandon me years ago. I was unable to understand that he had a good reason for allowing me to go through some horrendous experiences. I didn't trust in him as deeply as I needed to. He tested me in this, and I failed. This new Pastor would not be so pompous as to tell me that, but he did provide examples to allow me to see it myself. God is still here. He never left, even when I did. We can lose someone who's dear to us and wrongly blame God for it. We can lose a pet, a car, or not get the job we were praying for and wrongly blame God. We'll frequently wrongly blame him for not healing our marriage, healing our bodies, or healing our heart. Our comprehension is so infantile when compared to his wisdom. Yet we lean toward giving ourselves more credit for understanding a situation than we do his chosen solution. It seems as though many of us, myself included, feel, or have felt that if God agrees with our needs and requests of him, then he's right. If he doesn't, something is wrong, and it isn't us. I look back on these experiences that God has allowed me to go through and wonder if I've learned the lessons that he intended for me. Many times I've felt that the glass was half empty instead of half full. I've had to go around the mountain a couple of times to realize that I've been praying for just a little more glass. But if nothing else has been learned, and if I can relay anything to you, I would encourage you to take each of the experiences you've had, find the positive lesson, and they'll turn into adventures. The bad ones can frequently be more educational than the good ones. You don't want to go through your own bad ones again, do you? Learn what's there to be learned. Don't get mired down in the affects or outcome of that bad experience. Don't relive it with self-pity. Don't use a past experience as a tool to feel sorry for yourself. With each experience there is a choice of lessons. That's what experiences are for. Be sure to learn the lesson that was intended. Don't hold up your own progress by hindering yourself with pity. Don't use the bad outcome of an experience as a means of gaining attention from someone else. That's an invitation to self-destruction and a bad kind of attention. Don't latch onto that bad experience as a tool to elevate yourself to a higher level of importance. Don't let that experience devastate you to the point that you're unable to get up, move out, and move on. Don't camp in the Manzanita. That's not where you're going to find solace, consolation, or answers. If you have an inclination to believe that you can take care of your own life, you can handle your own difficulties, and you provide your own answers, then my experiences suggest that there's more that you might want to consider. I've lived with and without God in my life. I'm an independent man, who's believed that I could take care of myself. But I'd never experienced a loneliness like I had during the years after my conviction when I felt that God had abandon me. I focused on the experience and not the lesson. Therein lays the challenge for many of us. We're feeling the experience, and feelings carry a lot of weight. Both the good ones, and the bad ones. To turn that experience into a lesson is a major stumbling block for many, for as many varied reasons. Not the least of which is that it takes a lot of effort. "I'll worry about the lesson in this later," seems to be a common temptation in many of us. It was for me before I realized that it's this lesson that the experience is for. It's the lesson that's at the top of the pyramid, not the experience. Think for a moment about someone you know who may have had a sheltered life. Now think of someone adventuresome who has a logbook of experiences. Can you tell the difference in these two people? Sure you can. But the next step is the important one. Can you or he learn something from those experiences that he's had? This becomes the moment of truth where you have to evaluate yourself. I assure you it's a lot easier doing it with God alongside of you than it is without him there.

Can you take a chance going through life on your own? Take a look at mine and tell me what would have happened had God NOT been there. You've been through your own tribulations. Has God been there with you, or have you tried to endure it by yourself? Do you blame God for your troubles, or are you angry with him for not getting you out of them? I would say, Look Again! It's not likely that God put you in your position. It's more probable that he allowed you to get yourself there, generally because we didn't listen to him to begin with. God doesn't always protect his children from harm, he sees them through it. He wants you to love and worship him. Why not, he's God. And we're the only creatures he created that have the ability to worship. He made us this way for a reason. He wants us to choose to worship him, not comply by resentful obedience. How many of us with few experiences in life hold experiences dear? How many of us with experiences can declare that they were all good ones? You're correct, I read your mind. Now it's up to you to focus those experiences into something productive that will help someone behind you. If you waste your time with self-pity, no one will care or listen. Focus your past on someone's future, and they'll stop to lend you an ear. Listen to God when he speaks to you or ask him to speak to you. He will. Sometimes you won't want to hear what he has to say. Then be bold enough to tell God you don't want to listen to him. You may find that difficult to do. You should. But have an honest chat with God. You'll find that he's not only a good listener, but a gentleman. He just may not see things the way you do. On the other hand, sometimes God is just waiting for you to talk to him. He's prepared your plate and is giving you what you want, after you ask. I don't know the answers to what may happen to you during your experiences. I do know this about me. Without God, I'd either be in prison today, or dead. He's taken me this far and will see me the short trip home. In the meantime I look at my failures as clearly my failures. I have no delusions that they may be someone else's fault. You can now look ahead and avoid my mistakes.

Prepare for what I didn't and avoid what I couldn't. There's little worse than losing your vision and hope. Hear and obey God. His wisdom is greater than yours, and mine. To say less is folly, and a direct ticket to Hell. If you want to tackle life and its circumstances on your own, be prepared for failure of the utmost kind. You may win a battle, but you won't win the War. Dump your problems on God and make the outcome his choosing. He'll accept the responsibilities. The problems are bigger than you, but smaller than he. Could it be that he's allowed these problems to visit you to get your attention? He did mine. Now that it's over, I beg his forgiveness for not listening to him completely. If I could only say one thing to you, don't do as I did. Don't doubt God or fail to surrender yourself to his will. You need to talk to him, and you need to listen to him. For those first timers who think that strange or impossible, no, it isn't. God tells us exactly what needs to be done, and how. I'm not going to quote scripture here, you've heard it before, and if you don't know where it's at in the Bible, look it up. Search under Born Again and read the news.

You think the Bible is hard to read and it's just a story book? It can't be true. Ah, not so. Consider this for accuracy: The Bible is a library of 66 books, written by over 35 different authors, in a period of approximately 1,500 years. The authors were a cross section of humanity, both educated and uneducated, including kings, fishermen, public officials, farmers, teachers, and physicians. Included in the subjects are religion, history, law, science, poetry, drama, biography, and prophecy. Yet its various parts are so harmoniously united, as the parts that make up the human body. For 35 authors, with such varied backgrounds, to write on so many subjects over a period of 1,500 years in absolute harmony, with many of them not knowing the other, is a mathematical impossibility. It could not happen without the Holy Spirit of God talking to these men (Credit to The Open Bible Edition, Thomas Nelson Publishers 1977, page 1195). Further, as many a naysayer have tried to prove, there is nothing in the Bible that has ever been proven to be wrong, incorrect, or inaccurate, nothing, not one verse. Many of these men didn't have any reference material to study what the previous author had said. Yet everything matches exactly. Amazing isn't it? Impossible? Yes of course unless it was authored by the Spirit of God.

You don't believe that Jesus is the son of God? Or maybe it's not important and you just don't care. Then consider that there are no other credible religions that dispute that Jesus was here on earth. All of them have agreed that he was. Why, because he really was. The stupidity of denying that would be the end of their credibility. So if he really was here, and he did what has been written, which is un-refutable, then either he had a whole lot of magic (which we'd have to ask if magic was real as well), or he was given his powers by God, his Father. If God was his Father, and he the Son, then Jesus was exactly what he said he was, the Son of God. He told you who he was and no-one that wishes to have any credibility at all would accuse the Son of God of being a liar. The Bible says that only by believing in the Son, will you ever see the Kingdom of Heaven. That's pretty plain. If that doesn't scare you now, it will within your few final minutes before you go to meet him.

So what does God want you to do? It's not difficult. Listen to it in simple words. Get on your knees and ask God to hear your prayer. Admit to Him that you've sinned in your life. You know you have. Some of you may think you've committed too many or too big a sin to be forgiven. That's not true. God speaks directly to you when He says, "I'll forgive everything." Ask Him to forgive you for those sins and mean what you say. You don't need to review them with God, both you and he know what they are. Admit to God that you know he sent his Son, Jesus, to walk about this earth as a human being, and while here, Jesus allowed himself to be tortured to death to pay for the sins we, not he, committed. Somebody had to pay for them. God washed the earth clean during Noah's time to get rid of the garbage. Later, he did it again to the cities of Sodom and Gomorrah, yet we climbed right back up to our world of self-indulgence, and God was going to command a price once again. There was no way around it, we were going to pay for the sins we were committing. But instead of making us pay for it this time, he sent his perfect Son, who felt every tinge of pain that we do as human beings. Want another tidbit? Jesus could have denied his destiny and left us here stranded to pay the price of sin ourselves, but he didn't. He asked

His Father to take this cup from him, but only if God wanted to do it. Amazing, isn't it. He was about to be tortured to death in a sadistic miserable slow fashion. He had to have been terrified, yet he asked God to continue to have His own way.

Admit in your prayer to God that you recognize his son is the Son of God. He was, admit it. Thank Jesus for what he did for you. He didn't do it for just "anyone," or "someone else," He did it for YOU. He knew of you before you were born and knows the number of hairs on your head. He deserves your recognition. Then ask Jesus to come and join you in your life, as you hope to make it. Invite his Spirit to join yours. Submit your spirit to Jesus. He'll welcome the invitation and join you. Each of you will have your own experience, and each experience will be unique to each person, but without asking God to forgive you, asking Jesus into your life, and getting baptized, I'll guarantee you will never hear a word God has to say to you, you won't be able to obey him, you can't unload your problems on him, and you will not, NOT see his kingdom of Heaven when you die. Those aren't my words or my opinion. It comes directly from the Bible, the Word of God that he left behind for us to refer to. The book that tells the truth about it all. Take it or leave it, you've been advised as directly and truthfully as I know how to say it. Accept Jesus as your Lord and Savior, and you'll grow to love him. I promise.

Once you become Born Again, pray, and listen. You'll find a miraculous thing happen. Your spirit will feel the presence of God, you'll feel him talking to you, and you'll feel the comfort he graces you with. Shine it on as folly if you wish, but at your own cost. Think about the 1990 movie "Ghost" with Demi Moore and Patrick Swayze. It's only a movie, with little scriptural accuracy, but ask yourself, would you rather be the one ascending above, or the one dragged by demons down to Hell? Now take the time to watch the "Passion of the Christ," again. I know you've seen it at least once. Watch it again. Then try to convince yourself you'll pay attention to God later. Maybe when you're older, or maybe when you're through with this little adventure you're involved with now. God isn't here to slap you down and take away all your pleasures. If you have some sinful things in your life, and who doesn't, you'll work through them with him, at a pace he knows you can handle. All he asks you to do is try. He's not here to make a schoolmarm out of you. He uses all types of people with all types of personalities to accomplish his tasks here on Earth. Many of those who know me know well that I'm not a good representative of God according to accepted standards of practice. I'm coarse, direct, annoying, and perturbing at times. At other times, these seem to be the best traits I have. But God may have used me to speak to someone in this life's story. If so, maybe you'll bless me by finding a way to let me know. He can certainly use you, too. Take your chance if you must, but I've sealed my name with God, and I know where I'm headed. Unless he has some plan to use me somewhere or somehow that I don't envision I'll await His angel's gentle tap on my arm to tell me it's time to go. I'll be prepared to lay down on my face in front of Jesus before I humbly crawl up on his lap and ask him to hold me.

THE END

www.ingramcontent.com/pod-product-compliance
Lightning Source LLC
Chambersburg PA
CBHW021608120626
46545CB00001B/118